The Egyptian Strategy for the
Yom Kippur War

The Egyptian Strategy for the Yom Kippur War

An Analysis

DANI ASHER

Translated by Moshe Tlamim
Foreword by Shlomo Gazit

McFarland & Company, Inc., Publishers
Jefferson, North Carolina, and London

This book was originally published in Hebrew in 2003 by Ma'arachot, the IDF publishing house, which is affiliated with the Israel Ministry of Defence Publishing House. This book is a work of independent scholarship and was not sponsored by a government entity. It was translated by Moshe Tlamin. All photographs courtesy IDF and Ma'arachot Archives.

LIBRARY OF CONGRESS CATALOGUING-IN-PUBLICATION DATA

Asher, Daniel, Dr.
[Li-shebor et ha-konseptsyah. English]
The Egyptian strategy for the Yom Kippur war : an analysis /
Dani Asher ; translated by Moshe Tlamim ; foreword by Shlomo Gazit.
p.   cm.
Includes bibliographical references and index.

ISBN 978-0-7864-4253-9
softcover: 50# alkaline paper ∞

1. Israel-Arab War, 1973 — Campaigns — Egypt.   2. Israel-Arab War,
1973 — Decision making.   3. Israel-Arab War, 1973 — Egypt.
4. Israel-Arab War, 1973 — Participation, Soviet.   5. Egypt —
Military policy.   6. Egypt — Military relations — Soviet Union.
7. Soviet Union — Military relations — Egypt.   8. Civil-military
relations — Egypt — History — 20th century.   9. Strategy.   I. Title.
DS128.1.A8413   2009
956.04'8 — dc22   2009016895

British Library cataloguing data are available

On the cover: Egyptian President Anwar al-Sadat (center) flanked by
his military staff at his Army headquarters in Cairo on
October 15, 1973 (Associated Press)

Manufactured in the United States of America

*McFarland & Company, Inc., Publishers
Box 611, Jefferson, North Carolina 28640
www.mcfarlandpub.com*

To my family, who encouraged and supported me with all their love in the lengthy production of this work: my late mother, Ruth, who gave me boundless support; my late father, Avraham, who instilled in me the foundations of historical research; my son, Itai, and his family, my daughters Noa and Nurit; and most of all my wife and constant companion — Menucha.

Acknowledgments

During my years of service in the IDF (Israel Defense Forces), I had the opportunity to study various facets of the enemy and keep close tabs on "the other side." Between 1970 and 1971, I was the Southern Command's intelligence officer, and in this capacity was responsible for carrying out research on the Egyptian army and carefully tracking its lengthy war preparations. The Egyptians had analyzed the course of events in the War of Attrition and learned the lessons from this conflict. The army's training routine included specialized combat activities — such as bridging and water crossings — that were geared to the expected fighting conditions. On a few occasions I was able to observe the Egyptian forces, right under their noses, undergoing canal fording exercises.

During the "Year of Decision" — the year after the cease-fire went into effect in August 1970 — we waited for hostilities to break out every three months, and followed the Egyptians' ground preparations for a major water-crossing operation. We discerned intensive activity along the canal: preparations at the banks for a breakthrough, getting fording barges ready, and practicing descents into the water. We also noted the assembly and staging areas that they built close to the front, and observed how they were paving roads and constructing bridges to enable their forces to move from the assembly areas to the crossing points. In response we deployed artillery and antiaircraft missile batteries and cannons, set up headquarters and observation posts, and drew up as complete a picture as possible of the Egyptian plan for traversing the canal.

During this period I took part in operations and exercises designed to test the Egyptians' capabilities. One of these involved moving an amphibious force in the Gulf of Suez and the Bitter Lakes — a skill that the Egyptians put to great use in the war. On February 28, 1971, I participated in another drill to test the "Or Yikarot" system. This system was based on oil-storage facilities located at the canal, that could spread an oil slick on the surface of the water and then be ignited electrically, turning the canal into a flaming inferno. The Egyptians viewed this system as a major obstacle that had to be overcome before a successful canal crossing could be made.

My responsibility in Israeli operational planning and presenting the enemy's probable courses of action provided me with tools I have been able to apply to this study for understanding the Egyptians' preparatory stages of the war.

In 1973 I was sent to the Jerusalem Brigade as its MI officer. In September of that year, on Rosh Hashana (the Jewish New Year), I inspected one of the brigade's reserve battalions that was manning most of the strongholds on the Suez Canal. (Months later, with a team from the IDF's History Branch, I investigated what had happened to the battalion during the first days of the fighting.) Prior to the outbreak of hostilities I also monitored changes in the sector, although I was not involved in assessment analysis. Only in the last phases of the war did I return to the sector, this time with a brigade that had been transferred to Maj. Gen. Arik Sharon's division and ordered to hold the sector west of the Suez Canal in the "agricultural barrier" south of Ismalia, facing the Egyptians' Tomb of the Unknown Soldier. Again I was deeply involved in the canal sector and even met with Egyptian paratroop officers (170th Brigade) holding the line opposite us. This encounter took place during the initial low-level "peace talks" between Israel and Egypt prior to Israeli disengagement. We discussed local issues, area problems, and border questions. During the talks I was also invited to visit Cairo.

After serving in other sectors, including the Northern Command opposite the Syrians, I returned to the study of military doctrine. Between 1979 and 1984 I was in charge of analyzing the enemy's military doctrine. In this role, I examined the roots and principles of war, the Soviet army's development of its war doctrine, and the way the Arab armies — especially the Egyptian armed forces — adopted it and put it into practice. In this capacity I wrote dozens of papers and lectured to soldiers and officers, expanding their knowledge of this subject.

In the following years I collected material, visited libraries and archives, and met with scholars working on related topics. I kept abreast of the accounts and memoirs written by the commanders who fought in the war, and read the published material summarizing and formulating the lessons of the war.

When I joined the faculty at the IDF's Command and General Staff College, I realized the need to convey to officers — on their way to senior command and staff positions — information and critical explanations of the military situations and moves in past wars in general and Israel's wars in particular. I would like to dedicate this book to all my students, in the belief that its material will prove vital to them for the roles they will be called on to fulfill.

I began the task of gathering material for the research many years ago. The time and effort that I invested naturally came at the price of other obligations, and required the consent and understanding of many individuals — commanders, subordinates, military associates, and work colleagues — who recognized the subject's importance and encouraged me to pursue it. For this, I am deeply grateful to them.

I would especially like to thank my advisors at Tel Aviv University: Professors Shimon Shamir and Yehuda Wallach, whose encouragement and assistance enabled me to undertake this project; Prof. Eyal Ziser, who replaced Prof. Shamir when the latter became incapacitated; Dr. Mati Mayzel, for his help; and Prof. Yoav Gelber of Haifa University, who recommended a new version of this study, and facilitated its acceptance as a doctoral thesis.

Thanks are also due to the Jaffee Center of Strategic Studies at Tel Aviv University for the support it extended during my research; to the commander of IDF military colleges, Maj. Gen. Amos Yadlin, and the director of the Command and General Staff College, Brig. Gen. Yaakov Zigdon, for helping me obtain permission to have the work published as a book; and to Lt. Col. Hagai Golan, commander of the "Ma'arachot" publishing house, and my editor, Zvi Ofer, both of whom labored tirelessly in transforming the research into book form and getting it published.

Table of Contents

Foreword

by Major General Shlomo Gazit (Ret.)

On two occasions I visited the panoramic exhibition in Cairo glorifying the "October War" (once I even viewed its Hebrew version). The presentation is an impressive tribute to the Egyptian army's successful crossing of the Suez Canal and military accomplishments on the canal's eastern bank. However, I couldn't help but notice that any reference to the rest of the war — from October 8 to the Egyptian army's surrender two weeks later — when half of Egypt's land force, the Third Army, was surrounded by the Israeli Defense Forces (IDF) which had crossed the canal and deployed on the western side — was conspicuously omitted.

This book by Dani Asher adds a crucial perspective to our understanding of the Yom Kippur War — a perspective that the Agranat Commission (the official blue-ribbon panel that investigated the mishaps in Israeli intelligence that led to the war) did not examine. Since the fatal day of October 6, 1973, we've been running around in circles asking the same questions that continue to bedevil us. How to explain the Egyptian surprise? How to fathom the egregious oversight on the part of military intelligence and our other intelligence agencies? How to account for our negligence in furnishing an early warning of Egyptian and Syrian preparations to launch the war? The missing perspective focuses on our enemy on the strategic level — and our failure to understand Egypt's real intentions.

At the end of the Six-Day War, we all heard the much-touted statement by Egypt's president, Gamal Abdel Nasser: "What was taken by force will be returned by force!" From that time on Israeli intelligence was convinced that sooner or later Egypt would launch a war aimed at realizing this objective. Nevertheless, the Israeli intelligence community repeatedly affirmed: "According to our estimates, Egypt is still unprepared for war and will remain incapable of initiating war in the near future. No military initiative will occur within the next two–three years." This assessment, which was almost universally accepted in the Israeli intelligence community at the time, stated that Egypt had not attained operative conditions for embarking on a major campaign.

Brig. Gen. Dani Asher (Ret.), a former military intelligence (MI) officer, has carried out academic research that removes the shackles from the accepted view of the Israeli intelligence estimate. He meticulously analyzes and describes what happened "on the other side": the transformation in Egypt's strategic perception, and the change initiated by Nasser's successor, Anwar Sadat. Once Sadat became president, he analyzed the military balance of forces and withdrew his predecessor's assertion. Sadat realized that Egypt was incapable of forcibly retrieving all of the land that Israel had captured in 1967. Therefore he formulated an alternative strategic concept — the concept of an "all-out war of limited dimensions, designed to get the diplomatic wheels moving."

1

After Sadat outlined the war's aim to the military command, a plan was devised for fighting and dealing with Israel's security concept. The author presents a detailed description of the planning and preparations that began in the aftermath of the Six-Day War and created a military organization capable of accomplishing its assignments. Despite the Egyptian war planners' dislike of the Soviet military advisors operating in their county, they were willing to reap the maximum benefit from the Red Army's experience and warfare doctrine, adapting them to Egypt's operational plans that were being worked out in detail and implemented at different levels in the Egyptian army's assault and support units.

Thus, in early October 1973, on Yom Kippur — the holiest day of the year in the Jewish calendar — Egypt launched an all-out war whose objectives were limited to crossing the Suez Canal and constructing a military defense layout along a narrow strip on the canal's eastern bank. For the eastward advance to succeed, it was essential that the new layout east of the canal remain entirely within range of Egypt's surface-to-air missile umbrella — a layout of antiaircraft batteries that had been deployed west of and adjacent to the canal at the end of the War of Attrition (1968–1970). In effect, during the Yom Kippur War, the Egyptian army transferred its defense layout, that was protected by antiaircraft weapons, from the western side of the Suez Canal to the eastern bank.

Brigadier General Asher discusses a question both interesting and troublesome, that has not been sufficiently addressed until now: could Israel have countered Egypt's new strategic concept if its efforts at concealment had failed and Israel had not been tactically surprised? One can argue that as long as Egypt kept its forces from penetrating deeply into Sinai, lest they exceed the range of the air defense umbrella, it is more than doubtful whether Israel could have completely stopped the Egyptian crossing. Thus, the Egyptians' strategic objective — breaking the stalemate and getting the diplomatic wheels rolling — would have been achieved even under these conditions.

This book is the story of the Yom Kippur War from the Egyptian perspective. Until Egyptian military archives are opened (and it seems unlikely they ever will be), the author provides a thorough analysis of the war, basing his research on the wealth of documents captured by the IDF, which have enabled him to see the campaign through the Egyptians' eyes.

This book is required reading not only because it furnishes a clearer understanding of what happened to Israel thirty years ago, but also because its message is of utmost importance: *we must always be attentive and alert to the possibility of change in the other side's strategic concept.* Prevailing concepts of Arab strategy lead to inflexible thinking. The danger that lies on our doorstep — the danger that overtook us thirty years ago — was our own rigidity. Whoever repeats the mantra, "the sea is the same sea and the Arabs are the same Arabs," runs the risk of falling into a trap that he sets for himself.

Shlomo Gazit is a retired major general and former head of the IDF's intelligence branch. He also served as president of the Ben-Gurion University in Beer-Sheva for eight years. Currently he is a member of INSS (Israel National Strategic Studies) at Tel Aviv University.

Preface

The aim of this work is to examine the Egyptian war planners' answer — at the civilian and military levels — to the problems facing them on the Sinai front prior to the Yom Kippur War. Israel's "concept," that was formulated in the two years before the war, held that Egypt, under conditions at the time, was incapable of launching a full-scale offensive on the Suez Canal front. This concept was wrong. The Egyptian planners studied doctrinal issues, solved the problems that the IDF set up for them on the canal, prepared their army for combat, and embarked upon war. The Israeli security concept, expressed in the IDF's overall defense system in Sinai, was cracked by the Egyptians and destroyed on the waves of attacking forces.

The book explores all aspects of the Egyptian concept of war with Israel — goals, objectives, courses of action — and the changes that the concept underwent from the Six-Day War until the outbreak of the Yom Kippur War. The book describes the Egyptian political system — the conditions and constraints in which it operated at the domestic, inter–Arab, and international level — and in particular, Egypt's relations with the superpowers — the Soviet Union and United States.[1] The study also discusses the instructions that the Egyptian political level gave to the military commanders, and how these orders were translated into operational plans. The heart of the analysis deals with important changes in the Soviet warfare doctrine — ground forces in particular — in order to meet the Egyptian army's needs at the end of the Six-Day War, during the War of Attrition, and especially prior to and during the Yom Kippur War.

Egypt's preparations for the Yom Kippur War are practically the only effective example since World War II of an army adopting and applying the entire Soviet military doctrine. In general, the book has steered clear of an analysis of Egyptian military moves after the war broke out. When these moves are discussed, it is only to elucidate and illustrate various plans and preparations of the campaign, the chief subject of the study.

Military research in general — modern military history and especially the Arabs' moves in the wars with Israel — is an area still outside the Israeli academic world. A nation "that lives by its sword," that experiences "another round of fighting" every decade, has still not figured out how to pool its efforts into a comprehensive study of the background and stages of the wars themselves. The various works on the military history of the Jewish people since its return to its homeland are mostly "battlefield heritage" descriptions and memoirs, mainly intended to preserve the war stories and eyewitness accounts of officers and soldiers. The picture presented is not a complete one.[2] A lucid understanding of the past might improve our preparations for the future. An accurate comprehensive study of the background and facts might heighten our awareness of our limitations, revise our perception of favorable circumstances and their exploitation, and show us how to plan more wisely for future military situations. War is a two-sided affair. Awareness of the "other side" does not in itself provide a complete picture or give us an understanding of the "truth" in history. In order to gain a full picture of the events, we have to understand what the other side did, and equally important — what it planned to do.

The military history of modern Israel is still a new field. The Yom Kippur War, the largest of all the Arab-Israeli confrontations since the War of Independence, has been researched almost solely by official agencies. Academia's contribution to this area is still in its infancy. The official body — the IDF's History Section — made a great effort to study the enemy's strategy and tactics immediately after the war. But the section's publications are primarily for IDF use — only a few of them reach the general public; furthermore, they were carried out under conditions that created a stilted perspective. In my opinion, the proximity to the events, and especially the researchers' occupation in the prewar stages and the war itself, along with their emotional involvement in the conflict and its results, have marred the integrity of these studies. The initial research was not updated even when additional material was published, including memoirs by commanders on both sides.

Nearly all of the academic studies in this period deal with the strategic level, the policy and leadership circles, processes in the Middle East and beyond, the balance of forces, the reasons for the war, and its consequences. What is missing is a description at the operations level: a comprehensive examination of the war plan in light of its goals, an analysis of the war's stages in view of the plans, and an in-depth look at the preparations and their implementation. While much effort and resources were devoted to studying the IDF's moves at the time, the enemy's operational system was not analyzed. This book is intended to fill in part of the lacuna in academic research on the strategic level and the moves at the tactical level where the plans were implemented.

The book's innovation lies in its tracing the changes in the Egyptian concept of the war's objective and aims that came to expression in the operational planning from the end of the Six-Day War, through the War of Attrition, and up to the Yom Kippur War. The book analyzes Egypt's plans at the operational level, comparing them with the Soviet warfare doctrine, and examines how the Soviet warfare doctrine was adopted as a basic tier in preparing the Egyptian army for the Yom Kippur War. The study hopes to provide answers about the forces' course of action and how the Egyptian plan was formulated. The book discusses whether the plan, as the Egyptian minister of war stated, was "entirely different from the ideas that we heard from Soviet experts." Was the plan based on the Soviets' antiquated World War II warfare doctrine? If so, then according to some experts, this was an exception to the rule, almost sui generis; it was essentially the Egyptians' brilliant adaptation and application of a warfare doctrine developed on European soil.

Today, more than a generation has passed since the Yom Kippur War; the initial shock has receded, the emotional involvement reduced and perspective expanded. The time has come to reexamine the political, and more importantly the military plans and events prior to and during the war. The moves themselves have generated disputes on both sides of the border. Certain incidents serve as the basis for arguments and conflicting interpretations of the events, and their causes and results.

I believe that the key issue is linked to an understanding of the war's aims and their transformation into an operational plan by the Arabs — by the Egyptians in particular. Even today, thirty years after the war, the task that the Egyptian forces were assigned, their objectives, the bickering between Egyptian and Syrian commanders, and among the respective armies' commanders themselves still remain unresolved. Each side clings to its particular interpretation, and only the head of state (in the case of Egypt — the late President Sadat) can provide the answers.[3]

This dispute has spawned (and still spawns) interviews, statements, and published works; two of the most conspicuous are the account by the Egyptian chief of staff, Shazli, on the canal crossing, published five years after the war, and the memoirs of the Egyptian chief of staff, Gamasi, that was published later. Both generals had worked together in preparing for the war, and were "comrades in arms" (in the initial stages of the fighting, at any rate). Their concept regarding the war's aims and objectives, and the actual plan that the troops were supposed to carry out, are rent with controversy. Shazli, the father of the limited plan, believes that the plan went according to his instructions and accomplished its objectives. Gamasi, however, who supported the more ambitious plan, agrees with the Syrian version: that the Egyptians halted earlier than planned and failed to attain all of their objectives. The two conflicting versions did not become Israel's inheritance.

Israel's "official history"—that includes the backdrop to the war, memoirs, and later interpretations by Israeli scholars and commanders — portrays Egypt's achievements in the early stages of the fighting as a semi-victory. The war aims, at least the territorial ones that the Egyptian hoped to gain, such as the capture of the Gidi and Mitla Passes and Bir Gafgafa were not met. By basing the "official" Israeli version of the war on this shortcoming on the part of the Egyptians, Israeli commanders, commentators, and historians have been able to depict the war's events, even in the initial stages, as a much greater Israeli success than it actually was.

The "Egyptian armored attack" of October 14 is another example of a plan gone awry or being only partially completed. IDF commanders and MI officers waited for the Egyptian army's second echelon to join in a final attack in the heart of Sinai. But the offensive was postponed, and when it came it was carried out piecemeal, in limited strength, and with no attempt to reach objectives deep in enemy territory. By relying on the official Israeli version that highlights the Egyptians' failure to gain their objectives, certain elements in Israel can portray the IDF's capabilities and accomplishments in a rosier light than they were.

This book presents the Egyptian army's intentions, planning, and operations during the Yom Kippur War in a more objective and updated fashion than in the past. In other words, the study's purpose is to describe how the Egyptian army planned and prepared for military assignments defined by the political level. The updated presentation enables us to examine the Egyptian plan — its formulation and implementation — that was based on experiences in the Six-Day War and War of Attrition. The book also illustrates how the plan was influenced by the obstacles that Israel's defense lines set up on the Suez Canal front.

The Egyptian war concept, and its implementation, sets a precedent in modern military history. The Egyptians tried to launch an all-out war in very limited dimensions in all types of combat missions. To the best of my knowledge, this attempt runs counter to everything known in military literature published in Israel and abroad regarding the Egyptian army's goal and missions; it also enables armies, military academies, and scholars to derive basic lessons from this conventional war — the largest of its kind in the second half of the twentieth century.

The Opportunity

The case before us is unique because we have a wealth of primary sources related to the military aspects of the Yom Kippur War. Captured documents collected during the war are the main source of information for the prewar period.[4] This material, taken from the battlefield, and especially from the headquarters of military units, falls under six categories.

1. Doctrinal literature was studied in various courses in Egypt and the Soviet Union and transmitted to the commanders and troops. It includes, *inter alia*, collections of lectures and lesson plans for conducting the war and the battlefield, rules and regulations, and publications dealing with the warfare doctrine. The Egyptians took great pains to translate the material from Russian into English and Arabic.

Many publications from Nasser Higher Military Academy, the highest military college in Egypt, fell into Israel's hands. The works that were translated into Arabic between 1969 and 1971 also served as the basic material for studying the military doctrine at the operational level and relied almost exclusively on the Soviet doctrine. Some translations included minor adaptation supplements geared to the needs of the Egyptian theater and army.

2. Research — the Egyptians carried out research on specific doctrinal issues applicable to battlefield scenarios on the Suez Canal front and in the Sinai Peninsula.

3. Summaries include discussions at the Egyptian general staff level, and instructions — mainly from the Egyptian chief-of-staff — on general matters and special operational issues dealing with the war plan.

4. Plans and training outlines for units, in the years before the war, deal with tactical and technical-tactical matters and operational issues such as bridging and fording. The plans contain Soviet advisors' doctrinal recommendations and comments to Egyptian units at various levels.

5. Orders and operation maps cover a wide range of plans at different levels, including operational plans for defense ("Amalia 200") and several generations of offensive plans ("Granite 1," "Granite 2," and "Granite 2 Improved"), as well as exercises and training that were part of the war preparations. The material (in various degrees of detail) is from different periods.

6. Detailed Maps are at the battalion, brigade, divisional, and army level of war scenarios in Egyptian defensive and offensive plans.[5]

When the IDF crossed the canal and advanced west to a point one hundred kilometers from Cairo, it captured the main tactical and rear headquarters of the Egyptian army. Plans, orders, and detailed maps from the operational echelons of divisional level and army headquarters fell into Israel's hands. This material has provided an invaluable primary source for a comprehensive analysis of the campaign and has enabled us to understand the processes at work in the Egyptian planners' military thinking. Such material could only be found with senior commanders or in the Egyptian army's history unit. During my research I was able to compare the data and descriptions in my possession with those of the sacked chief of staff, General Shazli. In many cases we seem to have used the same documents in investigating the events.

Along with original Egyptian material, I also had access to a wealth of Soviet doctrinal matter gleaned from a number of sources, especially military publications that reached the West. These included: Soviet field regulations from 1962, encyclopedias,[6] and books on military subjects that could be purchased on the open market[7] in the Soviet Union after Stalin's demise. Some of the publications had been translated, published, and used by scholars in the West.[8] These included unclassified Soviet army publications[9] — monthlies and bulletins in Russian, German, and English. The most interesting of these were translated by the Americans in JPRS (Joint Publications Research Service) and circulated among subscribers.[10]

Other material included widely circulated studies and research papers by western military elements[11] — especially American — on Soviet military doctrine,[12] and publications from western research institutes that analyzed the Soviet warfare doctrine. Among these institutes were SASO (Soviet Army Study Office) located next to TRADOC (U.S. Army Training and Doctrine Command) at Fort Leavenworth, Kansas, an office that surveyed and circulated unclassified Soviet military publications, and operates today under the new name of FMSO (Foreign Military Study Office) and is engaged in tracking and publishing military material from the Eastern Bloc. The most up-to-date and comprehensive publication of Soviet military material at the operations level is the anthology of lectures given at the Soviet Academy of General Command, collected and edited by American academic and military researchers under the title *The Voroshilov Lectures, Issues of Operational Art,* Vol. III, 1992.[13]

The use of original Soviet material and other publications form the basis for a comparison and examination of the Egyptian army's application, adaptation, and transformation of the Soviet doctrine, which is at the heart of my research.

Introduction

The Egyptian Military Concept on the Eve of the Yom Kippur War

> "The plan that we implemented was unlike anything we heard from the Soviet experts."
> (Ahmad Ismail Ali — the Egyptian Minister of War,
> in an interview with Hassanein Heykal,
> *al-Anwar*, November 18, 1973)

The Egyptian leaders' concept of the war, its objectives and goals, on the Jewish high holiday of Yom Kippur in October 1973, went through several changes in the years preceding the outbreak of hostilities. The Six-Day War in 1967 left a serious stain on Arab honor. Arab countries lost vast areas of their homeland — territory that would not be returned in the near future. Egypt's rout from Sinai — minus its territory — and its failure to initiate political moves for altering the situation, soon gave rise to President Nasser's view of a pan-Arab war aimed at "returning by force what was taken by force."

Egypt's military weakness and its failure to find a political solution in the first two years after the debacle convinced it to use the army in a limited fashion as it had done in the War of Attrition. The "*Sitzkrieg* years" revealed a number of weak points on the Israeli side, even though the IDF held the Suez Canal's eastern bank which effectively blocked the canal's opening. The War of Attrition demonstrated Egypt's strength, but also proved to Cairo's leaders that they had to seek another track.

Egyptian president Anwar Sadat tried to break the political-military stalemate that was created because of Israel's occupation of Arab lands, especially Sinai. He viewed the logjam as a result of the "no war — no peace" situation. Political moves and initiatives, and mediation attempts by both Egypt and other parties had all failed. Sadat himself admitted, "Either they utterly failed or were rejected by our enemy."[1] Sadat studied the military options and at this stage already realized that only military force could jump-start the political process.

At various levels the threats to renew full-scale war were perceived with reservation. This stemmed from the military system's weakness or perhaps unreadiness, on the one hand, and from the need to find political solutions, on the other. The Egyptian army had been blamed for the defeat in the Six-Day War and was still not prepared for assuming large-scale military tasks. The army that Sadat inherited from Nasser was still licking its wounds, undergoing partial training for a full-scale military offensive, and continuously looking at a wide range of options. From the moment that Sadat ascended to power, he strove to avoid a reckless entry to war until all the preparations had been made on a "scientific basis."[2] The systems that had

9

been set up in the end of 1972 led to Sadat's concept of "an all-out war of limited proportions" as the means for goading the political process into life.

The decision called for the allocation of resources for the ongoing recovery and build-up of the "military machine" so that it could meet its tasks assigned. Egyptian army commanders learned the lessons of the Six-Day War. They tested and studied all aspects of the Egyptian and Israeli armies' relative weaknesses and strengths in the War of Attrition. The Egyptian establishment strove to come up with solutions. The army was given top priority in the appropriation of personnel, equipment, and the president's attention; in effect it became a state within a state. Although Sadat did not abandon the diplomatic front, he was personally involved in the army and issued instructions directly to senior commanders.[3]

The overall strength of Egyptian ground forces, up until the outbreak of war, included the following formations and meta-formation headquarters[4]:
- Two field army headquarters — the Second and Third Armies.
- Two armored divisions — the Fourth and Twenty-first.
- Three mechanized divisions — the Third, Sixth, and Twenty-third.
- Five infantry divisions — the Second, Seventh, Sixteenth, Eighteenth, and Nineteenth.
- Three to five independent tank brigades.
- Two independent mechanized brigades.
- Four independent infantry brigades.
- Three paratroop brigades.
- Twenty-four commando battalions.

The Egyptian ground forces order of battle (ORBAT) had the following fighting equipment:
- Approximately 2,200 medium tanks, mainly T-54/55s and T-62s.
- Approximately 2,900 various types of APCs.
- Approximately 2,400 artillery pieces of various sizes.
- Approximately 800 antitank missile launch systems.
- Twelve surface-to-surface rocket launchers (Frog7s).
- Nine surface-to-surface missile launchers (SCUDs).
- Various types of assault boats, amphibious trucks, ferries, rafts, and bridges.

The overall strength of the ORBAT for the offensive included two army headquarters in charge of five reinforced infantry divisions, two armor divisions, two mechanized divisions, and half the commando battalions.

Sadat made the crucial decision to take the "military option," that is, to make massive use of the armed forces in an operation designed solely to get the wheels of diplomacy rolling. In this way a war with limited objectives would prevent a détente from crystallizing, and would serve Egyptian interests without having to take pan-Arab goals too much into consideration. Sadat decided to embark upon a new course of action when he ordered the armed forces to launch an "all-out war of limited dimensions," a war that would restore Egyptian control over a limited area on the eastern side of the Suez Canal, force the Israelis to deal with the shock of their own fallibility, unfreeze the diplomatic stalemate, and push the two sides to the negotiating table. A by-product of this conceptual transformation was the change in and reduction of the war's aims. Army commanders were informed of the modification and ordered to translate it into operational plans for the coming campaign.

The "concept" that developed in Israel in the early 1970s was based on the IDF's air and armored superiority that had been demonstrated in the Six-Day War and War of Attrition, and its defense system that was based on ground obstacles — the Suez Canal, the dirt embankment on the eastern (Israeli) side of the canal, and the strongholds along the Bar-Lev Line (the Israeli defense layout on the eastern side of the Suez Canal). According to the Israeli concept, until certain basic conditions were met, such as Arab air superiority and strategic pan-Arab cooperation, the Egyptians would not dare to go to war. Israeli military superiority and the obstacles on the front forced the Egyptian planners and the entire military establishment to come up with solutions that would enable Egypt to launch a war, accomplish its objectives, and allow the country's leaders to realize their political goals.

From the moment that the decision for a war of limited dimensions was made, Egyptian military commanders and war planners began preparing the troops for battlefield objectives. In addition to developing a goal-oriented ORBAT, drilling for the canal crossing, and training specialized units, the military leaders were also ordered to plan the force's course of action.

The Egyptians' strategic planning and especially their operational and tactical solutions (or fighting methods) looked to the Soviet warfare doctrine that their army had adopted in the mid–1950s when it acquired weapons from the Eastern Bloc. But this doctrine, based on the experience of World War II and Soviet military thinking,[5] gave only a limited answer to the special problems that the Egyptian military planners faced. The Soviet warfare doctrine was partially rewritten, its dimensions altered, reduced, and adapted to the Egyptian army's needs on the Suez Canal front. The revised doctrine was studied and digested by military commanders and troops in the war's planning stages. The army adopted the principles of the new doctrine and trained according to it.

The Egyptians' operational plan employed by its army in the Yom Kippur War was also prepared on the basis of this doctrine. Like the Syrian case, this was the only time in the second half of the twentieth century when the Soviet offensive doctrine was studied and then applied on the battlefield. The plan's principles called for taking the offensive while crossing a complex water obstacle, destroying the Israeli force on the forward point of the front, establishing bridgeheads, and setting up a powerful defensive position to withstand the IDF counterattack. The offensive required Egyptian ground forces to be organized in four efforts. The two main efforts in the center of the sector were made up of the field armies that bore the brunt of the task.

The northern effort of the front was made up of the Second Army, which included three reinforced infantry divisions in the first echelon: the Eighteenth reinforced with the Fifteenth Independent Tank Brigade; the Second reinforced with the Twenty-fourth Brigade from the Twenty-third Mechanized Division; and the Sixteenth reinforced with the Fourteenth Brigade from the Twenty-first Armored Division. The second echelon consisted of two reduced divisions: the Twenty-third Mechanized Division and the Twenty-first Armored Division.

The front's southern effort was made up of the Third Army, that included two reinforced infantry divisions at the first echelon: the Seventh Division reinforced with the Twenty-fifth Independent Armored Brigade, and the Nineteenth Division reinforced with the Twenty-Second Tank Brigade from the Sixth Mechanized Division. The 130th Independent Amphibious Brigade was also slated for this front. At the second echelon were the Fourth Armored Division and Sixth Mechanized Division, both with only one mechanized brigade.

The secondary independent effort in the canal's northern sector was made up of the 135th Independent Infantry Brigade and a number of commando battalions.

The southern secondary effort, on the shores of the Gulf of Suez, consisted of the First Mechanized Brigade from the Sixth Division, and other commando units.

Most of the remaining forces were held in reserve at general headquarters in the Egyptian rear, a few were assigned to the Red Sea Area Command.[6]

With these efforts, the Egyptian army went to war. It used its infantry, commando, and armored forces in a complex operation that commenced with an offensive: the fording of a water barrier, capture of territory on the eastern bank, and erection of bridgeheads. After these assignments were accomplished, the army began digging in, building its defenses in a tight array with antitank weapons designed to repel the IDF counterattack. The campaign witnessed the integration of artillery, antitank units, engineers, and various types of logistical support. All of the fighting proceeded according to the operational plan whose roots lay deep in the combat doctrine.

The Egyptian army performed like a well-oiled machine and ran according to a systematic doctrinal blueprint. In the baptism of fire, the troops implementing the "Egyptian doctrine" on the battlefield shattered Israel's security concept, "smashing it to smithereens," and gaining military victories that eventually led to political ones and the realization of the war's aims as the nation's leader had defined them.

Minor deviations from the course of action and flaws in planning and performance did occur: the breach between army bridgeheads, the ferrying of armored forces to the eastern bank, and the delayed departure from the bridgeheads on the October 14 offensive, all detracted from the Egyptian achievement and enabled the IDF to cross the canal and occupy territory on the western bank. Nevertheless, the IDF victory could not prevent the Egyptians from attaining their main goal: the opening of political talks that eventually returned the entire Sinai Peninsula to their hands.

1

The Egyptian Army

*From the Six-Day War to the
End of the War of Attrition*

The Egyptian Army's Lessons from the Six-Day War

In May 1967 the Egyptian army received instructions from the political level, headed by President Nasser, to prepare for a military venture. In the Arabs' eyes, a decisive victory over Israel was guaranteed — not because of Arab military supremacy but because of their cultural superiority and the justice of their cause. Israel was perceived as a contrived, fragmented, weak statelet containing a faint-hearted, pusillanimous Jewish population lacking the nobility of spirit necessary for self-sacrifice.[1] Prior to the war, Nasser often proclaimed that the whole of Palestine would have to be returned to the Palestinian people, and that Israel, as a Jewish state and the realization of the Jewish national movement — Zionism — would have to be destroyed.[2]

The Arab world — especially Egypt — was traumatized by its abject defeat in the Six-Day War, and experienced an ideological crisis of the first magnitude as it engaged in soul-searching for the reasons of the failure. Arab self-image — previously that of a reinvigorated society and rising world power — plummeted to new depths. The Arabs now saw themselves as a socio-economically depleted nation; a technological, scientific, and cultural backwater wallowing in braggadocio and emotionalism, swept away by self-nourished illusion; a people that lacked the strength to get a job done; a superficial, imitative conglomerate of states incapable of understanding the essence of a problem.[3] This time, those who sought the reasons for the catastrophic failure could not pin the blame on "reactionary regimes" in the Arab world or Israel's collusion with the European powers. The debacle of 1967 was seen and felt as a calamity greater than that of 1948 because it occurred after the Arabs were certain that they had overcome their deficiencies and were fully girded for battle. For a second time the Egyptians were forced to face issues related to their vulnerability and impotence.[4] The defeat was recognized as national failure that the Arab regimes themselves were solely responsible for.[5]

The entire Arab world naturally tried to comprehend the scale of the "drubbing," but it was mainly the Egyptians who examined the following reasons:

- The leaders' responsibility for the method of decision-making style and issuing orders, and their conduct before and during the war;
- The strategic, operational, and tactical circumstances in the planning stages and during the war;
- War planning, modus operandi, conduct of operations, and battle moves; IDF activity in the southern front: strong points, blunders, and weaknesses.

13

The Egyptian army learned from its mistakes, and on this basis planned and prepared for the coming challenges: the War of Attrition and, to a much greater extent, the Yom Kippur War.

The Egyptian army entered Sinai on the eve of the Six-Day War having undergone wide-scale modernization with the aid of Eastern Bloc countries, especially the Soviet Union. In addition to absorbing of huge quantities of Eastern European arms and equipment in the 1960s, it also adopted several chapters of the Soviet combat doctrine, mostly those on defense. The army, especially its infantry divisions, grew in size. The main reason for Egypt's military strengthening in this period was its involvement in the civil war in the mountainous regions of Yemen.

The army was almost at full strength when its 1,050 tanks entered Sinai in May–June 1967.

Egyptian forces consisted of:

— One entire armored division — the Fourth Division — and the headquarters of another armored division (minus the troops);

— Two to three independent armor brigades;

— Four infantry divisions (comprising twelve brigades);

— Eight independent infantry brigades and fourteen reserve brigades;

— Six general headquarters (GHQ) artillery brigades: one antiaircraft, two field artillery, and three medium-sized brigades.[6]

The deployment in Sinai included a hastily assembled force of infantry and armor, taken from existing units.[7]

Almost all of the forces entered Sinai according to the "Kahar" Defense Plan. These formations integrated into the defense zones of General Murtaga's Eastern Command (Sinai) which contained one infantry division, two independent tank brigades (Murtaga's reserves), and the Fourth Armored Division (the GHQ's reserve force).

At his trial in February 1968, the former minister of war claimed: "We were one hundred percent certain that Israel would not dare attack or launch a first strike because any military move on its part would spell suicide for it. [We blindly believed] that it would be defeated in such an event."[8]

The Egyptian army suffered heavy losses in men, weapons, and equipment during the war. Almost every Egyptian unit was damaged and needed time for intensive recovery. By Israel's reckoning, 15,000 Egyptian troops were killed and almost 50,000 wounded in the Six-Day War.[9] [10] Of the 845 tanks in Sinai at the outbreak of hostilities, 590 remained in Sinai and the Gaza Strip. Only a handful of armored units managed to cross the canal back into Egypt without casualties. Most units were wiped out. The Egyptian air force lost 360 jet fighters and other planes. According to Egyptian accounts, 17 percent of the ground troops, 4 percent of the pilots, and 85 percent of the air defense forces were lost in the war. The Egyptians also admitted that 85 percent of their fighter aircraft and their entire fleet of light and heavy bombers were destroyed.[11]

Beyond the personal blow to Nasser's stature, to Egypt's position in the Arab world and the army's effectiveness as a fighting force, Egypt paid a heavy economic price for Israel's occupation of Sinai and the eastern bank of the Suez Canal. The closure of the canal and the loss of Sinai's oil fields wrested major assets from Egypt, curtailed its foreign currency input, and increased its dependency on outside elements. The IDF's deployment on the east bank put the canal cities, their inhabitants and infrastructure under imminent physical threat. Egypt's loss of its deterrent capability — because of reduced ranges — left its air force vulner-

Egyptian soldiers carrying supply to the east side of the Suez Canal.

able even in bases deep in the rear. Furthermore, the air force's ability to hit targets inside Israel was almost completely nullified.[12]

After the war, as stated, the Egyptians analyzed their war aims and preparations, Israeli activity and their responses to it, and came to several conclusions. They scathingly criticized the political level and government leaders in an all-out effort to understand what went wrong on the battlefield.

The analysts discovered that the war's objectives had not been clear or adequately clarified by the leadership — Nasser and others — especially Field Marshal (Mushir) Amar, the deputy commander of the armed forces, and Shams Badran, the war minister, who were directly responsible for military affairs and the running of the war.

The military scientists discussed at length Egypt's aim in demonstratively marching into Sinai in May 1967, but the issue remained unanswered. The Egyptian-Israeli border had generally been stable and calm in the decade between Israel's pullout from Sinai in 1957 and the Six-Day War (excluding a few cases of infiltration for smuggling and some isolated shooting incidents). However, the quiet along the border did not reflect the depth of hostility between the two countries after the Sinai Campaign. Egypt had a twofold account to settle with Israel: the 1948 reckoning and the 1956 score. During this ten-year lull Nasser was occupied with other problems, domestic and foreign, but he never forgot the open account.[13]

His decision in May 1967 to move his army overtly into the Sinai Peninsula was the first in a series of fatal decisions that changed the face of the Middle East and the balance of power in the Arab-Israeli conflict. It created an irreversible situation. The general impression in Israel was that Egypt's steps were designed to deter Israel from attacking Syria and strengthen

Nasser's status as the leader of the Arab world and defender of Arab states against Israeli aggression.[14]

Nasser hoped his moves would achieve a number of goals: magnify his status in the inter–Arab World, the international arena, and the conflict with Israel. On this occasion he tried to use an improved and expanded version of his ploy during the "Rotem" crisis of February 1960 when he embarked upon a sudden massive build-up of Egyptian forces in Sinai to deter Israel's activity against Syria (Operation "Tarnegol" [Rooster]) at Tawfiq in the southern sector of the Golan Heights. Israel's response to Egypt's saber rattling was the mobilization of its reserves, a step that convinced Egypt to withdraw its troops from the peninsula. The Israeli counteraction is known as "Rotem." This time too, it seems, Nasser had no desire to get embroiled in a full-scale war with Israel. But his limited "stratagem," implemented in the light of day and before the world's television cameras, spun out of control.[15]

IDF analysts, who kept close track of Egypt's advances, advised proceeding cautiously. They also took into account that Egypt might take far-reaching steps, such as blocking the Straits of Tiran or bombing Israel's nuclear reactor at Dimona, and took into account Egypt's willingness to incur an Israeli counterstrike because of its solid defense layout in Sinai that was built to repulse such an attack.[16]

On May 26 Nasser made his most explicit threat to Israel since the beginning of the crisis in mid–May. Appearing in Cairo before the representatives of the "Confederation of Arab Professional Unions," he spoke as though he had made up his mind to risk a head-on collision because of his confidence in victory: "Today the Arab world is different from what it was a decade ago, and the same is true for Israel. The Arabs are determined to realize their rights, and they will restore the rights of the Arabs of Filastin. We are certain of victory.... Closing the straits means a commitment to full-scale war with Israel. This has required preparations. When we felt we were ready, we did [what we had to do] ... If we're attacked, it will be war and our basic goal will be the liquidation of Israel."[17]

The political level's goal was apparently not sufficiently clear to the military commanders. Gamasi, the deputy commander of the western front, later posed the question: "What exactly was our mission? Was it just to concentrate our forces in order to pressure Israel, to prevent it from attacking Syria? Was it merely a demonstration of military power to deter Israel?" Gamasi felt that the important lesson to be learned was that not only the state had to devise a meta-strategy — from which the political, military, economic, and social strategies would be derived — but that staff and his key mechanisms must be alerted to the strategy's main objectives. These officers, too, must be given the opportunity to review the plans and discuss the ramifications of political decisions on military activity.[18]

After the war the Egyptians realized that the disunity at the top — the profusion of functionaries and mechanisms at the political level, in the intelligence services, and at military headquarters (such as the Eastern Command and General Murtaga's Eastern Region Command Headquarters stationed in a forward base in Sinai behind and in addition to the only Sinai field army HQ, a headquarters that proved useless during the war) — were all contributing factors to the debacle.

The Egyptians pointed to the following reasons for the strategic fiasco:

• The state lacked a meta-strategy that coordinated political activity with military activity. The national leaders and the state drifted into war at a time acutely unfavorable to them.

• Political and international conditions worked against Egypt.

• There was no inter–Arab cooperation and no joint military plans for Sinai and other fronts, a fragmented state of affairs that enabled Israel to deal with each front in piecemeal fashion.

• Egypt became entangled in war while one-third of its regular army was bogged down in Yemen, which meant that a large part of Sinai's defense was placed on the backs of poorly trained reserve units.

• The Egyptian army's assignments were revised and revamped even while they were being prepared or implemented.[19]

• The defense of Sinai lost its strategic balance.[20]

The only plan that was adequately prepared before the move into Sinai was the basic defense plan for the eastern front — the "Kahar" Plan.[21] Changes were introduced and its main objective altered during the waiting period. The field army was under the command of Lt. Gen. (Fariq) Salah Mukhsayn, who was also responsible for the defense layouts and for preparing a number of operations outside the approved plan (including a limited offensive). Among the changes[22]:

• An offensive plan for cutting off Eilat from the rest of Israel;
• Strengthening the Gaza Strip and preventing its fall;
• Securing the Sharm e-Sheikh region;
• Advancing the defense line in northern Sinai from el-Arish to Rafah.

On May 31 the commander of the field army was ordered to "prevent enemy forces from breaking through the defense lines, defeat them, and block them from approaching the Suez Canal." He was also ordered to "remain on standby to carry out a limited-size attack in the southern Negev in conjunction with GHQ reserves, the air force, and air defense units."[23]

The plan went through a number of changes during the waiting period. Many units, more than those allotted to the basic defense plan, were deployed in relatively advanced positions and in layouts intended for the screening force. The Fourth Armored Division, the GHQ reserve force, was brought into Sinai and deployed east of the mountain passes. Additional troops, more than the original plan called for, including hastily put together units, were transferred and spread out across Sinai. The Israeli feints also caused further changes to be made and troops to be rushed from one sector to another. The modifications in the "Kahar" Plan became so profound that its advantages were squandered.

In his examination of Israeli plans, Gamasi notes a surprising strategy whereby the IDF did not act simultaneously on all the fronts. It began with a cumulative attack: first "taking care of" Egypt, then Jordan, and finally Syria. The IDF's system consisted of a preemptive air strike followed by a ground attack, with the greatest effort being made against Egypt (Israel's major foe) in order to destroy the majority of its army, capture the Sharm e-Sheikh area, and lift the blockade of the Straits of Tiran. This took place while a minimum number of troops were engaged on the other fronts.

Gamasi examined the events at the tactical level and described the moves of the first day's fighting from the Egyptian point of view, basing his study on Chief of Staff Fawzi's analysis. Gamasi's reasons for his country's military failure:

• The IDF's intention on Sinai's northern axis was to open the coastal axis and cut off the Gaza Strip. During the fighting it encountered a hastily assembled, still-incomplete Egyptian layout at the portal to Pithat Rafiah (The Rafah Opening).

• The Abu Agaila layout on the central axis held out for over a day against the penetration efforts until the IDF broke through using a vertical flanking movement.

• The Egyptian armor repulsed an IDF diversionary attack on the Kunteila axis.

Summing up the first day of fighting, Chief of Staff Fawzi emphasized that most of the

Egyptian forward layout had held. It broke only in Rafah in the Seventh Division's sector. The second defense line remained intact. The Fourth Division planned a counteroffensive on the second day but canceled it because of Israeli air superiority. At the same time the Egyptian command post in Sinai was destroyed and the general order for a retreat sounded.[24]

The Egyptians tended to exonerate Nasser of responsibility for the fiasco and the decision to retreat, in particular.[25] They blamed his deputy, Field Marshal (Mushir) Abd al-Hakim Amar — who committed suicide afterward[26] — for giving the panic-stricken order to withdraw. The question of who gave the order became a subject of controversy among Egyptian writers. Another question that surfaced in the aftermath of the debacle was related to the organization of the withdrawal and supervision over the retreating forces. Where were the commander and army headquarters that were supposed to be in charge of the troops? A long list of questions followed.[27]

It turns out, for example, that the army headquarters of Lt. Gen. Salah Mukhsayn crossed the canal to the west, into Egypt proper, with the approval of Field Marshal Amar as early as June 6. In other words, the retreat began without even informing the Eastern Command's headquarters which was located in the Bir Tmade region and was supposed to have command over the entire front.[28]

The desire to lighten the catastrophe led the first wave of Arab commentators to make assorted excuses, such as attributing the opening air blitz to the western superpowers. Even after the truth was revealed, the Arabs repeated the false accusation in hundreds of articles and based on a potpourri of pretexts and testimonies. At a later point in the search for answers for the debacle, the Arabs drew upon explanations from the 1948 war, such as glaring inter–Arab disunity; the absence of a joint military command; the miscalculated trust in the international system which had assured that war would not break out; underestimating Israeli strength; a constraining spiritual and intellectual mind-set; the ineffectual dissemination of information; rhetorical hyperbole; lack of realism; absence of social justice; bad luck; and so forth. In addition, Harkabi notes, relying mainly on his perusal of the Arab press and literature, a list of social weaknesses that can be summed up by the term "weakness of the trigger" or, fighting in isolated units in which each individual acts as though he's on his own.[29]

When the Arabs sought the reasons for their miserable performance on the battlefield they divided along the following lines[30]:

• The reformers — these were liberals who blamed the defeat on Egypt's social backwardness that had bred technical and technological stultification. They stressed the need for accelerated modernization as the only way out of this debility.

• The establishment's players — these observers saw the defeat as an aggregate of blunders: the surprise attack, the air force's annihilation, flawed reporting, faulty command and control, and even the balance of power in Israel's favor. The combination of catastrophes created a situation in which the Egyptian soldier hardly had time to pull the trigger.

• The Islamists — these blamed the defeat on the social-cultural disgrace caused by the people's alienation from the strict observance of Islam and will of God.

• The revolutionary-Marxists — these believed that the defeat was the outcome of Egypt's lopsided socio-economic structure and self-serving Arab leadership.

Later military-research literature is also reluctant to face up to the Egyptian army's ineptitude on the battlefield. The authors prefer to pin the defeat on the element of surprise and the army's unfamiliarity with the enemy and its tendency to underestimate, if not disparage him. Gamasi's analysis of the Egyptian military system's breakdown notes many omissions, including the following:

• For five years the army was stuck in Yemen (since 1962) where the fighting was of a different nature from what was required in Sinai. The Yemen adventure worked to the army's disadvantage, especially regarding budgeting and the level of training, discipline, and technical development — all of this had an adverse effect on the army's operational capacity.

• Crucial steps against the enemy were inexcusably neglected. Egypt's defense belts had been improperly constructed and shoddily equipped. The commanders thought it sufficient to prepare only the first line of defense near the eastern border. The remaining defense lines, especially the mountain passes in western Sinai, had not been prepared.[31]

• The army lacked an offensive capability. The only operational plan for defending Sinai was the "Kahar" Plan that had been drafted in December 1966.

• When the war broke out, half of the Egyptian troops in the battle zone were reservists. The majority were untrained and hastily called up only after other reservists had been discharged earlier than planned, two months before the war. The slapdash call-up created serious gaps in the units' manpower.

• The annihilation of the air force while it still sat on the ground, and the chronic shortage of pilots, meant that Israel's air supremacy was absolute.

• Air defense and air warning systems were lacking.

• The army's 1967 training program had been neglected. A year of limited instruction was especially inauspicious.

As mentioned, the Egyptians analyzed the IDF's moves in the Six-Day War. The conclusions became an integral part of the military manuals taught in the Nasser Higher Military Academy in the interim between the two wars. The material appeared in the chapter on defense which defined the expected threat.[32] In the introduction to the academic program on offensive organization and management, Israel is portrayed as the main cause of tension in the Middle East. The Egyptians claimed that imperialist countries were aiding Israel in building up its military might and developing its operational doctrine and capability. Israeli officers studied the NATO doctrine and the America's lessons in Vietnam, adopting and adapting them to their needs. According to the IDF's combat doctrine, the basic tactic for defeating the enemy is the offensive, especially in a surprise attack. The offensive's goal is to destroy the enemy's forces and capture vital territory and facilities deep in his territory.

The Egyptians analyzed the IDF's ORBAT on the front and noted two main operative groups, each of which included a formation made up of a number of brigades augmented with artillery. During the war the Egyptians had been caught off guard by the IDF's penetration into areas least expected — areas where the terrain was difficult — and by the IDF's exploitation of nighttime conditions for penetrating Egyptian defense lines. This was how the Israelis made use of heliborne forces and feinting movements, including the use of decoys. The Egyptian manuals also gave a number of examples where the Israeli offensive momentum stalled chiefly because of the Israelis' fear of losses. The IDF preferred to outflank Egyptian defense layouts rather than attack head-on. In other words, a frontal breakthrough was made only when other ways proved impossible. In each case, the Israelis carried out an integrated attack that included a vertical flanking movement.

The lead force on the battlefield is the armor because of its maneuverability, its ability to deliver a decisive punch, outflank the enemy, and attack him from the rear — especially in desert terrain. The basic operational formation is the armored brigade, reinforced with forward and flanking protection that includes engineering units, mortars, and a battery of self-propelled artillery. The infantry battalion is retained as a second echelon or reserve force, and is also reinforced with a tank battalion and artillery.

Before making contact and attacking, Israeli ground forces are assisted by the air force. Artillery barrages are also laid down as part of the effort in softening up the enemy before the breakthrough. The time needed for these preparations may vary. The Israelis tend exploit their pre-battle intelligence — especially from reconnaissance flights — to complete the intelligence picture and acquire target updates. Reconnaissance patrols, including the use of helicopters, are employed at all echelons for collecting precise information during the fighting.

The Egyptians' attempt to sum up the IDF's probable modus operandi, according to the lessons of the Six-Day War, emphasized the following points that afforded the IDF an advantage:

• Moves based on the following war and battlefield principles: surprise, coordination, aggressiveness, and taking maximum advantage of day and nighttime conditions, reconnaissance, and protection elements.

• Deep and graduated activity in its combat structure, using armored units as a strike force;

• The preference to outflank and bypass the enemy's defense layouts, while feigning a frontal attack; the widespread use of vertical (helicopter) and naval flanking movements to assist the attack, while striking the enemy's rear defenses;

• The set up of tactical [division-sized] taskforces for improved coordination among the units.

The Egyptians noted that the IDF's weak points included the following:

• Extreme sensitivity to the loss of life and equipment, especially against an organized defense layout like the ones at Bir Lachfan and Jabel Livni;

• Landing small heliborne units too long before their link-up with the main force;

• The presence of non-mobile infantry units at the brigade level, second echelon, and in reserve;

• Ground forces dependent on air assistance;

• The relatively slow pace of pursuit and advance that gave the retreating force sufficient time to reorganize.

In the final analysis, the Egyptians studied the reasons for their colossal failure and sporadic successes in the war, and applied the lessons in their preparations for the Yom Kippur War. Gamasi, who considered himself the architect of the Yom Kippur War,[33] wrote in the preface to his memoirs: "There is no going back from discussing everything that happened in the 'June War' which influenced military operations in the October War. The lessons of the June 1967 war served as one of the most decisive elements in drafting Egypt's strategy in the Yom Kippur War."[34]

Conclusion

The Six-Day War left Egypt with an overwhelming sense of failure. The system in command and control of the battle fell apart. As the War of Attrition — and especially the Yom Kippur War — approached, Egyptian military leaders worked tirelessly to simplify the chain of command and clear up overlapping and unnecessary connecting points.

The army was rebuilt, restructured, and rearmed after the Six-Day War in all aspects of unit formations, weapons and equipment. It adapted itself to the tasks it was assigned in the main battle theaters on the eastern front.[35] At the same time, Egyptian planners drew up a detailed, yet simplified, defense plan for Egypt proper (west of the canal), and at a later date, they drafted an offensive plan for Sinai (east of the canal). These plans were broken down to their essentials and practiced repeatedly by the units that would be implementing them.

The Egyptian army was organized in a combat framework that suited its operational needs. Infantry divisions, that had borne the brunt of the Six-Day War, continued to be the mainstay of the army and its defensive missions, but they were now given offensive assignments that entailed fording the canal. The divisions were reinforced and fortified with anti-aircraft weapons and heavy armor so they could meet the challenge, independently, of Israeli tanks — the victors of the Six-Day War. On the eve of the Yom Kippur War, Egyptian divisions were beefed up with independent tank brigades and tank brigades transferred from other armored divisions. The tanks had permanent crews that had gone through rigorous training in order to minimize the errors so common among improvised forces.

The mechanized and armor divisions were kept in the second echelon as reserve forces. Even during the battle for the bridgeheads they remained outside the combat zone. The planners of the Yom Kippur War gave top priority to maintaining a balanced plan. This was another lesson that they learned from the Six-Day War: avoid making last-minute changes. This enabled the commanders and their units, who had prepared for their assignments, to remain relatively calm.

At the strategic level, in addition to their experience in the Six-Day War, the Egyptians learned from the IDF's modus operandi the importance of clearly defined war aims, detailed planning, professional relationships among senior commanders, and the training needed by the individual infantry soldier for destroying IDF tanks. They analyzed their abilities and advantages, and discovered the weaknesses and mistakes in their performance in the Six-Day War. Since the Egyptians planned to be the offensive side this time, they had to know how the IDF would operate as a defensive force in the opening stages of the war, and how it would respond in the later stages when it mounted a counteroffensive against the Egyptian defensive layout surrounding the bridgeheads on the eastern bank.

The supremacy of Israel's armored shock force on the battlefield, the absolute superiority of its air force against Egyptian infantry, and the failure of Egypt's air defense system to protect the troops fighting on the ground and retreating from Sinai led the Egyptian strategists, as stated, to derive the necessary conclusions and make sweeping changes. They prepared for a war that would return the army's honor that had been shattered in June 1967. They internalized the lessons from their battlefield debacle, found solutions for the problems the IDF had set for them, and steeled their army for the coming campaigns.[36]

The War of Attrition and Its Contribution to Egypt's Combat Experience

At the end of the Six-Day War it was obvious that the Egyptians would never agree to a status quo that had IDF troops stationed on the east bank of the Suez Canal. However the Arab leaders who participated in the Khartoum conference in August 1967 realized that they lacked the strength to launch a military venture at this point. Therefore they decided to take the political track.[37] In this light Khartoum may be seen as a turning point in Egypt's and Jordan's willingness to forego the military solution and embark upon the political path as a way to resolving the conflict. Before the 1967 war the Arab struggle aimed at liquidating "the artificial Jewish entity." The Khartoum Conference, however, decided to attempt the political route — with superpower assistance — to eradicate the remnants of the aggression. Nevertheless, the conference concluded with a unanimous decision that became known as "the three noes": "no negotiations, no recognition, and no peace with Israel."[38]

Along with the military defeat in June 1967, the devastation and demoralization of the Egyptian army, and the loss of Sinai, there were additional losses: the loss of income from shipping in the Suez Canal; the loss of oil fields; a significant drop in tourism; the reduction in foreign investments and the parallel rise in security expenses. All of these burdens had an impact on the general atmosphere in Egypt and necessitated changes.[39]

The biggest change in Egypt after the war was the creation of a new status quo in the military, socio-economic, and political spheres. Unlike Nasser's rigid approach prior to the 1967 war, after the debacle a small degree of flexibility appeared in Egypt's goals in the conflict and the means of attaining them.[40] The new status quo compelled the leadership to discard the radical aims and means for solving the conflict and adopt more limited objectives and means.[41]

Despite its weakness, Egypt realized that it could not remain idle in the face of the IDF's presence on the canal because of the threat that it posed to the country's strategic depth—and especially its interference with Egypt's ability to operate the canal. The conflict with Israel shifted from an external problem to a domestic one that was felt on many levels in the public domain. The conflict became a permanent daily factor in the lives of millions of Egyptians: the population of the canal cities that was forced to evacuate the region; the families of the war casualties, and later the families of the dead and wounded in the War of Attrition; and the bombings deep inside Egypt. Public pressure was released in various ways: from moderation and the search for a political solution to militarism and the call for aggressive revenge.[42]

The Egyptian army's incapability and its need to reorganize and replenish its arsenal led to a lull in hostilities on the canal (excluding isolated incidents) for over a year after the 1967 defeat.

The Egyptians see a number of dates for the outbreak of War of Attrition and various chronologies in it. Fawzi, the chief of staff in the Six-Day War and minister of defense immediately afterwards, begins his reckoning in the first days after the war's conclusion. He divides the War of Attrition into three stages:
- The holding stage (*sumud*)—from July 1967 to March 1968.
- The confrontation stage (*muaja'a*)—from March 1968 to March 1969.
- The resistance and deterrence stage (*altahadi waalrada*)—from April 1969 until July 1970.[43]

Other scholars who studied the background to the Yom Kippur War and the war itself, such as the three senior officers (Majdud, al-Badri, and Zahadi), point to four stages:
- The holding stage—from June 1967 to August 1968.
- The active defense stage—from September 1968 to February 1969.
- The attrition stage—from March 1969 to August 1970.
- The cease-fire stage—from August 1969 to October 1973.[44]

Field Marshal (Mushir) Gamasi, the deputy commander of the Canal Zone, the only army at the time, claims that the War of Attrition began with an artillery exchange in September 1968. In his memoirs, he states that the Egyptians' reason for heating up the line and launching the War of Attrition was "to create a military situation whereby the situation on the front did not lapse into a standstill."[45] This appears to be the main reason for the "three-year war."[46] During the War of Attrition each side struggled to either alter or freeze Israel's occupation of Sinai and the Suez Canal which, it must be remembered, was a strategic asset for Egypt and located slightly over a hundred kilometers from Cairo.

From the moment the flare-up began at Ras el-Ayish on July 1, 1967, and until the cease-fire went into effect in August 1970, many Egyptian combat branches took part in a large number of operations (and attempted ones), all of which contributed to the army's strengthening and rehabilitation. Several land, sea, and air units were involved in various military activities on the front and in the rear. Activity took place at the tactical level, as well as at the operational and strategic levels, and involved combat doctrine, the building and training of the forces, awareness of the enemy's system, and the search for ideas and solutions to counter the rationale behind the enemy's moves. In many situation estimates during and after the war, the Egyptians devoted prodigious effort in trying to understand Israel's security thinking and translating it into practical terms at the operational and tactical levels.

In addition to the Egyptians' desire to alter the situation, and the elite's interest in finding a political solution to the conflict, the War of Attrition may also be seen as a three-year training session for the army. The war furnished the troops with firsthand combat experience and afforded commanders the opportunity to work out solutions to urgent military problems.

Like any combat system the Egyptian army was subordinate to the political leaders and their objectives. They viewed the War of Attrition as comprising two main areas. First was the Palestinian problem, whose key issue was Israel's creation at the national and territorial expense of the Palestinians in particular, and the Arab nation in general. The second was Israel's occupation of Arab lands in the Six-Day War. The Egyptian leadership realized that an activist line aimed at attaining an immediate and total solution to both issues would end in failure. Therefore it chose to proceed in stages: first a solution to the 1967 problem, then a solution to the 1948 one.[47]

The trend to detach the immediate Egyptian goal — the liberation of the territories seized in June 1967 — from the long-range goal of solving the Palestinian problem, fit comfortably into Egypt's preference for giving priority to Egyptian affairs.

Thus, the national-strategic goal — according to Nasser's public statements and the decisions of the Khartoum Conference (September 1967) — was "the eradication of all traces of aggression."[48] This goal was designed to compensate Egypt for its catastrophic losses in the Six-Day War — losses that included not only territory but also self-respect and national honor.[49] The national-strategic goal resulted in systems goals in the spirit of "selfless sacrifice for the defense of Egyptian soil and liberation of the occupied territory," and on the principle of "what was taken by force will be returned by force."[50] The nullification of Israel's war gains became Egypt's operational objective, while the option for "liberating Filastin" remained intact but could take place at a time and in a manner that were not defined in a way that committed Egypt.[51]

Nasser acted on two levels — the military and political — to secure Egypt's aims in the conflict with Israel, focusing on a particular level according to current circumstances and the means at his disposal.[52] On November 23, 1967, he delivered a major speech on the integration of the political and military spheres. This came one day after the UN Security Council unanimously adopted Resolution 242 for settling the Middle East crisis — a resolution that Egypt supported.[53] Nasser insisted on the need to act simultaneously on two plains, the political and military, without stating a preference for either one (at least not at this stage).[54] Egyptian activity on the political level continued until the Egyptian president's death[55] and was designed to alter the status quo, advance Egypt's objectives in the conflict, and assist two other goals: gaining time to rebuild the army — absorbing new equipment and undergoing an intensive training program — and convincing the Soviet Union that a political solution to the conflict was no longer an option, and that Moscow would have to reply favorably to Egypt's requests for advanced weapons systems and strategic support in the event of war.[56]

The military goal required three main tasks to be simultaneously carried out:

• The rehabilitation of the army according to the following priorities: the air force, air defense, and ground forces — since these branches had lost most of their weapons, in addition to losing confidence in their commanders, morale, and fighting spirit;

• The planning and construction of a defense layout (troops and fortifications) on the western bank of the Suez Canal to defend the areas close to the front and, more significantly, to prevent the IDF from crossing the canal and advancing into Egypt;

• The search for a military solution and the preparation for the main campaign: fighting to return "self-respect" and the Sinai Peninsula to the heart of the Egyptian people.

Implementation of the three tasks was also a function of the intensive military activity before and during the War of Attrition. This activity took place as a parallel system that was influenced by and depended on the different stages of the political and military campaigns. It is unnecessary to look for a uniform, detailed master plan of the type that Minister of War Fawzi tried to present — and not only in retrospect — regarding the order of operations preceding each of the three tasks.[57]

The first task was the rehabilitation of the Egyptian army. The first step taken, even before the rebuilding of the units, was the reorganization of the command and control system that had totally broken down in the Six-Day War — especially during the retreat. Nasser took responsibility for the debacle and resigned, but he quickly returned to office. He removed Field Marshal Amar from all his duties, and appointed four-star general (Fariq Awal) Mahmud Fawzi,[58] a meticulous, hardened officer, as overall commander of the armed forces, and Lt. Gen. (Fariq) Abd al-Manam Riad, a highly professional and astute officer, as chief of staff. He also got rid of the commanders of the land, air, and naval forces, and other senior officers. He appointed new commanders in their place, whom he ordered to learn from the army's malfunctioning on the battlefield, and assume responsibility for repairing and strengthening the armed forces.

Another step was taken: a new law was enacted to bring order into the leadership level on command-and-control issues regarding security and the armed forces. The law was supposed to emend the previous situation that, according to Gamasi, had led to Egypt's defeat in the Six-Day War.[59] The law determined the areas of authority of the following three bodies: the National Security Council, the Armed Forces Supreme Council, and the Armed Forces Headquarters. It eradicated the awkward overlapping that characterized the Egyptian army in the Six-Day War, and "enthroned" the war minister in the position of general commander of the armed forces.

Another lesson that Egyptian strategists learned was that the ground, air, and naval services had acted independently without having received authorization for this from GHQ. To correct this error, the ground forces HQ was annulled, and the armed forces GHQ became the sole authority and control center for all branches of the military. Furthermore, in view of the results of the war, and based on Soviet advice, another air defense branch was established for dealing with Israeli air superiority on the battlefield.[60]

Gamasi notes a third step in the rehabilitation of the army and restoration of its esprit de corps: improved professionalism and military discipline that would inculcate into the troops such habits and qualities as conscientiousness, efficiency, and punctuality. All types of civilian assignments that the armed forces had been required to do were henceforth rescinded. No longer would the army have to engage in customs control, agriculture, transportation, and diverse supervisory roles. From now on the troops' time would be devoted exclusively to military matters. The intelligence services now became primarily concerned with collecting and analyzing reports on the enemy. Only a fraction of their time was spent on internal security matters and military counterintelligence.

Another aspect of the army's restoration involved closing the qualitative and quantitative gaps and restocking the stores of weapons and equipment that had been lost in the war or had grown obsolete. Naturally the Soviet Union was the main source for revitalizing the army, training the forces, and supplying the weapons.[61] The quantity of Soviet weapons that was channeled into Egypt had not been seen since the first arms shipments began in 1955. Heading the list were jet fighters and air defense systems, followed by artillery, tanks, and other weapons for building the defense layout adjacent to the canal. Some units on the front received the weapons directly from the Soviet Union. The troops trained with them, integrated them into their units, and used them in exchanges of fire with the IDF.

The Egyptian army's main shortcomings remained in the realm of organization, communications, intelligence, and the command infrastructure, not to mention demoralization and its severely bruised self-confidence following the 1967 calamity. A classified American estimate stated that the Arabs, especially the Egyptians, had no option for military operation.[62]

The desire to absorb advanced weapons and equipment as rapidly as possible required the assistance of experts. A large Soviet military delegation headed by General Lishenkov arrived in Egypt to help reorganize the Egyptian army and assist in its rearmament and training. Egypt's aim was to improve the military balance with Israel. Nasser brought this subject up in talks with President Podgorny and Defense Minister Zakharov, who came to Egypt in late June 1967. Soon after the meeting, arms supplies were rushed to Egypt, accompanied by nearly 1,200 Soviet military advisors.[63] The Soviets experts worked mainly in air defense, but they also supervised the absorption of the new weapons into the Egyptian units. Soviet Marshal Grechko described the army's reorganization in the following manner: "Today the Egyptian army numbers close to 220,000 soldiers; the Egyptians have 900 tanks, 300 planes, and over 1,000 artillery pieces. But all this equipment is in the hands of inexperienced soldiers— close to sixty percent of them are raw troops—since a large number of trained offices and soldiers were killed, captured, or simply quit the army. The Egyptians are short thirty-five percent of their pilot strength and almost thirty percent of their tank crews."[64] The supply of Soviet weapons, equipment, and advisors was extremely effective in boosting the morale and raising the combat proficiency of the Egyptian troops.[65]

In addition to rebuilding the army, from early 1968 to the summer of 1969 Egypt endeavored to reorganize the eastern front. Its aim was to set up two fronts opposite Israel: one in the west (Sinai), and the other in the east-northeast (Syria). It was hoped that inter–Arab activity on two fronts would increase the military pressure on Israel, increase the superpowers' involvement in the crisis and their determination to find a solution, and rehabilitate Egypt's impaired status in the Arab world. The efforts to establish two fronts at this stage, even in the limited format of the confrontational states, ended in failure, primarily because of inter–Arab contention.[66] Furthermore, Nasser's attempt to formulate a broad Arab consensus supportive of the Egyptian line of action — the two-pronged political and military activity — was a nonstarter because of inter–Arab bickering and rivalry.[67]

Parallel to the army's reconstruction, the forces on the canal front, under the command of Maj. Gen. (Liwa) Ahmad Ismail Ali, began to prepare the defense layout and continued maintenance of the front line. From the small number of forces (five infantry and two armored battalions) that was assigned to the area's defense immediately after the flight to the west bank of the canal, the number expanded dramatically to include the majority of Egypt's ground forces (five infantry divisions reinforced with artillery, tanks, and antitank weapons). According to Fawzi, by late November 1967 the deployment of the first defense line (including reserves) west of the canal was completed, and the danger of an Israeli crossing to the west of the canal was removed. The buildup and distribution of the forces continued uninterruptedly, and by late 1968 the ORBAT returned to what it had been on the eve of the Six-Day War.[68]

The Egyptians kept a wary eye on IDF activity on the east bank and in the canal's waters. In addition to daily observations, they sent deep penetration patrols across the canal to collect information on the enemy's deployment and layout. This stage was primarily geared to keeping the line stable and quiet so that the Egyptian army could channel its main effort and resources to rebuilding itself and completing its fortifications. This stage continued until August 1968, when the friction on the line increased and the Egyptians shifted to the stage of active defense.

Along with the routine defense activity of fortifying the canal front, a series of shooting incidents broke out. Some of them were initiated by the Egyptians, according to Gamasi, in order to sow unrest on the front, thereby hampering the enemy's troop movement and exacting from him a heavy toll in lives and equipment.[69] The first major incident was the battle of Ras el- Ayish on July 1, 1967.[70] A thirty-man Egyptian commando unit crossed the canal and ambushed an Israeli patrol of half-tracks and tank escort that was moving north of Kantara toward the Port Fuad region. The Egyptians also struck the IDF reinforcements that were rushed to the scene. The eastern bank's northern axis was difficult to defend and cost the Israelis many casualties in the War of Attrition and Yom Kippur War. The Port Fuad region (north of the canal) and the areas south and east of the port remained the only sections east of the canal where the Egyptians maintained a foothold until the Yom Kippur War. In addition to small aerial actions in this period, the Egyptian ground forces took pains to thwart Israeli shipping in the Suez Canal. The IDF's attempts to send rubber boats down the canal encountered withering Egyptian fire that was intended to sink the boats and kill their crews.

In October 1967 the military confrontation reached new heights. The political, economic, and military status quo was growing intolerable for Egypt. Dissatisfaction with the domestic situation and the fact that the international community relegated the Middle East crisis to the back-burner led some senior Egyptian officers to demand an escalation on the front.[71]

On October 20, naval activity suddenly entered the cycle of Egyptian-initiated combat operations. Two Egyptian missile boats armed with sea-to-sea Styx-type missiles left Port Sa'id and attacked and sank an Israeli destroyer off the Sinai coast. (The Egyptians claimed the event occurred approximately one mile within their territorial waters.)[72] The IDF responded with massive artillery fire, setting the oil refineries and depots outside the city of Suez on fire. The artillery exchanges caused casualties among the Egyptian civilians who resided in the canal cities. Since the Egyptian army needed freedom to act, it evacuated most of the inhabitants from the Canal Zone to the rear.[73] This population transfer had a major effect on Egypt's military activity, and especially on its attempts to secure a political settlement (for example, its adoption of Security Council Resolution 242 of November 22, 1967).

During this period the Egyptians observed that Israelis were trying to set up a temporary defense layout on the banks of the canal — a layout designed to bolster the line with small forces and minimum casualties. The Egyptians regarded the sparsely held line, in comparison to the deep contiguous defense layouts they had built, as a system based on rapidly available mobile forces that would provide immediate answers to the changing needs of defensive combat.[74] Jamal Hamad, the Egyptian army's historian, and a member of Nasser's Free Officers, and later the Egyptian military attaché to Syria, attributed the IDF's relatively slow entry into solid defensive fortifications on the canal to the fact that the IDF was basically an offensive force that was inexperienced in constructing a genuine defense line. Also, Israeli braggadocio and complacency incorrectly assessed the Egyptians' ability to recover from the 1967 defeat.[75]

The Egyptians had no intention of letting the military situation on the canal come to a standstill, so, once the armed forces regained part of their operational strength, and once the defensive layout stabilized, they went over to the next stage — active defense. Under Nasser's direction Egypt commenced a campaign of prolonged limited fighting whose strategic goal, according to Minister of War Fawzi, was to pierce Israel's Achilles heel — its limited manpower resources. According to Fawzi, the fighting was also intended to realize Nasser's aim: "To fight slowly and methodically so that the fighting would have a deleterious impact on the enemy at a rate that corresponds with the build-up of our forces."[76]

In early September 1968 the Egyptians unleashed a massive artillery barrage on the thin line of Israeli fortifications on the east bank of the canal.[77] The barrage served the new war's primary objective — attrition. A war of attrition would cause the enemy heavy losses and convince him that remaining in the captured territories would come at a very high price. The September 8 barrage covered the entire length of the front — from Port Sa'id in the north to the port of Adabia in the south. The artillery duel lasted five and a half hours. Ten IDF soldiers were killed and eighteen wounded. The shelling resumed on September 28, directed mainly against Israeli fortifications on the "Bar-Lev Line," that was in the first stage of construction. The Egyptians made the most of their artillery superiority, and suffered a small but painful Israeli reaction aimed at the canal cities of Ismalia and Suez. In another artillery shoot-out on October 26, that included an Egyptian commando crossing, fifteen Israelis were killed and thirty-four wounded. The IDF responded with an artillery barrage that set three oil depots in Suez on fire.[78]

In addition to artillery duels in this stage, the Egyptians employed small ground forces for raiding expeditions, ambushes, and mine-laying. Some of the raids were aimed at kidnapping IDF soldiers, other missions were planned for intelligence gathering but also as morale boosters for the army and nation. One commando

Nasser observing the "Bar-Lev Line" during the War of Attrition.

operation of limited success occurred in the Deversoir area. Its objective was to kidnap Israeli troops. But the raid failed and eight Egyptians were killed.[79] In other actions raiding forces succeeded in capturing Israelis. The heavy losses that Israel sustained demanded a new response, and Israel began calling in its air force. The fighting culminated in an Israeli nighttime heliborne raid on November 1, 1968. The commandos blew up bridges and electrical lines at Naga Hamadi in the Nile Valley in southern Egypt. The operation was designed to show the Egyptians the consequences of continued escalation. Eventually it brought about a lull in the fighting — when the Egyptians realized that they had to organize their rear. According to Fawzi, the Egyptian army quickly learned the lessons of this operation. It expanded its warning system southward to the Sudanese border, and new "people's defense units" were set up deep in Egypt, under a unified regional command.[80]

On March 8, 1969, only three days after the UN envoy, Gunnar Jarring, arrived in the region for another round of talks, a new chapter opened in the escalation of the fighting. The Egyptians shelled the still incomplete line of fortifications on the eastern bank in an enormous volley intended to demolish the Israelis' construction work and incur heavy casualties. The barrage lasted two days, during which forty thousand shells rained down on the Israeli fortifications. But already on the second day of the cannonade, the Egyptians suffered a severe blow. The chief of staff, Major General Abd al-Munam Riad, who was inspecting the forward defense lines north of Ismalia, was killed by Israeli rocket fire. His death led to an intensification of Egyptian activity on the front. The canal front commander, Maj. Gen. Ahmad Ismail Ali, was appointed chief of staff. The shelling continued with full force during March, April, and May, and reached its climax in June 1969. Following these artillery duels, hundreds of thousands of inhabitants of the canal cities fled their homes and escaped westward. The fighting spread to the entire front and penetrated deeper into Egypt. While the battles on the canal raged, diplomatic efforts to settle the crisis also continued. In mid–1969, as the recently elected and appointed Nixon administration was stepping into power and the Suez front was spiraling out of control, the United States increased its involvement in the conflict and tried to create a venue for an arrangement.[81]

On July 23, Egyptian president Gamal Abdel Nasser announced that a war of attrition had begun in earnest (although, as we have seen, it began even earlier). The Egyptians did their utmost to prevent a status quo on the canal, and looked to the War of Attrition for gaining a number of loosely defined objectives which must have included:

• Forcing Israel to make political concessions;
• Applying physical pressure on Israel to withdraw from the canal;
• Keeping the international community continuously aware of the Middle East crisis;
• Protecting Egypt's stature on the homefront and in the Arab world and projecting the regime's image as an undefeated warrior still on its feet and fighting back.[82]

The Egyptians adopted the new strategy of the "limited goal" or "Fabian strategy" that was designed to alter the balance of forces by wearing down the enemy's strength without coming to a head-on clash.[83] It is not clear if the Egyptians believed that victory would be won by attrition,[84] but at this point they definitely felt that they would not be able to defeat the IDF in a single large-scale event.[85] Nasser called the war an "*harb istinizaf*" (Arabic; a war of bloodletting), but he may have intended to launch a war of attrition like the one waged by the German chief of staff, Erich von Falkenhayn, against the French in Verdun in 1916 — i.e., to make Israel pay a heavy price, on the assumption that it was extremely sensitive to the loss of its men.

According to Gamasi, who quoted Magdub, Egypt's goal was to hurt the Israeli war machine by inflicting grave damage on its weapons, equipment, and strongholds in Sinai, in addition to causing the loss of life. Such a blow was expected to deter Israel from a confrontation with Egypt, exact heavy casualties, shatter the morale of the IDF and the country, pin down forces on the front (including reservists), and inflict a nationwide economic and social disaster.[86] The Egyptians assumed that Israel's shortage of personnel and other resources would preclude it from sustaining a war of attrition which, by its nature, demanded long-term endurance and the ability to suffer losses — the exact opposite of the lightning wars that Israel was accustomed to. The Egyptians hoped that Israel would be overcome by dissatisfaction and angst that would force the government to concede its Six-Day War territorial booty.[87] The Egyptians weighed the possibility of a military option to regain their land, but removed it from the agenda because of their armed forces' inability to "liberate" Sinai.[88]

Morale was also an important issue for the Egyptians. The Egyptian soldier began to regain his self-confidence and his faith in his commanders and weapons. His combat proficiency improved in the actual canal crossings under battlefield conditions of concentrated fire and heavy aerial bombings. Many units took part in these operations, especially special forces (commandos) but also infantry and engineering units.

The size of the forces taking part in the canal crossings and the assaults on the east bank increased from small teams to battalion-size formations. In the night of July 9–10, 1969, a raid was made for the first time under the command of the recently established Third Army. An Egyptian commando battalion crossed the canal in the Suez southern sector, attacked an Israeli force in the tongue of Port Tufiq, knocked out three tanks, killed and wounded a number of soldiers, and withdrew with a small number of wounded. In other sectors, sometimes directly opposite Israeli fortifications, the Egyptians succeeded in overtaking IDF positions on several occasions and hoisting the Egyptian flag. In addition to regular combat operations, the Egyptians carried out intelligence forays to gather information on the enemy's layouts and deployment along the canal. On June 30 the IDF responded with a heliborne raid on a high-tension electric station near the city of Suhaj in the Nile Valley, and on July 19 with a seaborne assault on Green Island, north of the Gulf of Suez.

The escalation on the front and the large number of casualties in the Green Island raid forced the IDF to undertake "counter attrition" and play its trump card — the air force. In a series of operations beginning on July 20, 1969, the Israeli air force became, in effect, "flying artillery," especially targeting artillery batteries, gun emplacements, and the antiaircraft missiles protecting them. Egyptian aircraft and air defense units found it difficult to challenge the attacking planes because of Israel's absolute air superiority. Nasser demanded an answer. He badgered the Soviets for long-range bombers that would allow him to attack in-depth targets in Israel,[89] but the Kremlin consistently turned down his requests. Egypt tried to improve its air defense system by receiving massive assistance from Soviet defense experts, as well as Soviet pilots and aircraft.[90] In a study compiled on Egyptian air activity during 1969, Fawzi notes that of the 2,900 sorties that Egyptian planes carried out, only 170 were against ground targets. In twenty-two dogfights, in which 110 planes participated, twenty-three Egyptian jets were shot down to Israel's fourteen.[91]

On September 9, 1969, the IDF landed an armored raiding force on the western shore of the Gulf of Suez against an Egyptian guard post and radar installation at Za'afrana. The force operated for over six hours before returning to the eastern bank. Two Egyptian patrol vessels moored in the vicinity were sunk. The raid had major repercussions on Nasser and senior military commanders, especially because of its timing — it came on the heels of a conference in Cairo of the confrontational states: Egypt, Syria, Iraq, and Jordan. The conference had hoped to revive the idea of the eastern front, with the strategic aim of using military force to destroy the enemy and return to the borders of June 5, 1967.[92] The Egyptians' abysmal failure in identifying the IDF raiding force prior to and during its operation and their disgracefully ineffective response created medical problems for Nasser and led to the resignation of Chief of Staff Ahmad Ismail Ali and his replacement by Maj. Gen. (Liwa) Muhammad Sadaq.[93] The commander of the Egyptian navy was also dismissed. Additional steps, personal and operational, were taken immediately after the lessons were learned.[94]

Egyptian intelligence analyses of the factors that contributed to the IDF's success point to the element of surprise, the selection of a region with meager forces located a great distance from Egyptian troop concentrations and the air force. The main lesson from the Israeli raid was that the Egyptian armed forces' had to improve their intelligence capability and surveillance of IDF ground forces near the front; they had to keep constant track of the air force, especially helicopter activity; and follow Israeli naval movement, particularly at landing sites.

The Egyptians' response to the Za'afrana operation was quite unexpected. Despite the weakness of their air power, they sent out sixty planes to bomb the fortifications along the canal and other targets deep in Sinai. But Egyptian losses were heavy. Twelve of their aircraft were shot down. The attack, whose main objective was to elevate the morale of the troops on the front, ended in failure.[95]

On December 27, 1969, the Egyptians suffered another military setback. An Israeli raiding party seized the P-12 air radar position at Ras Ghareb in the area of the Red Sea Command. Heavy helicopters lifted the radar and transferred it to Sinai. This operation, too, had a ruinous effect on Nasser's health, and again the area commander was dismissed — Maj. Gen. (Liwa) Bahi al-Din Nofel. Militarily, the operation was of minor importance, but its psychological implications were devastating, especially for the morale of the troops.[96] The blow came after the Rabat Conference in December 1969 had promised to allot Egypt and the other confrontational states assistance and money, weapons and military forces. The conference came to no decisions and reached no agreement. Nasser's hopes for pan-Arab solidarity were crushed.

Again the Egyptians tried to derive lessons from the Israeli operation.[97] After analyzing the modus operandi, the general staff officer of the 112th Infantry Brigade who signed the report listed the factors that led to the IDF's success and its lessons for Egypt: the importance of early planning, the need for realistic training exercises on a regular basis, the preparation of the reserve forces for all contingencies. The writer also emphasized the importance of defending and protecting isolated vital targets[98]; the need to prepare appropriate reserves for every possible route to the enemy; the importance of secrecy and perimeter defense; training technical troops for combat roles; the commanders' roles in combat operations; perfecting methods of foreseeing and countering IDF raids; measures that had to be taken against helicopters and heliborne troops; and the importance of training exercises to counter such operations.

In late 1969 the Jarring initiative and other diplomatic efforts to halt the fighting and hammer out a solution to the conflict reached a dead end. At the same time the War of Attrition on the canal escalated. The Americans felt that if the fighting continued while the Soviet Union was increasing its military involvement in Egypt, the situation would spiral out of control into a major international confrontation. Therefore they decided to prevent further exacerbation. Secretary of State Rogers devised a plan that entailed increasing American pressure for a solution the Middle East crisis through direct mediation between the sides. The keynote feature of plan was its shift from the search for a comprehensive resolution of the Arab-Israeli conflict to the search for an arrangement in the Egypt and Israel sectors based on an Israeli withdrawal and the mutual recognition of international borders.[99] The parties in the conflict rebuffed the plan and its thirteen sections. Israel completely rejected it, regarding it as a veritable threat. Egypt, too, did not accept it but neither did it officially reject it. It saw the plan as an attempt to isolate it from the rest of the Arab states through a separate agreement. The Egyptians noted that the plan did not call for Israel's withdrawal from Sharm e-Sheikh and the Gaza Strip. Egypt preferred to work for the full implementation of UN Resolution 242.

On December 25 the Israeli air force launched its largest air strike since the Six-Day War, across the entire canal front to a depth of twenty kilometers inside Egypt. The attack lasted eight hours and seriously damaged the greater part of the Egyptian layout, destroying twelve surface-to-air SA-2 missile batteries that had just arrived from the Soviet Union.[100] Another step in the escalation occurred in January 1970. Israeli planes not only hit targets along the length of the front but also civilian and military targets deep in Egypt. The aim of Israel's in-depth offensive was to increase domestic pressure on the leadership, perhaps leading to Nasser's ouster and create a new military situation that would force the Egyptian public and the decision makers in Cairo to realize that their continuation of "attrition" would exact an unbearably heavy price.[101] Egypt had not considered an Israeli "counter war of attrition." While the Egyptian public, exposed to actual fighting (bombing) in densely populated areas, was demoralized and under stress, the armed forces stood by impotently. Fear was now accompanied by the real pain of being hurt at home and suffering many casualties in the front and the rear.

In light of Israel's freedom of action and Egypt's inability to make an adequate response — such as long-range bombing raids — Egypt made a concentrated effort to come up with answer whose first stage would be an improved air defense system. After a series of consultations Nasser concluded that Egypt would have to pressure the Soviet Union to supply it with a more effective air defense system, train Egyptian pilots, and furnish it with the latest attack planes.[102] On January 22, Nasser and Minister of War Fawzi flew to the Soviet Union to request greater Soviet involvement in Egypt in the form of Soviet-manned antiaircraft units and aircraft that would be integrated into Egypt's air defense layout. At first the Soviets were suspicious, but after serious discussions with the Egyptian leaders, they finally consented.[103]

In late January, the president of the Soviet Union, Leonid Brezhnev, announced that a Soviet force would be sent to Egypt. The force included one division of SA-3 antiaircraft missiles and three air brigades (ninety-five advanced MiG-21s, and their commanders and pilots). Most of Nasser's requests were fulfilled (excluding the one for long-range TU-16 bombers). Egypt received sophisticated radar systems and advanced technical equipment. Photo-reconnaissance and spy planes arrived and began taking off from Egyptian airfields. Soviet naval vessels and aircraft stopped at Egyptian bases on the Mediterranean coast. The United States did not remain indifferent to all this activity. President Nixon sent a memo to the National Emergency Conference for Peace in the Middle East stating that the United States was studying the strengthening of Egyptian force and that it would not hesitate to supply friendly countries in the area with equipment if circumstances required it. Indeed, the Americans increased the shipment of upgraded Skyhawks and Phantoms to Israel.[104]

The peak of Soviet involvement came in the dogfights with Israeli pilots. Ground activity also continued. On January 21, IDF forces raided the island of Shaduan in the Gulf of Suez, wounding Egyptian soldiers and taking several prisoners. This operation precipitated a Soviet response. The Egyptians made repeated raids on the canal front, with the express aim of killing and capturing IDF troops. In a naval commando action on February 6, the Egyptians damaged Israeli vessels in the Port of Eilat. Throughout this period ground activity continued with massive use of artillery. On May 30 the Egyptians ambushed Israeli patrols twice on the same day, killing thirteen, wounding four, and capturing two. In response, the IDF's "Shaked" reconnaissance unit struck on June 11, assaulting Egyptian fortifications north of Kantara.

The Russians and Egyptians made a joint effort to whittle down Israel's near-total freedom in the skies. Egyptian forces underwent training, and the groundwork of an air defense layout was established in the front and rear. Egypt invested vast amounts of energy and resources in constructing antiaircraft missile emplacements west of the canal. The work proceeded even when Israeli air strikes caused many casualties. In the final tally, four thousand Egyptians were killed in the air attacks.[105]

The Soviets' direct involvement in Egypt's air defense peaked in June 1970 when they assumed overall responsibility for operating the system.[106]

The air war came to a head on July 25 and July 30 when Israeli and Russian pilots tangled in dogfights. Despite Israel's bombing campaign, the Egyptian "missile wall" on the canal managed to score a number of Israeli Phantoms in late June and throughout July.[107] The Soviet antiaircraft missile brigades and aircraft deployed deep in Egypt enabled the Eighth Egyptian Air Defense Division, with its twenty-seven battalions of upgraded SA-3 missiles and batteries of antiaircraft guns, to "crawl" forward and take up positions on the western bank of the canal.[108] This layout allowed the Egyptian air force to resume its patrols and sorties in Sinai, albeit on a limited scale.

Egypt deployed its completed antiaircraft layout despite Israel's unremitting attempts to knock it out. The missile transfer and stabilization of the air defense system on the front — and in Egypt in general — were the two factors that broke the wings of Israel's planes at the end of the War of Attrition (and three years later in the Yom Kippur War).

The onset of a new American initiative on June 19 was preceded by contacts with Nasser, contacts that accelerated after the Egyptian president's May 1 speech in which he expressed willingness to renew ties with the United States. The U.S. secretary of state, William Rogers, sent a memo to the Egyptian and Israeli foreign ministers calling for an immediate end to the War of Attrition. Egypt changed its stance and agreed. Nasser returned to Moscow with the express aim of convincing the Soviets to accept the American initiative. A ninety-day cease-fire was announced on August 7. This cease-fire would remain in effect over three years until the outbreak of the Yom Kippur War.[109]

The Egyptians used the period between the two wars to hone the army for the main campaign. According to Egyptian sources, the lessons learned from the War of Attrition had a crucial influence on the preparations and planning of the October War. Gamasi[110] felt that the War of Attrition had been a vital practical experience that enabled Egypt to decide on the Yom Kippur War. It was also proof of Egypt's endurance, determination, and dedication to the goal of liberating the occupied land. Gamasi quotes Maj. Gen. (Liwa) Taha Magdub who described the War of Attrition, with all its suffering and losses, as a crucible in which the professional Egyptian fighter grew to maturity. The positive results of the war brought enormous, long-term benefits to Egypt, and served as the training ground for the October War.

The War of Attrition provided the Egyptian armed forces with the opportunity to gain firsthand knowledge of the Israeli soldier and his fighting methods. The Egyptian soldier recouped his faith in the chain of command, his weapons and equipment, and last but not least his self-confidence.[111] The intense preoccupation with this issue enabled the Egyptians to plan for an all-out war of limited scope, a war in which the IDF's weaknesses were identified, solutions found, and maximum advantage made of the Egyptian system in general and the individual soldier's role in particular.

The experience gained during the War of Attrition in planning and executing offensive operations, as well as defensive ones, assisted the Egyptian army when its forces forded the entire length of the canal. The war proved to the Egyptian planner that his army was capable of crossing a wide and treacherous water obstacle.[112]

The close familiarity with the Israeli fortifications through observation and actual combat enabled the Egyptian planner to detect the errors inherent in the Israeli system of frontline fortifications. The forts' weaknesses and their marginal contribution to Israel's defense layout, the gap between the strongholds, the closing of some of them and disrepair of others after the War of Attrition — all these factors induced the Egyptian tacticians to design an attack plan based on outflanking the majority of the fortifications in the first stages of the war and capturing them later from the rear.

The size of the IDF's armor units near the canal and their role as reinforcements and as an offensive force against the opposite bank during the War of Attrition reflected a fixed pattern whereby the Israeli locus under attack would be quickly reinforced by a tank platoon on standby. The Egyptians analyzed the standard Israeli response and discovered how to block the armor reinforcements with antitank weapons and mines. This modus operandi, which had already been of great use to the Egyptians in the War of Attrition, was doubled and applied to its fullest capacity in the initial fighting in the Yom Kippur War when Egyptian infantry, equipped with antitank weapons and a small amount of mines, blocked the tanks' approach routes to the crossing points, inflicted heavy casualties, and enabled the Egyptian armed forces to continue streaming across the canal and construct bridgeheads.

The Egyptian infantry's relative advantages because of its sophisticated, lightweight, antitank weaponry and its ability to operate in "low signature"[113] in desert terrain were doubled to meet the parameters of the general operational plan that envisioned battalions, brigades, divisions, and even entire armies deployed in defensive bridgeheads. From these positions they first blocked the IDF tanks attacking from the east, and then destroyed them.[114]

The inferiority of the Egyptian armor layout that had performed poorly in the Six-Day War, and was idle during the War of Attrition, meant that its role in each of the stages of the crossing and subsequent fighting was kept to an absolute minimum. During most of the Yom Kippur War the Egyptians' large armor formations (tank divisions) remained west of the canal. When they did join battle, in the October 14 attack for example, their performance was spotty and irresolute. Their main function was on the west bank when the Fourth Armored Division was pitted against IDF units advancing to the west and south on the Suez-Cairo axis.

The importance of the artillery layout as a support weapon in preparing the offensive and pounding the enemy in his allegedly protective strongholds and armored vehicles was also learned during the War of Attrition and applied successfully in various stages of the Yom Kippur War. While the artillery supported the troops crossing the canal, its main job was to provide cover for the forces on the bridgeheads on the east bank.

During the last days of the War of Attrition Egypt's air defense layout and "missile wall" in the forward areas succeeded in watering down Israel's air supremacy. This tactic was applied on a large scale in the Yom Kippur War. The Egyptian army was able to ford the canal with minimum casualties thanks to the missile umbrella to the west which neutralized Israeli planes. The masses of Egyptian infantry that poured across the canal were of low signature, which made it difficult for the Israelis to locate and subdue them. The use of low-signature infantry as the main attack force, and the limited employment of armored units on the front — and especially on the east bank — also meant that the Egyptians were minimally exposed to Israeli air strikes.

For three years the Egyptians had experienced intense defensive combat alongside sporadic offensive activity. They integrated this experience into their attack plan. The Yom Kippur offensive began with the wide-scale crossing of the canal and consolidation of limited objectives, thus recreating, this time on the eastern bank, a solid contiguous defense layout so well-known from the War of Attrition, and against which the IDF's armored fist was broken.

2

Israel's Defense System
on the Sinai Front

The Israeli Defense Concept in Sinai

Israel's defense concept on the Sinai front — from the time the IDF reached the Suez Canal in June 1967 — was based on a defense layout that underwent constant readjustment because of operational circumstances and changing needs. At first the layout was designed to meet the routine security requirements of the units patrolling the canal bank. Later the layout was revised to meet the challenges of the War of Attrition. The question of preparing for full-scale war was undoubtedly discussed in this period, but answers were not forthcoming. Possible solutions remained in a perpetual state of debate, so that when the Yom Kippur War did erupt, Israel's defense layout on the Suez Canal was caught unprepared and without the necessary infrastructure and a clearly formulated operational doctrine. In short, the IDF found itself without a decisive answer to Egypt's modus operandi.

The Egyptians wasted no time in overcoming the obstacles the IDF had constructed on the eastern bank. They closely monitored — and internalized — Israel's altering defense concept. While they formulated their operational plans, they identified the Israel's strong and weak points and sought ways to apply this knowledge to their troops' advantage once a military campaign was underway.

The Egyptian analysis included the following elements:
• Monitoring ground developments, such as defense construction, road paving, fortifications building, the setup of training programs, and improvements in the size and deployment of units;
• A theoretical study of Israel's defense system, comparing it with the Egyptian system, and attempting to locate the advantages and disadvantages in both systems;
• An analysis of Egyptian ground activity during the War of Attrition and the IDF's responses to it on both sides of the canal as well as in the interior of the country;
• Formulating a picture of the IDF's modus operandi in all areas of its defense layout on the east bank against a possible Egyptian crossing.

Israel's political level issued orders to the army during a meeting with Chief of Staff Rabin on June 9, 1967 — the fifth day of the Six-Day War. The government had decided earlier to halt the troops twenty kilometers before the canal, but in light of the continued military activity on the ground and the Americans' intention to endorse a cease-fire resolution in the UN Security Council, Israel allowed its troops to advance to the eastern bank until the cease-fire went into effect. Defense Minister Dayan issued the order with the approval of the Knesset's Foreign Affairs and Defense Committee. Dayan believed that once hostilities abated and the armistice went into effect, the IDF's distance from the canal could be determined, and in this way the Egyptians would be able to reopen traffic and resume normal life in the Canal Zone. Furthermore, the United States proposed to the Security Council that the combatants be kept at a distance from the canal, but this proposal was rejected.[1]

The reopening of the canal appeared in all of the proposals for a military arrangement with Egypt. The Israeli government used the issue as a bargaining chip in its various contacts, but at the end of the day its instructions to the military remained in effect: maintain a presence of the canal's eastern bank and block the passage of vessels.[2] Despite the Rogers Plan, the August 1970 cease-fire, and statements on Israel's intentions to withdraw from the canal, nothing changed. Israel grew firmly entrenched in its military presence and political position and chose to remain where it was.[3]

In July 1967, almost one month after the termination of hostilities, several firefights erupted on the banks of the canal. The Egyptians violated the cease-fire in an attempt to prevent Israel from enjoying the fruits of victory and turning its dazzling victory into a fait accompli. Israel, for its part, tried to create facts on the ground and define the cease-fire line as the middle of the watercourse rather than only up to the canal bank. To back up its assertion, Israel sent rubber boats down the canal. The government ordered the IDF to see that the borderline along the canal was not breached and that the canal remained out of commission, in the hope that its closure would spur the Egyptians to enter negotiations. Instead, the skirmishes continued and the casualty rate rose.

This was the state of affairs facing Lt. Gen. Haim Bar-Lev when he was appointed chief of staff on January 1, 1968.[4] Along with the main task of preparing the army for the coming war, he also had to deal with the new reality of daily firefights and mounting casualties.

In March 1968 Hassanein Heykal, the editor of the daily *al-Ahram* and Nasser's chief speechwriter, formulated the following declaration of intent: "What was taken by force will be returned by force." On March 10 Nasser visited a joint Egyptian-Sudanese stronghold on the Suez Canal and announced that Egypt was at present striving, and would continue to strive, to go from the "standing fast" stage (*tsoomood*) to the "defense" stage (*dafa'a waka'i*) and from there, to the "liberation stage" (*tahrir*) and final victory. In the meantime, he published his "stages doctrine,"[5] and in July declared the end of the first — "standing fast" — stage, which heralded the rearmament of the army, the rehabilitation of its esprit de corps, and the start of the second state — deterrence through active defense.

The War of Attrition erupted in early September 1968 when the Egyptians translated their intentions into a series of heavy artillery barrages against the Israeli troops on the eastern bank. The IDF responded with artillery fire, which elicited an Egyptian counter-response of further shelling and commando raids. Another escalation in October triggered a stiff Israeli answer: the shelling of the oil refineries in the city of Suez. In the wake of the massive damage, Nasser ordered the cities evacuated and a reduction in military activity. IDF commando operations deep in Egypt's interior (especially the helicopter raid on the night of October 31–November 1 against the Naga Hamadi transformation station and the Qina Bridge on the Nile in the heart of Upper Egypt) led to a freeze in Egyptian military acts.

The Israeli system of makeshift fortifications on the east bank of the canal was based on fixed emplacements and communications trenches. Egyptian overhead covers that had been left in the area were used to protect Israeli observers but were insufficient to safeguard the troops against heavy artillery fire. Therefore it was decided to create a new defense layout. The timetable allowed the IDF to reorganize.

Chief of Staff Bar-Lev convened the commanders for a series of discussions on the government's directive that ordered the IDF to hold the water line lest the Egyptians exploit the breaks in the defense and storm the eastern bank in an attempt to gain a foothold and neutralize IDF troops.[6] None of the participants in the meetings disagreed with the political directive. According to the Israeli intelligence assessment presented by Major General Yariv, the Egyptians would be able to ford and regain control of the canal with three armies in less than three years, perhaps by 1969. According to Yariv's evaluation, the Egyptians would satisfy themselves with obtaining a limited strategic objective—up to the line of the mountain passes—rather than capturing all of Sinai. Yariv gave teeth to this assessment by showing that the areas planned for the crossing were situated opposite the main longitudinal roads that led into the heart of Sinai.

The officer in charge (OC) of the Southern Command, Major General Yeshayahu Gavish, presented his command's view that Israeli had to deploy its forces on two lines: a forward line to be held by mobile armored forces and a rear line—at the passes—that had to be built as a permanent defensive line and serve as a stable base from which local large-scale counterattacks—with the assistance of additional mobile forces—would be made against Egyptian units crossing the canal. During the discussions, the possibility of an "offensive" defense was broached, in other words, parallel to the Egyptian crossing into Sinai, the IDF would cross westward into Egypt proper.

Summing up the meetings, the chief of staff stated that the layout "has to be based on a structure at the appropriate places, dug in as necessary, and on strong armored reserves that can reach any point within two to three hours, and, of course, on the air force." The minister of defense, Moshe Dayan, who attended these discussions, ordered a timetable to be drawn up within four months, in anticipation of the Egyptian move. It was also decided that an inter-branch team would be established to draft a new defense layout. General Adan, the team leader, immediately set out to inspect the length of the line, after which he held a marathon of meetings concerning the IDF's redeployment.[7]

At the same time the Southern Command prepared the "Sela" (Boulder) defense plan, and began constructing a line of fortifications as part of the plan's implementation. The command's basic assumption was that the Egyptians might try to cross the Suez Canal in "fording areas" close to the Israeli roads leading to the canal and, once securing them, proceed in depth into Sinai. These areas were: in the north—opposite Kantara; in the center—opposite Firdan, Ismalia, and Deversoir; and in the south—opposite the Gidi and Mitla roads and the Suez area. According to "Sela," additional regular army troops had to be assigned to the Sinai front as well as (and mainly) reservist units. Southern Command planned to deploy the lion's share of these units in layouts on the east bank. This necessitated preparing the fortifications. Opposite each of the anticipated crossing areas, a huge square yard was constructed and surrounded with dirt embankments two to three meters in height and with ribs two kilometers long. The yard and embankments inside it were designed as positions for an infantry brigade. Tanks were planned to operate from inside the yard, taking advantage the embankment for firing positions.

General Adan (Bren) and his team pointed to two basic flaws in the Southern Command's plan: one—it called for the deployment of a large number of forces in permanent defense positions on the banks of the canal; two—until the arrival of the reservists, each yard would have to be held by a very small number of conscripts who would be scattered in isolated groups, in distant positions, incapable of defending themselves and preventing the Egyptians from taking over the entire yard. Bren looked for solutions to several complex problems: how to hold the line with minimal forces while at the same time guaranteeing their high degree of protection against barrages and raids; and how to devise a defense plan in stages that would enable the buildup of strength and a simple and smooth entry into the line before and during the battle.[8] Meanwhile, in order to guarantee the troops' safety, especially from shelling, a team of officers headed by the OC of combat engineers, Elhanan Klein, broached the idea of using train tracks (taken from the Kantara-el-Arish railway line) as overhead covering to prevent enemy shells from penetrating the bunkers. When an experiment with the tracks proved successful, the idea was quickly put into practice.

Bren deliberated over the advantages and disadvantages of the two basic defense systems: the permanent one — based primarily on static ground deployment in a rigid forward layout with two or three deeper defense lines held by mobile armored forces ready to counterattack; and, the flexible mobile system — where the front was held by a small number of forces assigned to deterrence and covering tasks, and where the main force, concentrated deeper in the layout, held the ground and was ready to attack at the time and place of its choosing. The team recognized the inherent advantages in the mobile defense system for a small army like the IDF with the armored force as its backbone. Nevertheless, concern was voiced — at the political level — that the Egyptians might decide to capture only part of the territory that was evacuated (and not pursue their advance into Sinai), and then call for a cease-fire once they regained this territory.

The plan that Bren arrived at was, as he put it, an integration of the two systems: organizing the forces for battle and the fighting method, both of which were taken from the mobile defense system. But he could not accept the flexibility to be gained by ceding territory and choosing the place of battle. He recommended that the battle be fought on and adjacent to the waterline. He also recommended that the small units act as trip wires until the main force — the mobile armor — arrived from the rear.

According to Bren, the integration of the two systems was made possible mainly by the formidable water barrier on the front. Bren believed that the time needed for the enemy to cross the canal, overcome the high dirt embankments and set up bridges, would allow the IDF to rush armored reinforcements to the crossing sites and smash the enemy before he had time to advance his main force — the armored units — eastward. This scenario, which was based on the assumption that the main battle would be fought on and close to the waterline, eliminated the need to remain in the rear and have the warning forces armored and mobile.[9]

From a ground analysis on the canal bank, the Israeli team concluded that the linearity of the artificial water obstacle could be closed in an unbroken line of ten-kilometer spaces with the help of an electronic system. The idea was also broached that the warning points could be built ten kilometers apart — a distance that would enable optical surveillance in daytime and electronic warning at night. However, until such an electronic system became operational, the line would have to be maintained by ambushes set up between the points in order to partially cover the area. The plan called for the construction of twenty such points. When the OC of Southern Command reviewed the plan, he added a number of extra points at those areas considered particularly sensitive: Kantara, Ismalia, Firdan, and the Mitla and Gidi Passes. Chief of Staff Bar-Lev also added a number of points, mainly in the front's northern and southern extremities.[10]

The need to defend the small forces from Egyptian raids and artillery barrages gave birth to the idea of the stronghold (*ma'oz*) model, a type of fortification based on Bren's experience in the Negev during the War of Independence for defending small settlements. Bren's plan envisioned an outpost of small-dimensions: four positions, manned by fifteen to twenty soldiers protected by dug-in emplacements and small adjacent shelters. The stronghold would be surrounded by a dirt embankment with built-in sentry positions, a network of communications trenches, and several layers of fencing made up of coiled barbed wire and mine belts. Each outpost would be provided with a half-track, mortars, and other weapons, including surveillance equipment.

Bren assigned the main role in the defense battle to the armored forces, supported by infantry, artillery, and the air force. For this to succeed, he recommended developing an infrastructure of access roads. "Artillery Road," eight to ten kilometers from the eastern bank of the canal,[11] was intended to enable artillery batteries to be deployed at effective ranges along its length, and to leap-frog and integrate effectively into the mobile defense system. "Lateral Road," thirty kilometers east of canal, would allow the passage of large forces and supplies from sector to sector. "Artillery Road" was also designed to allow the concentration of forward armored units capable of reinforcing the strongholds within thirty to sixty minutes, while "Lateral Road" was planned for the sectors' larger armored reserves which would carry out the main counterstrikes and crush the Egyptians' attempts to bring their armor units across the bridgeheads.

The line of mountain passes on the ridge that blocked the open areas east of the canal was unprepared for a defensive battle despite its topographical advantage. The Egyptians seem to have attributed greater importance to this region than the Israeli planners did. Egyptian strategists, who incorporated the passes in their preparations for the offensive, came to the conclusion that "if we examine the enemy's tactical doctrine and fighting method, his main effort can be expected to be based on defending the passes and narrow defiles. This area will most likely serve as a strong base that he will want to defend and sally forth from in counterattacks against our advancing forces."[12] The Israelis only used this line of defensive deployment to set up active and passive electronic command and control centers for MI, the air force, and Southern Command. MI units controlled the high spot in the area — Jabel Um Hashiba — and later the air force and Southern Command's command posts were also established there.[13]

When the general headquarters (GHQ) discussed the plan, no one refuted the basic idea of integrating the various defense systems into the "rigid defense" at the waterline. Differences of opinion revolved around the essence of the strongholds and the employment of small groups of warning forces.[14] A very concerned chief of staff asked "if a plan exists for blocking the penetration of Egyptian forces into the known crossing areas," and was told that "the areas will be fenced, mined, and closed."[15]

General Ariel Sharon, the head of the GHQ Training and Doctrine Section, supported defense at the waterline as part of the defense layout, and regarded the concentrated tank units and aircraft as the force that would break a full-scale attack. Sharon proposed paving additional east-west access roads and replacing the stronghold with an observation point on the dirt embankment, which would be provided with a shelter for a thirty-man force. This point would be concealed on the embankment's rear slope and would have communications trenches leading to the top of the embankment.

Major General Tal, commander of the armored forces, was the most outspoken critic of the plan. Although he agreed that it might solve routine security tasks and limited Egyptian attacks, he felt that an all-out war had to be prepared for, one in which only a limited number of IDF troops remained in full control on the waterline, with the main force deployed in the rear. Tal, who believed in armor's superiority, claimed that "defense on the waterline would be effective only with tanks and antitank missiles." Therefore he wanted to deploy large units along there. Regarding a full-scale war, he stated: "I propose not fighting on the waterline; that is, not holding a rigid defensive line. Militarily speaking, it is obviously preferable to let the enemy cross and bring 500 tanks into Sinai, and then destroy them. But we did not recommend this since we too understand the goals of war.... Our goal is not to destroy 200 hundred tanks but to sit on this side of the canal. The debate is over to achieve this goal. The forward line is extremely important but will not determine the fate of a crossing attempt, and we should not expect it to. The line's specific function is to serve as a trip wire and give us a delay of twenty-four hours to know what's happening.... Within the framework of the offensive, an attempt at a canal crossing poses no special threat for the troops stationed there other than barrage fire. The strongholds themselves will not fire a single shot when the Egyptians mount the crossing. The battle will be decided by the mobile forces that we succeed in concentrating."[16]

Yitzhak Hofi, assistant commander of GHQ, pointed to the absurdity in the fortification plan's vast scale and recommended concentrating the defense at the fording areas and reducing it elsewhere. "We have the capability of brushing off any Egyptian force advancing across the canal."

The chief of staff, Lieutenant General Bar-Lev, summed up the discussion, approved of the plan, and gave his signature to what became known as the Bar-Lev Line: "Our goal is to sit on the waterline and prevent the Egyptians from making any territorial gains...." Bar-Lev believed that the mission could be accomplished with the help of four elements: permanent deployment along the canal, with a tank battalion divided among the strongholds; mobile armored forces; artillery fire and various innovations as needs arose[17]; and the air force."[18] He concluded that the IDF had to deploy for two different situations: an IDF offensive, and a full-scale crossing by the Egyptian army. He pointed out that "it was impossible to say with certainty that the solution to an Egyptian attack will be the simultaneous crossover to their side. We'll probably have to defeat the enemy by burying him in his crossing attempt." Regarding the layout on the line: "We've based it on regular forces [as opposed to reserves]. Two brigades will have to hold the line until the second [?] brigade or reserve brigades arrive. If a catastrophe occurs, and we fail to smash the enemy in two or three days, we'll have more battles to fight."[19]

The debate over the correct defense procedure on the Sinai front has yet to be resolved. Proponents and opponents have remained steadfast in their views. Gavish asserts: "The strategic depth that was attained with the capture of the Sinai Peninsula allowed for a defense plan based on a forward line and mobile forces that could buy time and delay the enemy until the reserve forces arrived. It was ridiculous to expect the strongholds to block Egyptian divisions pouring across the canal. Such an idea had been raised in the past. The only alternative was to leave the canal and pull back twenty kilometers to the mountain passes. It was suggested that if the Egyptians crossed the canal, we could hit them in the open territory between us and the canal. But if you pull back twenty kilometers then the enemy advances twenty kilometers and brings over its armor and antitank weapons, and operates in topographical conditions similar to yours. And if the war opens on his initiative, then no obstacle will stop him."[20]

Israel Tal, too, has stuck to his views from that period:

Mobile or static defense ... is a system, not the goal.... The government ordered the IDF to hold Sinai and prevent the Egyptians from forcibly retaking territory or crossing the canal. The IDF's strategic task was a rigid defense.... The aim was not the destruction of the Egyptian army, but the retention of territory. The debate was over the system. Bar-Lev, Bren, and others spoke about building a fortified line along the canal, with the addition of mobile armored forces deployed along its entire length. And we said that the water line had to be defended, but defended wisely.

We'll have daytime and nighttime lookouts, control systems, and patrols. We won't be glued to permanent positions. And, beyond the range of the enemy's artillery and observation posts, we'll keep our strong mobile armored fists coiled, ready to rush to wherever necessary.[21]

Writing in retrospect, Tal explains his opposition to the establishment of a line of strongholds: "In the case of an all-out attack, the strongholds will contribute nothing toward stopping a full-scale offensive.... Instead of IDF ground troops and the air force trying to pulverize the enemy and gain a victory, they'll have to rush to the aid of their comrades in the strongholds and attempt to rescue them."[22]

After the decision to establish the fortification line, preparations proceeded at a fast pace in the awareness that time was short and a war of attrition was imminent. The only armored brigade that was active in the Canal Zone had a sister brigade added to it. Bren went to Sinai and set up "a headquarters for armored forces," while he organized and built the IDF's first armored division made up of conscripts. He was also instructed to implement the GHQ's decisions and the conclusions of the committee that he headed: continue planning Sinai's defense and building the fortifications' infrastructure for directing the battle.[23]

Bren took charge of the enormous project of strong-

Diagram 1: Israeli Deployment on the Canal Front (the "Ma'oz" Plan 1968–1969)

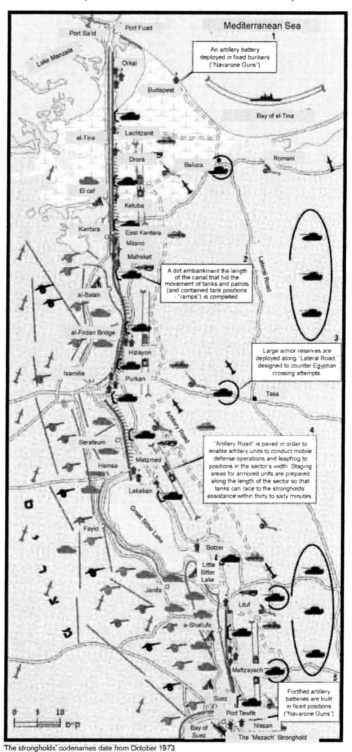

The strongholds' codenames date from October 1973

hold construction. When Defense Minister Dayan visited the line in January 1969, work was going on at thirty-three locations linked by dirt roads. Between the strongholds and the canal a dirt embankment was raised to provide firing positions and conceal the activity going on behind it. In March, when Nasser announced the start of the war, the strongholds were almost complete. Thirty-two forts, each protected and ready (excluding three in the south: el-Balach Island, Tusan, and Deversoir), "welcomed" the defensive troops on the waterline.[24]

The Egyptians opened the war with the "provocation and deterrence" stage, or as President Nasser termed it, the "preventative defense" stage.[25] On March 8 the Bar-Lev Line weathered a massive artillery barrage. Using the shelling as a screen, small Egyptian units crossed the canal and attacked the strongholds and tank parks, setting up ambushes and laying mines. In March alone, nearly 140 incidents were recorded, and in April the number rose to 570. The IDF withstood the barrages and returned artillery fire. The stronghold troops and the reinforced tank units repulsed the Egyptian attacks, but suffered scores of casualties. The Egyptians fired almost 40,000 artillery shells a day; the Israelis paid the price in seventy to one hundred casualties a month.[26] *How Many Cas in 1967 war*

The fortifications layout transformed the Canal Zone, that had been empty of vulnerable Israeli targets up to now, into an area brimming with static Israeli targets, especially the road network for maintaining the strongholds. Intense daily activity took place in the strongholds for administration and service tasks that exposed vehicles, troops, and even civilian laborers to enemy fire. The IDF provided the Egyptians with static, soft targets. Over 1,200 soldiers were injured in the strongholds on the canal front. A large proportion of them were wounded not in combat activity, guard duty, or surveillance, but when traveling between the strongholds or to the rear for R & R, or when transporting supplies or in administrative tasks in the vicinity.[27]

The controversy over the defense concept in Sinai did not let up. GHQ reviewed an evaluation report on it in April 1969 that pointed to the deep breath needed by the IDF in order to maintain the present situation over a long period of time. The chief of staff opened the discussion: "We're planning for the next war — not the one that was — yet we need answers for the war that is currently being fought."[28] The IDF's difficulty in this period was how to end the war of attrition without being exhausted by it and without having it interfere with its planning for a major one. Also, how to maintain the contact line with minimal forces, while at the same time training the rest of the army? And lastly, how to wear out the smallest number of tanks and artillery pieces in a war of attrition — that is, how to preserve the army's resources and train the troops?[29]

The IDF called in the air force on the canal line and sent commandos deep into Egypt. Armored forces raided the coast at the Gulf of Suez, and an entire radar facility was captured and "choppered" back to Israel, but the artillery duels and raids on both sides of the canal continued unabated. Airplanes — flying artillery — were used to pound Egyptian antiaircraft batteries and bag Egyptian aircraft. The introduction of top-of-the-line U.S. Phantom planes enabled Israel to carry out bombing raids deep in Egypt for nearly three months.[30] Soon a pattern in the War of Attrition emerged: each side responded to the other in an ever widening cycle of escalation. The ongoing attacks and growing list of casualties[31] took a heavy toll on the IDF at the front and civilian population in the rear.

In January 1970 Maj. Gen. Ariel Sharon was appointed OC of Southern Command and began to set his ideas in motion. He proposed abandoning the strongholds on the water line and instead to survey the canal with long-range observation posts and mobile, armored patrols.[32] Besides various proposals for offensive action adjacent to the canal and deep in

Egypt, he also proposed "building a deeper line ten kilometers from the canal and a third line thirty kilometers further back, where sophisticated electronic devices could be deployed."[33] His recommendation to reduce the number of forces on the water line and make greater use of manned and unmanned surveillance equipment on the front was rejected, but GHQ continued to debate the issue. General Hofi (the head of Training & Doctrine Section), David Elazar (the deputy chief of staff), and others supported the idea of staying on the canal. Bar-Lev added: "It's impossible, in fact, to stabilize a line more suited to us than the Suez line." The minister of defense, also present at these meetings in June–July 1970, stated that he "saw no alternative to the water line. [But] we also need a second line, and some strongholds may have to be abandoned."[34]

Sharon, now responsible for the canal line, followed GHQ's order to the letter in buttressing the fortifications. Larger strongholds began to be constructed ten kilometers from the waterfront as sites for concentrating tank companies. During this period many new access roads to the canal were paved. Dayan viewed the construction of the fortresses as a new defense line which served both defense concepts still under contention in the GHQ.[35]

On July 22 Nasser accepted the Rogers Plan for Israel's withdrawal and the opening of bilateral negotiations — Israel also accepted it the following week — and the ninety-day cease-fire went into effect on August 8. Israel paid a heavy price in the War of Attrition on the Egyptian front — 367 of its troops were killed and 999 wounded.[36] These figures stood in the center of rancorous debate in both the public and military circles.

General Tal, who had been transferred to the defense ministry in this period, drafted a proposal for another system for retaining control of the Sinai front: adjacent to the strongholds, infantry squads would be put on Armored Personnel Carriers (APCs) for daytime patrols and used at nighttime for ambushes and in listening posts that would be set up at four to five kilometer intervals between strongholds, instead of the current ten to thirty kilometer intervals. Besides the infantry-laden APCs, the front's defense would be based on two fully-manned tank brigades responsible for six battalion-sized sectors from Kantara to Ras Sudar. Each battalion would be divided into three companies: one deployed next to the battalion's headquarters on "Lateral Road"; the second in a fortress on "Artillery Road"; and the third divided into platoons on the canal line. In addition to the large outlay in personnel and weapons, there were also other drawbacks in the proposal, such as the danger of tanks being damaged by Egyptian tank traps east of the canal. But Tal assured his critics that a solution even to this problem could be found in a dynamic process. Bren criticized the plan. He felt that the difference between Tal's plan and the original one lay only in the use of a mobile, armored warning instead of the warning system of the strongholds. He also claimed that Tal envisioned the main defense battle taking place near the water line rather than in killing areas deeper in the peninsula.[37]

The cease-fire held, and at the same time preparations continued for the resumption of fighting. The OC of the Southern Command, who in the past had opposed the strongholds plan, now acted on two levels: one — reducing the number of strongholds; two — building a line of fortresses, bunkers constructed on the rearward slope near "Artillery Road," on mounds that partially dominated the plains to the west. In times of quiet, the fortresses were intended to serve as assembly areas and places for preparing the tank companies that could reinforce the strongholds on the canal. In wartime they would serve as bases for reserve forces and create a tactical depth behind the contact line. Thirty-one strongholds and eleven fortresses were built on the canal, the shores of the Bay of Suez, the two Bitter Lakes, and the southern coast of the Mediterranean. Some of them were built with tank positions, others with "snapirs" (long dirt embankments on the strongholds' flanks or a short distance from them).[38]

The debate over the defense concept in Sinai resurfaced when Lt. Gen. David Elazar was appointed chief of staff in early 1972. Sharon, who favored "mobile defense" and opposed the stronghold system for holding the canal line, obtained the chief of staff's approval to evacuate some of the forts. The picture on the ground — approximately one and half years after the cease-fire went into effect — was that of a loosely held line of sixteen manned strongholds located at the entrances to the main roads. Each stronghold had between sixteen and sixty soldiers. According to Major General Gonen's testimony before the Agranat Commission, on the eve of the Yom Kippur War there were only fourteen manned strongholds on the canal line out of the original thirty-one. Gonen also testified that the unmanned strongholds had been "deserted and blocked up: some were totally abandoned and others used only for daylight observation. When the possibility of reopening the vacated strongholds was studied during an inspection on October 2, they were found to be blocked up and destroyed. Therefore it was decided not to reopen them during Operation 'Shovach Yonim' (Dovecote)."[39]

In late May 1972, Chief of Staff Elazar held an exhaustive discussion on the "the defense concept in Sinai."[40] Among the participants, in addition to the permanent generals, were Major General Gonen, the chief of Training & Doctrine Section, who was designated to become OC Southern Command in July 1973; Maj. Gen. Dan Laner, commander of the armored division in Sinai; and his predecessor, Maj. Gen. Shlomo Lahat, the adjutant general of GHQ. The chief of staff presented his basic view: "We have to do everything we can to prepare for the coming period — not only for a full-scale crossing or a major war, but also for a campaign of limited goals." He did not mean an all-out attack of limited dimensions, as the Egyptians eventually carried out, but limited Egyptian activity as in the War of Attrition in the form of assaults on the east bank to capture an Israeli stronghold and raise the Egyptian flag. At any rate, this was the accepted assessment of the enemy's modus operandi at the time. Elazar continued: "The defense of the canal, the cease-fire line, and [the rest of] Sinai will be the responsibility of the armored forces — tanks and mechanized infantry.... There is no division of authority with the strongholds on this matter.... We'll build an optimal tank layout of [at least] three armored brigades. We want to see the armor used at company-sized and larger formations." Regarding the fortifications, he added: "The stronghold is a major contribution to the strengthening of our defense layout.... [It] lessens the number of potential crossing points. We may assume that the fording will occur opposite a stronghold [actually the Egyptians sidestepped the strongholds in the Yom Kippur War and crossed at significant distances from them, dealing with most of them in later stages of the war — D.A.]. Taking all of this into account, I would say — use [the strongholds]." As the discussion turned to doctrinal matters, the chief of staff ordered a new operative plan to be prepared, one that would take into consideration the evacuation of the strongholds, on the one hand, and creation of an additional armored brigade, on the other hand. This order does not seem to have been carried out.[41]

In early August 1972 Southern Command held a war game — "Ayle Barzel" (battering ram).[42] The Training & Doctrine Section, under the command of Major General Gonen, prepared the exercise which was designed to test operational maneuvers in the event of a full-scale Egyptian attack on Sinai and Gaza (the Egyptian modus operandi that Israeli MI presented[43]). The scenario depicted the Egyptians crossing the canal on three bridgeheads with four infantry divisions that included 380 tanks. Following this force would come two additional tank brigades, one independent and the other from the Fourth Division. These forces would immediately proceed eastward from the bridgeheads and reach "Lateral Road" near Rumani, Baluza, and the gateway to the Gidi and Mitla passes. Israeli counterattacks by regular army units would commence two hours from the time of the Egyptian crossing. They would have to fight off the Egyptian offensive on their own until the third day of the war and push them back toward the canal. It would be left to the single reservist division that arrived on the third day to cross the northern sector and transfer the fighting to the western bank. The chief of staff summed up the exercise, noting the army's optimism but also the unrealistic results. He too believed that the main campaign would be fought after the IDF crossed to the western side. This could be achieved, he stated, only by crossing in another sector and creating a fourth armored division that would be integrated into the fighting.

Maj. Gen. Albert Mendler was appointed commander of the armored division in Sinai in September 1972. He immediately set about making a comprehensive reexamination of the front's defense, especially the strongholds on the water line and the adjacent tank ramps. Mendler proposed increasing the number and quality of the soldiers manning the strongholds on the first line, and, given the threat posed by the Egyptians' long-range antitank weapons on the huge ramps they had built on the opposite bank, he also ordered construction of a second line of ramps, 2,000 to 2,500 meters from the canal, that would serve as tank positions. During the IDF's "Blue and White" alert in May 1973, General Mendler repeated his demands, but only received a guarantee that when the time came the reservist force on the front would be replaced with a unit of regular army paratroopers.[44]

The defense plan that was formulated in this period was designed primarily to provide an answer to an attack the size of a "large raid" in a narrow sector — which was essentially an Egyptian attempt to seize a foothold on the eastern bank. The plan called for additional forces to be integrated, or prepared to be integrated, in the defense of the area.[45] These included eight tank platoons (twenty-four tanks) that would fight in platoon formation alongside the strongholds, or in positions inside a stronghold; eight additional companies that would be deployed behind the strongholds; and an additional tank brigade behind the companies in a third line. The brigade's three battalions would be deployed at great distances from one another: in the north, the Kantara sector; in the center, the Ismalia-Tasa area; and in the south, the exit from the Mitla-Suez sector. These battalions would remain concentrated in the rear and sally forth in local counterattacks against the enemy that had managed to cross the waterway.[46]

GHQ, Southern Command, and the armored division in Sinai labored to complete the redrafting of offensive and defensive operative plans. In July 1973 Major General Gonen (Gorodish) replaced Major General Sharon as OC Southern Command, and vigorously began reinstating the plan. Circumstances dictated that most of the attention was accorded to the offensive plans which were intended to provide a decisive answer to any attempt at a major Egyptian crossing. As for defense, two plans may be discerned.[47]

"Sela" was basically a carefully organized defense plan whose ORBAT included reservists designated to the Southern Command's western front. "Shovach Yonim" was a defense plan for the deployment of regular army forces (conscripts). It included additional regular army troops and reservists as an initial answer to an Egyptian offensive. The plan was designed to afford adequate opening positions in a defensive battle, and enable the switchover to the full-scale defense plan — "Sela" — or to attack plans, such as "Tzefania," for traversing the canal in the Kantara area.[48]

"Shovach Yonim" was drafted in December 1972 and issued as an order to the Sinai division in January 1973.[49] It was planned as the initial defense layer of regular forces that would eventually be joined by the reserves in the event of a full-scale war. From the beginning, the plan envisioned an answer to only limited Egyptian moves. It dealt with the deployment of the regular army units in the Sinai armored division — reinforced with infantry and artillery — on the canal front.[50] According to "Sela," the division's forces would deploy in three brigade sectors: from the north to south of Kantara — an area brigade reinforced with a tank battalion and infantry battalion headquarters; in the center of the front and the south — two tank brigades. The plan took into account a forward line based on strongholds that were strengthened with infantry. Because the strongholds were isolated and access to them difficult, they would have a permanently stationed tank platoon on hand. Most of the strongholds would be reinforced within half an hour — and only when efforts at Egyptian crossing were observed in their area — with tank platoons from the companies concentrated on the rear line and in the fortresses on "Artillery Road." The tank platoons' missions would be to secure the embankment, assist the strongholds, and smash the crossing attempts. A brigade-level reserve battalion was planned for deployment on a more rearward line, on "Lateral Road,"[51] and was supposed to reach the water line within two hours from the moment the order was given.

The divisional reserve of an additional armored brigade was planned for deployment in the middle of the front, where it would counterattack the enemy's main crossing effort.[52] Another brigade was added that was not organically part of the Sinai division. Ordinarily, the Seventh Brigade was given this assignment, and even drilled it with one of its battalions stationed permanently at Refidim. On the eve of the war the Seventh was transferred north and replaced by a brigade from the Armored School.

The deep layout in the crucial areas of the Mitla and Gidi passes was supposed to be held by a reduced infantry battalion.[53] A small amount of artillery pieces were also deployed next to the tanks. The artillery consisted of two battalions of self-propelled howitzers in the northern and southern parts of the sector, a long-range artillery battery in the central sector, and another self-propelled artillery battalion planned to reinforce the central sector.

All told, the "Shovach Yonim" forces were designed to provide an answer to an Egyptian attack by means of regular army forces, whether or not an early warning was received, though, it should be emphasized, this warning was absolutely vital for mobilizing the reserves in time. The task of the regular army forces, the conscripts, was to delay the crossing and prevent the enemy force from establishing itself on the eastern bank of the Suez Canal.

"Sela" was a comprehensive defense plan for the front that envisioned the deployment of two additional armored divisions of reservists[54] behind the forward division that had been deployed according to "Shovach Yonim." The two reservist divisions would enter the battle during the Southern Command's counterattack. They would be used offensively in the direction of the canal[55] immediately after the stabilization of the line and return to the status quo ante. In a worst-case scenario, if Egyptian armored divisions penetrated the front in depth, the counterattack would be directed against these penetrations. The allotment of two divisions was an initial one. GHQ would reinforce the front with additional formations according to inflowing intelligence data.[56]

The Israeli air force — "flying artillery" — had proved its tactical superiority when it struck Egyptian frontline forces and in-depth targets deep during the War of Attrition. This continued until it found itself in the midst of missile ambushes in July 1970. Now, in the post–War of Attrition period, the air force was given an important role in all the GHQ's plans. Its main task was to keep the skies "clean" above the Israeli troops. Its first priority was to knock out Egypt's air defense systems and aircraft in order to create suitable conditions for its primary missions: to provide close assistance to the ground forces and impede Egyptian ground forces as much as possible.[57]

Critics point to the shortcomings in the Sinai defense plan[58] that was designed solely on

Diagram 2: The Deployment of Forces on the Canal Front on the Eve of the Yom Kippur War

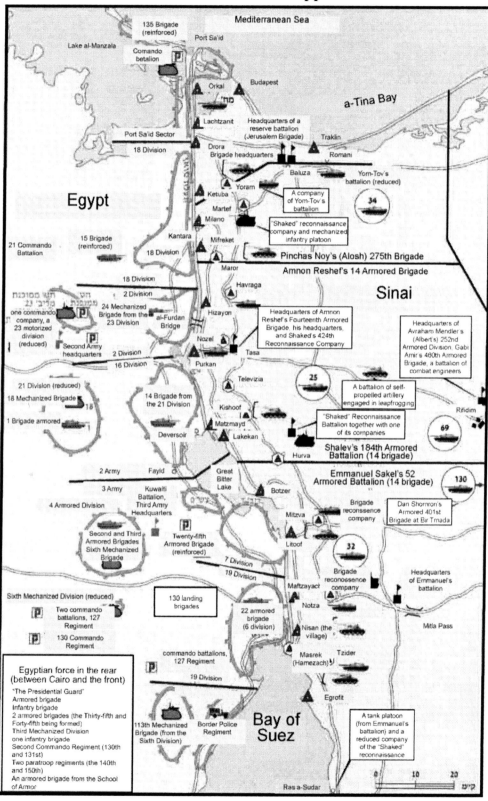

the tactical level. Limited engagements were planned for the sectors and formations, but a comprehensive, overall defense plan at the operational level was lacking. The Israeli strategists assumed that tactical defensive battles would be fought on the water line, and that an all-systems campaign would develop only when IDF forces went on the offensive. Later, reserve reinforcements would arrive, after they had been mobilized under the cover of defense engagements. In the meantime, however, the "holding battles" would be waged by the regular army troops.

In addition to the shortcomings in the defense planning, another important factor went almost unnoticed. In February–March 1973, GHQ and Southern Command made a thorough administrative study designed to curtail costs, mainly by reducing the regular army's ORBAT. Among the ideas "entertained" was a multipronged plan: reduce the division's forces in the tank brigade; eliminate the regular army artillery group; and even dismantle divisional headquarters and convert it into a reservist headquarters, thereby placing all the remaining forces in Sinai directly under Southern Command headquarters.

This plan was apparently canceled because of "Blue White" events in April–May 1973.

The defense plans on the Sinai front — "Shovach Yonim" and "Sela" — were actually "alternative plans." A great deal of time and thought had been had invested in them based on military knowledge and combat experience acquired in past wars and the most recent one — the War of Attrition. Even if the Israeli planner failed to construct defense plans capable of answering all of the battlefield's needs, the plans were intended to withstand the baptism of fire. The Egyptian military planner, who observed and analyzed IDF exercises on the east bank of the canal, and deduced Israel's defense plans, looked for ways to undermine the rationale on which the Israeli strategy was based. These solutions included the intelligent exploitation of all of the Egyptian army's advantages and the neutralization of its weaknesses; in addition, they discovered almost all of the omissions in the IDF's planning and application of its strength.

The Israeli Intelligence Concept

One of the primary reasons for the Israeli MI failure to warn of Egyptian plans to launch an imminent war may be attributed to the intelligence chief's mind-set in what the branch termed "the conception."[59] Two years before the Yom Kippur War the "conception" had become all but axiomatic in the intelligence community. Basically, it assumed that Egypt would avoid war with Israel until it had the air capability of attacking in-depth targets — especially Israel's main airfields — so as to paralyze the Israeli air force.[60]

The MI chief testified before the Agranat Commission, the blue-ribbon panel that investigated the events of the Yom Kippur War. Major General Zeira stated: "One of the cornerstones of the situation estimate was that Egypt would not attack until conditions in the air enabled it to attack airbases deep in Israel.... I would say that this concept came from the research department.... The second condition was [the acquisition of] bombers. He [Sadat] did not receive [them].... The problem was the conception."

Zeira also testified, "Our estimate[61] was based on [certain][62] assessments that, on the one hand, Egypt would lack the strength — especially air power — to launch an attack until it had [x number of] long-range bomber squadrons capable of striking our airfields ... [and] until other elements pushed Egypt, it would refrain from going to war."[63]

In his postwar memoirs,[64] Zeira presented the basic "intelligence material"[65] that he received and that formed his own concept of Sadat (and, in his opinion, the political level's too): "Egypt's military precondition for initiating a war is the basic change in the balance of air power. To achieve this, Egypt has to acquire two types of equipment. First, the requisite number of advanced, low-flying, long-range, adequately armed squadrons capable of reaching Israel's airbases and other deep targets. Second, Scud-type surface-to-surface missiles capable of threatening Israel's population centers and deterring Israel from attacking targets deep inside Arab countries."

The Agranat Commission attempted to clarify and define the conception: "*Egypt would not launch an all-out war until it had obtained [x number of] long-range bomber squadrons that could attack Israel's airfields and paralyze our air force, thus thwarting Israeli air strikes deep in Egypt, or retaliate against the air strikes by bombing Israel's population centers.*"

The commission based its views on General Zeira's testimony that when he assumed his role in October 1972, he studied the situation and was told that "Egypt was incapable of attacking Israel not because of the balance of ground forces, but because of the balance of air power. The Egyptians realized that until they achieved the necessary balance of air power and the strength to make long-range forays into Israel — especially against its airfields — they would put their plans for a major offensive on hold." Zeira added that the material on which he relied had estimated that "Egypt would not initiate a war until it had attained air capability — and until that time he assumed that its intentions were not being directed toward launching a war or crossing the canal."[66]

In trying to explain the development of the concept, Zeira noted that Israeli analysts compared Egypt's capabilities with its intentions, and concluded that "the [Egyptian] ground forces were capable of crossing the canal but [Egypt's leaders] feared to test this capability because they realized that we would hit them in depth. [Since] they lacked the means to retaliate, their intentions would not be realized."[67]

When the Agranat Commission examined the "evolution" of the concept and the reasons for its adoption by the chief of MI, it observed that this had been the generally accepted view in Israeli intelligence corridors since 1971, and that when Major General Zeira became head of MI in October 1972 he adopted the concept after being convinced that it was correct. Zeira's opinion of its accuracy was strengthened when he noted that in three previous attacks (late 1971 — termed by the Egyptians the "Year of Decision"; December 1972; and April–May 1973) it had proven itself.[68] Zeira admitted that information was coming in from various other sources regarding Egypt's intention to open a major offensive. This information on military preparations in the canal sector included the movement of troops and equipment, the deployment of artillery, the elevation of alert levels in the air and ground forces, and other pertinent data. Despite this, on each occasion the Egyptians refrained from going to war, which cemented the Israeli intelligence analysts' perception that its concept was sound. According to General Zeira, the concept proved its credibility on the following three occasions[69]:

• In November–December 1971, during the "Year of Decision," when Sadat made a public announcement that Egypt was on the path to war;

• In December 1972, when information arrived from covert sources that Egypt was about to launch a war;

• In April–May 1973, when intelligence experts estimated that Egypt was not headed for war.

The April–May 1973 alert and Israel's view of these events has been discussed by Brig. Gen. Yoel Ben-Porat in his book on Israeli MI in this period and its submission to the "concept": "The Egyptians won't attack us because they're not ready yet. And since they're incapable of attacking us, they have no desire to. Syria won't dare to attack us alone, since it depends on Egypt. The likelihood [of a Syrian-initiated attack] is lower than low....[70] On three occasions Sadat announced publicly or secretly that he was about to launch a war. [Our intelligence] experts analyzed the situation according to the conception and came to the conclusion that he would not go to war."[71] Indeed, each time Sadat backed away. In the meantime he worked exhaustively in preparing the army. In the end he chose his own time to open hostilities. MI also received reports of unusual signs of military activity in Egypt and Syria. These reports came in two waves (from mid–April until late May 1973 and especially from mid–September until the outbreak of the war) but did not change the branch's basic concept or assessment.[72] The conception that denied the likelihood of an Egyptian attack failed the test. When war broke out, the concept was blown to smithereens by the Egyptian ground forces crossing the canal on their way to redeem their country's lost honor.

Egypt's View of the Israeli Conception

The concept of the Egyptians' need for long-range air capability seems to have been at the base of Egyptian military thinking. The Egyptian strategist who drew up the battle plans sought answers to the army's operational needs.

The Six-Day War opened with a massive Israeli air strike against several key targets deep in Egypt, destroying in one fell swoop the Egyptian air force's ability to take part in aerial and ground fighting. Given these results, the Egyptian high command demanded a similar capability. Field Marshal Abdel Ghani El-Gamasi noted in his memoirs that already in 1967 Nasser asked the Russians for a new type of long-range bomber to counter Israel's monopoly in the skies. Gamasi relates that Egypt's MIGs had a shorter range than Israel's Mirages and Mystères (which were capable reaching Marsa Matruh from their bases).[73]

Part of the Soviet Union's military doctrine after World War II was based on air strikes deep in enemy territory capable of knocking out the maximum number of aircraft and other quality targets. This was a crucial factor in the preparatory or opening stages of the war. The Egyptian planners, too, regarded this aspect of the Soviet combat doctrine as essential.

Egyptian staff officers, the strategists who had been planning the next war since the 1967 debacle, proceeded according to the goals defined at the political level, the main objective being the recapture of the Sinai Peninsula. The war aim stipulated that air superiority alone would enable the army to advance in-depth.[74] Air superiority would provide full protection to the lines crossing the canal, and moving into the heart of Sinai, and then all the way to the international border (the Green Line). The Egyptians had learned the bitter lessons from the 1967 deluge when, in their retreat from Sinai, the Israeli air force had bombed and strafed the long lines of fleeing troops in open desert terrain, especially in the Gidi and Mitla defiles.

Added to the concerns over Israeli air superiority was also the fear of Israel's armor superiority. The Israeli conception may have paid little attention to this matter, but the Egyptian military planners were very much occupied by it.

Defense Minister Fawzi, who initiated the offensive plan in the first years after the 1967 debacle in light of Nasser's aims, was urged by his staff to obtain the necessary weapons to supply the advancing ground forces with contiguous air cover. The air force's arsenal, which included equipment received shortly after the last war, would not provide sufficient air defense to the troops moving into the heart of Sinai and away from the surface-based air defense umbrella at the canal. The various types of MIGs that formed the backbone of the Egyptian air force were incapable of reaching Israeli airbases, most of which were located in the center of the country.

The Egyptians' wish to launch a preemptive air strike, like Israel did to them in June 1967, was beyond their technical ability. This was why long-range aircraft were needed, and this technical deficiency explains the Egyptian leadership's tireless efforts and repeated petitions to the Soviet Union — their main (and perhaps only) weapons supplier — for planes with the necessary capabilities. Israeli MI officers who analyzed Egypt's needs, the pressure it was exerting, and its attempts to procure such aircraft, undoubtedly incorporated this information into their conception.

The pressure for advanced planes, which began in 1968, received added momentum in the War of Attrition. The Israeli solution to Egypt's expanded campaign of mainly artillery fire was to call on its air force to take an ever increasing part in the fighting. Israel's use of its aircraft against targets deep in the enemy's rear awakened the Egyptians to their need for a similar capability. Gamasi claims that the entry of American-produced planes in the war zone magnified Egypt's sense of inferiority and its realization that the solution lay with the Soviets.[75] When Nasser and the Russians held discussions in Moscow on June 30, 1970, the Egyptian president asked for long-range bombers. The Soviets agreed in principle to supply him with Tupolov TU-16s, but preferred to postpone delivery to a later date. Hints and signals that were leaked from the closed meeting added further layers of conviction and certainty to Israel's intelligence concept of Egypt's plans.

General Sadaq, the Egyptian minister of war and Fawzi's successor, searched desperately for solutions to the unconditional demand that Egypt's new president, Anwar Sadat, issued: equip the army with an offensive capability. Like others, Sadaq recognized the critical need for long-range bombers, but at the same time he was painfully aware of the army's shortcomings. He doubted that his predecessor's plans could be implemented, and his doubt strengthened Israel's conviction in the veracity of its concept. The Egyptian general's apprehensions stemmed mainly from the air force's offensive weakness, as well as from the IDF's superiority in all areas of battlefield mobility.

Sadaq was greatly troubled by the army's deficiencies in general, and the Egyptian soldier's in particular, to meet Israel's overwhelming armor superiority. Israeli intelligence seems to have gotten wind of the pessimistic mood that Sadaq infected his staff with. The combination of the Egyptian leadership's awareness of its army's technological inferiority and lack of self-confidence put the final nail into the coffin of the concept that Israeli intelligence analysts had constructed.

The turning point in Egypt's situation estimate that began at the end of the "Year of Decision" probably translated into a more limited objective by late October 1972.[76] On October 24 the Supreme Council of the Egyptian Armed Forces convened in Sadat's office in El Giza. During the meeting the president made a number of decisions, the main one being "to have the military put some muscle into the matter." This is the meeting where Sadat seems to have announced that Egypt would go to war "with the weapons it currently had."[77]

The new minister of war, Ahmad Ismail Ali, who was appointed on October 28, 1972, and the GHQ, headed by Shazli and Gamasi, understood perfectly the implications of Sadat's order. They changed both the objective and operational attack plan. They diminished its scope, and adapted it, first and foremost, to the Egyptian soldier's abilities, thus reducing, or circumventing, the army's technological deficiencies.

Sadat and the GHQ realized that it was not only the lack of long-range fighter-bombers that prevented Egypt from making an all-out attack and "returning by force what had been taken by force." The reasons for Egypt's caution and hesitations were more complex. Its aircrafts' inability to hit airbases deep in Israeli territory was one factor in the mosaic that had to guarantee the attacker's protection. The multisided mission that began with an offensive thrust — canal crossing and consolidation of the bridgeheads — also required the construction of a vital air umbrella and a comprehensive ground defense against Israel's armor with its superior maneuverability and firepower.[78]

The Egyptian plan to penetrate into the depths of Sinai, and seize and occupy the entire peninsula, would put the advancing force at a great distance from its starting positions, where they had been protected by antiaircraft batteries, and would leave it vulnerable to air and ground attacks. Moreover, the plan to limit the mission to the mountain passes (fifty to seventy kilometers from the canal) — that recalled the modus operandi that Israeli MI believed Egypt would probably adopt[79] — also encountered similar difficulties.

The Egyptian strategists received the full backing of the political leadership and developed a new track. Facing seemingly insurmountable handicaps — the main factors in the Israeli conception — they found a chink in the Israeli armor that afforded an alternative path. The issue was no longer the recapture of all of Sinai or just the mountain passes: *it was the capture of a narrow strip, eight to twelve kilometers deep on the eastern bank of the canal.*[80] The strip would be protected by ground-based antiaircraft units (with an emphasis on antiaircraft missiles), reinforced with antitank missiles and launchers, and planted with minefields. Together, this weaponry would supply the requisite air and ground protection to the crossing force. This mission was adapted to the abilities of the entire Egyptian army: from the grunt on the ground to the divisional level, to the field army, air defense, air force, and finally to GHQ.

Israeli intelligence failed to detect the tactical shift in Egypt's strategic thinking. Intelligence analysts who warned that the enemy was planning to capture all of Sinai (or even just the western part of the peninsula) also pointed to Egypt's limited use of force, such as the capture of a single IDF stronghold. But Israeli assessment experts failed to detect the enemy's eventual modus operandi.

Zvi Lanir, one of the senior staff members in MI's information collection department on the eve of the war, claims that Israel knew about Egypt's strategic concept for a limited war aimed at achieving a political objective, and that the Israeli intelligence community had noted this possible modus operandi long before the Yom Kippur War. The possibility of a limited war appeared in the intelligence branch's annual situation estimates in 1972–1973 (that is, from late 1971–early 1972) as a reasonable modus operandi, whose goal would be to capture a narrow strip of land on the east bank of the canal.[81] This modus operandi referred to a "quick grab" — that is, an Egyptian presence in a narrow limited area by overtaking an IDF stronghold on the eastern bank.

Even in the Agranat Commission's conclusion on the concept, the writers failed to understand how Egypt really acted. In discussing the weak points in implementing the conception, they noted that the Egyptians chose the "limited plan" — crossing the canal in order to seize territory on the eastern side as far as the Mitla and Gidi defiles — as opposed to the plan for capturing all of Sinai. This tactic was raised by the chief of Israeli intelligence at a GHQ meeting on May 14, 1973, in which he announced, "Sadat wants war. He wants to take all of Sinai, the mountain passes at the very least."[82] This plan was presented as the Egyptian plan in the war — but this was not the plan that was carried out.

Conclusion — Why the Concept Failed

The concept that developed in MI was correct in its time, as long as the Egyptians intended to cross the canal, capture the strongholds, and penetrate deep into Sinai. But the

Egyptian decision (which was apparently made in late 1972) to limit the military objectives and narrow the dimensions of the war pulled the rug out from under the Israeli conception. The Egyptian army no longer needed long-range aircraft. And even though it persisted in trying to acquire them and even managed to obtain a guarantee that MIG-23s and Sukhoi bombers would be supplied, this was no longer a sine qua non to going to war.

In an article in the Israeli daily *Ha'aretz* entitled "The Still Open Story," Yossi Melman quotes a GHQ officer in the intelligence collection main unit. Describing the conception, Bril admits that MI believed that the Egyptians would not go to war until they had acquired long-range bombers and surface-to-surface missiles capable of threatening Israel's military bases and population centers. According to Bril, MI predicted that Egypt would obtain this operational capability only in 1975 or 1976, so that until then, the chances of a war breaking out were low.[83] Efraim Kam, too, writes that an Egyptian attack was considered unlikely before 1975 — the earliest date when Egypt could procure and absorb the necessary air capability.[84]

The Israeli layout, which appeared justified during the War of Attrition and in 1972, the "Year of Decision," because of Egypt's inability to launch a full-scale attack, further strengthened its conception. The misleading Israeli alert in April–May 1973 known as "Blue White,"[85] reflected the GHQ's fear of an Egyptian attack and encouraged national security experts to present the concept as a barrier against a possible Egyptian attack.

After poring over captured Egyptian documentation, I failed to come up with any justification for the "Blue White" alert. On the contrary, during this period the Egyptian GHQ had already finished the details of the plan for a full-scale limited attack and was in the process of absorbing the doctrine, battle techniques, and military exercises at the individual and unit level.

The conception became a rock-solid assessment in the intelligence branch regarding the danger of war. As in "Blue White," so also in September 1973 (when thirteen Syrian MIGs were shot down) and in the critical first week of October, the concept served as the basis for the Mossad's assessment that the likelihood of Egypt and Syria opening a full-scale war against Israel simultaneously on two fronts was very slim.[86]

During his testimony before the Agranat Commission a few months after the war, the head of intelligence stated that he realized only in retrospect that at some point in the spring or summer of 1973 that Sadat had changed his concept of the coming clash. And, the intelligence chief added, "For some reason, I still don't know when he altered it." But the authors of the report note that from the material that the intelligence chief made available to them, the conclusion could be drawn that a shift was apparent in Egypt's position already in early 1973 when Sadat realized that his army would meet the IDF on the battlefield only with the weapons it currently possessed, even if it had not acquired long-range bombers in sufficient numbers to guarantee air superiority. In other words, this was a case of doctrinal change on the Egyptian side that contradicted Israel's rigid mind-set.[87]

"How did it happen that we were caught by surprise?" Colonel Yoel Ben-Porat asked. (Ben-Porat had been the commander of the central information collection — SIGINT — unit in MI before and during the war.)[88] He claims that intelligence assessment resembles an architectural design. Just as architects are enamored of their own concepts, rendering them incapable or unwilling to change their form or color, so the "artists" in military intelligence fell into the captivating embrace of their own dogmatic conceptualization without paying attention to the inflow of contradictory information and without wishing to change any part of their estimate regarding the low likelihood of war erupting. In another article Ben-Porat compares the intelligence branch to a man suffering from a special form of color blindness, where instead of seeing all the colors of the rainbow he sees only those that he likes. The national layout created a screen through which only the information that corresponded with the concept was able to pass. Other information, especially if contradictory, was blocked out and left unanalyzed — and if it was not examined critically, then it was not understood and even tossed away.[89]

The Israeli journalist Aryeh Arad discovered other reasons for the erroneous conception, especially regarding the Soviet combat doctrine's development which the Egyptians absorbed and adopted.[90] According to Arad, the strategic surprise was the natural result of its timing, and was able to happen because of the mistaken premise that the Arabs would not attack until they had attained air superiority which would enable them to neutralize Israel's air and land forces. This premise was based on the view that the Soviet doctrine assumed a priori that western-equipped and/or -trained forces were superior to Soviet ones and would remain so in the foreseeable future because of the East-West technological gap in electronics and complex materials.

Another mistaken assumption was that the Arabs' and the Red Army's military capability in firepower and movement was inferior to Israel's. What was unbeknownst to Israeli intelligence pundits[91] was that the Soviet combat doctrine, which had been adopted by the Egyptian army, had found a way to neutralize the West's advantages in general and Israel's in particular, and had developed two families of advanced surface-to-air and antitank missiles.[92] The Israeli chief of staff's ignorance of these missiles and their significance enabled the Arabs to catch Israel sleeping. In other words, the Arabs' ability to overwhelm the IDF tactically with devastatingly accurate missiles enabled them to surprise Israel strategically.[93]

According to Ben-Porat,[94] the Israeli conception could be summarized in the following way: The Arabs had no option for war because Egypt lacked the air power to go to war. The information that Israeli intelligence received stated specifically that the goal of the coming war was to set the political process in motion, and that the ground objective was a few kilometers on the east bank of the canal. In order to achieve this objective — Ben-Porat adds in his attempt to explain why the concept failed — the Egyptians acquired antitank missiles and a large quantity of antiaircraft weaponry as an alternative to their air force in protecting the crossing operation.

Also trying to clarify what happened, Brigadier General Levran (a colonel at the time), deputy director of MI research, states "In retrospect the inflexible, unalterable view of one particular estimate was undoubtedly the source of the blunder." According to Levran, reliable information that supported the intelligence analysts' versions blinded them and hampered their ability to perceive what was happening on the ground. Accurate, reliable information was not updated, or to put it more correctly, was updated retroactively for a certain period, while the enemy's volte-faces and his decision to go to war went unheeded.[95]

Israel's attitude at the leadership level can be summed up in the words of the defense minister, Moshe Dayan, who confessed to Sadat that Israel had known all about his military moves but refused to believe that he was capable of launching an offensive and crossing the canal.[96]

Twenty-six years after the war, Lt. Gen. (Res.) Amnon Lipkin-Shachak (a former chief of staff and MI director) wondered how we arrived at the "concept that war would not break out." He describes how on becoming chief of MI he read through archival material on intelligence assessments of the year preceding the Yom Kippur War[97]: "The Egyptians began preparations months before the war. These included the construction of massive dirt positions, laagers for fording equipment, and a missile layout. Months before the 1973 war, Southern Command received reports on unprecedented engineering operations on the Egyptian side — clear-cut evidence that a canal crossing was being planned. You see that the entire intelligence establishment is strained and tense and realizes that something big is going on. The reports continue to flow in, four months later they mention fording exercises and practice runs at breaking through the embankment on our side. And military intelligence estimates that this deployment will enable an immediate shift to the offensive, but they gauge it is as [only] an exercise despite the fact that two fully mobilized armies are now stationed on the border in attack position."

The Agranat Commission summed up the issue, stating that overreliance on the conception as the main criterion guiding the intelligence community produced a limited and rigid approach to thinking instead of intellectual flexibility, which is crucial in the field of assessment.[98] In the article, "If Only I Could Discover the Truth as Easily as I Refute the Lie,"[99] Brig. Gen. Yitzhak Ben-Israel adds that Israel's failure to predict the Yom Kippur War was basically a lapse of logical thinking and not a psychological or sociological omission.[100]

I believe that a methodical study of Egypt's strategic activity, doctrinal changes, training programs, instructions and orders could have resulted in a change in the Israeli assessment. An investigative approach to the "mosaic of activities" and a regularly updated analysis of Egypt's moves would have freed the intelligence assessors from their captivity to a particular concept. In my opinion, Egyptian military planning was characterized by flexible thinking that eventually led to military solutions and enabled the Egyptians to go to war and break the "concept" in October 1973.

3

Egypt Prior to the Yom Kippur War

Acceptance of the Soviet Warfare Doctrine

Egypt's War Aims

The system's aims are the heart and soul of every area of life: political, military, economic, and so forth. The aim is determined in advance by the system and reflects its achievements or influence.[1]

The war aim is the basis of the military level's activity and determines troop assignments. The assignments determine the force's objectives and modus operandi. The final aim is determined at the highest political level. The war aim is the main expression of the strategy that the political level implements (or intends to implement) when it turns to the military level for a solution to its problems. Defining the goal, especially in military operations, is a complex process that entails planning the entire campaign. The stages in this hierarchical process may be outlined in the following manner:

• The highest political level decides the aims and political-strategic limitations, defines the objectives and strategic limitations, apportions the necessary resources, and engages in a dialogue with the national strategic authorities (the defense, foreign affairs, internal affairs, and economic establishments).

• The appropriate strategic authorities (the defense ministry and GHQ) clarify the systems idea, define primary objectives, formulate plans, and define the tactical missions of the various command systems.

• The tactical command creates a battle plan for executing tactical missions.[2]

The term "strategy" refers to "grand or high strategy" that the British historian and commentator, B. H. Liddell Hart, defined as "policy being implemented." Strategy adapts and directs "all of the nation's, or group of nations,' resources toward attaining the war's political objective — the aim defined by the basic policy."[3] This is a broader definition than Clausewitz's, which views strategy as "the art of employing combat as a means of achieving the war aim." Strategy shapes the war plans, designs courses for the different systems that take part in the war, and oversees the battles fought in each campaign.[4] The term "strategy" was expanded by the French military theoretician, General André Baufre, to include "the art of deciding on the use of force as an effective contribution to obtaining political aims."[5] Today most observers see strategy as the way the senior command plans and conducts war in order to achieve supreme political objectives.

In preparing for the Yom Kippur War, the presidents of Egypt and Syria served as the supreme commanders of their armies (in addition to fulfilling their political roles), which explains the absence of a clear distinction between the political and military levels in all aspects of strategic decision making.

The war's main goal was to break the stalemate in the political process for resolving the Middle East crisis. The source of this stalemate was the continued state of "no war — no peace" that developed at the end of the War of Attrition (August 7–8, 1970). The cease-fire ended the hostilities without the Egyptians having achieved their war aims. The source of Egypt's military strategy in the coming years can be discerned in the basic structure of the War of Attrition: a war of limited dimensions and objectives that was fought for a relatively long time.

The war's limited goals included:
• Breaking the international deadlock;
• Weakening Israel and forcing it to give up the captured lands because of heavy casualties and economic strain;
• Salvaging the Egyptian regime's prestige by demonstrating its willingness and ability to continue fighting despite the crushing defeat in 1967.[6]

The ongoing "no war–no peace" situation had far-reaching, negative implications in all areas of Egypt's national life. Not only was Sadat's government in danger of being replaced, but so was the regime that had been in power since the 1953 revolution.[7] Sadat summed up the situation in a nutshell: "The entire world has lost faith in us, and even we have begun to lose faith in ourselves."[8]

The ignominious defeat in the Six-Day War was a traumatic experience for the Arab world, but Egypt suffered the most. Egypt, which had dragged all of the "confrontational states" into the war, now became the main party responsible for the catastrophic defeat. Even more difficult for the Egyptians was the debacle's impact on their self-image and their confidence in their ability to rise to the level of the modern world. The strength that the Officers' Revolution amassed for fifteen years was a source of hope for prosperity and self-respect, but along with the sudden collapse of this strength, the Egyptians' dreams for the future were also shattered. The defeat undermined the revolution's efforts to bring about a national awakening, and ruined the messianic vision of a glorious Arab nation reawakened under Nasser's heroic leadership. The trouncing that Egypt received, the loss of Sinai and the Suez Canal, and the evacuation of the large cities in the Canal Zone became tangible symbols of Egypt's weakness and the deadlock it was caught in.[9]

Immediately after the war the need to come up with a solution was expressed in the national slogan: "Eradicate All Traces of Aggression!" The banner epitomized Nasser's approach to the problem: overcome the loss by returning as close as possible to the *status quo ante bellum*.[10]

Crystallization of the War Aim

Nasser's main goal was to prevent Israel's military victory from turning into a historical victory for Zionism. The radical aims that Nasser had sought until the Six-Day War were no longer realistic. After the defeat he formulated two new war aims: Israel's withdrawal from all of Arab territory lost in the war and the restoration of Palestinian people's national rights. Between 1967 and 1970, when Egypt realized that these two objectives could not be achieved simultaneously, it gradually began focusing on the first goal, leaving the Palestinian problem to a future date. Egypt's acceptance of UN Security Council Resolution 242 in 1967 and the Rogers Initiative in 1970 bear witness to this trend.[11]

Under these circumstances, Nasser informed his war minister, Mahmud Fawzi, of Egypt's strategic aims.[12] Nasser announced that the first stage of the initiative would be in Israel's hands because of its military superiority, but he hoped that the initiative would progressively pass into Egypt's hands. He estimated that a three-year time frame would be needed for the armed forces to attain the capability of launching "a war of liberation," warning that if four years were required, it would not bode well for Egypt.[13]

In accordance with Nasser's instructions, Fawzi defined the "the armed forces' strategic goal" as the "liberation of occupied Sinai by force, reaching the Egyptian-Palestinian border, and defending the land." Nasser's strategy combined the "military solution" with the "political solution."[14] These goals were based on five principles, the fifth being "attrition," which became the main component in the strategy in March 1969. Nasser integrated "attrition" into his four-stage concept — resistance, deterrence, eradication of aggression, final victory — for attaining the strategic goal.[15] Although the Egyptian army underwent rehabilitation and reorganization, the Arab states rejected Nasser's grandiose plans for mobilizing an all-Arab force under Egypt's command.[16]

The Kremlin's predilection to involvement in the Arab-Israeli conflict was part of Nasser's strategy. Ironically, because Soviet troops took part in combat on the canal there was a heightened danger of a superpower confrontation, and this situation convinced the Soviet Union to seek a de-escalation in the conflict. Nasser sought to neutralize the United States. Although the U.S.-sponsored Rogers Plan inclined toward the Egyptian position, Washington continued to demand a peace settlement between Egypt and Israel. And while foreign governments maintained their support of the Arabs, none of them, excluding the two great superpowers, had any influence of consequence in the Middle East.

Just as Israel suffered in the War of Attrition, Egypt too paid a heavy price. In July 1970 Nasser was forced to agree to a cease-fire. This effectively slipped the rug out from under his strategy. His plan to reach a solution through military means proved a failure. The stalemate remained intact. Attempts by Egypt, Syria, Jordan, and the Palestinians to force Israel — and through negotiations — to change the status quo, also came to naught.

Just before Nasser's death, his general offensive strategy ended in defeat. In its place a new strategic-political-military conception began to unfold, one that was suited to the Egyptian reality, conditions in the Arab world, and relations between superpowers. This new outlook perceived military force as complementary to political activity.[17]

On October 15, 1970 Sadat succeeded Nasser as president of Egypt and supreme commander of the armed forces. Sadat, who was now captain of the state, realized that at present he was incapable of solving Egypt's basic problems. He faced four main challenges: consolidating his position in the regime; dealing with economic-social issues that had deteriorated since 1967; redressing the imbalance in Egypt's relations with the two superpowers and with the majority of Arab states; and taking the lead in the Arabs' struggle against Israel.[18]

The conflict stood at the center of every attempt to formulate and implement foreign and domestic policy. Sadat's oft-repeated declarations on Arab-Israeli relations proved that his basic positions were similar to Nasser's. On many occasions before the war he avowed that "Egypt's national goal is to eradicate the Israeli occupation of Egyptian territory."[19] He regarded the removal of the occupation as a means of liberating Egypt, at least in the long run, from the intolerable stress of the Israeli conquest.

Practically speaking, Sadat's ascendancy to political power offered a golden opportunity to reevaluate Egypt's position and adopt an innovative, more pragmatic approach to the conflict based on first an Israeli withdrawal from Sinai, and only later dealing with the Palestinian issue.[20] A review of the national strategy gave Sadat a free hand to formulate a new course for Egypt, especially since Nasser's strategy had reached a cul de sac. In retrospect, Sadat seems to have been blessed with just the right doses of flexibility and audacity to use this window of opportunity to the best advantage in order to devise a concept different from his predecessor's.[21]

One of Sadat's first decisions was to extend the cease-fire on (that was due to end on November 8, 1971).

The political changes that he initiated in his first months in power reflect his search for a direction. He was willing to consider a partial settlement that did not entail Israel's unconditional pullout from Sinai, as long as it revived the momentum of proceeding gradually toward Egypt's basic goals.[22] He examined various political options, and proposed an intermediate agreement for a limited extension of the cease-fire[23] in exchange for opening the Suez Canal. On February 15, 1971, he informed UN mediator Gunnar Jarring that he would agree to a peace settlement with Israel in exchange for an unconditional withdrawal from the territories captured in June 1967.[24] Israel's replies reflect its interest in maintaining the "no war–no peace" condition for as long as possible. Under these circumstances, and given Egypt's weakened situation on the homefront, Sadat had trouble managing the affairs of state.

Despite his announcement that 1971 would be "The Year of Decision," Sadat agreed to further extensions of the cease-fire, mainly in order to buy time for planning the massive military option — the Yom Kippur War.

"The Year of Decision" had been touted with fanfare, yet it passed without any change in the status quo on the Suez Canal. Domestic pressure increased. Student protests, first in January and then in October and November 1972, precipitated bitter criticism of Sadat's ability to deal with internal and foreign affairs, not to mention the Arab-Israeli conflict.[25] In light of the political stalemate and mounting domestic pressure, Sadat made a crucial decision: to opt for a "military solution" and the massive use of force.[26]

This course was an integral part of Sadat's political strategy and aimed at breaking the logjam that had overtaken the Middle East, a standstill that he believed was the result of the "no war–no peace" situation. He pursued the political track by every means possible,[27] in the realization that at this stage military power would serve as a catalyst for accelerating the political process toward a resolution of the conflict.

The decision meant that Egypt had to overcome its fear of Israel's power as well as its own self-doubts (that were especially felt by certain members of the leadership who dismissed the military option and inclined toward negotiations with Israel in order to deal with Egypt's internal problems). In addition to surmounting these hurdles, Sadat's decision required that Egypt rebuild its armed forces and plan meticulously for a full-scale military operation suited to its capabilities. Sadat's policy was based on a concept that diverged from the one that had been in vogue in Nasser's days.[28]

Instead of Nasser's progressive, cumulative, multifaceted application of pressure, Sadat's concept focused on a concerted two-stage effort, whose first step would be based on a large-scale military offensive with limited objectives in order to thaw the freeze in the political process and alter the balance of forces. The second step — embarking upon an aggressive diplomatic offensive on the heels of the military move — would incorporate a vast range of renewed Arab pressures designed to attain the war aim.[29]

Adopting this strategy meant that Sadat had to make a number of crucial decisions. According to Professor Shamir, two of them were of paramount military significance:

• The resumption of fighting had to occur in the course of a major war, while Egypt made full use of its military resources in a concentrated offensive.

• The offensive had to be in conjunction from its first step with only one Arab state — Syria.

The difference between Sadat's approach and Nasser's is obvious. Instead of progressively mobilizing the Arabs' military potential, Soviet involvement, and international backing for an Arab victory, Sadat chose a single-state operation that made maximum use of Egypt's current resources. The key element in his strategy was the ingenious concept of an "all-out war of limited objectives" that was part of a greater political design.

Hassanein Heykal too, Nasser's faithful follower, admitted that "it took Egypt a long time a long time to get used to the idea of a limited offensive that was aimed first and foremost at opening political prospects."[30] Sadat's approach was essentially a breakthrough in strategic thinking.

Another of Nasser's supporters, the war minister in the War of Attrition, Mahmud Fawzi, claimed that the "limited strategy" concept was a mistaken assessment by military commanders who misunderstood President Sadat's initiatives and his plans to divide the war into a series of stages. Fawzi believed that the idea of jettisoning the "correct" strategy of an "all-out war of liberation to eradicate all traces of Israeli aggression" stemmed from the erroneous concept held by the heads of the military command. According to Fawzi, these officers misread Sadat's refusal to sign a decision to go to war no later than the spring of 1971 (three months after Nasser's demise) — the date that Nasser determined for opening hostilities.

According to Fawzi — who cannot be accused of over-modesty — his successors (especially Major Generals Saad al-Din Shazli and Ahmad Ismail Ali — the latter being the head of military intelligence) lacked a comprehensive picture of the armed forces' true capacity because of their remove from planning and preparations centers.[31]

Israeli battlefield superiority obligated Sadat to postpone the date and modus operandi for the coming war. His concern over Israeli strikes deep in Egyptian territory — which had become a recurrent nightmare since the War of Attrition — made the Egyptians see that a military option depended on a long-term strategic cease-fire and especially on surface-to-surface missiles and MIG 23s.[32]

Sadat was desperate for these weapons, but the Soviets consistently refused to supply them. On March 1, 1971 he made a secret trip to Moscow accompanied by Fawzi. During the talks a rift opened between Egypt and Russia, especially regarding military acquisitions. Again the issue of long-range attack planes was brought up. Brezhnev agreed to supply them, but on condition that the Kremlin have final say on their operational employment.[33] Nor did President Podgorny's signing of the Soviet-Egyptian friendship pact in Cairo on May 27, 1971, produce the gains that Egypt had expected. Immediately upon his return to Moscow, Podgorny promised that the weapons would be transferred to Egypt, but months passed and nothing arrived.[34] Finally, in late October, after Sadat and his new war minister, Muhammad Sadaq, visited Moscow, did Soviet hardware begin to reach Egypt (albeit at a slow and desultory pace).[35]

Sadat realized that if the Russians intended to scotch Egypt's war plans, then their presence in the country only impeded Egyptian interests.[36] Thus, he concluded that it would be better to have a military option with the current arsenal than to cancel the entire program for gearing Egypt up for another confrontation with Israel. In July 1972, following further deterioration in relations with the Kremlin, Sadat ordered the Soviets to pack their bags.[37]

The first public expression of Sadat's change of strategy came on October 26, 1972 with the replacement of War Minister Muhammad Sadaq by Ahmad Ismail Ali.[38] Ali, who was appointed war minister almost a year before the Yom Kippur War, agreed to carry out the limited offensive plan. This plan was based on the weapons that Egypt had already amassed.

Ali's willingness ran counter to the opinion of the recently ousted war minister, who still held that the only way to achieve tangible results was to retake all of Sinai. Sadaq favored the all-inclusive offensive plan and believed that an Egyptian-initiated war without sophisticated weapons was doomed to failure.[39]

After a long period of deliberation over the path to be taken, Sadat and a select group of advisors made the decision to go to war. The choice narrowed down to two possibilities[40]: a new version of the War of Attrition, or an aggressive offensive based on Egypt's full military might.

At this stage it was relatively easy to decide on the modus operandi. Egypt had suffered three years of war that ended in 1970 "without having made a crack in the deadlock."[41]

Sadat described the war aim to Field Marshal Ali as an attack in Sinai to gain limited objectives, restore Egypt's self-respect at the price of Israel's, and force the superpowers to commence diplomatic activity toward a "solution" that Egypt regarded as a return to the 1967 borders.[42]

These objectives appeared in the speech Sadat delivered on September 28, 1974 (Nasser Memorial Day). "When we planned the war and defined its objectives, we assumed that the number of kilometers of the occupied land [that we recaptured] was not important. Demolishing Israel's security concept and overcoming international disbelief in our words and ability to do so were more important to us than crossing the canal and seizing the Bar-Lev line."[43]

Sadat defined "smashing the concept" as the basic war aim, and the direct confrontation between Egypt and Israel as "dealing with Israel's security doctrine and totally destroying it."[44] On another occasion he referred to the war aim and Israel's basic defense doctrine as "the tasks that I assigned the Egyptian army: the maximum destruction of the Israeli armed forces, since Israel believes, whether justifiably or not, that its security lies in its deterrent strength and that armed force is the instrument for maintaining it. That is why we must deal with the [enemy's] armed force. Israel will lose its primary means and goal if our armed forces obtain a decisive political triumph through military action — that is, they must forcibly shatter the Israeli defense doctrine."[45]

On October 1, 1973, Sadat conveyed instructions to the commander of the armed forces[46] that explicitly stated that the army's strategic objective was to smash Israel's defense doctrine by causing the enemy devastating losses and proving that the continued occupation of Egyptian territory would exact an intolerable price.

The Egyptian analysis of Israel's defense doctrine identified a number of key elements: the IDF's incontestable military and technological superiority; its ability to divide the Arabs' military effort, quickly transfer a campaign beyond Israel's borders, and wage a blitzkrieg; and its goal of avoiding loss of life.[47]

The Egyptian political leadership's instructions to the military planners pointed to four "strategic goals" that the operational plan had to be based on[48]:

• Forcing Israel to fight on two fronts simultaneously[49];
• Incurring an intolerable number of casualties on the IDF;
• Corralling Israel into a drawn-out war;
• Strengthening Arab solidarity.

The following goals were translated into strategic assignments and conveyed "as a strategic dictate" to the war minister on October 5[50]:

• End the stalemate on the front and break the cease-fire.
• Cause the enemy maximum losses.
• Liberate the occupied lands in stages according to the army's capability and the development of events.

According to the strategy and political level's definition of the war aims and missions, the senior military command carried out its orders: it prepared an offensive plan, implemented the Soviet combat doctrine (adapting it to the Egyptian army's needs), developed an Egyptian combat doctrine of the basis of the Soviet one (which enabled the detailed planning of war moves), drilled and trained the troops, and commanded them during the war.

> The Egyptians claimed that Soviet military thinking was based on the experience of World War Two, where the fronts were 3,000 kilometers long. The Egyptian army, on the other hand, would never find itself operating on a front longer than 150 kilometers.
> [Hassanein Heykal's Memoirs, *Ma'ariv*, April 28, 1975]

The Soviet Warfare Doctrine — The Basis of Egypt's Military Doctrine

The combat doctrine at the tactical level, or as it is also called, "the warfare doctrine," contains a set of principles and rules that determines the planning and command of military forces in combat. The doctrine is intended to instruct military planners and officers on how to engage the enemy on the battlefield. It consists of a collection of formulas, recommendations, and guidelines on how various activities should be carried out (in accordance with "doctrinal instructions" at the strategic and operative levels).

Seen in this light, the warfare doctrine is the link that connects the defense doctrine (the strategic level) to the army's operational planning (the tactical level). It is intended to guarantee that operational plans are directed toward achieving the political objectives as efficiently as possible, and are compatible with the army's capabilities and with political requirements and constraints.

A dynamic reality, changes in the defense policy's objectives and political needs, and — above all — shifts in the military balance of the combatants regarding ORBAT, weapons, deployment, warfare doctrine, battle theater, and systems-level objectives, all demand a reevaluation and at times an updating and renewal of sections of the defense doctrine and those parts of the warfare doctrine that are relevant to it. Such changes may create excessive problems — some basic, most organizational and operational. We will discuss these problems regarding Egypt's preparation of its layout as the Yom Kippur War approached.

The Egyptian planners had to devise a doctrine that overcame the obstacles in Israel's military layout.

Although Israel's defense strategy was traditionally based on preserving the status quo and lines of deterrence, during its first three decades it had to adopt an offensive concept whose main principles were transferring the fighting to the enemy's territory and carrying out a preventative strike (if possible).[51] After the Six-Day War, Israel still clung to these principles, while its troops were deployed on the banks of the Suez Canal, far from the homeland the army was supposed to defend.

The Egyptian military planner dreamed of toppling the Israeli system by going on the offensive and destroying Israel's military layout. The Egyptians' meticulous, brilliant analysis of the relative advantages and disadvantages of the Egyptian and Israeli military systems resulted in a revolutionary, courageous military plan on the eve of the war. The Egyptian military planner, who was versed in Soviet doctrine, realized that the offensive is what wins wars and produces tangible gains on the battlefield. The physical obstacle — the Suez Canal — forced him to wage an offensive campaign, beginning with the water crossing and consolidation of the bridgeheads. Nearly all of the moves in the later stages of the war were planned and executed as a defensive campaign. The Egyptians permitted the Israeli war machine — that proceeded according to the offensive doctrine — to smash itself to pieces against the defense layouts that Egypt hastily established on the east bank.

The Egyptian planner designed a campaign that could be described as a large-scale war, or to be more accurate, "an all-out war"[52] that the entire armed forces took part in. According to the Egyptian leadership, the war's raison d'être was to break the political stalemate, and enable the military tactician to draw up plans that did not require the enemy's army to be routed nor call for vast swaths of territory to be recaptured. The Egyptian military planners came up with a modus operandi based on an all-out war of limited dimensions.

Although the country's leadership devoted all of its military resources to the war, at the same time it limited the war's dimensions, thus enabling the operational forces to reduce the depth of their activity, shorten the dimensions of the attack, and adapt the troops' tasks to their performance capability.

The War Doctrine — The Soviet Concept

The Soviet military doctrine is the Eastern concept of the nature of contemporary warfare and the method of preparing and employing armies in combat. Its general principles regarding national security policy and all facets of building the army are its political basis. There are two sides to the combat doctrine.[53] The first entails basic premises that reflect the social-political nature of the war, the importance of the aims and missions, and the demands regarding the armed forces' structure and the methods used in preparing and waging the war. The second entails the organization, structure, training, arming, and employment of the armed forces in war. This aspect of the doctrine determines the main directions in developing the art of war, and the nature of the technical means for strengthening the state's defenses and improving the troops' combat readiness.

The two sides of the war doctrine are inseparable and interdependent. The state's military-political goals in war must be compatible with its economic resources and military capability. A war doctrine is realistic only when it accurately reflects the armed forces' military and technical abilities, and when its assessment of the army's preparedness and skill on the battlefield corresponds to the state's strength and resources.

Both sides are mutually dependent on the warfare doctrine. On the one hand, capabilities and changes on the military-technical level influence military-political goals and the state's duties; on the other hand, the state's political goals are in proportion to its military potential and the changes it is undergoing.

Since armed struggle is a means for implementing policy, it is subordinate to and dependent on policy. This being the case, armed conflict is granted a certain degree of independence and autonomy in its rules. The Soviet doctrine's task is to make a meticulous study of the laws of armed struggle.[54]

The warfare doctrine includes principles of an exclusively military nature that deal with the training and application of the armed forces. The principles also determine the direction the art of war will take — strategies, tactics, and the campaign itself — and the method of arming and equipping the armed forces. The Soviet doctrine is like a basic state law regarding self-defense. Its principles are expressed in the Soviet army's regulations and orders.[55]

More than any other people, the Soviets considered the warfare doctrine to be a science.[56] They claimed that it is a doctrine that analyzes warfare; in other words, a system of sciences that deals with general problems related to war: operations, battles, planning, and military training.[57]

The main objective in the art of war is to obtain victory by skillfully wielding the state's power and arsenal. War demands careful planning and organization — and even in the best of circumstances it is a very complex and risky undertaking. The doctrine is an indispensable element in the art of war — it is the force that mobilizes the army's consciousness.[58]

The combat doctrine is extremely useful. It deals with the theory and practice of war in general, and the employment of the armed forces and their use in combat operations. It covers a wide range of subjects, the most important of which are[59]:

• Planning combat operations;
• Organizing the armed forces, bringing the formations up to full quota, arming and equipping the units;
• Deciding on fighting methods and constantly improving them;
• Acquiring knowledge and experience in the deployment of troops and weapons, and putting the principles of strategy and tactics into practice in order to win the war;
• Determining the methods for taking command and control of the troops during wartime operations.

The Soviet concept divides military science into three areas[60]:

• Military strategy — command and control of the troops and use of the armed forces. This entails missions: preparing for war, directing the fighting, calculating the number of forces and means for conducting the war, defining the aims of the armed struggle and the methods of conducting the war in order to attain these goals. Strategy is implemented according to the way the army's high command operates large formations.
• Operations — a key link in the art of war, coming between strategy and tactics. Operations provide solutions to combat missions in order to attain strategic objectives. Operations determine the methods of preparing and conducting combat activity of the various branches and formations taking part in the campaign.
•Tactics — fundamental to the art of war. Modern tactics are extremely complex.

Operations and tactics are important links in the art of war. Even more than strategy, they determine the actual forms and systems used in managing the armed forces in time of war, and they direct the efforts being made by all of the units, formations, and larger groups to achieve the war's strategic aims.

The Soviet combat doctrine combines a decisive, bold, offensive spirit with a comprehensive scientifically based situation assessment and guaranteed supplies to all of the troops' needs. In practice, the integral elements of the doctrine include: a scientific view of reality; objective situation analysis; a realistic assessment; understanding of the laws involved in developing situations; new fighting methods and formations for organizing the troops; and plans drawn up for combat operations.[61]

From the outset wartime activities are characterized by their extreme complexity. The lightning speed of the attack, the in-depth breakthrough, the absence of contiguous fronts, the isolated nature of battlefield activity, the need to overcome radioactively contaminated areas[62] — all of these conditions weigh heavily on the troops' spirit.

The modern age is characterized by the shift from individual arms, based on the skill and muscle of a single soldier, to team-operated weapons. This change has dramatically raised the importance of organizing and strengthening military units. A large number of officers and individual soldiers unite into a smoothly functioning team. Coordination among military units operating under wartime conditions can be achieved through effective leadership and discipline, as well as by raising the soldiers' level of political education.[63] An army that demonstrates the greatest endurance and best operational plans has a better chance of victory. The laws of armed struggle are not automatic. Skillful application of these laws calls for military leadership that is capable of accurately evaluating a developing situation, and is dedicated to planning correctly and achieving the objective. When these elements are combined, victory is all but guaranteed. Bold, solidly based war plans depend on flexible, dynamic, creative thinking, and not on a mindset limited by routine patterns and bland formulas.[64]

Warfare According to the Soviet Military Doctrine

The principles of war are an integral part of the warfare doctrine. They are the basic rules and axioms derived from the principles of war, and are put to practical use in all areas of combat.

Soviet war principles exhibit flexibility in their ability to adapt to changing circumstances. The doctrine and its principles developed in three main stages after World War II:

• From the end of the war to 1953 improvements were made in weapons, mobility, and firepower.

• From 1953 to 1960 war plans were made in a nuclear environment.

• From 1960 the Soviets assumed that the next war would integrate conventional arms and weapons of mass destruction (WMDs).

The principles of modern warfare were based on analytical research: decisiveness, mobility, sudden situational changes, vast geographical dimensions, and asymmetry in battle development.

The principles of the Soviet doctrine at the strategic and systems level may be summed up as[65]:

• Heightened combat readiness;

• Decisiveness and activism;

• Coordinating war aims and missions to the forces, weapons, and fighting methods;

• Coordination and cooperation among all branches[66]; joint operations in battles and campaigns;

• Pressure and focus on the main effort in the sector exactly when needed;

• Saving forces at the sacrifice of secondary sectors or subsidiary efforts;

• Providing troops with complete logistical backing in the conduct of the war;

• Building up reserves and stockpiles (manpower, weapons, food, oil, etc.) in preparation for unexpected developments;

• Exploiting successes;

• Achieving maximum command and control, and integrating it into independent initiatives at the secondary levels.

Soviet military academies taught the principles of modern battle from textbooks in the years prior to the Yom Kippur War. Most of the principles are still applicable, and have been updated for both conventional and nuclear warfare.[67] The Egyptians adopted these principles and adapted them to their own needs, emphasizing offensive tactics, as the following list illustrates[68]:

• Concentrating troops and weapons in order to gain superiority over the enemy at crucial axes at a given time. Forces must be concentrated on the axis chosen for the main effort; with minimum forces and weapons allocated to secondary efforts. Such a concentration is possible when a narrower sector is designated and greater firepower and a deeper combat layout are appropriated for the main effort.

• Dispersion of troops the length and width of the front in order to strengthen their chances of survival.

• Cooperation and coordination between the forces and types of firepower assigned to the mission, objectives, and time.

• Continuous activity based on uninterrupted contact with the enemy; throwing fresh troops into battle at the right moment and continuing operations day and night and in all types of weather until the mission is completed. Ongoing activity will obstruct the enemy in organizing, deploying his reserves, and establishing a line.

• Surprise gained through deception; concealing preparations; rapid troop movement; night attacks; innovative use of weapons and modus operandi, powerful; sudden, unexpected strikes; and feints.

• Initiative and creativity; operations under the most inhospitable conditions; bold decisions; and the exploitation of every possibility for achieving success.

An American attempt to understand the principles of the Soviet combat doctrines resulted in a slightly different list[69] made up of seven principles:

• Mobility and speed in war[70];

• Concentration on the main effort and building a force and arsenal superior to the enemy's in critical places at the right moment;

• Surprise; and safeguarding the operational plan;

• Preserving the operational capability of friendly forces;

• Activism — boldness and decisiveness;

• A focused, realistic definition of the goal;

• Cooperation between the forces and other elements in the battle and campaign.

The Soviet Military Advisors

Russian interest in the Middle East goes back to the beginning of the eighteenth century. Soviet interests spread across all areas of foreign policy, including strategic matters: politics, economics, culture, religion, ideology, and military activity.[71]

The Egyptian army was basically a colonial army — organized, equipped, and trained along the lines of the British army. This orientation dictated the army's development in the years following the 1948 War. Egypt tried to replace British assistance with American assistance but had to be satisfied with substitutes, mainly because of the embargo on military equipment to the Middle East. At first it welcomed the help of Italian experts, acquiring Italian equipment. Later, it sought help from German officers, scientists, and engineers.[72] German advisors were involved in Egypt's debate over the defense layout in Sinai.[73] They founded the Egyptian armored corps, trained its officers, and taught them the principles of coordination between armor and other braches.[74]

The "Free Officers" revolution in July 1952 sent shockwaves throughout the Egyptian army. Gen. Muhammad Naguib, King Farouk's successor, tried to reorganize the military. He sought military experts and sources that could provide a stable supply of weapons and equipment. (The Arab world regarded the British army, still deployed in Egypt in defense of the Suez Canal, as the primary enemy in this period.) The ongoing conflict culminated in 1954 with the evacuation of the British troops from the canal, and the United States refusal to supply Egypt with weapons. This policy seriously incapacitated Egypt's ability to build and train its army. The IDF's retaliations along the Egyptian border and in the Gaza Strip also hurt the Egyptian army.

This situation created fertile soil for increased Soviet involvement.[75] The Soviet-Egyptian romance commenced in the mid–1950s after Nasser diverted Egypt's political orientation to the Third World and increased Egypt's ties to the Eastern Bloc. First the Czech arms deals and later direct military assistance from the Soviet Union obligated Egypt to strengthen its relationship with the Eastern Bloc in technological, technical-tactical, and doctrinal matters.

Building their army on Soviet weapons meant that Egypt had to adopt the Soviet military doctrine. As Soviet-Egyptian relations expanded, the doctrine's influence on Egypt's military structure, organization, and modus operandi increased enormously. Soviet military thinking led to a doctrinal shift in the Egyptian army's modus operandi.

A gradual transition took place in Egypt in the early 1960s with the adoption of the Soviet Union's doctrinal recommendations, especially regarding defensive warfare. The army's general layout — especially its ground defense in eastern Sinai — that was under Israeli observation, was rebuilt and reorganized along the lines of the "Red Army's" experience on European battlefields in World War Two. (The integration of the Soviet defense layout based on long lines with flanks in areas of limited passage, forced the IDF to learn the Soviet concept and prepare for it accordingly. The IDF's solutions came to expression in the Six-Day War in the breakthroughs at Um Katef and Rafiah.)

The Arabs' defeat in the Six-Day War resulted in the Soviet Union's increased penetration into the Arab world in general and Egypt in particular. Proof of this can be found in the "Vinogradov Paper" — a briefing for Soviet diplomats who served in the Middle East — that viewed the Arab military collapse in June 1967 as a giant step toward bringing the United Arab Republic into the socialist camp.[76]

After analyzing the reasons for the Arabs' debacle, the paper defined the principle of the Soviet Union's basic policy in the Middle East: the establishment of Soviet military power that would rid the region of western influences once and for all. The paper also discussed Soviet interests in detail, and mentioned the need to strengthen Soviet bases in Egypt (part of the strategy for defending Egypt), prevent Egypt from making rash moves against Israel, preserve Soviet gains, and secure Soviet superiority in the region.

Some observers considered the Arab defeat in the Six-Day War as a failure of the Soviet combat doctrine and as proof of the inferiority of Soviet arms and equipment vis-à-vis western arms. The Egyptians' battlefield debacle sullied national pride and forced the Soviet Union — which had prompted Egypt to launch the war but had refrained from coming to Egypt's help — to move quickly in order to salvage its prestige in the region.

The Arab collapse provided the Russians with a golden opportunity to enter the region. The most tangible example of this was the increased activity of the Soviet fleet. Soviet naval presence in the Mediterranean Basin, which began in 1958, expanded in 1963 but suffered from the lack of ports of call. Under these circumstances, the Six-Day War was a windfall for the Soviet navy. One month after the war, a Soviet flotilla entered the ports of Alexandria and Port-Said.[77] By late 1967, especially after the sinking of the Israeli destroyer *Eilat*, Soviet naval presence in Egyptian ports became a long-term fait accompli. The Soviet vessels' visit in the Egyptian ports was lengthened in January 1968, and in April a five-year agreement was signed granting port services to the Soviets. In the same month a squadron of TU-16 aircraft from the Soviet air fleet landed in Egypt for permanent deployment.[78] The long-term presence of Soviet naval and air forces, and the services provided for them, meant that Soviet experts, too, had to be stationed in Egypt, and ammunition, equipment, and replacement parts stockpiled. Presumably this was done for Egyptian needs, but in reality it aptly served Soviet interests.

After the 1967 defeat, the Soviets worried about a further decline in the Arab world. To counter this possibility, the president of the Soviet Union, the deputy defense minister, and the Soviet chief of staff arrived in Egypt on June 20, 1967 and made the following announcement: "We will prove that our visit here means more than words."[79] Ninety-one Soviet officers accompanying the three Soviet leaders stayed in Egypt for almost two months.[80]

Nasser asked the Russians to increase the number of advisors and integrate them at the battalion level (very few Soviet instructors had served with the Egyptian army until this time). Egypt also offered the Soviets command of the air force and air defense, but Chairman of the Presidium of the Supreme Soviet of the USSR Nikolai Podgorny rejected the offer, while promising massive assistance for rehabilitating the Egyptian army.

The Soviet Union agreed to supply all the equipment that had been lost in the war, and a full-scale layout of military instructors to rehabilitate and train the Egyptian army, on condition that Egypt introduced changes into the army's structure and organization. One of the Soviet chief of staff's first "suggestions" was to purge over one thousand Egyptian officers with western orientations, and replace them with officers who had received training and instruction in the Soviet Union and had proven themselves.

Immediately upon Podgorny's return to Moscow, Soviet arms began flowing to Egypt. By mid–October 1967, 80 percent of the Soviet-made weapons were restored (including hundreds of tanks and planes, and later, top-of-the-line APCs, antitank guided missiles, surface-to-surface rockets, artillery, antiaircraft missiles, and so forth). The arms supply became the Soviet Union's exclusive domain, and naturally demanded an increase in Russian advisors for absorbing and operating the weapons.[81]

The Soviet chief of staff remained in Egypt to supervise Russian assistance and the rebuilding of the Egyptian army. The first groups of Soviet advisors helped the Egyptians absorb the weapons and equipment, and endeavored to raise the Egyptian army's level of professionalism and the individual soldier's performance so that the weapons systems would be put to effective use. Much attention was given to training and skills acquisition. Such comprehensive and intensive activity called for a greater number of Soviet advisors: engineers and technicians to operate and maintain the systems; instructors to absorb and operate the weapons; and advisors to inculcate the warfare doctrine that these systems were based on into all of the Egyptian army's branches.

In the first stage, 1,500 advisors were deployed in headquarters (up to divisional level) and assigned to all brigade commanders.[82] Later, when the instructional layout was significantly expanded, the advisors worked alongside battalion commanders. The advisors became involved in all aspects of Egyptian military activity, training individual crews, and holding field maneuvers and exercises in bases for entire units.

But the Russian presence could hardly avoid becoming a source of friction. Although disputes and arguments broke at all levels of the military hierarchy, Nasser turned a deaf ear to them, and refused to allow matters of pride and prestige to interfere with the army's training program and rehabilitation. His catchphrase in this period was: "The Egyptians have to learn."[83]

The presence and influence of the instructors grew steadily. Their say in training and exercise programs for individual units and headquarters spilled over into other areas, such as planning and operations.[84] This trend became even more pronounced when the Russians became involved in the appointments and promotions of Egyptian officers.[85]

A captured document dated January 9, 1969 defines the role of the Soviet advisors in the following manner[86]: "The Soviet experts are working with the armed forces at Egypt's request.... Their aim is to use their practical experience to elevate the combat proficiency in units and sub-units, and maintain the armed forces' level of combat readiness. The Russian experts will extend practical assistance to commanders and officers in the following areas: the preparation of troops and command centers, field training, operational planning, control and improvement of combat readiness, instruction of individual soldiers in secondary units."

Egypt's fiascoes in the War of Attrition — especially the Israeli armored raid on the coast of the Gulf of Suez and the Israeli Air Force's (IAF) bombings deep in Egypt — resulted in the Soviet decision to intensify their involvement and assume responsibility for Egypt's security.[87] The concern that additional mishaps on the battlefield would reflect upon Soviet weaponry, Soviet doctrine, and the Soviet advisors themselves, compelled the Russians to strengthen their support and even engage directly in combat missions, such as defending against Israeli air activity over Egypt.

Following a comprehensive meeting with Soviet military leaders, Brezhnev informed Nasser that the Soviet Union had agreed to assume responsibility for Egypt's strategic air defense.[88] The Soviet effort was also designed to lighten Egypt's burden on the canal front and curtail the IAF's effectiveness. The transfer of Russian advanced weapons systems and military personnel to Egypt commenced.

The Soviet military presence in Egypt grew exponentially. The preparations for sending and deploying a large force (an air defense division) seem to have begun in December 1969.[89] By early 1970 the Soviet military layout included instructors, pilots, and antiaircraft battery crews. In March, Soviet personnel numbered between 6,500 and 8,000. Their involvement in Egypt — following the Soviet-Egyptian agreements and the War of Attrition — was so significant[90] that on April 14 Moshe Dayan admitted: "The Soviets have become our main problem."[91]

During this period a new command — air defense — separate from the air force, was set up in the Egyptian army, and consisted of surface-to-air batteries equipped with advanced antiaircraft weapons.[92] This air defense system was probably the densest, most sophisticated, and best planned antiaircraft layout ever built. Thousands of Soviet troops were dispatched to Egypt, where they received command and control of air defense bases covering entire areas. Their presence and autonomy in Egypt grew rapidly.[93] The Soviet ORBAT eventually came to five SA-6 missile battalions and twenty-two SA-3 battalions. Their deployment in Egypt widened. The Egyptians (or more precisely, the Soviets) advanced the surface-to-air batteries eastward to the banks of the canal — an act which violated the agreed-upon status quo — and kept them there until the Yom Kippur War. When the war broke out the missiles gave the Egyptian troops an effective air umbrella and contributed significantly to the crossing operation.[94]

In April 1970 Soviet fighter pilots began taking part in combat missions, flying in UAR-marked aircraft. Five Soviet air defense squadrons, each consisting of twenty to twenty-five aircraft, were stationed in Egypt. Their activity peaked on July 30 when four Soviet-piloted MIGs were shot down (and a fifth seriously damaged) in dogfights with the IAF. Again Soviet prestige received a painful blow. In response, the Russians escalated their involvement in the war zone, bringing over additional shipments of advanced weapons. Thus, Egypt was transformed into the largest reservoir of modern Soviet weaponry outside the Eastern Bloc.

The end of the War of Attrition, Nasser's death, and Sadat's succession opened a new page in Soviet-Egyptian relations. The Russians, who perceived the continuation of their massive involvement in Egypt in a positive light, began to strengthen their political relationship with Egypt. On March 1, 1971, Sadat arrived in Moscow on his first visit (at the Soviets' request). The Kremlin wanted to meet the new Egyptian president and learn his political views, but Sadat was only interested in strengthening his army and preparing it for war. His primary reason for coming to Moscow was to get the Soviets to supply Egypt with weapons equal to those in Israel's arsenal and capable of upsetting the balance of power. If this was achieved, then the war option would be realizable.

On May 27 Sadat signed a friendship pact with the Soviet. His alacrity in signing the pact apparently stemmed from the need to tighten cooperation with Russians in order to enhance Egypt's defense strength and improve its ability "to eradicate the results of aggression." Put another way, this meant enabling Egypt to liberate Sinai.

Despite their demonstrated willingness to help Egypt, the Soviets were not prepared to accommodate it with all the armaments in their arsenal (even after the signing of the defense pact). The Kremlin refused to send over long-range, surface-to-surface missiles and long-range attack planes.[95] Be this as it may, Soviet advisors and instructors continued to arrive in Egypt. Their involvement grew in key areas of military activity, especially in the creation of the force being built and in the absorption of the Soviet combat doctrine.[96]

In October Sadat returned to Moscow with a renewed request for offensive weapons. Again the Soviets turned him down, and continued to provide only short-range defensive weapons. Throughout "The Year of Decision" Sadat persisted in his attempts to obtain long-range weapons,[97] until he came up with a new solution — a military plan that would liberate Sinai without this type of weapon.[98]

On July 17, 1972, after repeated complaints to the Kremlin over its refusal to supply Egypt with the type of weapons it demanded, Sadat informed the Russians that their advisors were no longer needed (those who had been in Egypt before the massive influx were allowed to stay).

The Soviets announced that their personnel had completed their mission and could return home. In the course of the month, nearly 20,000 Soviet military advisors (with their equipment) left Egypt. About one thousand advisors stayed in Egypt (along with many older models of surface-to-air missiles). The naval presence remained docked in the ports.

In the year before the war, the remaining Soviet advisors accompanying Egyptian units seem to have reduced their activity to a minimum. Their 1973 training schedule (captured by Israel[99]) describes in detail the assignments they had to carry out in the ground forces' battalion and brigade headquarters:

For the first half of 1973 they were supposed to help battalion and brigade commanders update their alert plans — with an emphasis on defense — and oversee the preparation and execution of routine training exercises at the company and battery level.

In the second half of the year, the advisors were supposed to take part in tactical training at the battalion level. The program included exercises for reinforced infantry battalions attacking an enemy deployed in heavily defended positions. The operational exercises entailed contact with the enemy and movement in daytime and night conditions, in open terrain and mountainous areas. The advisors also took part in antiaircraft and artillery exercises at the battalion level, and in defensive and offensive maneuvers held by tank companies. But the final exercises that the advisors were supposed to assist in were only at the individual level to the company level.

Most of the Soviet instructors left Egypt just before the Yom Kippur War erupted. To the best of my knowledge, not a single Soviet advisor was involved in actual combat.

As stated, the Soviet advisors integrated into almost every area of Egyptian military activity after the Six-Day War. In addition to technical instruction, they also participated in all aspects of ground activity, from advising officers and soldiers, to planning units' training programs; from organizing the composition of the force, to closely accompanying operational planning at different levels. The advisors who took an active part in determining the nature of battalion, brigade, and divisional exercises also engaged in defense planning and, apparently, in offensive planning at the staff level.

The advisors came to Egypt equipped with proven principles of warfare and the orders to apply them according to the Soviet combat doctrine. While the doctrine suited the Egyptian army's weapons and equipment, it did not necessarily fit the operational needs of the Egyptian army and character of the troops. Many differences of opinion and verbal altercations sprang up between Soviet advisors and Egyptian officers. Despite the generous assistance that the Soviets extended, only a handful of Egyptian officers really liked the Russian instructors. In fact, most Egyptian military personnel loathed the Soviets' self-righteousness and heavy-handed involvement in all levels of the army.[100] When the Russians' departed in mid–1972, a sigh of relief could be heard from both sides.

Senior Egyptian planners gained considerable self-confidence. Those who internalized the principles of the Soviet doctrine were now free to do as they pleased and adapt it to the conditions, abilities, and requirements of the Egyptian army.

Opinion is divided regarding the reasons for the expulsion of the Soviet advisors. Some claim that it was because of the Russians' refusal to back Sadat's plan to launch a war against Israel. Others claim that the Soviets themselves wanted to terminate their massive commitment to Egypt and waited for the opportunity to pack their kit bags.[101]

Each signatory to the aid pact had its own interests. In addition to assisting in the strengthening, rehabilitation, and improvement of the Egyptian army, the Soviets had a strategic interest in Egyptian territory and facilities. Soviet aid was designed primarily to restore Egypt's defensive capability, not to furnish Egypt with the capability of launching a new war. This was why the Kremlin refused to supply Egypt with sophisticated, top-of-the-line weapons. The Soviet advisors' presence and authority in the Egyptian army was instrumental in guaranteeing that Egypt's military orientation remained defensive.[102]

This issue, however, was a constant source of friction between the two countries. Egypt wanted a broad spectrum of Soviet aid in order to build up its military power. At the same time it jealously guarded its independence and tried to restrain Soviet intervention in its domestic and military affairs. Egypt demanded more arms, more equipment, and more instructors, experts, technicians, and advisors, but it absolutely refused to allow the Soviet Union to dictate its military policy, and it had no intention of allowing Soviet military personnel and advisors to assume command or administrative positions in Egypt.[103]

During his visit to Israel in November 1977,[104] Sadat recalled Egypt's relations with the Russians and the Soviet Union's influence on Egypt. According to the Egyptian president, the main feature of his rule in the seven years since Nasser's death (1970) was the "liberation of the national will" from the bonds of Soviet patronage.[105]

Sadat claimed that he told the Soviets that if Egypt has a "national will," then it is Egypt's alone. By the same token, Egypt acknowledged and was grateful for the immense Soviet support, the quantity and quality of the weapons, and the cooperation and advice that it received which proved essential to Egypt's success. General Israel Tal sums the issue up this way: "During the War of Attrition, the Russians' massive supply of antiaircraft systems, their command of Egyptian combat systems, and the development of the Soviet warfare doctrine enabled the Egyptians to plan the Yom Kippur War in a way that made it impossible for the Israeli air force's firepower to stop the canal crossing. The Egyptians, as well as the Russians, had learned the lessons of the War of Attrition, so that when they launched the Yom Kippur War they were already well-trained and fully confident in their antiaircraft capability."[106] Tal emphasized the antiaircraft issue, but I will try to prove that the Soviet doctrine's contribution in other areas too was of inestimable value.

4

Potential Problems in the Campaign

Planning the Military Solutions

The supreme commander's first task is to decide what to do, examine the means at his disposal for surmounting the obstacles the enemy is likely to place before him, and, after he makes his decision, do everything in his power to overcome them.

(Napoleon, *Military Maxims*, Ma'arachot, 1991)

Problems Facing the Egyptian War Planners

Between 1967 and the outbreak of the Yom Kippur War, Egyptian strategists were able to pinpoint the sources of the problems facing them in the Israeli defense concept. Some were purely military problems, others of a geopolitical nature. They may all be categorized according to the level of the decision-maker dealing with them and the solutions called for.

Problems at the strategic level

A. Loss of territory — Israel's capture of the Sinai Peninsula in the Six-Day War put the Egyptian army almost 250 kilometers from the international border and Gaza Strip — territories that Egypt had controlled since 1948.

B. Loss of prestige — The 1967 defeat was a harsh blow to Egypt's leadership status in the Third World and especially in the Arab world. Egypt is the most populous and well-endowed Arab state.

C. Tarnished honor — Egypt's dismal performance on the battlefield and the destruction of the greater part of its military capacity stained national pride and the army's self-respect.

D. Closure of the Suez Canal — In the aftermath of the Six-Day War, the Suez Canal, one of Egypt's most lucrative international assets, was blocked to shipping. This loss was a major blow to the country's revenues and Egypt's standing.

E. Vulnerability to an Israeli attack — Israel's military presence close to Egyptian population centers was intolerable. Egypt suffered heavily in the War of Attrition when IDF commandos carried out deep penetrations and the Israeli air force pounded the homeland with impunity. The air strikes tapered off in the last months of the war when the Egyptians moved surface-to-air missile batteries to the front and succeeded in shooting down a number of Israeli warplanes.

Problems at the operational level

A. Israeli air superiority — The IAF mercilessly pummeled Egyptian air and ground forces during the Six-Day War and demonstrated its prowess as "flying artillery" in the War of

Attrition. The Egyptians were forced come up with a solution to Israel's absolute air superiority, especially in the combat zone. According to the standard warfare doctrine, a canal crossing, concentration of forces prior to the crossing, construction of bridges, and consolidation of bridgeheads were all easy prey for air strikes. A "missile umbrella" was one solution to this critical problem.

B. Improved maneuverability on the ground — In the Six-Day War, the IDF's rapid penetration — especially by its armored units — into Sinai, and the dash to the Suez Canal, forced Egypt to recognize Israel's superior mobility. Most Egyptian formations were infantry units of low-level mobility. The Egyptians also had to deal with the IDF's ability to mobilize its reserves on extremely short notice and rapidly shift the centers of combat operations from one sector to another. Egypt tried to solve these problems by upgrading the antitank capability of its infantry units.

C. An organized defense layout — The IDF's deployment on the east bank (especially during the War of Attrition) meant that a solid defense layout had to be constructed. The Egyptians perceived it not just as a defense line, but also as a fortified area based on a series of wisely built assembly areas for armored reserves, artillery positions, antiaircraft systems, and so forth, running eastward 30–35 kilometers from the canal to the mountain passes and protected on all the sides with formidable natural defenses. The Egyptians observed that the layout, excluding the fortifications on the waterline and further to the rear, included diverse obstacles, minefields, interlacing roads, headquarters, command and control centers, and logistical bases.[1] The Egyptians distinguished between the earlier impromptu layout and the new carefully conceived and constructed one,[2] and now had to devise operational solutions for attacking and capturing the latter. The complexity of the water obstacle only added to their headaches.

D. A large, powerful reserve deep in the rear — Israel's reserve formations created major problems for Egyptian planners (as well as for Israeli tacticians). The fog that engulfed the size, location, and timetable of the enemy's forces left many key elements in the Egyptians' offensive plan dangling with question marks.

E. Offensive deployment and the parallel need to remain defensively positioned — The Egyptians stationed their forces defensively for the most part in five infantry divisions the entire length of the front. This created problems in preparing the offensive and attack method, and in masking their activity.

Problems at the tactical level

A. The canal obstacle — The Egyptian planner described the Suez Canal as the most complex and formidable water barrier in the world. Its length, depth, angle of concrete banks, flow rate — all required precise planning for the crossing.

B. The eastern embankment — During the War of Attrition, especially in its last year, Israel elevated the dirt embankment that had gradually been built up from the soil excavated from the canal. Rising to a height of twenty meters, the mound was designed to serve as an obstacle to block the Egyptians from crossing the canal and securing foothold on the eastern bank, and obstruct any attempt to advance eastward. The Egyptians gave much thought to this problem.

C. The "Or Yikarot" ("Burning Light") inflammable system — "Or Yikarot" was a system of pipes and oil tanks for storing inflammable material that would turn the canal into a flaming inferno. The IDF installed the system in a number of caches opposite likely crossing areas. The Egyptians discovered most of the decoys, and the plan was jettisoned. Even though they were aware of its shoddy performance, the Egyptians continued to look for ways to neutralize the system.

D. The strongholds — The strongholds' strength (especially their ability to withstand artillery barrages), on the one hand, and their lengthy dispersion, small-sized garrisons, and partial dismantling, on the other hand, did not pose special problems for the Egyptians. Although the Egyptians invested copious energy in figuring out how to destroy and capture the forts, for the most part they preferred to bypass them in the first stages of the offensive and deal with them later, usually by a rear attack.[3]

E. Tanks versus infantry — The IDF's tanks were incontestably superior to Egypt's in number, strength, mobility, and firepower. The Egyptians had to come up with a viable operational plan. Their plan to transfer tanks to the eastern side during the crossing stage was based mainly on their infantry's tank-hunting teams — especially commandos — with sophisticated antitank weapons. Antitank reserve units employing mostly Sager missiles also took part in the offensive. The plan also called for mobile units to rapidly plant dense minefields.

Egypt's Solutions

The Egyptians rigorously studied the Soviet combat doctrine and heeded the Soviet advisors who were attached to Egyptian army units up to battalion level.[4] They also drew up their own plans for adapting the advisors' recommendations to their needs and capabilities. Problems were solved at various levels by corresponding them to the Egyptian soldier's abilities and skills.

Solutions at the strategic level

Egypt's loss of territory and severe damage to its stature as the leader of the Arab world forced it to launch an all-out initiative. Since all of the attempts to generate such a move by political means had failed, Egypt realized that it would have to broaden its military activity. Armed operations had the potential to break the logjam and retrieve Egypt's honor by effectively opening the canal and removing the Israeli threat to Egyptian territory. The efforts to procure Soviet weapon systems that would provide a capability similar to Israel's for long-range strikes came to naught. The Egyptians had no alternative but to go on the offensive.[5]

There were many advantages to a "joint offensive" launched simultaneously by a number of states on several fronts. Egypt tried to induce other partners to join the war wagon but in the end it only managed to muster Syria because of Damascus's similar interests (though it did receive the blessings of other Arab states).

I will not go into the diplomatic moves that accompanied the war preparations. Chapters 3 and 4 discuss in detail the strategic solutions, the instructions to the military commanders, and the path that the politicians eventually chose.

Solutions at the operational level

Israeli air superiority was absolute. Given the conditions of this period, Egypt realized that an attempt to neutralize the enemy's air superiority by raising the standards of the Egyptian air force, acquiring sophisticated weapons, and intensifying the training programs was doomed to failure. In addition to drilling the combat troops under conditions of air inferiority,[6] the Egyptians adopted another solution that had proven partially successful at the end of the War of Attrition: the massive procurement of surface-to-air missiles, including mobile

SAM-6s which could be deployed close to the troops, and the installation of a "missile umbrella" above critical war zones — in extremely shallow areas. While the IDF continued to believe that its planes could function as "flying artillery," it was suddenly faced with an entirely new reality.

Since Egypt lacked an air arm and long-range missiles,[7] it avoided advancing its ground forces too deeply into the Sinai Peninsula. Such a push could have led to greater IDF activity into the heart of Egypt without the Egyptians having a parallel capability.[8]

The Egyptian operative plan, based on "an all-out war of limited dimensions," was intended to provide an answer to the IDF's superior maneuverability. The plan required neither a deep incursion nor comprehensive maneuverability on the troops' part. The gradual consolidation and expansion of the bridgeheads, and the reliance on state-of-the-art antitank weaponry enabled the Egyptians to wage a static defense against Israel's armored units. The absorption and use of Sager antitank missiles in all Egyptian units — including the reserves — and the integration of tank-hunter teams armed with these missiles and launchers in the front and flanks proved devastatingly effective against Israel's standing army armored units at the first level of the defense layout. Israel's armored reserves' counterattacks at the second level were also blocked in the same way.

The Egyptians obtained detailed information on the IDF's deliberate layout (commonly known as the Bar-Lev Line). The cutback in the number of frontline and second-level strongholds enabled the Egyptian planner to practically brush aside the entrenched layout. Even the

An Egyptian bridge crossing the Suez Canal from west to east.

first-line fortresses facing the Egyptian crossing areas were minimally operational as minor forward observation posts. The Egyptians circumvented the strongholds wherever the topography permitted so, and constructed the bridgeheads' bases in the gaps between the forts. Most of the Israeli strongholds were neutralized by Egyptian artillery fire, and were captured in later stages of the campaign, generally from the rear.

In additional to reducing the bridgeheads' depth, the Egyptians also tended to bypass Israeli headquarters, command-and-control facilities, and logistics centers, preferring to attack some of these targets with their air force or surface-to-surface "Frog" rockets. Almost none of the planned commando raids were carried out.[9]

The Egyptians regarded IDF reserves as a powerful force that could alter the situation on the battlefield. They assumed the IDF capable of rapidly mobilizing its reserves and throwing them into the fray. Given these assumptions, a solution to this threat had to be found. The best way to neutralize Israel's reserve forces was to limit the scope of the Egyptians' tasks to establishing and expanding divisional bridgeheads, and connecting them to army-level bridgeheads. In this way the Egyptians could immediately shift to the defensive after the crossing and consolidation of the canal front before the mass of Israeli reservists arrived.

The other method was to have special forces (SF) isolate the battlefield by cutting communications axes deep in enemy territory. This plan, as stated, was not carried out; instead, only ambushes were set up on the margins of the front. One commando force on the northern axis, in the Rumani area, was wiped out by an Israeli armored unit and a "Shaked" reconnaissance team; another force on the Wadi Sudar axis, south of the front, was destroyed by Israeli paratroopers. The Egyptians' small-scale use of commando forces was another facet of the "limited plan."

Defensive deployment on the western bank, according to defense plan "Amalia 200," enabled the Egyptians to launch an "attack from contact" along a "broad front"—in effect, the whole length of the canal. This modus operandi, unlike an "attack from movement," demanded preparations for launching the attack from defensive positions. Since some of these preparations were observed by the IDF in the strongholds and by air reconnaissance, extreme measures had to be taken to conceal them.

Fearing the loss of surprise, the Egyptians carried out deliberate activities to safeguard the operation. This was generally done under the cover of attack exercises codenamed "Tahrir 41," which the Israelis perceived, as in the past, as deception.[10] In my opinion, all of the Egyptians' moves were designed to camouflage their preparations. It is impossible to discern, not even retrospectively, genuine acts of deception whose primary goal—according to the universal deception doctrine, and especially Soviet *maskirovka*—was the construction of "another facade" (the real deception) according to which the Egyptians would operate or attack.

Solutions at the tactical level

The Egyptian planners also devoted a great deal of time to tactical problems. The solutions they devised were often issued by the chief of staff himself, as instructions and explicit orders to field units. These solutions that would eventually be implemented by military commanders were mostly based on the combat doctrine that had been worked out to the last detail by professional research and administrative institutes.

The Egyptians dealt with problems such as crossing the canal, breaching the eastern embankment, neutralizing the inflammable systems, and overcoming enemy strongholds defended by tank platoons and other obstacles. This would be accomplished by collecting information, maintaining surveillance, carrying out detailed studies, and issuing instructions.[11] The

Diagram 3: IDF Defensive Deployment in the Suez Canal Theater

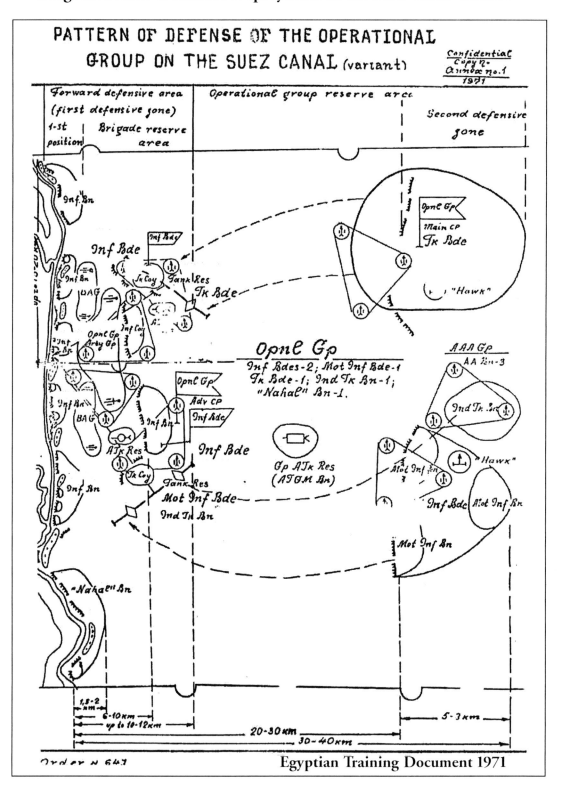

Egyptian Training Document 1971

problems were meticulously analyzed, their advantages and limitations recognized, and finally the most effective way of dealing with them chosen. The Egyptian planner's greatest wish was to quickly overcome all delaying factors by sidestepping them whenever possible and reducing the need to deal with them.[12]

The War Plan

The Egyptians worked out an offensive plan for the 1973 "October War" which — like all operative plans — was based on war aims defined at the political level by President Sadat, and on missions formulated by Sadat and interpreted by the general staff. The plan naturally underwent modifications in the period between the 1967 defeat and the noon attack on Yom Kippur 1973.

The roots of the plan, which can be traced to Nasser's designs and the proposals of his war minister, Fawzi, went through numerous stages. From 1967, strategic plans were studied and numerous attack plans drafted.[13] The first plan dealt with the capture of all Sinai but was later changed to more limited objectives much closer to the eastern bank and jump-off bases. The plan took into account the army's operational needs and realistic capabilities. On the basis of the warfare doctrine, a military solution was hammered out that provided a definitive answer to the president's most cherished goals. The final plan, and the one that was eventually implemented, can be seen in the moves on the battlefield, and especially in the documents that Israel captured (most of them at the battalion, brigade, divisional, and even army group level)[14] as well as from the memoirs of Sadat, Ismail Ali, Shazli, and Gamasi.[15]

The Plan for an All-Out Attack — Stages in Its Formation

The master plan of an attack is an integral part of any military planning system. The Egyptian GHQ seems to have prepared its offensive plans at the end of the Six-Day War. The first draft was completed during the War of Attrition and was supposed to be an answer to the declaration broadcast by the supreme commander of the Egyptian army, President Nasser: "What was taken by force will be returned by force." Fariq Awal Mahmud Fawzi, the commander of the armed forces, four-star general who was appointed war minister on January 24, 1968, claims that in 1967 Nasser ordered him to prepare the army for retaking the entire Sinai Peninsula in three years.[16] Fawzi states that in a meeting with Nasser on June 11, 1967, the Egyptian president was convinced that all that was taken by force would be returned by force. According to Nasser, this force had to be equipped with advanced weapons and the troops had to undergo rigorous training. Both requisites called for "tightening our relations with the Soviet Union and giving its leaders the impression that they shared the defeat with us. This is necessary so that they [the Soviets] will accept responsibility for rebuilding the armed forces on purely scientific foundations and strict discipline." Nasser added that he believed it would take the armed forces three years to reach the necessary capability for launching a war of liberation.

Following these instructions, Fawzi summed up "the armed forces' strategy [as] the forcible liberation of the occupied land in Sinai and the army's advance to the Egyptian-Palestinian border."[17] Thus, he argued that his plan for the recapture of the entire peninsula would accomplish the goal as defined by the head of state."[18] Fawzi worked round the clock to prepare the retaking of Sinai, and at the same time he endeavored to rehabilitate the armed forces and create new army groups.[19] The chief of staff appointed Lt. Gen. Abd al-Munam

Riad as officer in charge of the plan's details. Fawzi refers to the plan by its code name: "Plan 200."[20] This plan was supposed to be revised every six months in pace with the army's rehabilitation. The plan was presented to Nasser, who demanded that it keep to the original objectives and instructions, while strictly following the timetable for training the combat formations that would be carrying out the operation. In January 1968 "the operation was running full steam in every army group."[21]

Fawzi, who has never been accused of being too modest, presents the War of Attrition, which occurred during his watch, as though it was only the backdrop to the army's preparations for liberating Sinai. Fawzi claims that everything was foreseen and planned (excluding a minor setback in the timetable due to Nasser's death) and that the army was prepared, armed, and trained according to Fawzi's plan for recapturing Sinai. He also informs the reader that after the 1967 War he decided on the necessary ORBAT for "liberating the land." He says that he planned the ORBAT "based on the Egyptian people's potential, the enemy's capability, and his estimate of the arrival of Soviet supplies and the army's ability to absorb them." The buildup of the ORBAT was supposed to take three years and to be based on five infantry divisions, three mechanized divisions, and two armored divisions. In addition there would be three independent armored brigades, a reconnaissance brigade, two paratrooper brigades, forty-four commando battalions, and two air transport brigades. The air force needed 600 fighter-bombers, two air groups of light bombers, two air groups of heavy bombers, two transportation air groups, and 130 training planes. Air defense required eight divisions, each made up of three to five missile and antiaircraft cannon brigades.[22]

According to Fawzi, in July–August 1970 Egypt attained military superiority over Israel. The last draft of the Egyptian air force's operational plans for liberating Sinai was made in July, and presented to Nasser for approval.[23] Fawzi tried to implement the plan, convinced that the Egyptian army had completed its rehabilitation and was capable of putting the plan into practice. He recalls that when the cease-fire went into effect on August 8, 1970, the Egyptian forces had already reached the stage where they could initiate military moves.[24]

Fawzi also states that during a meeting in late August 1970, attended by Nasser, he (Fawzi) expressed the armed forces' readiness to launch the campaign, and Nasser promised to approve of military plans in another meeting that would be held in Marsa Matruh in the first week of September. According to Fawzi, Nasser showed him maps of the general plan ("Plan 200"), the stages plan ("Granite"), and detailed plans of army groups, including air, naval, air defense, artillery, signal, and logistics branches. According to Fawzi, the president approved of the plan orally, and it was only Nasser's sudden demise that cut short further planning and the final implementation.[25] Many scholars reject Fawzi's claims and consider his plan to have been unrealizable. The Egyptian military historian Gamal Hamad, one of Nasser's supporters on the Revolutionary Council and later a general and military attaché to Damascus, dismissed Fawzi's assertions, noting that "Fawzi liberated Sinai on paper," and expressed doubt regarding the Egyptian army's ability to undertake the liberation stage at that time.

A number of sources refer to the attack plan's code name as "Granite." The first version of the plan was called "Granite 1."[26] According to Heykal, it was completed in the first half of 1970, after the deployment of surface-to-air missile systems close to the Suez Canal.[27] Previously there were three "Tahrir" exercises (Tahrir 1, 2, and 3) that tested a number of possible scenarios in a canal crossing, consolidation of bridgeheads, and IDF counterattack.[28]

Fawzi states that because of Nasser's death the main exercise for testing the offensive plan was put off from the end of 1970 to the spring of 1971 (March 14–15). This exercise was intended to examine the armed forces' ability "to attain all of the objectives in the 'Granite' plan, and carry out the general plan — 'Plan 200.'" This meant that the first stage would concentrate on crossing the Suez Canal and capturing the area between the waterfront and the Gidi and Mitle mountain passes ("Granite") as part of a general framework for the liberation of the entire Sinai Peninsula up to the international border in the Negev ("Plan 200").[29]

Taking part in the exercise, disguised as a war game, were five infantry divisions (three mechanized and two armored), three independent tank brigades, three reconnaissance battalions, a brigade of marines, and airborne forces. The entire force was provided with air and naval support and air defense. The objective was to capture the Mitle and Gidi Passes, the area between them, and the canal, in the course of five days. After the passes were taken, tank units and mechanized forces would advance, enter the main battle zone, and engage and destroy the Israeli armor. Afterward the Egyptian forces would continue to the international border and gain control of it.[30]

The exercise included a nighttime crossing with five divisional bridgeheads (in addition to alternative bridgeheads prepared for each army group) under the cover of a dense air defense layout. On the night of the crossing, heliborne troops would land at the eastern ingresses to the mountain defiles in order to block the arrival of Israel's strategic reinforcements. The main force was supposed to arrive at the mountain passes four days after the crossing and wage the main mobile battle against the IDF's tanks. Having destroyed the Israeli armor, the Egyptians would proceed to the international border and surround the enemy's forces in southern Sinai.[31]

Diagram 4: The Egyptian Plan for Retaking the Entire Sinai Peninsula

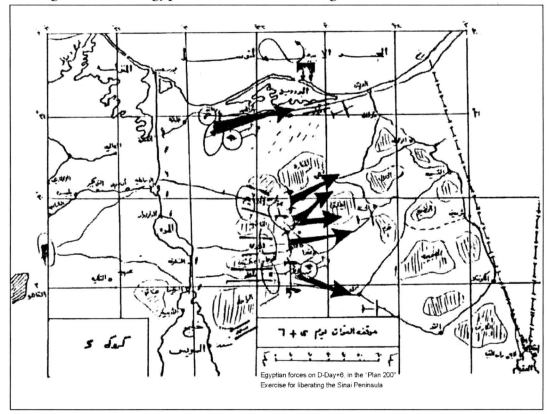

Egyptian forces on D-Day+6, in the "Plan 200"
Exercise for liberating the Sinai Peninsula

Fawzi's book contains detailed diagrams of the routes of advance and the different stages in the exercise. The author carefully outlines the shift to the second stage after the completion of "Granite" and the start of the "liberation of Sinai" on the fifth morning of the exercise. At this point he requested the president's approval to bring two armored divisions as well as an independent tank brigade into the battle against IDF tanks east of the passes. The battle that was fought on the seventh and eighth days of the war went to the Egyptians and enabled them to continue their push east. On the tenth day the main force would reach the international border, and two days later gain control of all of Sinai. It would take the Egyptian army twelve days to accomplish all of the tasks in "Plan 200."[32]

Sadat, Nasser's successor, tries to magnify his part in preparing the military option, and claims in his memoirs that his predecessor left him no offensive plan whatsoever.[33] Be this as it may, the operational plan for the attack that was prepared in Fawzi's period seems to have served as the basis for future plans, doctrinal solutions, and instruction and training.

This maximalist plan was apparently used as the groundwork for the updated and comprehensive plan that was later drafted when Sadeq became war minister. Sadeq expanded and improved the plan and called it "Granite 2." This revised plan included the canal crossing, seizure of the passes, and advance to the international border. "Granite 2" then evolved into "Granite 3" which also contained the entry into the Gaza Strip.[34] These general plans apparently reflected Sadeq's estimate that the Egyptian army was not ready yet to go to war and capture all of Sinai. Sadeq's views, and perhaps those of his predecessor, influenced the reservations and restrictions that had to be removed before the Egyptian army could launch an offensive. Sadeq was of the opinion that these plans required more men and weapons than the Egyptians currently had.[35]

While Sadeq was war minister, additional "Tahrir" exercises were held, including "Tahrir 23" (December 1971) and "Tahrir 24" (March 1972) — with troops participating in both of them. The exercises were carried out between 1969 and 1971 as bilateral staff exercises — that is, with Soviet advisors playing the role of Israeli commanders.[36]

On October 26, 1972, with Ahmad Ismail Ali's appointment as war minister and overall commander of the armed forces, the plan was completely revised. Ali, together with Chief of Staff Shazli and the head of GHQ, Gamasi, prepared a new plan of limited dimensions that was in line with President Sadat's perception of the war and its goals.[37] The drafting of the plan in its new version was completed in the first half of the January 1973.[38]

The development of military thinking and the stages that the Egyptian plan went through in the two years prior to the war can be understood from later accounts of its planners. Gamasi, who was appointed head of the GHQ in January 1972, claims that the nature and dimension of the offensive was determined according to the anticipated change in the political and military balance in the region and preparations for employing all of Egypt's power factors. According to Gamasi, Egypt's combat strength (vis-à-vis Israel's) and the strategic situation facing the two sides had to be taken into account.[39]

Gamasi states that the war's strategic objectives were to shift the military balance in the region while demolishing the Israeli defense concept. The Egyptians' offensive concept and the capture of territory "in stages" were designed to crush the IDF by inflicting heavy losses in life and arms that would force Israel to return Egypt's soil.[40]

Egyptian strategy and war planning were based on a number of principles intended to achieve this goal. In addition to the lessons gained from the Six-Day War, the detailed planning that went into preparing various sectors of the country for war and the effort to build as a large a coalition of Arab states as soon as possible, the principles were rooted in the desire to shatter Israel's security concept. The Egyptian planner tried to locate the power centers in the Israeli system and neutralize or nullify their influence. Weak spots were recognized that could be exploited at the right time.

According to the plan, Egypt would deliver the first strike in order to preempt the Israeli initiative (that had characterized the previous Arab-Israeli wars). However, a number of formidable problems first had to be surmounted[41]:

• The complex water obstacle and defense fortifications on the eastern bank;

• Israel's powerful air force that could only be neutralized with a sophisticated antiaircraft layout;

• Israel's desire to wage a lightning war on one front.

Gamasi believed that the Egyptian strategy favored a single offensive action aimed at liberating the entire Sinai Peninsula.[42] This operation would require Egyptian military superiority, superiority that did not exist and that would entail several years of arms and equipment acquisitions from the Soviet Union. The problem, as Gamasi saw it, was that the Kremlin did not welcome the Egyptian military solution. Thus, Egypt had no choice but to plan the liberation of Sinai in stages that were compatible with the development of the armed forces' combat potential. However, since Egypt could not wait indefinitely, it would have to launch the offensive with the weapons it currently possessed, despite Israel's military superiority. The Egyptian planner had to be realistic and adapt the plan to the army's capability.[43]

In addition to Israel's military superiority, Gamasi noted another serious obstacle facing the attacking force: the Suez Canal. This was "the only water obstacle of its kind with such formidable technical and natural characteristics." Every Egyptian offensive plan entailed crossing the canal and breaking through the embankment on the opposite bank in the teeth of heavy enemy resistance solidly entrenched in a fortified defense front — the "Bar-Lev Line."[44] So complex an operation demanded meticulous planning.[45] Gamasi also points out that each plan for a strategic offensive campaign required cooperation and coordination with the Syrian offensive plan which envisioned its forces fighting on the Golan Heights (simultaneously with Egypt's campaign in the south), and whose objective was the Jordan River line and eastern shore of the Sea of Galilee.[46]

Shazli recalls that when he became chief of staff in May 1971, he found the army without any serious offensive plan. But, he adds, "Granite" was on the table and envisioned forays into Sinai, though this was far from being a genuine attack plan. Discussing the offensive exercises that began in 1968,[47] he states that the gap between the plans and the army's capability was virtually unbridgeable. The exercises had an unrealistic aura to them, and were based on the unfounded premise that Egypt possessed personnel and resources far greater than what it really had.[48]

Regarding the army's state of readiness in this period, Shazli claims that its defensive capability, including the air force and air defense units, was realistic. On the other hand, even if the frameworks were expanded, the ground forces would still be incapable of allocating enough troops for a major offensive. In addition to a shortage in personnel (and despite the superiority in artillery fire) Shazli refers to the Suez Canal, and the fortified Bar-Lev Line that overlooked it, as an obstacle that most military experts regarded as a hard nut to crack. Another problem was Israel's air superiority and its implications for the Egyptian mechanized force that would be advancing on open desert roads without air cover.[49]

Based on the relevant data and operational parameters, the Egyptian chief of staff drew the conclusion that the Egyptian army lacked the strength to deliver a major blow capable of destroying the IDF's concentrations and forcing the enemy to retreat from Sinai and the Gaza

Strip. In his opinion, the Egyptian armed forces could, at the most, carry out a "limited attack" that included the canal crossing and destruction of the "Bar-Lev Line."[50] Any additional, more aggressive moves demanded larger quantities of equipment, more intensive training, and infinitely more preparation.[51]

Shazli enumerated the factors that led him to see the advantages of a "limited attack"[52]:

• The Egyptian air force's weakness, and below standard, poorly controlled operability which could result in its loss.

• The static air umbrella which covered an area of only nine to twelve kilometers from the water's edge. This required reorganization after the crossing. Attempting to advance without the protection of mobile antiaircraft missiles was an invitation to disaster.

• The need to force Israel to fight in unfavorable conditions by stabilizing the Egyptian defense layout after the crossing to ten to twelve kilometers east of the canal. When the IDF attacked this layout, it would suffer heavy losses on the ground and in the air. Such a move would also require long-term fighting, a tactic that went against Israel's preference for a blitzkrieg.

• The Egyptians' lack of experience in a wide-scale offensive. Only a limited operation would succeed and in so doing amend the Egyptian army's wounded pride.

Shazli recalls that the first offensive plan of limited dimensions was prepared in early July 1971—less than two months after he became chief of staff. The plan was presented to the war minister, General Muhammad Sadeq, for approval, but he rejected it outright.[53] He based his decision on the combat doctrine, but above all he claimed that it was a matter of gain and loss, i.e., such an operation would be politically unprofitable, the main reason being that the Egyptian defense line on the western bank was far superior to one that would be hastily set up on the eastern bank. The new defense layouts installed on the eastern side, at the end of a limited operation, would have to fend for themselves without the canal as a frontal defense barrier, and they would also require a new network of communications routes across the canal that would be especially vulnerable to air strikes.

Sadeq was convinced that the offensive — if and when it took place — would have to be overwhelming and unlimited in scope. He recalled an identical plan drafted by his predecessor, Fawzi — a large-scale plan for advancing Egyptian troops across Sinai in the direction of the Gaza Strip, during which they would annihilate as much of the enemy's forces as possible.

This plan was similar to Soviet exercises and war plans. It should be noted that the influence of Soviet advisors in Egypt reached its climax in this period, and the task of translating Soviet doctrinal material for study in Egyptian military academies was completed. The goals and dimensions of the European battlefields had considerable influence on Egyptian military thinking, especially on senior officers, some of whom had just returned from study programs in the Soviet Union.

Shazli claims that he agreed in principle with the basic operational idea, but had serious reservations regarding Egypt's ability to realize it. He presented Sadeq with an analysis and the reasoning that led him to favor the limited plan, but the latter bluntly dismissed it a second time. Sadeq instructed Shazli to prepare a plan that would lead to the liberation of all of the occupied territories.[54]

After further attempts at convincing Sadeq, Shazli finally agreed to a kind of compromise plan that was limited to seizing the mountain passes forty-five to sixty kilometers east of the canal.[55] According to Shazli, this plan was called "Operation 41," and was supposed to be prepared jointly and in full cooperation with the Soviet advisors. To the best of my knowledge, and based on captured documents from later periods, this plan was code named "Granite 2."[56]

Shazli informs us that parallel to the known plan he began to prepare, with Sadeq's approval, a "more limited" one that was termed "The High Towers" (al-Ma'athin al-A'aliya)[57] — a practical, realizable plan that was supposed to reflect the Egyptian army's true capabilities. The plan's limited mission, according to Shazli's proposal, entailed the penetration into the eastern back at a depth of only seven to nine kilometers. The secret planning began in September 1971. The so-called "Egyptian Original" plan was devised by a small team without the assistance or even knowledge of the Soviet advisors. Even the name of the plan was kept secret and appears in no other source. Nevertheless, the objectives recall "Granite 2 — Improved," which formed the basis of the Yom Kippur War.

The planning of "Operation 41" was also completed in September 1971, but it required a long list of acquisitions. Although the Soviet advisors were privy to the plan, the Kremlin was not forthcoming with the necessary materials. Of critical importance were one hundred MIG-21 planes and a brigade of mobile surface-to-air SAM-6s. These weapons were intended to provide an air umbrella for the bridgeheads, and be of crucial importance for the forces advancing east beyond the protection of the air defenses and stationary missile systems.[58]

Gamasi, who, it will be recalled, was appointed chief of staff in early 1972, mentions only one offensive plan — the "Bader" plan — and presents himself as its chief architect. The plan entailed fording the canal with two armies, while a third operated along the canal front.[59] The armies' bridgeheads would be established at a depth of fifteen to twenty kilometers and include five divisions and the force from the Port Sa'id sector. The entire force would be protected by air defense systems.[60] The attack would develop eastward — with or without a "tactical pause"[61] — with the goal of capturing, holding, and consolidating the mountain passes.

While the Egyptians were engaged in planning the offensive, the troops continued their training, honing their skills, and going through actual water-crossing drills.[62] The end of the massive presence of Soviet advisors in the Egyptian army in late August 1972 meant that the Egyptians had to deal with most of the military activity by themselves. The units continued to train according to the Soviet doctrine, which the Soviet instructors had recommended, but the operational planning, such as that which was carried out in October 1973, became a solely Egyptian enterprise.

At the end of October 1972, Lt. Gen. Ahmad Ismail Ali was appointed war minister. Although his attitude regarding the armed forces' unpreparedness was known,[63] he began working in the spirit of Sadat's order: "War under the present conditions." On Ali's first day on the job, Sadat instructed him to prepare the army for a major confrontation according to a plan that would be exclusively Egyptian.[64] When Shazli presented Ali with the two master plans for the offensive, the latter ordered him to stick to the plan entailing a "very limited offensive" — the "Granite 2 — Improved" plan — and to continue working on it.[65]

In his memoirs, Gamasi tends to minimize the chief of staff's part in the war planning, and describes his first meeting with the new war minister, in which he, Gamasi, expressed his determination to complete the war preparations as quickly as possible. The war minister stated that he believed in the quality of the Egyptian army's weapons but he had doubts about their quantity. Ismail Ali ordered him to draw up realistic plans that corresponded to the effectiveness of the weapons and equipment in the army's arsenal — plans that would enable the missions to be carried out.[66] In answer to Ismail Ali's question as to when the armed forces would be ready for war, Gamasi replied that the army would need a year to make progress in three important areas:

• The troops had to "leave the defensive positions and advance into open territory." They had to train for offensive operations with an emphasis on planned assignments.

Diagram 5:
The Egyptian Offensive Plan "Granite 2" Up to the Mountain Passes

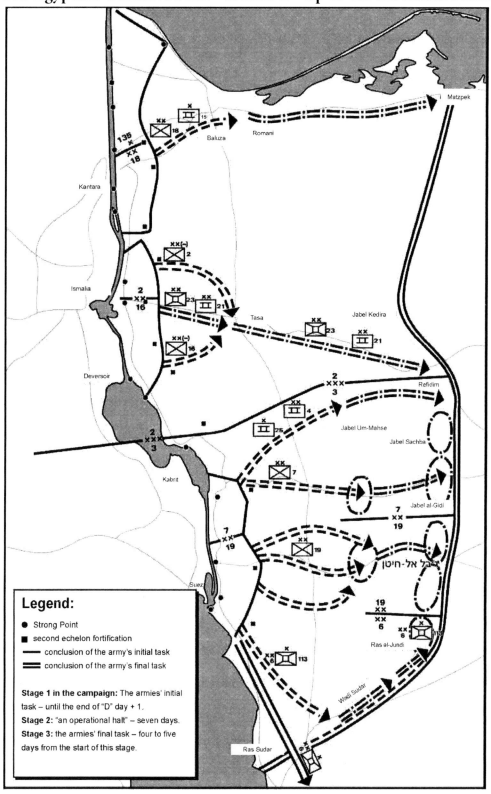

• The planning had to be completed and suited to the weapons and equipment currently in stock. There was no time to wait for new hardware.

• Joint planning with the Syrians had to be completed.

When Ismail Ali received Gamasi's time estimate, he told to him to shorten it.[67] In talks and conferences with military commanders at various levels, the new war minister repeated his instructions that the army would have to fight within the limits of its capabilities, without obtaining new weapons.

At this point the detailed planning went into high gear. The main problem was the canal crossing. The Egyptian planner had to devise solutions for a whole range of problems stemming from the Israeli defense systems on the eastern bank. According to the stages of their advance, the Egyptians would have to face the following challenges:

• Developing the ability to concentrate the crossing force on the western bank;

• Devising technical-tactical solutions for all phases of crossing the water obstacle and breaking through the dirt embankment;

• Neutralizing the enemy's ability to unleash withering fire from the strongholds and canal bank against the crossing force;

• Building a bulwark against IDF counterattacks as quickly as possible in order to protect the troops erecting the bridgeheads.[68]

Shazli pointed to three levels of IDF counterattacks that the Egyptian army had to prepare for:

• Local counterattacks — from the tank platoon to the tank battalion — fifteen to thirty minutes after the initial crossing;

• Division-sized counterattacks by reinforced tank brigades two hours after the crossing;

• Counterattacks by the Israeli Southern Command using tank and infantry brigades — that is, with larger than division-size forces — beginning thirty-six to forty-eight hours from the crossing.

The likelihood of these attacks forced the Egyptian strategist to come up with realistic solutions. He also had to consider the possibility that Israel would launch its main counteroffensive much sooner, six to eight hours, for example, from the outbreak of the fighting (if the IDF received an early warning).

The basic contours of the offensive plan were completed in January 1973.[69] The full plan for crossing the canal and building the divisional bridgeheads was drafted in March 1973 as "Chief of Staff Order No. 41"[70] which had the infantry crossing the canal first and taking up defensive positions against Israeli counterattacks. The solutions for this contingency included:

• Heavily equipping the first-wave troops with antitank weapons (taken from second echelon reserves)[71];

• Intensified operations in the enemy's depth in order to isolate the battlefield[72];

• Infantry units that constructed the bridgeheads assigned limited ranges of advance.[73]

The first waves of infantry forces would advance only five kilometers, then halt and wait until heavier reinforcements arrived: artillery, tanks, and APCs. Shazli summed up the basic concept at this level: "By consolidating the bridgeheads from the rear and narrowing their scope, we were able to concentrate our defensive fire more effectively, increase the density of our antitank guided weapons on each kilometer of the front, and improve the likelihood of repulsing counterblows. These new, narrower bridgeheads would also receive artillery and antitank support from the western bank of the canal which was in our hands. In addition, at this stage our infantry would be protected by a surface-to-air missile umbrella deployed on the western bank, until its unwieldy advance to the east bank was possible."[74]

The basic principle guiding the operation was that the crossing and the attacks would take place on a broad front so as to enable Egypt's infantry divisions, which were spread out in defensive position the length of the canal, to reach their assembly areas, cross at the designated sectors, and erect the bridgeheads across from their permanent and nearly contiguous defense layouts.

This tactic would split the enemy's efforts. Naturally the Israelis would carry out air strikes, local counterattacks, and, later, counteroffensives at a number of sectors along the front. Thus, even if the IDF decided to make a concerted effort in one sector and destroy one or more bridgeheads, others would remain intact and enable the mission to be successfully accomplished.[75]

The "limited" plan that the Egyptian GHQ under Shazli's command formulated contained the following elements.[76]

The first stage was planned to take eighteen to twenty-four hours, during which five infantry divisions would cross the canal, each of them reinforced with a tank brigade (a reinforced tank brigade was either independent, part of a second-echelon mechanized division, or even from the Twenty-first Armored Division). Only the Fourth Armored Division, with its three brigades, would remain on the western bank — antitank units, artillery, and antiaircraft batteries.[77] Each division would cross at a five-kilometer sector. Divisional bridgeheads would extend to an eight-kilometer depth, destroying the enemy on the front line and blocking his counterattack. At the end of this stage the bridgeheads would have reached a twelve-kilometer depth.

The second stage would require another twenty-four hours, to close the gaps between the bridgeheads and create a continuous army-sized bridgehead.[78] In the following twenty-four hours the bridgeheads would be widened and a defense layout constructed and consolidated the entire length of the eastern bank up to a depth of twelve kilometers from the waterline. The plan called for seaborne and airborne commando operations against enemy headquarters in order to isolate the battlefield and delay the arrival of Israeli reserves.[79]

According to Shazli's account, sometime in April 1973 War Minister Ismail Ali ordered him to draft a plan for capturing the mountain passes. The minister explained that the operation was necessary because the Syrians had declared that they would not go to war unless the Egyptians advanced at least fifteen kilometers. The chief of staff, who was one of the key proponents of the "limited plan," explained why the more ambitious plan — "Granite 2" — could not be implemented. Shazli claims that Ismail Ali suggested a compromise solution: Shazli would prepare the plan for crossing the canal, as well as another plan for expanding the offensive to include the capture of the defiles. The minister stressed that he would not order an attack on the passes unless an exceptional opportunity presented itself.

Shazli states that he obeyed the orders, and prepared and circulated a plan for seizing the passes: "Granite 2 — Updated."[80] The planners explained to their superiors that the two stages — the canal crossing and the rolling offensive in the direction of the defiles — were completely separate.

Like Shazli, Ismail Ali doubted the practicality of the plan. In late March he told Shazli that "the armed forces will carry out operations according to their capabilities."[81] Armed with these instructions, the chief of staff continued working on the plan. In September, the date October 6 was chosen for launching the war. The campaign was designated "Operation Bader," after Muhammad's legions' first victory in battle. In early October the plans and the army's capability were united in a single operational effort.[82]

Opinion is divided over the final offensive plan and its objectives. The "official IDF history" states that the mountain passes were the limited war's objective. This relatively deep line appears in a number of the plan's early versions as the final mission, but to the best of my knowledge, and according to Shazli's detailed explanation, the objective was abridged, or at best was not specifically intended to be implemented.

The Egyptians too disagree over the true intention of the war plan. Gamasi claims that "the truth as far as I know it was that the plan did not limit the capture of the Bar-Lev Line as the final objective. The plan envisioned the obtainment of a strategic military goal: consolidating the line of the mountain passes as the final objective."[83] In my opinion, Gamasi's subsequent reference to the plan was designed to give an official and formal answer to Shazli's defiance.

While the offensive plans go into great detail on the intermediate objective, the final objective is retained solely as an option. The more that the Egyptian strategist worked on the plan, the more he realized that "a limited plan," based on the construction of bridgeheads ten to fifteen kilometers from the canal, was better suited to the abilities of the Egyptian army and the war aim.

The basic version of "Granite 2" entailed relatively deep missions. The final objective of the two field armies was defensive deployment east of the defiles. The initial plan visualized the troops reaching a deep line: in the north, Sabhat Bardawil (in the area of Nachal Yam); in the center, Bir Gafgafa; in the south, the eastern openings of the mountain passes (the Gidi, Mitle, and Wadi Sudar passes in the Ras Jundi region).[84]

According to the official version, these objectives would be attained in three stages[85]:

Stage A (the main and most detailed stage): crossing the canal on a broad front with five infantry divisions reinforced with tanks, antitank weapons, artillery, and combat engineers; capturing bridgeheads on the eastern bank, and expanding and stabilizing them to a depth of ten to twelve kilometers.[86] This was the "daytime assignment" of the first-echelon divisions until the end of "D-Day+1."[87] During the canal crossing, airborne forces would land at the approaches to the defiles and on the eastern coast of the Bay of Suez. Their assignment was to secure the entranceways and isolate the area of operations.[88]

At some point before the war, in line with the changes in the war plan and reduction of its objectives, the Egyptians canceled the plan for the massive landing of commando forces at the approaches to the passes.

Stage B: Completing the deployment; consolidating the first echelon divisions' bridgeheads for blocking IDF counterattacks. This stage, whose timeframe depended on the development of the fighting, would be reinforced with additional troops, tanks, antitank weapons, artillery, and air defense units crossing the canal. The authors of the official history refer to this stage as the "operational halt"—a term borrowed from the Soviet warfare lexicon. The "operational halt" was intended to allow the in-depth concentration of troops at the front in preparation for a new offensive effort.[89]

Stage C: In this stage two armored divisions might be thrown into the battle, followed by two mechanized divisions supported by troops at the bridgeheads. The combined force would advance eastward and capture the mountain passes and consolidate a defense line further to the east.[90]

Although the Egyptian planning enabled, or at least took into account, the rolling development of the attack, the objectives were limited to the canal crossing, capture of the "Bar-Lev Line," and construction of massive bridgeheads on the east bank of the canal under the protection of antiaircraft missiles. The cutback in the scope of objectives was part of the concerted effort to learn the doctrinal problems, adapt them to Egypt's needs and capabilities, and drill the troops according to them in preparation for the campaign.[91]

Shazli claims that no one really contemplated ordering the troops to take the defiles. The army's intensive activity from the end of 1972 until the October War involved military research, rewriting the combat doctrine and orders, carrying out exercises and training that focused on limited objectives, generally to a distance of ten to twelve kilometers from the canal.

The entire plan seems to have reflected Sadat's vision, which he developed in Nasser's

Figure 6: The Egyptian Plan for "An All-Out Attack of Limited Dimensions" on the Canal Front (drawn from author conclusions)

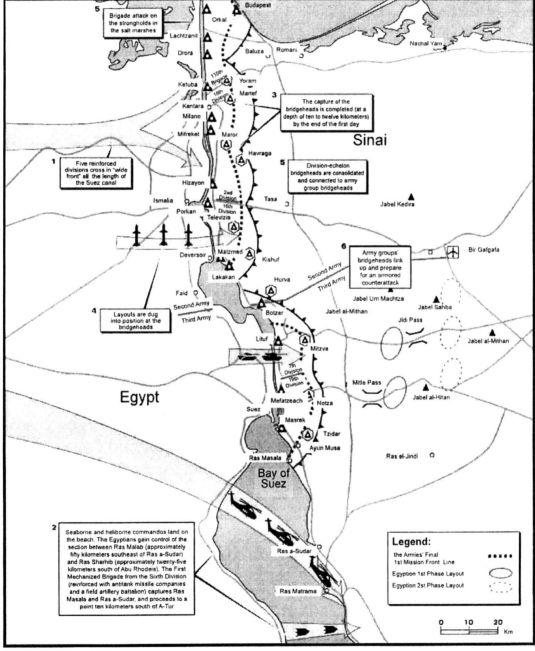

time: "If we can retrieve even ten centimeters of Sinai and establish ourselves there, no force on earth will be able to move us, and the entire situation will have changed."[92]

The Egyptian army retained the option to pursue the attack from the bridgeheads with armored and mechanized forces to the Bir Gafgafa area and the mountain passes. But these operations were relegated to the "sidelines" and their implementation was considered feasible only under extremely favorable conditions. Also, the "armored attack" that the Israelis were eagerly expecting, never materialized. Israeli intelligence was convinced that it had cracked the "Egyptian plan,"[93] and waited for the Egyptian tanks on the second day of the war, but they never appeared. Because of the decision to limit the war aim, the mountain passes did not have to be taken. The order to the armored forces to push east from the bridgeheads in the second week of the war seems to have been issued without a specific task in mind and only under political pressure.[94]

Deception and Feint: The Preparatory Stage of the Yom Kippur War

"All warfare is based on deception.... Hence, when able to attack, we must seem unable; when using our forces, we must seem inactive; when we are near, we must make the enemy believe we are far away; when far away, we must make him believe we are near. Hold out pieces of bait to entice the enemy. Feign disorder, and then crush him."
(Sun Tzu, c. 544–496 B.C., Chinese author of *The Art of War*)

The use of deception according to the Soviet warfare doctrine
(See also Appendix B)

The essence of operational deception (in Russian: *maskirovka*), according to the postwar Soviet warfare doctrine, is to guarantee the element of surprise when attacking the enemy; misleading and confusing him regarding all aspects of the objectives, loci, and timing of the approaching strike; and concealing preparatory steps and troop concentrations.[95] Responsibility for planning deception is assigned to the front echelon. However, field armies too have to devise deception tactics to support the main battle plan on the front.[96] At the army level, the main effort should be made in realms of security, concealment, and dissemblance. The army must also carry out deceptive moves to confound the enemy's discovery of the operation's objectives and modus operandi.

Egyptian vehicle crossing the canal in the Nineteenth Division's sector (Suez Canal-Kubari) (IDF Archives).

Red Army officers gained additional experience in deception tactics after World War II. Every political and especially military move contained basic elements of deception.[97] These tactics can be observed on two occasions when the Soviet Union invaded rebellious satellite countries: the 1956 invasion of Hungary and 1968 invasion of Czechoslovakia. In both cases the Soviets blanketed their preparations and troop concentrations and movements under the cover of military exercises.[98] Egypt's leaders and GHQ carefully applied these and other Soviet lessons in their planning and preparation for the Yom Kippur War.

Deception is an integral part of the planning and implementation of every large-scale military action. It is one of the basic means to achieve surprise and superiority on the battlefield.[99] Barton Whaley, a leading scholar in the application of stratagem, defines deception as "an act intended to outwit the victim or mislead him."[100] Whaley also claims that a number of differences exist between deception and surprise. Surprise is "a sudden military action perpetrated by the enemy ... unforeseen and totally unexpected by the designated victim." While surprise can occur without applying deception, successful deception generally contains the element of surprise. Therefore it may be regarded as a means of attaining surprise.

In his study of "Barbarossa" — the German invasion of Soviet Russia in June 1941— Whaley saw that surprise was associated with deception.[101] According to the author, deception is intentional activity whose "noise" is perceived by the enemy as a "signal."[102] This happens in the following ways:

• Providing the enemy with information from credible sources;
• Carrying out acts of deception in order to reinforce the enemy's basic (mis)conception;
• Maintaining strict operational secrecy by employing concealment and camouflage.

Deception combines initiative, actions, and methods that are designed to "drip" information into the enemy's intelligence assessment and in this way influence his thinking in the direction that the attacker wants. A flawed assessment can lead to significant results at a relatively small cost. Deception is sine qua non in the war effort and must be integrated into every operational plan.[103] It should be seen as an obligatory and rational action, since it serves as a booster, that is, it increases the attacker's strength by a significant margin.[104]

According to Michael Handel, who has studied various types of deception, an inverted relationship exists between the strength of the force and the motivation to use deception. In the case of asymmetrical enemies, deception (and surprise) is liable to compensate the weak side on its numerical inferiority or other weaknesses. On the eve of the Six-Day War, Israel estimated its military power to be acutely inferior to that of the Arabs. In order to compensate for its perceived weakness it employed deception. After the Six-Day War and until the outbreak of the Yom Kippur War, the trend reversed. Israel increasingly relied on its military might and less on deception, whereas the Arabs —first and foremost Egypt, who had experienced an ignominious defeat in the Six-Day War — turned to deception.[105]

Handel mentions several practical ways deceptive activity is carried out,[106] all of which are designed to dupe and confuse the enemy in two basic areas: the attacker's intentions and capabilities. One form of deception tries to divert the enemy's attention, causing him to concentrate his forces in the wrong places. In so doing, the attacker impairs the principle of concentration of forces, which creates an advantageous balance of forces for him in a given sector. The second type of deception seeks to hurt the enemy by damaging the principle of preserving strength. The objective is to cause the enemy to exhaust his resources and divert his efforts to secondary, inconsequential directions. Decoys, diversions, and an exaggeration of one's capabilities will avert the enemy's attention and force him to expend his resources on misguided goals which detract from the main effort. A third type of deception, similar to the first two, is designed to surprise the enemy by creating a situation that appears routine but in effect leaves the enemy unprepared for action.

The various systems of deception are intended to dull the enemy's state of alertness and create the impression that large-scale military maneuvers are taking place, rather than actual preparations for an offensive.

Deception, accompanied by military moves, is common in warfare. It is relatively cost-efficient and does not require a large outlay in labor or resources. On the other hand the relatively small costs can reap enormous dividends. Deception achieves the element of surprise, which increases the chances of a quick and decisive military success. Effectively applied deception will cause the enemy to exhaust his resources, spread his troops out thin, reduce or completely remove his troop strength at the critical moment of the attack, and deploy large numbers of troops in the wrong place at the worst time. Deception will divert the enemy's attention from vital matters or areas, blunt his preparedness, lower his level of alert, and bedevil his sense of certainty.[107]

Many methods and means have to be employed in order for the enemy to buy the deception ruse. The enemy has to be convinced of deception's accuracy, and his intelligence units have to absorb it from as many reliable sources as possible so that he will act on the fed information.

Deception's basic aim at the operational level is to support the advancing forces in carrying out their missions in two main areas: forcing the enemy to make moves that serve the attacker's interest, and concealing weaknesses and deficiencies in various stages of the attacker's planning and in his implementation of the mission.

The Egyptians planned their moves down to the minutest detail before and during the Yom Kippur War. They even sought to dupe Israeli leaders and senior military commanders at the strategic level regarding all aspects of Egypt's war plans. During the fighting, however, they expended less energy on deception than on actual operations.

In my opinion, the surprise that overtook Israel at the beginning of the war led it to stress the importance of deception more than the actual magnitude of the Egyptians' moves. Analytical studies, many of them written by members of the Israeli intelligence community who were to blame for not sounding the warning in time or recognizing the signs of the surprise attack, tried to locate the processes and events that had blinded Israel. Many of the authors pointed an accusatory finger at Egypt's highly successful deception tactics.

Analyses of the Egyptians' successful application of surprise and deception also appeared in many scholarly papers and journals.[108] My study deals mainly with the practical application of deception at the systems level that was an integral part of the Egyptian war plan. The Egyptians employed the Soviet combat doctrine which was based on years of experience. Here too activity was divided between the strategic level, which produced the main results, and secondary activity at the troop level, which dealt mainly with the concealment and timing of the operation, not with actual feints on the battlefield.

When Sadat decided to go to war, he ordered two-pronged activity to be carried out: preparing a strategic deception plan that would parallel the preparatory stage and, as far as possible, the stages of actual combat. This plan was based on a comprehensive analysis of the Israeli security concept and the exploitation of its shortcomings.[109] Thanks to the Israeli media, the Egyptians had no difficulty whatsoever in locating the crux of Israel's security concept. The Egyptian team in charge of strategic deception planning made maximum use of the Egyptian media in order to fatten up the Israeli concept that the Egyptian army was incapable of launching an all-out war. In the months preceding the hostilities, the Egyptians padded the accepted estimates in Israel. The Egyptian media participated in the ploy by emphasizing the following so-called facts[110]:

• The negative influence resulting from Egypt's expulsion of the Soviets;

• The schism in the Arab world, especially the "irreconcilable" differences between Egypt and Syria;

• Egypt's intention to forego the military path since it realized that soaring oil prices were a more effective weapon for pressuring Israel (this would nail home to Israel that its deterrent strength and technological superiority left the Arabs no choice but to abandon the military option).[111]

Aharon Zeevi (Farkash) (former director of Israeli military intelligence), who studied the Egyptians' use of dissimulation in the Yom Kippur War, observed that the main steps in their strategic deception appeared in President Sadat's prewar moves and speeches. Farkash assumes that the majority of Egyptian ministers had been kept in the dark about the deception plan, and that unbeknownst to them had become pawns in their own government's stratagem. Zeevi also notes that five months before the war, Egypt set up an interdepartmental team comprising the foreign ministry and war and information ministries to arrange deception activity. The team's main task, in addition to supervising the implementation of the deception plan, was to coordinate the release of disinformation. Zeevi lists the following maneuvers that were taken:

• Announcements and leaks to the foreign press regarding Egypt's shortage of weapons and their sorry state;

• Circulating articles in the press pertaining to basic disagreements between Egypt and Syria — implying that these differences of opinion precluded the possibility of military cooperation between the two states;

• Publishing dozens of articles relating to the efficacy of the oil weapon as a means of pressuring Israel to withdraw from the occupied territories.[112]

According to Zeevi, this stratagem contributed to the Israeli conception that the Egyptians had abandoned the path to war (at least in this stage), and preferred to solve the conflict via political and diplomatic efforts. Sadat, too, contributed to the dissimulation in his speeches from June 1973 to late September 1973, speaking in a milder and much less radical tone than he did previously and stressing the need for an increased effort in the political sphere. All of these feints were carefully planned to influence the Israeli assessment that Egypt had no intention of embarking on war.

Zeevi mentions other, nonmilitary steps that Egypt took prior to the war[113]:

• Passing on reports to diplomats in Cairo who were aware of military movements that the Egyptian army was deploying defensively against a possible attack due to the tension on the Israeli-Syrian border;

• Announcing the visit of the Romanian minister of war, and the scheduled meeting with his Egyptian counterpart on October 8;

• The Egyptian foreign minister's talks with the American foreign minister, Henry Kissinger, held as planned, in Washington on October 5;

• Four Egyptian ministers were outside the country when war broke out;

• The Morgan oil field's furnaces left burning until the opening of hostilities;

• Most of the civilians in the canal vicinity evacuated only after the fighting commenced.

Political dissemblance was a major part of the Egyptian strategy and was designed to bolster the military plan in general and the deceptive element in particular.

A look at the Egyptian deceptive plan at the operative and strategic levels reveals a wide range of concealment activity but almost no dissimulation on the battlefield.[114]

The main purpose of the deception activity was to support the plan for the army groups to take part in war games and from thence to proceed to the real thing. By preparing for war under the guise of a general exercise, Egyptian forces were able to attain the highest level of readiness, and advance to the front while their true intentions were almost completely masked from the enemy.[115]

Beginning in 1968, the Egyptians held a series of staff exercises — code named "Tahrir" (liberation) — at the strategic-operational levels. From the outset, and until the Yom Kippur War, the Egyptian army practiced one or two Tahrir exercises every year. Units at all levels participated in the war games, in cooperation with headquarters from various branches. The exercises entailed moving units to the front, crossing the Suez Canal, destroying the enemy's forces, and capturing the Sinai Peninsula and at times the Gaza Strip too. Combat engineers also took an active part in the exercises. The army's performance was closely monitored.[116]

The Egyptian planners concealed the breakout to war in the last exercise in the series, termed "Tahrir 41."[117] Israel captured an order stating that the "exercise" was planned to "organize and launch a strategic-operational offensive by initiating a breakthrough to the Suez Canal, destroying the enemy's local reserves in contact engagements, reaching the international border and Gaza Strip and consolidating the defense."[118] The timing, which pertained to the headquarters and tactical forces, was determined for "sometime between October 1 and 7, 1973." Ahmad Ismail Ali, the war minister, was given overall responsibility for the exercise. Under the pretense of a military drill, the Egyptians took the following steps[119]:

• Mobilization and discharge of reservists: On September 27 (under the guise of "Tahrir 41") 120,000 soldiers were mobilized in two groups. Twenty thousand were released on October 4, in accordance with the deception plan.[120]

• Transporting bridging and fording equipment to the canal: Bridging equipment was advanced to the front under the pretense of a military exercise. Convoys loaded with equipment arrived at the canal by various routes; some of the convoys were seen returning to the west on transporters. The vehicular movement was timed to occur so that all of the equipment would be at the front on October 6.

• Advancing army formations and units to the front: Second-echelon divisions and brigades, those not stationed permanently on the canal's banks, were advanced to the front as part of a military maneuver prior to the exercise.

• Military academies shut down and then reopened: According to "Tahrir 41," the Nasser Higher Military College would shut down on September 30, and the cadets would join their units "in order to ensure that every soldier and officer gained the maximum benefit from taking part in the tactical maneuvers with the troops currently deployed for the exercise." Studies at the military institutions would resume on October 9 at the conclusion of the exercise.

• Circulating information regarding soldiers receiving permission to go on pilgrimage to Mecca: The press published these reports, and the information was simultaneously conveyed to the units.

• Creating an "idyllic" atmosphere on the waterfront: In the days leading up to the war — and especially on the morning of October 6 — Egyptian troops on the canal acted in most unsoldierly fashion: sauntering down to the shore without weapons or helmets, fishing, and goofing off, thus creating the impression of utmost tranquility on the front.

This use of a combat exercise as a cover up for the Egyptians' real intentions was, in my opinion, the key — and perhaps only — feature of deception activity at the military level. It employed mainly radio transmissions, since the Egyptian planner correctly assumed that Israeli intelligence would be eavesdropping.[121] The deception tactics and other concealment ruses were carried out piecemeal. Except for a few cases involving decoys — dummy bridges and antiaircraft weapons — no other use was made of deception or dissimulation.

The bulk of the activity was designed to camouflage the operational plan so as to achieve the element of surprise. Stringent steps were taken to maintain secrecy and concealment. Only a handful of people knew of the war plan, while others who were involved in the training schedule, were informed of the real goal and date of the operation only in the later stages, close to "D-Day."

General Zeira, the Israeli chief of intelligence, refers to the concealment as "the Egyptian army's deception." In his view, Sadat and a small coterie of confidantes had to establish three basic conditions:

• Ascertain that the time for launching the war remained a state secret and was issued only at the last minute.

• Cancel all patrols before the war.

• Devise as basic and simple a war plan as possible, one that precluded the need for specific readjustments or complex revisions once hostilities commenced.[122]

Indeed, the offensive plan in general, and the crossing of the canal and consolidation of the bridgeheads in particular, was a simple crossing-with-contact plan based on the egress from divisional sectors, from crossing points that the troops were familiar with. This was the plan that had been internalized and practiced at various levels on a number of occasions since 1971.

Zeira points to additional aspects of concealment.[123] Basing his evidence on books by Hassanein Heykal[124] and Shazli, the Israeli intelligence chief notes that concealment included full cooperation with the Syrians, leaving most of the Egyptian government ministers in the dark, and even duping the Soviets, whose hundreds of officers in immediate contact with the Egyptian and Syrian armed forces had no clue that a war was about to erupt until forty-eight hours before it began.

Zeira devotes a special chapter in his *mea culpa non* to the possible use of human sources ("HUMINT") for conveying, via the Mossad (Israel's CIA), potential dates for war between 1971 and 1973. Zeira claims that all of the information leaked to Israel was part of the deception plan and designed solely to lead Israeli leaders and intelligence analysts astray from Sadat's real plans, since the only date that had been decided on was October 6, 1973.[125]

It is difficult to discern active dissimulation by Egypt at the operative level. A careful review of its war preparations and battlefield performance fails to detect a deception plan or feinting maneuvers[126] that might have thrown dust in the IDF's eyes regarding Egypt's true intentions, the army's tasks, the fording areas, directions of the offensive, types of the operational troops and their strength, and so forth. Israel may have believed that Egyptian armored divisions would cross the canal and that the attack would gather momentum from the bridgeheads—a move that the Israeli chief of intelligence and the entire GHQ expected but that in the end did not take place. Israel's blindness may have stemmed from years of Egyptian deception that culminated in the initial days of the war. But here too I found no evidence to corroborate the thesis.[127]

The scholar Michael Handel, who identified different forms of deception, notes that the Egyptians, in effect, abandoned the first two types of deception that could have tilted the balance of forces on the battlefield to their favor and exhausted the IDF by forcing it to deal with marginal efforts or feints. Instead, the Egyptians concentrated exclusively on dulling the Israelis' alertness so that they could surprise Israel as a whole and the army as the body responsible for the campaign. I found no examples of Egyptian troops engaging in deception activity during the fighting; only few attempts at setting up dummy layouts, mainly those that had been deployed on the front in the years preceding the war.[128]

The Egyptian troops who crossed the canal from their defense positions had no need to concentrate near the front, excluding fording equipment which called for a special conceal-ment plan. The buildup of the Egyptian crossing force was done in its defense layouts in prepa-ration for a defensive battle, and included the in-depth concentration of forces to counter a surprise IDF attack.[129] The divisions, supported by infantry as well as mechanized and armored units, were deployed in defensive layouts proximate to the front, from where they could leap across the canal. Reinforcement of the ground troops was carried out by the army in an ini-tiated maneuver to and from the front.[130] The push east went according to the combat doc-trine: from contact with the enemy, not from movement. This is the recommended method for concealing forces deployed a considerable distance from the front line for an attack from staging areas. The concentration of the force was carried out during a three- to four-month period, under the guise of preparations for a war exercise.[131] The regular artillery layout, as well as the reinforced one, had been positioned along the line in the early stages of the prepa-rations as part of the routine defense system. Artillery and antitank missile battalions had been ensconced in these advanced layouts since the end of the War of Attrition. Minor reinforce-ments, like the larger additions, were added under the facade of a combat exercise.

No decoys of troop layouts were set up in staging areas or elsewhere on the front.[132] The main decoys were artillery and antiaircraft batteries, and radar installations that had been deployed before the war. During the crossing, a number of phony bridges were built, how-ever, not to make it look like there were crossings in other sectors, but in order to lessen the chances that the real bridges would be damaged.[133]

Five infantry divisions crossed the canal (from areas that had been prepared over the years) to establish bridgeheads on the eastern bank. No attempts were made at feinting moves and no decoys were planted in other crossing areas. No dummy unit or real unit tasked with appearing to be another effort or another unit was detected.[134] The Israelis and the Egyptians knew the directions of advance and the areas where the bridgeheads would be built. The Egyptians took no trouble to lead the Israelis astray or pretend that another effort was being set in motion.

All activity at the operational-tactical level was focused, as stated, on the effort to con-ceal the war plan — especially its most crucial stage: the crossing. The hour chosen was when the sun was in the Israeli lookouts' eyes, but the critical operation of the actual crossing was carried out under cover of darkness, and, later, under a thick smoke screen[135] which was planned to minimize the likelihood of Israeli troops — especially the IAF — wreaking havoc on the crossing force.

The Egyptians made massive use of smoke screens, mainly to camouflage the bridging operations and the forces engaged in crossing the canal. During my tour of service and other visits to the western bank, I encountered scores of diesel-fueled smoke apparatuses. These devices were densely deployed and operated most effectively in the first days of the crossing.

The little that the Egyptians did in all aspects of deception and dissimulation at the tac-tical and operational levels indicates that these areas were of minor importance. Nevertheless, the Egyptian planner and the combat troops succeeded in obtaining the element of strategic surprise. Israeli intelligence failed to comprehend what was really happening. The lure of a military exercise corresponded perfectly with the Israelis' unquestioned "concept."

The dictionary of military terms defines surprise as an act against the enemy, and whose timing, place, strength, modus operandi, and weapons are unexpected." The Egyptians attained the element of surprise in the Yom Kippur War. Their success in timing, weapons, modus operandi, and especially in the use of antitank weapons during the crossing from the bridgeheads was superlative. Place — areas selected for the crossing; strength — divisions, brigades, and battalions; weapons; and even the principles of implementation: all were known to the enemy — the IDF.

The Egyptians' strategic surprise in the use of deception (even though it was applied mostly passively) and the Israelis' conceptual blunder created surprise on the battlefield. The Egyptians launched a complex battle, crossed a formidable water barrier, consolidated their defense lines opposite the IDF's armor, and paid a lower price in human lives and material than what they estimated. The surprise that they achieved by employing concealment and deception, and their brilliant use of antitank weapons, and integrating them into the modus operandi, were the main factors that enabled them to accomplish their missions and achieve the war's objective.

5

The Soviet Warfare Doctrine and Its Application by the Egyptians

"As Operation Bader drew near, we had no illusions about the discrepancies in the quality of the equipment between the two armies. Therefore, given our limited military means, we looked for an unconventional way to deliver a devastating blow."
— General Abd al-Rahim Hajaj in an interview with the Israeli journalist, Yoram Binur. "Akhathna Tharna" ("We Got our Revenge"), *Hadashot*, September 24, 1995

Tactical Principles in the Soviet Warfare Doctrine*

The offensive has always been the primary method of fighting. The Soviet warfare doctrine recommends the attack as the preferred method of battle. The doctrine holds that the only way to rout the enemy and attain the war's final goals is by delivering devastating blows on the enemy and using one's forces to their full capacity. In the best of circumstances, defense will detract from the enemy's offensive capability and create conditions conducive to a counterattack. But defensive acts alone will not achieve victory.[1]

In general, the objective of the attack at the operational level is to capture key political or economic areas in the enemy's rear, while eliminating the military units defending them.[2] Offensive combat is typically carried out on one front under a single command.[3] The front's headquarters, which is responsible for operational efforts, contains a number of field armies supported by airpower, missile layouts, and reserve troops from GHQ.

The attack plan must define the objectives, the forces taking part in the primary and secondary efforts, and the routes of advance.[4]

Planning must be based on a comparative analysis of the strengths and weapons of the offense and defense. An attack's success depends, inter alia, on a minimum manpower ratio of 3:1 in the offense's favor. A lower ratio is possible only at the secondary effort.[5] A similar ratio is also required for weapons — especially artillery concentrations.[6]

A field army carries out an offensive[7] in two ways:

• Attacking and breaching the enemy's layouts on one axis, in order to split and separate his defensive forces;

• Attacking on several axes in order to encircle the defender in-depth.

In both cases, the remains of the enemy's forces and layouts will be mopped up from the rear only in the advanced stages of the fighting.[8]

The various stages in the operation are planned according to two key factors: the aggres-

---

For details on offensive tactics in the attack at the field army and divisional level, see Appendix A.

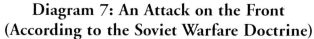

Diagram 7: An Attack on the Front
(According to the Soviet Warfare Doctrine)

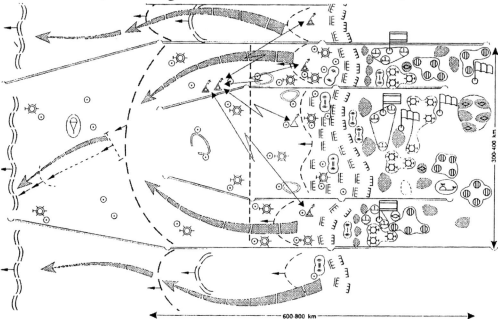

sor's intended depth and operative objectives. In the European theaters of war the objectives are divided according to the level engaged in them:

- The field army's tactical objective is to reach the rear of the divisional defense layout.
- The offensive front's immediate objective is to penetrate the defense at a close operational depth.
- The front's long-range objective is to achieve an in-depth breakthrough at the defense's army group layout.
- The front's ultimate strategic objective is to capture and consolidate the enemy's government, and logistical and economic centers.

Task allocation in an offensive campaign calls for an analysis and planning of priorities in the following areas:

- Breaching brigade-level forward defense layouts;
- Penetrating the enemies' echelons at a tactical depth, and attacking his divisional reserves in the forward defense layout;
- Destroying or neutralizing enemy forces (including corpus reserves) at a close operational depth;
- Capturing an area so that second-echelon units can enter the battle, attack the enemy's strategic reserves, and attain strategic depth (the front's ultimate objective).

A front consisting of three or four field armies attacks in a single primary effort and one or more secondary efforts. An offensive sector can reach more than three hundred kilometers in length, depending on the front's tasks and objectives, and the nature of enemy forces and deployment in the sector. Mission depth may be up to two hundred kilometers.[9]

The offensive is carried out mainly by two echelons, each of which is made up of a number of types of field armies. In addition, one division (armored or mechanized) will remain in reserve at the front.[10]

Diagram 8: Attack by a Field Army — Mission Depth
(According to the Soviet Warfare Doctrine)

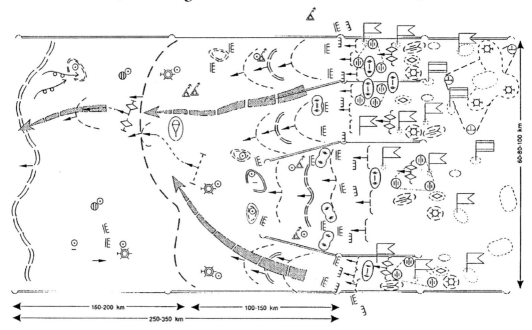

A field army attacking on the primary effort's axis will deploy in a relatively narrow sector (forty to fifty kilometers in length). A field army engaged in secondary efforts will attack an eighty-kilometer sector. Mission depth at the first echelon can reach from 100 to 150 kilometers.[11] Long-range missions, such as those incapacitating the enemy reserve's assembly areas, can attain ranges of 150 to 200 kilometers.[12] The front generally breaches the enemy's defense layouts in two sectors (one of which is the primary effort). Sometimes the front breaks through in only one sector. Whatever the case, the depth of penetration will be no less than twenty to twenty-five kilometers. The length of the field army's breaching sector will be between eight to ten kilometers.[13]

An Attack at the Divisional Level

The division applies the principles and tactics of the offensive, confronting the enemy with overwhelming firepower, aggressive assaults, in-depth penetration, encirclement, and splitting and destruction of his forces. A divisional attack will encompass the following basic elements: firepower, shock, superior maneuvering.[14]

Offensive operations at the tactical level are based on the following basic elements: movement to the line of attack; assault with concentrated firepower; locating and repulsing counterattacks; exploiting success on the battlefield by advancing rapidly to the depth.

Soviet tactics insist on the use of massive firepower in order to paralyze key objectives at the front and in the enemy's in-depth defense layout, and to serve as a cover for the attacker's aggressive movements. While advancing, the aggressor will try to circumvent and outflank the enemy's heavily defended layouts.[15] The offensive battle will proceed dynamically according to developments. Influencing factors include the nature of the enemy's defenses (hastily set up, organized, fortified, or located on the waterline or close to a water obstacle); the nature of the terrain; season; daylight or nighttime conditions.[16]

Offensive maneuvering depends on circumstances — a frontal attack will merge into a close flanking and deeper envelopment. The aggressor will attempt to exploit gaps in the enemy's defenses and move against his flanks and rear.

The attack may be carried out from movement. The attacking force may advance through units already engaged in contact, or the attack may commence from positions already in contact with the enemy. According to the Soviet doctrine, speed is a key element and provides the greatest advantage to the attack in movement.[17]

The element of surprise is also of utmost importance in an attack, and is naturally given special emphasis in the Soviet doctrine. The ground forces conducting the attack must also employ various types of deception and subterfuge.

A division engaged in an offensive operation under the command of an all-branch army may be ordered to act at the first echelon, at the second echelon — on the axis of the primary or secondary effort, or as a reserve force.[18] The division's role and place in the field army's layout depends on its battle concept and fighting ability.[19]

The use of a first-level division on the axis of the primary effort depends on its ability to break through and destroy the enemy's main forces. The battle's ultimate success depends on this stage. The division's success in the secondary effort may cause a shift in the effort's value and transform it into the primary effort. Infantry divisions are usually employed at this echelon.

The use of second-echelon divisions or reserves is intended to increase the attacker's strength and exploit success. The division leading the attack on the main axis of the primary effort has a decisive role to play in destroying the enemy's reserves.[20] At this level mobile divisions — armored and mechanized — are generally employed.[21] While the attack is developing, they will be used in the first echelon and on the axis of the primary effort during the breaching of improvised defensive layouts.

Division-level missions

The division's missions depend on the following factors: the main battle concept; the enemy's strength, modus operandi, and defensive network; the division's fighting ability and amount of assistance given it (including air support); the nature of the terrain; weather conditions.

At the tactical level the operative plan determines the attack. In other words, the attack routes are part of a wide-scale maneuver. The plan calls for the following operational activity: cutting the enemy's defense layout; destroying specific units; determining how and when enemy objectives will be captured.[22]

The division's combat mission is usually planned for a twenty-four hour period,[23] and includes the capture of a specific area and the enemy's destruction in a particular sector. The mission consists of a series of consecutively implemented moves that enable the most effective use of troops and weapons, the best organization, coordination, and control of the forces participating in the battle so that maximum results are achieved.

The division's combat mission is divided into: the primary task, follow-up task, and daily task. At the brigade level, instead of a daily task, the attack will proceed in the direction of the route.[24]

This arrangement allows for a particular line to be held, part of the enemy's forces destroyed, and suitable conditions created for pursuing the attack. The arrangement also enables the attack to continue while maintaining the combat layout and same system of coordination. Mission depth is adapted to the formation's fighting abilities.

The division's tasks (depth and goals) proceed according to the following scheme[25]:

• Primary task: breaking through the first defense layout and destroying the enemy's first echelon brigade.[26] Mission depth depends on the brigade's deployment — eight to ten kilometers.

• Follow-up task: breaking through the enemy division's secondary defense layout and destroying his second-echelon or reserve forces. Mission depth will be approximately twenty kilometers. If the defense strip is deeper, the breach becomes the division's daily task.

• Daily task: The development of an in-depth attack; (together with local forces) destruction of the enemy's operational reserves; consolidating a convenient line for defense or pursuit of the attack to a thirty kilometer depth.

A brigade, whose primary task is at the first-divisional echelon, will break though and destroy the enemy's first- and brigade-echelon battalions to a depth of three to four kilometers. Its next task will be identical to the division's primary mission, completing the breakthrough to a depth of eight to ten kilometers. After this the brigade will attack its appointed axis. The daily mission of a brigade operating on an independent axis should reach a depth of twenty kilometers.

Egyptian documents present the primary mission as the capture of the line fifteen to seventeen kilometers from the canal. This task includes crossing the canal; destroying enemy covering troops; breaching the first strip (while in movement); wiping out the enemy's brigade and first echelon forces, and overtaking the artillery deployment area.[27]

The follow-up mission develops the deep attack; completes the breakthrough (including the destruction of the first-echelon brigade and consolidation of the line twenty-five kilometers from the canal). The daily task calls for consolidation of the line thirty to thirty-five kilometers from the canal.[28]

The rate of advance influences mission depth. The infantry's advance through the enemy's defense layouts is less than one kilometer per hour. The infantry brigade will need three to four hours to complete the three kilometers — the depth of the primary task. Beyond the main defense layout the rate of advance will be one and a half kilometers an hour. At this rate the division will be able to complete the breakthrough and drive back enemy counterattacks. A ten- to fifteen-kilometer-depth mission will take eight to nine hours (even up to twelve hours) to complete.[29]

As the fighting continues (and until the daily task is completed), the rate of advance will be two to three kilometers (or more) an hour. At this rate the division will need fifteen to twenty hours to complete its task. The first day is the toughest and slowest. Afterward the rate of advance will increase.[30]

The command level determines the length of the division's attack sector. The length depends on the following factors: battle concept and combat mission; the division's operational capability; the amount of support it receives; enemy strength; nature of enemy defenses; terrain. The sector's length must provide the attacker with superiority, especially in the breaching zone, and the best conditions possible for maneuvering, command, deployment, and dispersal of the forces.[31]

An infantry division generally attacks on a front eight to ten kilometers long. If a mechanized or armored division makes the attack, the length extends to twelve kilometers.[32] This is the recommended dimension for a division attacking with two first-echelon brigades. The length of an infantry division with two battalions, with an interval between them, is four kilometers. This is the case when each battalion attacks along a line one and a half to two kilometers in length.

In the case of an enemy's organized or fortified defense layout, a shorter length is employed at the breakthrough sector so that the first echelon division or brigade engaged in the attack will have a numerical superiority of at least 3:1 in men and weapons. By limiting the sector's length, the attacker obtains superior firepower, which hastens the enemy's capitulation.[33] The divisional breach may be up to four kilometers in length,[34] that of a brigade only two kilometers.

The Attack at the Suez Canal Front — Application of the Soviet Warfare Doctrine

The Egyptian army adopted the Soviet warfare doctrine. The planning, preparations, and implementation of the moves in the first part of the Yom Kippur War were based on this doctrine. Nevertheless, the Egyptians were flexible enough to adapt the doctrine to their particular needs, abilities, and conditions in the combat theater.

The decision for war meant that Egypt had to launch an all-out offensive. This was the only way it could convince other parties, namely Syria, to hop on the war machine whose ultimate goal was to break the deadlock over the captured territories. The Egyptians had tried to melt the impasse in the War of Attrition, but failed. In the Yom Kippur War, however, they drafted an attack plan that went far beyond the Soviet doctrine's guidelines.

The Suez Canal had to be forded and Israel's fortified defense layout breached. This meant that the Egyptians had to plan "an attack from contact," that is, an attack from fixed positions on the defense line. The attack took place on a broad front. Egyptian forces advanced to a limited depth and made separate efforts on a number of axes. By choosing the strategy of an all-out attack of limited dimensions it was hoped that the Egyptian troops would be able to split the Israeli force in all of the sectors under attack.

Egypt's inferior maneuverability and shortage in armored and mechanized formations (not, however, in infantry formations) also influenced their choice of modus operandi. Egypt's infantry, deployed along the entire length of the canal front, bore the brunt of the burden. Egyptian foot soldiers crossed the Suez Canal, built the bridgeheads, and, from their hastily organized defense layouts, managed to push back Israeli counterattacks on the east bank.

Other mobile forces, armored and mechanized, that were designated to carry out an "attack from movement" according to the Soviet doctrine and advance rapidly by exploiting their success, were left in the rear as second-echelon units or for an equally important task — as a second-echelon defense in the event of an Israeli crossing. The second echelon's primary task was to reinforce the divisions that had crossed the canal. The second echelon included artillery, antitank and antiaircraft units, as well as tank brigades, all of which boosted the Egyptian army's ability to withstand Israel's expected counterattacks.

A detailed Egyptian combat plan curtailed the hierarchy in the attack. In other words, the plan for a quick advance to key objectives in the enemy's depth was shelved. Once the Egyptians realized that the capture of a relatively narrow area, adjacent to the canal, would also attain the war's goals, they abandoned the tactical in-depth objectives. Airborne and/or seaborne ground forces would not have to attack in the enemy's deep layouts. There was no longer a need for the second echelon to make a rapid, determined effort to reach the enemy's well-defended rear.

The offensive consisted of two stages: a massive barrage in the initial stage — as the Soviet doctrine called for — followed by the canal crossing and construction and consolidation of the bridgeheads.[35] The dimensions of the attack — mission depth and rate of advance — were less than the doctrine's recommendations. The field armies (and divisions) were reduced to securing the defense lines in the extremities of their "primary mission."

At this stage the attack consisted of local improvements on the bridgeheads' forward line. From this point on, all Egyptian combat activity became defensive. The sole exception was the uncoordinated attack of October 14, carried out by a number of tank brigades in a few halfhearted efforts in unconnected sectors in northern, central, and southern canal fronts.[36] This irresolute operation only weakened the Egyptian defense layout and facilitated the IDF's canal crossing.[37] Israeli forces made a deep penetration into Egypt, capturing large tracts of land on the western bank and encircling Third Army bridgeheads from the rear.

Crossing the Canal and Securing the Bridgeheads

The Suez Canal, the largest artificial water barrier in the world, divided the Egypt's layouts on western bank from the IDF's defensive positions on the eastern bank. It seems that the devastating results of the Six-Day War convinced the Egyptians to learn how a canal crossing should be carried out. However, despite the numerous water obstacles in the Nile Valley and Delta, and the canal itself, the only aspect that seemed to concern them after the war was the administrative movement of forces in the rear.

Diagram 9: Mission Depth in a First-Echelon Division Attack — Three Situations (Egyptian Document, 1971)

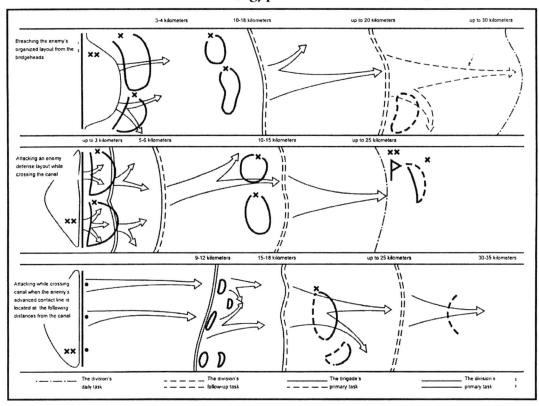

The need to get to the other side and "do what had to be done" forced the Egyptian planner to deal with the complexities of a water crossing. In order to facilitate this task, the Egyptians turned to the experience of others—the Soviets and their warfare doctrine.[38]

The Basic Principles of the Soviet Doctrine Crossing Water Obstacles

The Red Army's warfare doctrine considered water obstacles an issue of major importance. Undoubtedly this was because of the vast number of rivers and streams in the European theater of operations in general and Russian theater in particular.

In the postwar period, the Soviet Union earmarked huge investments for the development of its warfare doctrine, the production of special water-fording equipment, and training programs for the ground troops designated for large-scale water-crossing operations. The Soviets devised new techniques for getting combat troops across water barriers, and practiced them at the tactical and operational levels.[39]

The Soviet doctrine[40] views a water obstacle (river, stream, canal, and so forth) as a delaying factor in an attack. The obstacle is not the objective per se but one of the intermediate objectives that the aggressor has to overcome in order to complete his mission.

The complexity of an aquatic obstruction, the defender's advantage behind it, and the vast resources needed to cross the obstacle and overpower the enemy's defense layouts make a water crossing an extremely complicated enterprise—perhaps the most difficult of all offensive operations.

One goal is to get the fighting forces across as quickly as possible so that they can pursue the attack. Combat units have to be transferred in the same battle formations they will be in when fighting to secure the bridgeheads and advancing into the enemy's in-depth layouts.

The huge strides that have been made since the Second World War in the development and use of weapons (such as modern bridging equipment) have completely altered fording operations.

According to the Soviet concept, the enemy's entire layout, including the line protecting the water barrier, can be overcome. The attacker's main problem is to cross the barrier in as short a time as possible with minimum losses.

Therefore, technical information about the obstacle becomes a key factor at the tactical and operative levels when planning the operation, even before the enemy's strength and location in the defensive layout are taken into consideration.

The starting point in the Egyptian plan was to locate areas in the littoral leading to approach roads on both sides of the obstacle. The most serviceable sections had to be found for approaching and descending to the water, and operating an unprecedentedly large amount of modern fording equipment. A road network to the water line had to be constructed so that the attack could proceed develop at a fast pace to the eastern shore.

The Soviet method for crossing a water obstacle went through numerous changes over the years. In the sixties and early seventies it envisioned a broad front with all levels of the army involved in the operation.[41] Several efforts would be made, more or less equidistant from one another. In the late 1960s the doctrine recommended that the crossing take place in a relatively narrow sector at the operative level, and on a broad front at the tactical level.

The first echelon would exert maximum pressure on the enemy, assaulting his layouts in as many places as possible and as early as possible. In the sector where the largest crossing occurred, a large force would race toward the tactical objective. This was the recommended modus operandi when employing mechanized and armored forces capable of advancing rapidly.

The width and depth of the water obstacle were the main parameters that had to be taken into account. According to the Soviet doctrine, the obstacle's importance was proportional to the amount of attention that had to be given to control over the attacking forces, their weapons, and the fording equipment. Based on this equation, various solutions were needed for overcoming obstacles according to their width, importance, and difficulty.

Narrow rivers and canals could be crossed independently by brigade- or division-sized units. A medium-sized river crossing (up to 300 meters in width) was generally assigned to a field army. And the largest water obstacles fell to army groups.[42] At the tactical level, a brigade or division was direct responsibility for the crossing.

An analysis of the crossing methods focuses on two main techniques: "crossing from movement" and "crossing from the contact line." "Crossing from movement" is generally made during a successful attack that begins at a great distance from the obstacle. This type of crossing is intended to generate momentum for the attack. "Crossing from the contact line" is made when the sides are directly opposite one another and the enemy is dug in behind heavily fortified defense layouts.[43]

"Crossing from movement" is planned as a regular maneuver made by forward units that have completed the first stages of the crossing and have progressed into enemy territory as far as possible before the arrival of the main force. In order for the "regular crossing" to succeed, meticulous planning is necessary.[44]

"Crossing from the line of contact" demands painstaking preparation, intensive planning and control at the highest levels, and the use of men and weapons on a vast scale. It is carried out at the tactical level along a broad front, and may require much time and entail many casualties.

According to the Soviet doctrine, the commander should strive to implement a "crossing from movement," and avoid a "crossing from the line of contact."

Both methods consist of five basic stages that are undertaken either simultaneously or integrated in succession:
- Intelligence gathering, planning, and preparation;
- Approaching and securing the local bank[45];
- First-echelon assault forces making the crossing;
- Transfer of the main body to the opposite shore, and capture of the enemy's forward defense layout;
- Exploiting the initial victory — bringing across troops from the second operational echelon (generally armored or mechanized forces), capturing the enemy's in-depth layouts, and proceeding to the tactical objective.

The standard Soviet field army was a multi-branched force made up of three mechanized and one or two armored divisions. (The Egyptian field army consisted of two or three infantry divisions, and one mechanized and one armored division. The mechanized divisions were usually in the first echelon and the armored ones in the second echelon.)

The Soviet doctrine stated that a field army should cross with two or three first-echelon mechanized divisions. Each division should be divided into two tactical echelons; the first consisting of at least two mechanized brigades.

Armored divisions should generally be used in the second echelon in order to exploit the success. During a "crossing from movement" the armored divisions should generally be sent across first in order to pursue the enemy and advance into his area. These divisions will be reinforced with infantry or mechanized forces, depending on circumstances, in order to eliminate the enemy's resistance.

Second-echelon forces will be used at as early a time as necessary, moving through the first-echelon forces, penetrating the enemy in depth, and seizing the tactical objective.

If the echelons are organized in this manner prior to and during the crossing, the attacker will maintain the initiative and gain momentum.

A successful crossing depends on a combination of several factors:

• Collecting information on the water obstacle — its banks, defensive strength, and enemy deployment — in order to determine the safest and most effective crossing areas.

• Achieving a tactical surprise regarding the time and location of the crossing. This will be attained through deception and dissimulation.

• Crossing on as broad a front as possible in order to prevent the defender from discovering the primary effort, thus dividing his efforts and forcing him to use his armored reserves at any early stage.

• Employing a fast-moving force in the approach stage, crossing, and securing of a foothold on the opposite shore. Speed can be attained if the obstacles are removed at an early stage, equipment effectively employed, existing passageways overtaken at an early stage, and the movement of forces toward the obstacle and the crossing itself meticulously organized and supervised.

• Exhibiting an aggressive fighting spirit in the different stages of the crossing, from the approach to the deep penetration of the enemy's layout.

• Early neutralization of the enemy's sources of fire that could hamper troop assembly, the crossing, and erection of bridgeheads, by concentrating one's firepower and using all weapons with maximum effectiveness.

• Avoiding troop and equipment concentrations close to the waterline.

• Providing an effective air umbrella during the crossing and fighting on the opposite shore.

• Establishing lateral axes on both banks so that the efforts can be shifted from one crossing area to another.

In regular offensive operations, a water obstacle can be crossed at an acceptable rate of advance in attack operations only if the forces, including tanks and artillery, transfer across without any special difficulties. In order to achieve this goal, mobile fording equipment with high lift capacity and specially-designed rafts and bridges were developed after World War II.

Modern crossing equipment consists of amphibious (and non-amphibious) military vehicles, assault boats, pontoons (floating metal sections), rafts, and mechanized bridges[46] that enable the transfer of both troops and weapons. (Prior to the Yom Kippur War Egypt procured a huge quantity of modern fording equipment.)

The Soviet doctrine holds that troops should make maximum use of their organic fording equipment during the crossing: vehicles and assault boats, pontoons, rafts and ferries. Only later will floating bridges be erected (and dismantled or hidden before daylight to protect them from air strikes or other sources of damage), and gradually transformed into permanent bridges.

The technical side of getting the forces across the canal depends on overall conditions, the equipment, and the data that has been collected about the obstacle. Forces have to cross a canal in amphibious armored vehicles, assault boats, or rafts; and in shallow water on ferries or bridges.[47] Under certain conditions, tanks are also capable of crossing by submerging, but this method is not suited to conditions at the Suez Canal.

The method finally decided on called for the concentration of forces in areas that had access to a relatively smooth descent into the water. The exit from the canal on the distant shore would be organized only in the course of the crossing itself.

Crossing with amphibious equipment would be the basic method used by the forces of the first tactical echelon since it would provide a quick passage across and the development of an in-depth attack in the enemy's layout. The equipment would be rotated: after each crossing, the equipment would return to the starting point. The ideal crossing method would be in "waves," with the assault forces attacking from their landing craft.[48]

Various types of rafts — especially self-propelled vessels — could be used for transporting tanks, artillery, non-amphibious APCs, and other vehicles and weapons, mainly in the first stages of the fighting. Later in the operation they could be used for building bridges that would serve as the main means for transferring large numbers of forces to the eastern bank.

Bridge construction was planned to begin only after a tract of land on the distant bank was secured and safe from the enemy's direct laying fire.

"Crossing from the contact line"

"Crossing from the contact line" is an initiated attack made in the face of strong opposition from an enemy situated in heavily fortified defense layouts. The Soviet doctrine states that a 3:1 proportion is required for such an attack to succeed. Assaulting a fortified layout, not to mention one located behind a water obstacle, calls for a much higher proportion of forces.

The defenders will probably be supported with heavy artillery, aircraft, and combat engineers. In this case, the crossing operation may take a long time, with the aggressor suffering heavy losses.

Since the crossing from the contact line is a preemptive operation, the aggressor may wish to gain tactical surprise regarding place, time, and size of the attack.

The forward troops on the contact line will make the necessary preparations; the main crossing force will come up from the rear and carry out a crossing from movement.

Crossing from the contact line demands meticulous groundwork preparation in the form of engineering and artillery deployment and troop concentrations.

Much of the engineering work takes place in the aggressor's layouts on the contact line long before the operation begins.[49]

The combat engineers' primary tasks in preparing the crossing include:
• Patrols to examine the water obstacle, its banks, and the enemy's defense facilities and fortifications;
  • Preparing concentration and deployment areas;
  • Preparing crossing points and descents into the water;
  • Establishing command-and-control and medevac positions;
  • Clearing and safeguarding the area from mines and sabotage;
  • Ensuring engineering support for the troops making the crossing and advancing into enemy territory.

Artillery softening up

When the time for "crossing from contact" approaches, artillery softening up is used as in the preparations for an attack against a fortified layout. The softening up consists of a lengthy and devastating barrage produced by a massive concentration of artillery. The artillery's push forward during the crossing must not detract from the continuity and accuracy of the artillery fire.

Artillery support consists of a barrage lasting until the first crossing force enters the water, and covering fire until the assault force reaches its objectives.

Artillery pieces from field-army units and higher formations will take part in the softening up. The barrage will generally last forty to sixty minutes. Its roles consist of:
- Destroying the enemy's chemical and nuclear weapons launch pads[50];
- Paralyzing the enemy's artillery layouts;
- Destroying the enemy's fortification system (that includes observation posts and communications facilities);
- Knocking out enemy reserves.

Covering fire will continue for ten to fifteen minutes. This is the amount of time needed for the first waves to cross the obstacle, gain a foothold on the distance bank, and approach the enemy's defense positions. The main tasks of the covering fire are:
- Destroying enemy positions and fortifications capable of dominating the crossing areas with fire;
- Paralyzing the source of direct and indirect laying fire capable of sweeping the crossing area;
- Repulsing local counterattacks against the first wave;
- Protecting the troops' flanks;
- Laying down a smokescreen when entering and exiting the water.

Air support too will be integrated into the artillery softening up. Air support will cover the crossing area and hit targets beyond artillery range. The air effort will also be part of the concentrated destruction of the enemy's forward defense fortifications before the first assault wave crosses. At the same time, artillery fire will neutralize the enemy's air defense layout.

The crossing forces will assemble at the last possible moment. Prior to H-Hour (on the night before the operation) the troops and their equipment will concentrate in rearward assembly areas and advance to the deployment areas adjacent to the canal. The crossing will take place in daylight, at which time the forces and crossing gear will advance under cover of artillery fire.

The first-echelon troops will cross on a broad front to make it difficult for the enemy to pinpoint the direction of the primary effort, thus forcing him to disperse his reserves. Second-echelon forces will be used in sectors where the greatest progress has been made. From here they will gradually move into a narrow fighting zone, up to the enemy's defense layout.

The Egyptians' Application of the Crossing Doctrine — The Plan

After the June 1967 war and the creation of a new contact line with the Israelis, the Egyptians realized that they had to develop a combat doctrine for a water crossing. The routine activity in the Canal Zone (especially during the War of Attrition) and Egypt's war plans drafted by War Minister Fawzi called for a doctrine that would provide practical answers for the battlefield. As stated, the Egyptians turned to their time-tested benefactors, the Soviets, whose warfare doctrine contained a treasure of material adaptable to the Canal Zone.

Egypt's intense involvement was expressed in a number of ways. The vast doctrinal literature, some of which fell into Israel's hands as war booty,[51] contained details of a water obstacle crossing. This was the main subject in the training programs of many units. Most of the Egyptian army's assault echelon was geared for this mission. The Suez Canal crossing became the main subject in the training program from 1971 until October 1973, and was integrated into almost in every military exercise.

The Egyptians built training facilities deep in the country where the units practiced the technical aspects of the crossing. These facilities in Fayum and Dahashur in the Nile Valley, in Bikrash and Tel al-Kabir in the Delta, and in Katzatzin, located on the freshwater canal, provided realistic training grounds that included actual water obstacles. After the 1970 ceasefire, the Egyptians set up a training facility in the Balah Island region in the western extension of the Suez Canal. Beginning in February 1971, infantry units sent there were able to practice on the canal itself and carry out exercises in capturing the eastern bank.[52]

In addition to the training program, Egypt acquired many new types of fording equipment from the Soviet Union, including modern machinery. The Egyptians also began producing equipment for their own needs. Special units became part of the bridging brigades and took part in crossing exercises with the assault forces. Some of the equipment was moved to the canal front during the War of Attrition.

The doctrinal literature includes Egyptian army training manuals, program schedules, and especially the material taught in the military academies.[53] This material proved extremely useful. Another important publication was Order No. 41, issued by the Egyptian chief of staff, Shazli, in March 1973, which contained details of the crossing operation.[54]

The introduction to the training brochure[55] discusses the Egyptians' need to learn the subject. The authors emphasize that "the preparation of the commanders, headquarters, and units for breaking through the Suez Canal and consolidating the bridgeheads on the east bank should be considered the most important task given to the armed forces in actively readying for operations."

The document states that the Suez Canal is a complex water obstacle whose breakthrough will require surmounting many problems and securing temporary bridgeheads on the eastern bank in order to conduct a successful offensive operation.[56]

Crossing the canal

The Egyptians believe that crossing the canal was the heroic and crucial stage in the war. In his memoirs, and in his famous Order No. 41,[57] Shazli describes the crossing and construction of the bridgeheads in mostly technical-tactical terms.

Technical instructions appear in the operational orders to the troops. An abridged document[58] based entirely on the chief of staff's order was published with operational orders, the ORBAT, battle plan and timetable which stated that

• The infantry will assault the dirt embankment from boats.

• Breaches will have to be made in the embankment and landing areas prepared on both shores. This will take five to seven hours from the start of the attack.

• Ferries can be employed after the embankment is breached and landing areas on the near shore prepared.[59] This may be possible two hours after the start of the attack.

• Ferries may be used to transfer vehicles and artillery after landing areas have been prepared on the far shore. This may be possible five to seven hours after the start of the attack.

• Once a bridge is in place, every type of vehicle and tank can cross it, seven to nine hours after the start of the attack.

Based on this timetable, the division planned to cross in two main groups (*majmu'ot*), the first consisting of infantry and all the weapons, ammunition, and equipment they can carry (partially with carriages), and the second consisting of tanks, heavy weapons, and various kinds of vehicles.

The first crossing called for 32,000 troops[60] in twelve waves to proceed according to the following plan:

• Four waves of first echelon battalions. The first wave would be comprised of first-echelon companies and observation officers for 82-millimeter mortars and artillery batteries; the second wave would be made up of second-echelon companies and infantry battalion headquarters; the third wave would bring up the support weapons, recoilless guns, heavy machine guns, and mortars; the fourth wave would transfer the ammunition for the support weapons.

• Four waves of second-echelon battalions: The fifth wave — second echelon battalions; the sixth — command centers of the first echelon brigades; the seventh and eighth waves — the division's forward headquarters.

• Four waves of second echelon brigades: The ninth wave would slice through the first-echelon battalions of the second-echelon brigades; the tenth wave would bring over the brigades' forward headquarters, and the remainder second-echelon battalions.

The second group (*majmu'a*) had a six-stage list of priorities[61]:

• First — tanks, antitank companies, 120-millimeter mortar batteries, communications vehicles, and jeeps (approximately 200 tanks and 750 other vehicles);

• Second priority — ammunitions carriers for the weapons already across, field artillery, and intermediate-sized cannons with one round of ammunition (approximately 700 vehicles);

• Third priority — vital administrative equipment at the infantry battalions' echelon (approximately 600 vehicles);

• Fourth priority — administrative elements at the brigade level (approximately 400 vehicles);

• Fifth priority — administrative elements at the divisional level (approximately 250 vehicles);

• Sixth priority — other vehicles; troop transports only if the progress of the battle permits them to be used (approximately 800 vehicles).

Each of the five divisions that crossed the canal used the following fording equipment:

• One hundred and forty-four "NDL-10" assault boats;
• TPP (heavy floatation) bridges;
• PMP foldable floatation bridge made of truck-transportable parts;
• Three ferry bridges capable of sustaining fifty ton loads;
• Four amphibious mobile bridges (apparently GSP amphibious ferries);
• Four-ton bridges — decoy bridges but capable of bearing lightweight vehicles[62];
• Two infantry hanging bridges;
• 288 rope ladders;
• 410 man-portable carriages.

The following timetable, dated October 5, 1973, contains the amount of minutes each mission was allotted on the first day of the crossing[63]:

• First concentrated air strike — from H-Hour minus 15 to H-Hour plus 15.

• Artillery softening up and tank-hunter crossing — from H-Hour minus 15 to H-Hour plus 38.

• First FROG missile barrage by the Luna Brigade — H-Hour minus 15.

• First artillery barrage and commencement of Thirteenth Marine Brigade crossing — from H-Hour minus 15 to H-Hour.

• Second artillery barrage and commencement of main force crossing — from H-Hour to H-Hour plus 22.

• Third artillery barrage — from H-Hour plus 22 to H-Hour plus 27.

• Fourth artillery barrage (deception) — from H-Hour plus 27 to H-Hour plus 32.

• Fifth artillery barrage — from H-Hour plus 32 to H-Hour plus 40.

- Commencement of main-force takeover of Israeli strong points (Israeli forts?) — H-Hour plus 40.
- Commencement of opening of passageways through the embankment — from H-Hour plus 60 to H-Hour plus 6 hours.
- Transfer of first-echelon brigade's forward headquarters — H-Hour plus 60.
- Transfer of first-echelon division's forward headquarters — H-Hour plus 90.
- Beginning of transfer of first-echelon battalion of the second-echelon brigades — H-Hour plus 110.
  - Second air strike — from H-Hour plus 130 H-Hour to H-Hour plus 205.
  - Transfer of second echelon — H-Hour plus 140 plus an additional three hours.
  - Ferries begin to move — H-Hour plus 230 plus an additional four hours.
  - Second missile barrage — H-Hour plus three hours.
  - Rafts enter water — H-Hour plus four to six hours.
  - Bridges enter water — H-Hour plus four to seven hours.
  - Heavy bridges put into water — H-Hour plus four to nine hours.
  - Third missile barrage — H-Hour plus six to eight hours.

The Egyptian operational plan[64] for putting the rafts in the water, building the bridges, and beginning the transfer of tanks, heavy weapons, and the higher echelons[65] was as follows[66]:

- Rafts weighing from 50 to 90 tons enter the water — H-Hour plus six hours.
- TPP heavy armor vehicle bridges — H-Hour plus eight hours.
- Four-ton decoy bridges — H-Hour plus nine hours.

The Egyptians were not sure when to make the crossing: in daylight or at nighttime. Shazli discusses the various considerations[67] and explains that until early 1972 the Egyptians preferred a nighttime crossing because of Israeli air superiority. Upon examination of the plan, he came to the conclusion that a night crossing was impractical. Thus, from mid–1972 it was decided that the first attack would be carried out under cover of darkness but the bridges would remain open during the day in order to facilitate, at a later stage, the quick reinforcement of the crossing force.[68] It will be remembered that the crossing began at noon and the bridge construction continued into the night.

Capture and Construction of the Bridgeheads — Mission Depth

The Egyptian chief of staff's Order No. 41 — a document pertaining to an infantry division crossing[69] — discusses the capture and construction of bridgeheads, which are presented as conditions for the overall crossing activity: crossing on a wide front or a surprise crossing in several areas. The bridgehead is "a land area on the distant bank that has to be captured and consolidated by our forces." It can be tactical or operative according to the need, and can absorb a battalion or reinforced division. It must enable the deployment of forces and weapons needed for conducting an offensive aimed at defeating the enemy.

The brochure presents the canal crossing and capture of the bridgeheads as an initial stage in the offensive and as an all-out attack on the Sinai Peninsula aimed at routing the enemy.[70] Air and naval forces would also be needed, in addition to field army units and reserves. Crossing the canal and securing the bridgeheads would require an effective air umbrella above the battle zone.

The forces taking part in the operation had to be coordinated, organized, and directed according to the goals, timetable, and locations designated for them, and according to a single plan under the command of a single senior officer. Therefore, the canal crossing and securing of bridgeheads had to be planned as a special operation commanded by a field marshal according to GHQ instructions.

The Egyptians' analysis of the terrain — and the roads leading from the canal area into the heart of Sinai — showed that one bridgehead had to be built in the Third Army sector and two in the Second Army sector. The study made no mention of the need to combine the armies' bridgeheads.[71] It recommended that two divisions be deployed in the southern area and three in the north, two for the primary effort in the Ismalia sector facing the Ouja road (the Ismalia-Nitzana road), and one in the Kantara sector facing the el-Arish road.[72]

The size of the bridgeheads in each sector would vary according to local needs. In the Suez region in the south, the first echelons of the two divisions that made the crossing would secure a bridgehead ten to twelve kilometers long and six to seven kilometers deep. Thus, the size of the armies' bridgeheads would be fifteen to twenty kilometers. The two divisions in the Ismalia area would consolidate smaller bridgeheads — four to six kilometers wide and three to four kilometers deep. The entire bridgehead layout would be eight to twelve kilometers.[73]

The task of securing the bridgeheads and the enemy's fortified positions inside them generally falls to a reinforced infantry division. The basic force taking part in for the operation is the well-equipped, highly trained infantry battalion. Heliborne troops may also be used for seizing mountain passes, obstructing the enemy's reserves from approaching from the rear, and supporting the attack force at the front.[74]

The length of the crossing and depth of the missions depend on a number of factors: terrain, the enemy's strength, and the warfare doctrine. The recommended length of a division's offensive front is approximately ten kilometers. As the war approaches, the length of the division's crossing sector will be reduced to six or seven kilometers.[75] The brigade's sector is approximately four kilometers. The bridgehead's depth has to allow the deployment and operation of the forces and their weapons. Because of the special nature of the Suez Canal and the conditions that might develop during the crossing, mission depth for the field army would generally be smaller than that recommended in the doctrine.[76]

The primary mission of the division making the canal crossing was the destruction of the enemy's forces, the takeover of first-echelon fortifications, and the construction of bridgeheads three to four kilometers in depth, all of this had to be accomplished by H-Hour plus 180 minutes.[77] The expansion of the bridgehead to eight kilometers in length and five kilometers in depth were to be completed by H-Hour plus 240 minutes. This task was to be carried out by infantry units from first-echelon brigades, reinforced with antitank weapons. The bridgehead depth would not be expanded until tanks and artillery moved up.[78]

The following mission would be the destruction of the enemy's first echelon, blocking counterattacks by enemy reserves, and expanding the bridgehead depth from six to eight kilometers and its length to sixteen kilometers. This mission, performed mainly by a second echelon mechanized brigade and tank battalions from the infantry brigades, would begin at H-Hour plus fifteen hours and conclude at H-Hour plus seventeen hours.[79]

The daily mission for a division reinforced with a tank brigade would be to augment the bridgehead and complete deployment at it. This mission was identical to the field army's primary mission.

The first echelon brigade's primary mission was to cross the canal, seize the distant bank, destroy the enemy's first echelon battalions, and consolidate the bridgehead at a depth of two kilometers until H-Hour plus 120 minutes. Its next mission would be similar to the division's primary mission, and its daily mission would be the establishment of the bridgehead, and to

Figure 10: A Reinforced Infantry Division at a Bridgehead (East of the Suez Canal) (According to Egyptian Chief of Staff Order No. 41, March 1973)

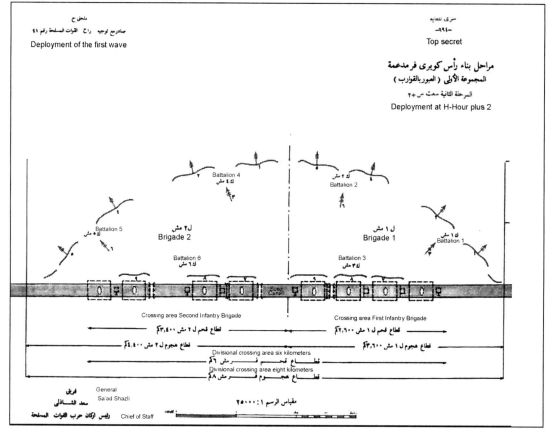

block the enemy's counterattack, destroy the enemy's second echelon forces, and augment and improve deployment at the bridgehead.

The Structure and Reinforcement of the Units Crossing the Canal

Given the expected problems and threats involved in the crossing, the assault division needed the support of air defense, combat engineers, and fording equipment.

The Egyptians learned from their exercises that an infantry battalion crossing a water barrier like the Suez Canal had to be reinforced with an artillery battalion, mortar battalion, one company of antitank missiles, one company of 85-millimeter antitank cannons, two companies of combat engineers, one platoon of light flamethrowers, and thirty fording vessels. The battalion also had to be supported with eight additional artillery battalions. A division had to be reinforced with mortars, heavy artillery, and one battalion of antitank missiles from levels above the division.

The air force had to provide two bomber or fighter squadrons to prepare for the attack and defend against Israeli air strikes. The crossing battalion required the protection of air defense: five regiments and four battalions of antiaircraft cannon, two battalions of light surface-to-air SA-7 "Strela" missiles, as well as SA-2 and SA-3 missile brigades.

Each battalion crossing the canal would be augmented with two companies of assault engineers and additional rafts, amphibious trucks, and boats. The brigade would be reinforced with up to one engineer battalion and crossing equipment; and the division would receive two combat engineer battalions, two bridging battalions and extra fording equipment. The forces engaged in the crossing would be provided, as stated, with antiaircraft units and chemical warfare defense personnel.

The battle formation crossing the canal would be identical to that of regular operations: a first echelon, second echelon, and reserves from various branches that included artillery groups, air defense units, antitank reserves, and mobile bridging units.[80] In addition, special forces (SF) would land from the sea and air for encirclement and deployment in the advancing forces' exposed flanks. At the division level SF would consist of a reinforced infantry battalion or company (or smaller unit) whose main job would be to isolate the battlefield, capture the Israeli strongholds, and securing the open areas. During the war, divisional level SF were not used.

Other units with specialized tasks would include encirclement companies (from a reinforced infantry company to a battalion) whose job would be to surround the strongholds from the exposed flanks or the gaps between them. The capture of the strongholds would be a more complex task requiring special training.

Assembly and Deployment of the Forces Designated for the Crossing

In its initial stage, the crossing operation requires the assembly and deployment of forces on the western bank. Deployment areas will be built from the defense layout and capable of absorbing units prior to the operation. Most of the troops will enter these areas one or two nights (or more) before H-Hour.[81]

The first troops to arrive will be the divisional and army group artillery forces and antitank reserves. Then the artillery groups and brigades' antitank reserves will move into position. On the eve of the attack, tanks, mobile artillery, and direct trajectory antitank missiles will enter prepared firing positions. Weapons will be camouflaged and entrenched in bunkers, emerging and opening fire only proximate to the commencement of the barrage. The tanks designated for direct support will already be on standby the night before the crossing, approximately twenty kilometers from the canal, and will advance to their jump-off points when the crossing begins.

Air defense units at the canal front will be fully prepared to protect the assault forces from air strikes, and will be deployed in firing positions to defend the forces waiting in the deployment areas, and also later when they make the crossing.

Administrative support layouts will become operational. Intelligence and chemical defense units, combat engineers, camouflage, electronic warfare, and logistical support troops will participate in the general deployment according to their missions at the time of the crossing.

The combat engineers' jobs will include breaching the dirt embankment, neutralizing obstacles (such as the incendiary systems),[82] and building and securing the bridging layouts. The Egyptians assigned specially tasked troops to bridge construction and landing craft operation during the crossing. Camouflage and deception were also among the specialized tasks. Camouflage's main function was to conceal the preparations for the crossing and the crossing itself.[83] This activity included decoys (such as fake bridges), and smoke (which was used to great effect as the Soviet doctrine recommended). Smoke screens, produced with various means — especially ground-based mechanisms[84]— hid the crossing forces, the bridges, and the newly blasted openings in the embankment.[85]

Crossing the Canal and Building the Bridgeheads

The crossing will be preceded by a heavy barrage — carried out mainly by artillery and aircraft. The aim of the barrage is to paralyze, demoralize, and eliminate enemy troops and weapons at a tactical depth, thus preventing the enemy from building organized layouts in front of the attacking forces.[86] Flat trajectory fire will also be part of the artillery barrage and will be used especially against weapons and strongholds facing the western bank. This fire will come from antitank cannons and missiles, artillery, and tanks. The air force's main targets will be strongholds, artillery positions, air defense batteries, communications facilities, and reserves — especially tank reserves — outside the range of enemy artillery.

The recommended artillery softening up was based on the experience gained in the military exercises: thirty minutes of seven-, eight-, and ten-minute volleys. The barrage would end with a massive concentration of fire at H-Hour plus two or three minutes, when the first waves were crossing. The barrage would last until the support fire for the breaching forces commenced.[87] The fire support accompanying the attacking forces would be augmented with "rolling smoke screens" and fire concentrations against selected targets according to the original fire plan and operational requirements.

The plan called for first-echelon forces of secondary units — first the companies, followed by the battalions — seizing the western bank on a wide front under cover of artillery and air support, facing the targets.[88] The first wave would reach the eastern bank and secure it until the arrival of the second wave. When the second wave reached the dirt embankment, it would advance 200 meters. Both waves were supposed to remain in their positions until the arrival of the third and fourth waves that would proceed to join the secondary units. This stage was planned to take approximately sixty minutes.[89] Reinforced with antitank weapons, flamethrowers, and engineering equipment, the assault force would advance, and seize and secure the strongholds and dirt embankments to make them safe for the rest of the troops to cross.[90]

With the transfer of first-echelon combat troops to the eastern shore, the attack would advance along the length and into the depth of the enemy's layouts in order to expand and link up the bridgeheads. This would enable intensive bridging activity to begin so that the main fighting force could be transferred to the eastern bank. The forces advancing with the support tanks, antitank teams, obstacle-laying units, antiaircraft and artillery batteries[91] would then exploit the breaches in the enemy's defenses and make quick flanking movements as unobtrusively as possible in order to consolidate deeper lines.

Once the enemy's first echelon was subdued, firepower would be directed to support the advance of the brigade and divisional reserves. While the advance in the bridgehead was in progress, the troops would have to be constantly prepared to meet and neutralize the enemy's counterattacks. Enemy reserves would have to be destroyed as early as possible, preferably when still in their assembly areas, so as to preclude their attack. Their flanks and rear should be hit while in movement, but with fire from fixed defense positions.[92] This explains why it was vital to establish and beef up the defense layout in as short a time as possible so as to enable the reinforcement and maneuverability of forces engaged in destroying the enemy.

According to the doctrine, while the bridgeheads were being strengthened, the flanks of the units that had already crossed the canal would have to be protected and the layouts had to be defended in the direction of the enemy's expected counterattacks.[93] The bridgehead would have to be reinforced with a series of in-depth defense lines. This would come about by augmenting the troops and being in coordination with antitank reserves and mobile obstacle units of all echelons.[94]

The divisional bridgehead would be built on three defense lines[95]: a first line of first-echelon reinforced battalions; a second line of second-echelon battalions, brigade antitank reserves and mobile obstacle units; a third line of general reserves — divisional antitank reserves and mobile obstacle units, and in some cases army group antitank reserves. The distance between the lines would depend on the maximum range of the antitank weapons. In other words, if the enemy penetrated one line, it would immediately be exposed to antitank fire from the next echelon. The layout had to be constructed so that it could be defended — especially with antitank fire — on all directions simultaneously.

Combat engineers would plant obstacles at the bridgeheads — mostly antitank minefields — in the direction of the enemy's expected thrust. At the same time battle positions would be set up that included command posts for directing and controlling fire, and defense layouts for soldiers, weapons, equipment, and administrative needs. Fortification construction would proceed according to a carefully prepared plan.

Fortification priority would be given to firing positions for all weapon types and to exposed trenches used by troops and headquarters. Later, other positions and trenches could be dug and provided with overhead covering. At the end of the day, sections of the trenches would be covered and command-and-control centers would be prepared in light bunkers and pillboxes. The preparation for individual and group positions (infantry), tank and artillery emplacements, and exposed lookout posts would take between five and six hours to be com-

Diagram 11: A Reinforced Infantry Division at the Bridgeheads (East of the Suez Canal)

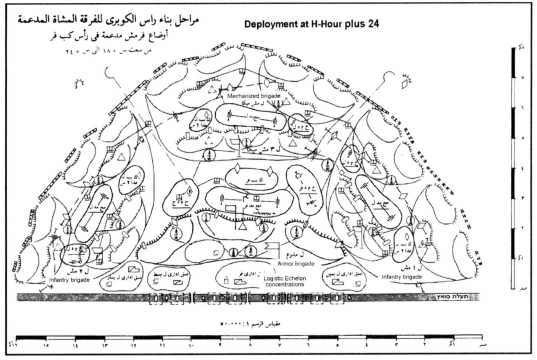

pleted. Trenches for infantry troops and artillery crews, alternative tank positions, covered observation points, and open trenches for all the troops will be prepared within ten to twelve hours. Fortification improvement will continue around the clock.

The Structure of the Stronghold and Its Capture[96]

The Egyptians' 1972 analysis[97] that was based intelligence reports refers to the IDF layout which had been rebuilt and strengthened after the August 1970 cease-fire. The study states that the IDF had more than twenty heavily fortified strongholds on the eastern bank of the canal, large enough to hold an independent company or platoon. Also, the strongholds were separated from one another by four kilometers.

All of the strongholds on the dirt embankment had bunkers and watchtowers made of reinforced concrete, tank ramps, firing slits for machine guns, communications trenches, and anti-vehicle obstacles. The stronghold was surrounded with coils of barbed wire and minefields. Protected firing positions for tanks and artillery had been built in the gaps between the strongholds along the canal.

The company-size stronghold stretched 1,200 to 1,800 meters on the front and was 800 meters wide. The platoon-size stronghold stretched 300 meters along the front and was 200 to 300 meters wide. (Some time later the Egyptians realized that the strongholds which had been strengthened during the cease-fire were considerably smaller than what was previously believed, measuring only 120 by 160 meters.)[98] The company-size strongholds contained eight to ten concrete bunkers, five to six tanks, six 120-millimeter mortars, six to nine tank positions, six to twelve antiaircraft machine guns, twelve machine-gun positions, and four antiaircraft machine-gun positions. The platoon-size stronghold contained four concrete bunkers, three tanks, the tank positions, four machine-gun positions, and two antiaircraft machine-gun positions. The bunker's size was a permanent feature, measuring two by two and half meters and protected with iron railroad tiers, concrete, and carefully camouflaged sand. The roof or upper layer was five and half meters thick.

The IDF raised a thirteen- to fifteen-meter-high dirt embankment (inclined at a forty-five degree angle) along the length of the canal. On the banks of the western side of the embankment, land mines were planted, with oil tanks and pipes hidden in them that could be ignited, transforming the canal into a blazing inferno. The embankment became one of the most formidable obstacles facing the invaders.[99]

Opinion is divided between the instruction manual (cited here) and material based on captured documents (that appears in the appendix to this book) regarding the allocation of forces in the capturing of a stronghold. A captured document which appears to have been written later than the manual attributes minor importance to the strongholds. The plan calls for outflanking the Israeli fortifications in the initial stages of the operation and capturing them later with second-echelon forces.

The manual states that a reinforced battalion must be used for capturing a company-size stronghold, and a reinforced company for taking a platoon-size fort. First and second echelons of the brigades and divisions would be assigned this task. A battalion or company given the assignment would prepare a breaching company.

According to the warfare doctrine, each company engaged in the breakthrough would be reinforced with the following strengths: one or two tank companies; artillery and antitank units; one battery of antitank missiles; one or two companies of combat engineers; one squad of amphibious vehicles; one platoon or company of light flamethrowers; one battery of mobile antiaircraft artillery; and one or two platoons of the "Strela" portable antiaircraft missile system. Later, the Egyptians made a realistic appraisal and concluded that these reinforcements were impractical since it meant apportioning twelve battalions to the Second Army's sector for this task alone[100]—another reason for the change in plans regarding the capture of the strongholds.

The manual recommends that the breaching company divide into teams according to the number of bunkers that have to be destroyed. One or two teams must be kept in reserve. The breaching team included one infantry platoon; one recoilless cannon platoon; one or two teams with machine guns and grenade launchers; one team (or platoon) of combat engineers; and one team of light flamethrowers. The teams would be equipped with demolition and mine-removal equipment, smoke bombs, and communications gear.

The breaching teams would be further divided by special tasks[101]: a clearing team, a takeover team, a covering team, and a back-up team for independent fire. The flamethrower unit would destroy enemy troops in their firing positions, trenches, and bunkers.

Regarding the capture of the strongholds, [102] once across the canal the breaching team would head to the bunkers and capture them while killing the enemy troops. This would take place with the battalion covering the teams' flanks and rear. The clearing team would move forward in the direction of the fortified bunker, clear the way through the obstacles girding the stronghold, and secure a passage for the takeover and covering teams. The takeover team would advance through the breach, enter the bunker and eliminate the enemy troops, fortified positions, and entrances and exits. The covering team would secure the breach and the takeover team's movement to the bunkers, and would block the enemy from attacking from the depth.

The Egyptian plan for capturing the IDF's defense layouts was based on three possible methods.[103] In the first, the main force would attack the gaps between the strongholds from the flanks and rear. The second would be a frontal attack (since most of the strongholds had been built at the "ideal" spots for the Egyptian canal crossing). This method demanded serious preparation: the destruction of neighboring fortresses by artillery and air strikes prior to the assault. The second method was recommended only if no alternative existed. The third method called for a simultaneous attack from the front, flanks, and rear — a combined assault by the main forces from the flanks, landed forces from the rear, and a breaching company from the front.

Later, the Egyptians seem to have devised a fourth plan of attack — bypassing most of the strongholds in the first stages of the operation and passing between them, even if this contained special problems.[104] They chose to pin down the strongholds during the crossing with artillery, mortar, and direct-line

Egyptian GSP heavy amphibious ferry, one of the best means used by the Egyptians to cross the Suez Canal (IDF Archives).

antitank and cannon fire from the front. The capture of the strongholds was put off to a later stage, when the Egyptians encircled them from the rear, strangled them, and attacked them only under the most favorable conditions for such an operation.[105]

Combat Engineer Support During an Attack — Application of the Warfare Doctrine

Engineering support is vital during an attack — especially one involving a water crossing. Wartime experience taught the Soviets the crucial role that combat engineers play in the fighting doctrine.[106] Elsewhere in the book I have discussed the combat engineer contribution to the campaign. Now I will look at the doctrine and characteristics of the engineering operation itself, as it was implemented in the Yom Kippur War according to the Egyptian offensive plan.

Egyptian PMP mobile floating bridge unit used to build the heavy bridges on the Suez Canal (IDF Archives).

Amphibious K-61 troop carrier, used by the Egyptian infantry on the first waves of the crossing of the Suez Canal.

Facing unprecedented engineering challenges, the Egyptians sought the experience of others. In July 1970 they came out with a study on the warfare doctrine entitled "Combat Engineers Assistance to Brigades and Divisions in an Offensive Campaign."[107] A comparison of the study with other material shows that the Egyptians copied and translated the Soviet source, changing the content to suit their particular needs. In my opinion, the Egyptian tacticians relied heavily on this work when they planned the Yom Kippur War.[108]

The Soviet army put great stock in the corps of engineers, rapidly expanding and developing the branch during and after World War II. The modern battlefield proved that engineer units had to be organized and integrated into most operations. In addition to the organic infantry units and armored groups, task-oriented engineering formations[109] were established for bridge building, assaults, camouflage, water supply, obstacle laying, operating mechanical equipment, and so forth.

Military engineers were

almost always in demand by the officer in charge of operations. In the final stages of the war the number of engineering units increased to the point where one or two platoons of engineers were attached to each attack and breaching battalion. The tactical density of combat engineers on the front came to four to six companies per kilometer.

The Egyptians' main engineering force — like the Red Army's — was the assault echelon. Each division had an engineering battalion[110] consisting of three companies,[111] and each brigade had one company of engineers. Altogether — six organic companies.[112]

The Egyptian engineers' roles were based on the Soviet doctrine: preparing the best conditions for an attack in a given timeframe with minimum casualties, and then participating in the effort to maintain the momentum and effectiveness of the offensive.[113]

The engineers' main tasks in an offensive battle:

• Patrolling enemy territory (mostly) in order to gather information on obstacles the assault teams were likely to encounter[114]; guiding recon units that were leading the troops into battle[115];

• Preparing assembly and deployment areas before an operation and constructing defensive layouts after the operation (building firing positions, gun emplacements, and fortified command and control posts, bulldozing roads, laying obstacles,[116] and camouflaging areas);

• Preparing corridors and breaches through natural and artificial obstacles (especially minefields)[117] in one's own territory, on the contact line, and in the enemy's layouts and rear; preparing and securing roads, protecting the forces moving through the corridors prior to, during, and after the operation;

• Participating in antitank fighting (together with the task-oriented forces) as mobile mine-laying reserves[118]; during a battle, serving as a "mobile blocking force" for obstructing roads being used by enemy armor,[119] halting the armor columns, and then destroying them[120];

• Helping consolidate the lines and supplying fighting units with fortification material.[121]

The Soviet doctrine assigned combat engineers with the job of supplying water to the troops during the fighting. Because of the harsh conditions in the desert, the Egyptians established an independent water directorate in late 1971, under the command of the GHQ quartermaster branch.

The Soviet warfare doctrine states that the preparation of the layouts prior to the war depends on the amount of time that the force has. A field army reinforced with combat engineers can prepare assembly and deployment areas and jump-off positions in a matter of days.[122] The Egyptians had seven years (from the end of the Six-Day War) to build their defense layouts along the canal. After the 1970 cease-fire, intense engineering activity could be observed on the western shores of the canal, which could have meant only one thing: the Egyptians were engaged in ground preparations for a water crossing.

The Egyptians went on a construction frenzy, building hundreds of protected firing positions for all kinds of weapons, preparing roads, erecting above-ground bridges, and paving shallow areas for vehicle crossings at the freshwater canal (west of the Suez Canal) and cement-lined descents to the waterline. Positions were set up for the front-line forces and for the reinforcements and support units taking part in the preparatory stage of the war. In addition to these positions, ramps were also constructed (elevated sites for tanks, antitank weapons, and infantry that afforded observation and firepower domination in areas overlooking the eastern bank).

Air defense positions — especially for surface-to-air missile batteries — received special attention. Some of these positions had been prepared when a huge number of missile batteries were moved forward in the last stage of the War of Attrition; the rest were built and constantly improved on up until the outbreak of the war.

The command-and-control positions with headquarters bunkers, the commanders' observation posts, protected emplacements, vehicular and communications truck parks, helipads, and defense positions in the strongholds and observation posts were all part of the defense layout in the area west of the canal and, according to the doctrine, also served as a launch base for the attack.

The road network recommended by the doctrine was part of the defense scheme, but also served the assault forces. The Soviet attack doctrine called for 500 to 600 kilometers of roads in each field army's sector. The Egyptians seem to have strictly followed this requirement, preparing a sufficient number of longitudinal roads to the canal front and latitudinal roads near the front and in the rear.

The doctrine had the combat engineers playing a major role in concealment and camouflage operations. Although most of this work is supposed to be performed by the regular fighting forces, engineering units are responsible for the more complicated aspects of the task. Camouflage is an integral part of deception and includes the masking of assembly and deployment areas and troop concentrations, and propping up dummy positions and decoy layouts. The Egyptians learned the importance of concealment in the War of Attrition. After incurring heavy losses from Israeli air strikes, they began to successfully deploy fake layouts. Egypt invested an all-out effort in the construction of dummy positions — especially air defense systems (surface-to-air missiles and antiaircraft cannon).

Every Egyptian attack plan was based on engineering solutions to overcome the enemy's defense layout — mine fields, antitank trenches, road obstacles, and barbed-wire fences. Each division had an engineering unit annexed to it and breaching equipment for making a number of permanent breakthroughs that would facilitate the troops' advance to their objectives. The canal's specific parameters — width, depth, shoreline gradient, and embankment dimensions — transformed it into an extremely tricky obstacle to cross. The Egyptians referred to it as the most demanding, complex obstacle ever placed before an advancing army.

Later in this chapter I will discuss the specific solution that the Egyptians applied in the crossing operation, but at this point it may be said that the crossing and immediate breakthrough succeeded mainly because of the outstanding efforts made by the combat engineers, bridging units, and rest of the troops.

The engineers were also responsible for constructing the defense layouts against enemy counterstrikes after the attack phase of the war was completed.[123] In addition to fortifying the defense line, the combat engineers had to set up obstacles on their front and flanks, and prepare a road network on the eastern side of the canal for their reserve units that would be meeting the expected Israeli counterattack. The engineers were also ordered to lay minefields on the defense layout front and flanks.

The Egyptian chief of staff's instructions for organizing the crossing and bridgehead construction[124] also contains a large chapter on mining. Minefields should not be laid while the bridgeheads are being established or they might get in the way the advancing forces. Minefields should be emplaced only when an IDF armored counterattack is imminent or when errors or delays have occurred in bridging operations. In such cases — and only if four to six hours have elapsed from the time of the crossing — would minefields be planted in front of the infantry forces assigned to blocking the attack.[125]

Mine-laying was planned for the first stage of the bridgehead construction, before tanks and antitank cannons arrived. Mines would be strewn on the ground (and only in special cases buried) so that friendly forces would not detonate them in their advance east.

Once the bridgeheads were in place and the shift to a defensive stance made, the minefields would be laid according to standard practice. Mines that had been hastily planted in the first stages of the attack would be carefully unearthed or detonated and their exact number recorded so as to prevent accidental detonation by friendly forces.[126]

Much of the Egyptian document deals with the transfer of mines across the canal and through the embankment to the bridgehead. According to the chief of staff's general instructions, first-echelon infantry companies and battalions were forbidden to carry the mines with them since lightness and mobility had to be maintained at all costs. Each second-echelon infantry squad would carry fourteen mines — two mines per soldier.[127] If this number was kept, each first-echelon brigade would bring 630 mines with it and each second-level brigade 1,134, so that each infantry division would be in the possession of 2,394 mines on the eastern bank.[128] Back-up units would transfer additional mines to the front-line units.

A separate chapter in the chief of staff's instructions discusses the role combat engineers would play in laying mines in areas where an enemy attack was brewing. This mining reserve would be a key element in the antitank forces. In effect, it would serve as a mobile force responsible for intercepting and destroying the Israeli counterattack.[129] Each brigade would have a company-sized, mobile mine-laying unit attached to it, loaded with 1,200 mines. Minefields would be planted at a ratio of one mine per meter (1,200 square meters per brigade).

The first waves also brought mines across with them, which were used extensively at the bridgeheads and on the routes of the expected IDF counterattacks. Many IDF casualties, especially in the first days of the fighting, were caused by Egypt's effectively placed mines.

The combat engineers had two additional assignments (that Egyptian planners and troops had little need to concern themselves over): preparing roads for the advancing units and supporting the field army's second echelon in carrying out its mission. The Soviets, with their vast experience in large-scale war zones, had specially tasked engineering units paving and improving road networks during the fighting. In the Yom Kippur War, the Egyptian field armies' need to advance was limited since almost all of the fighting took place at a shallow depth at the bridgeheads. These conditions, along with the relatively complex road network the IDF had paved east of the "Bar-Lev Line," freed Egypt's combat engineers from having to deal with such problems.

The Incendiary Pipeline — "Or Yikarot" ("Bright Light")

One special engineering problem that the Egyptians had to deal with was the "Or Yikarot" incendiary pipe system. This was the name of the system that the IDF had devised for

The author on the Suez Canal East Bank during the trial run of "Or Yikarot," February 1971.

flooding the Suez Canal with inflammable liquid opposite expected launching areas and igniting the water during an Egyptian crossing attempt.

The system was installed in a number of places on the eastern bank in the last stages of the War of Attrition. As war appeared on the horizon, the Egyptians took the threat very seriously, investing much time and effort in figuring how to overcome it. Engineering commandos and construction specialists reconnoitered the canal to locate and examine the system. Their conclusion was that the inflammable pipeline's effectiveness had been grossly exaggerated.

Shazli refers[130] to the system as one of the major problems that the Egyptians had to surmount prior to the crossing. He says "Or Yikarot" — Israel's secret weapon — was capable of transforming the canal into a flaming sea.

The Soviet warfare doctrine was carefully studied. The Egyptians undertook intense activity to find a way to neutralize the system. They even classified the relatively simple system "an unconventional weapon." A 1972 study published by the Nasser Higher Military Academy on chemical and biological weapons[131] devoted a whole chapter to "Bright Light." In addition to the fear of other secret weapons, the study stressed the need to defend against various types of inflammable materials — especially against burning liquid on the canal. "It is vital to remember the enemy's ability to install an incendiary obstacle on the Suez Canal by spreading oil-based materials across the water and igniting them when the crossing begins."[132]

The document estimated that "at the start of the crossing operation the enemy may be capable of discharging crude oil onto the water and setting it on fire. These fire-screens could present serious difficulties during the crossing, and, based on reliable estimates of the enemy's crude oil supply in the strongholds he should have enough reserves for no more than two to three hours of burning. Therefore we should carry out feints and deceptions in order to encourage the enemy to ignite the canal and deplete his oil supply before the main crossing. This will neutralize his ability to create lengthy fire-screens."

Shazli, who credited himself with many technological solutions, has a short chapter on them in his book.[133] He claims that the engineers brought a "rough idea" to him in June 1971. The idea called for protectively clad firefighters putting the flames out. Another proposal entailed the formation of amphibious fire-fighting units. Shazli rejected both ideas when he realized that the best way to fight the inflammable system was to obstruct the enemy from using it in the first place. He ordered the oil pipes to be blocked or blown up, and the reservoirs sabotaged or destroyed by artillery.

The Israelis captured several operational plans dealing with two types of solutions to this problem.[134]

The IDF installed a number of such systems underneath the dirt embankment but due to various shortages and shortcomings, the whole idea was shelved. On February 28, 1971,[135] an experiment was made to inflame the canal which, it was hoped, would serve as a warning to the Egyptians not to dare attempt a crossing.

In practice only two facilities remained barely operational: one in Hizayon (an Israeli stronghold) near the Firdan Bridge; and the other in Matzmed, in the vicinity of the Deversoir Crossing (where two of the system's operators were taken prisoner).

Egyptian reconnaissance teams located approximately twenty such systems (fourteen opposite the Second Army, and eight across from the Third Army). Egyptian intelligence estimated that the facilities had become ineffective and inoperative since late 1971 when their maintenance was abandoned.[136] This estimate was apparently accurate. Most of the systems had been plugged up and destroyed during the intensive fortification activity and elevation of the dirt embankment immediately after the August 1970 cease-fire went into effect.

Egyptian combat-engineer recon teams were dispatched to check the installations (excluding those built inside the strongholds) and reported back that the systems were merely decoys.

One report[137] describes the system (apparently a decoy) in the following manner: "A pair of pipes two inches in diameter lying four meters apart. The pipes are buried in the mud; no napalm drums behind them. The other end of the pipes is buried in a flat area of unknown content."

The report[138] sums up its estimate stating that the enemy has probably given up on the system after the experiment failed but has kept it in place as a deception and psychological deterrent. The author of the report adds: "After verifying that most of the incendiary facilities deployed outside the strongholds were decoys, then in the worst case scenario only those inside the strongholds might be operable."[139]

Gamasi mentions the flammable installations and gives high marks to the Israelis for the technological surprise that could have had been a decisive factor in delaying the Egyptian offensive, inflicting heavy losses, and even preventing the crossing in a number of sectors.[140]

He also lauds Egyptian intelligence's ability to gather information on the facilities, but he forgets to mention their assessment: that most of the system was a merely a decoy. He accepts the descriptions of the heroism Egyptian commandos displayed in neutralizing the facilities on the day before the war. The Egyptian version presented for public consumption describes how commando teams cemented the pipe openings on the night before the war, thus blocking their use.[141] In an interview published in May 1975 Gamasi refers again to the Egyptian commando mission.[142] I found no evidence that such an operation ever took place.[143]

Shazli knew that most of the system was a decoy and that its effectiveness was extremely limited.[144] He disagreed with the Israelis whom he claims denied that such a system existed because they were "un-gentlemanlike," and he attributes their non-use to his credit. He repeatedly praises[145] the engineering recon teams who, on the night before the attack, checked whether the inflammable liquid pipes had been blocked, and he presents the information that they returned with as an outstanding Egyptian victory.

What we see here, then, is another incident that both sides claim to have detailed information on and that each uses for its own interests.

Breaching the Embankment

In addition to standard engineering activity, Egyptian combat engineers had to carry out the difficult task of breaching the dirt embankment which the IDF planners had buttressed. During the War of Attrition — and especially during Sadat's "Year of Decision" — and parallel to the Egyptians' ground preparations for the crossing, the IDF embarked upon a massive engineering operation: elevating the dirt embankment.

Bulldozers added tons of sand to the earthwork, creating a giant wall that was intended to prevent the crossing force from gaining a toehold on the eastern bank, and impede any attempt at scaling the rampart or employing mechanical equipment to prepare landing areas.[146]

The Egyptian engineers who dealt with this obstacle struggled to come up with a solution. They had to find a way to open corridors through the enormous mound[147] without which it would be impossible to establish bridges and transfer equipment to the bridgehead sites. Experiments with dynamite proved ineffective. According to Shazli, opening a breach would require 225 kilograms of dynamite, sixty men and one bulldozer working under concentrated fire for five to six hours.[148]

Finally, a young engineer came up with a brilliant idea for breaking through the embankment: blasting out a corridor with high-powered water hoses whose energy would be supplied from on-board pumps using the canal's water. In June 1971— even before the cease-fire went into effect — a successful experiment was carried out. British and German pumps were capable of cutting a hole in the dirt barrier within two hours (if not under enemy fire).[149]

When the war broke out, the first troop waves included combat engineer platoons[150] and water pumps. Work began in about seventy locales.[151] The engineers operating the "water cannons" used 350 pumps and blasted out thirty corridors in a matter of hours.[152] In a detailed report of events between of 18:30 and 20:30 on the first day (i.e., until H-Hour plus 6), the chief of staff noted the difficulty entailed in this engineering feat but that sixty breaches had been made in various sectors. The Third Army, however, encountered muddy soil in its southern sector which delayed[153] bridge construction and slightly delayed the entire crossing operation.

Defense of the Bridgeheads — The Warfare Doctrine and Its Application

The Egyptian warfare doctrine, like the conventional Soviet doctrine, was based on the belief that victory on the battlefield is gained only from an attack, that defense is a temporary tactic[154] to be employed only when absolutely necessary. A defensive posture may be taken at the beginning, middle, or end of an operation depending on developments on the battlefield. Generally, the aim is to block the enemy's superior forces, inflict heavy casualties, retain vital areas, and create optimal conditions for implementing the crucial offensive.[155]

Egyptian military planners of the Yom Kippur War viewed the defense of the bridgeheads on the eastern bank — like the crossing stage — as a sine qua non for attaining victory.[156] They planned the crossing to be launched from fixed defense layouts on the western bank, followed by the layout's transfer to the eastern side where it would seize vital territory in order to block Israel's armored counterattack and inflict heavy losses.[157] By implementing a two-staged maneuver — a crossing and immediate shift to the defense — Egyptian military leaders hoped to establish optimal conditions on the ground for political negotiations that would achieve greater territorial gains than whatever an attack into Sinai's interior might gain.

A number of doctrinal defense missions are required, depending on the particular situation: defense of territory, as stated, is designated, first and foremost, to repulse enemy attacks. Egypt had been preparing its army since 1967 to defend the western bank because of the fear that Israeli would seize additional land in an attack, this time in Egypt proper. The Egyptian layouts were built to meet other defense needs as well, such as gaining time so that Egyptian forces could be assembled to block an attack and establish deployment bases for troop concentrations and a canal crossing, and then advance into the peninsula.

Egyptian bridgehead planning envisioned additional goals that would be gained from a defensive battle. These included securing objectives seized at the time of the crossing and ensuing attack; protecting the bridgeheads and the flanks of the assault forces; and most importantly, repelling a counterattack by the enemy's superior armored forces. Egypt's defense layouts on the eastern bank were not intended to answer another doctrinal need, providing cover for a withdrawal. The Egyptian planner based the campaign on achieving short-term objectives. There was no place for a retreat from the bridgeheads back to the western bank. Furthermore, such a maneuver was so complex as to render it conceptually and physically impractical.

The combat missions of the troops on the defense line included destroying the enemy in his deployment area and attack preparations; repelling an assault against the forward line; and destroying enemy forces that penetrate the defense layout. For these missions to succeed, Egypt's defense had to be stable and dynamic.[158]

Stability is attained when the defense layout is based on a number of echelons, deployed in depth, especially along the expected route of the enemy attack, that exploit the terrain for digging in and establishing cover from enemy fire and protection for the flanks. Firepower also plays an important role in creating defensive stability. Stability is further gained when firepower, consisting mainly of cannons and mortars, can be fluidly transferred to various quadrants on the battlefield and integrated into the obstacle layout.

A defense layout is most effective when it continuously hammers away at the enemy's troops by maneuvering, delivering deadly counterstrikes, and employing massive firepower especially in the critical sectors. Artillery and antiaircraft systems are also of key importance in preparing a dynamic defense layout just prior to the attack.

The shift to the defense can take place in two basic situations — in close contact with the enemy or without contact with the enemy. In close contact that the Egyptians predicted would happen at the bridgeheads, the shift to defense was made under the pressure of fire and enemy attacks that had to be thrown back while the defensive layout was being deployed.

The field army's first- and second-echelon divisions and brigades could defend the length of a "regular-sized or broad front." The difference in area would influence the defense's effectiveness. When the enemy's main effort was about to be made in crucial sectors, a division would generally be deployed in two echelons in order to provide greater stability to the operation. The defense of a broad front required close deployment of the troops in secondary sectors only when there was a shortage of troops. Under these circumstances, brigades and divisions would be deployed in a single echelon, and a reserve force built in the rear.

The Egyptians planned to build the bridgeheads east of the canal at a standard width. The canal's length, where five infantry divisions would operate, enabled regular deployment. (Each division was reinforced with an additional armored brigade). This ORBAT allowed a reinforced mechanized brigade to be assigned to the bridgehead and, in most cases, on the main defense route, both sides of which were protected by infantry brigades. The armored brigade and a divisional tank battalion were deployed in the second echelon and created the required depth without the need of building an improvised special reserve force.

The Egyptian warfare doctrine, like the Soviet one, perceived the infantry division as the field army's first echelon. All of these divisions were transferred to the eastern bank. The mechanized and armored divisions — most of which were ordered to reinforce the infantry divisions with an armored brigade — remained in the layouts on the western bank as the field army's second echelon. The near-total separation between the two echelons did not permit the divisions to engage in counteroffensive activity. The Egyptian army apparently had no plans for an in-depth offensive campaign or the use of mobile divisions — mechanized and armored — as a task force for counterstrikes at the bridgeheads.

Defense would take place on a "strip" where first echelon divisions — usually infantry — were deployed. The frontline strip would be protected with covering forces while second-echelon divisions deployed in the rear of the second defense strip. Each defense strip would have a division spread out in three or four defense layouts.

For many years the Egyptian infantry divisions had been organized and strengthened in a defensive strip on the western bank. Some of the mechanized and armored divisions were parked in the rear of the defense strip in a relatively light state of protection. According to the defense plan "Amalia 200," the divisions would move out of these deployment areas and create a strategic depth on the main penetration roads leading to the delta, and join the field armies in the counterattack on the front's main defense line. After the crossing, the assault divisions created a first defense strip on the eastern bank. The main defense line was composed of an almost continuous connection of bridgeheads. The mechanized and armored divisions remaining on the eastern bank formed the second defense strip, while employing some of the layouts on the western side that had served the first-echelon infantry divisions for many years.

The length of the defense sector depends on the division's mission, the importance of the route it has to defend, the nature of the terrain, and the enemy's estimated defensive strength. A battalion is the standard used for determining the length of a breaching sector. A two-echelon infantry or mechanized battalion is deployed in a sector four to five kilometers in length and approximately two kilometers deep. The deployment of a one-echelon battalion is expanded by approximately five kilometers and its depth reduced to one or one and half kilometers. The two-echelon infantry or mechanized brigade is deployed in a sector measuring seven to eight kilometers in length and in equal depth. If a one-echelon brigade is deployed, the length of the sector may reach up to fifteen kilometers, but its depth will be narrowed to five. A three-brigade, one-echelon infantry division is deployed in a sector twelve to fifteen kilometers long and up to fifteen kilometers in depth. A one-echelon division will fan out in a sector up to thirty kilometers in length, but this will take place only in secondary sectors (at the level of a second-echelon field army, along the coast, or when there is a serious shortage of troops).

Many different forces are deployed in a divisional defense layout in a kind of combat array. These forces may include the following task-oriented troops: a divisional artillery group, brigade groups, antiaircraft units, antitank reserves, a mobile obstacle-laying force (including minefields), reserves from other branches (such as chemical engineers), and commando teams that act as covering forces in the protective strip or forward layout.[159]

Most of Egypt's artillery groups and antiaircraft units remained on the western bank where they assisted the troops at the bridgeheads. Antiaircraft weapons provided an air umbrella for the forces on the opposite shore. The main reinforcements for the troops on the eastern bank were deployed in the antitank layout. A considerable portion of this task force was integrated into the first echelon combat layouts. Additional antitank units served in advanced positions as tank hunters for the covering forces because there was no room to build a protective strip at the bridgeheads. Only a small number of antitank units—those equipped with cannons rather than missiles—remained in reserve in the layout's center.[160]

A division that has been set up in the defense strip will build a defense area made up of a number of elements, the main ones being the defense layout themselves. Three or four defense layouts can be established in a divisional sector, with first-echelon brigades securing the first and second layouts, and second-echelon brigades maintaining the third layout and sometimes the fourth. Layout depth of infantry battalions is approximately two kilometers.

The Egyptian units at the bridgeheads were deployed in two divisional echelons, according to the importance of the defense sector.[161] The assault divisions' original brigades—the mechanized brigade and two infantry brigades—were deployed at the bridgehead, each of them in two brigade-level echelons. The armored brigade that reinforced each of the assault divisions was responsible for the divisional second-echelon defensive close to the eastern bank. An independent divisional tank battalion was deployed to the rear of the forward brigade echelons—between them and the tank brigade—as the division's reserve force.[162]

The role of the first-echelon division: to repulse attacks on the forward line and prevent the enemy from penetrating the center of the layout. Together with its primary mission, the first echelon was supposed to cause the enemy heavy losses, retain vital areas, and prepare a counterattack for the headquarters level above it.[163] This echelon would be reinforced with antitank weapons, combat engineers, and artillery. First-echelon battalions of infantry and mechanized brigades would also be reinforced with tanks from the brigade's tank battalion (the rest of the brigade's tanks at this echelon would remain concentrated in the second echelon or with the brigade's reserves).[164] The Egyptians knew that their tanks were inferior to the IDF's. This is why they preferred to employ antitank missiles at the first echelon. The Egyptians' use of tanks at this echelon was negligible. Tanks were transferred to the eastern bank only in the later stages of the offensive, and generally only after the bridges were in place.

The role of the second-level divisions: to block the enemy that penetrated the first-echelon layouts, prevent him from carrying out a flanking maneuver, and eliminate him with firepower and counterattacks. In the Yom Kippur War this echelon consisted of tank brigades that were attached to the infantry division, and was deployed on the eastern bank in the final stages of the crossing. During the war, it was not used in the static defensive battle but in a counterattack against the IDF's thrust to the canal (before it succeeded in crossing to the western bank).

In addition to the defense echelons, artillery groups in the division and brigade will also be in the defense layout. These groups need to have the independent use of firepower during the fighting. Organic artillery units in the brigades and divisions will be reinforced as much as possible by second-level units, reserves, and higher levels. Every first-echelon, defensive infantry battalion will be allocated up to one artillery battalion. The divisional artillery group will be deployed between the first and second layouts, as well as in the second layout itself.

The Egyptians at the bridgeheads will receive artillery support, but the main artillery force will remain in its positions and generally stay within the radius of its ranges.

The division's antiaircraft defense will be reinforced with extra antiaircraft battalions from the rear. The antiaircraft guns will defend frontline first-echelon units, artillery concentrations, command bunkers, and reserve forces.

Egypt's air defense in the Yom Kippur War was carried out mainly by surface-to-air missile units that were part of the air defense system. These units usually operated from well-protected positions on the western bank where they provided an air defense umbrella for all the forces at the bridgeheads. Only a few antiaircraft missile batteries crossed the canal in the later stages of the war.

According to the doctrine, Egyptian defense on the western bank had to have a superior antitank capability in order to diminish the need for antitank reserves as an independent layout. Instead of using these reserves to intercept and destroy IDF tanks that penetrated the Egyptian defense layout, the bridgeheads were heavily guarded with antitank weapons (including missiles) along their entire length and flanks. Less modern antitank reserves replaced the antitank cannon batteries that had been deployed between divisional and brigade echelons and in their flanks.

According to the warfare doctrine, a mobile obstacle-laying force must be established. Its job would be to plant mines and create improvised obstructions during the fighting. This force, consisting of combat engineer platoons at the brigade level and sapper companies at the divisional level, was planned to protect deployment areas where the Egyptian counterattacks would emanate from by sowing minefields on the enemy's routes of attack. The force was used both independently and in coordination with the antitank-tank reserves.

Various levels of obstacle-laying forces became an integral part of the bridgeheads' defense.[165] Mines were planted in the first stages of the bridgeheads' construction and on expected routes of attack by the IDF. The reserve forces planted mines in the advanced stages of layout strengthening and when IDF troops began their push west for the canal crossing.

Hasty Bridgehead Defense

The Soviet warfare doctrine considers defense tactics as temporary missions until the attack can be resumed. During the attack, defensive measures are also considered as short-termed moves necessary for quickly organizing a defense.[166] The final stages of an improvised defense might look like the initial stages of an organized defense layout.

The authors of the Soviet warfare doctrine perceived the improvised defense (like the one at the Egyptian bridgeheads) as a more prevalent form of defense than the organized one. The main problem was creating it while in contact with the enemy, since this left no time for solid, carefully arranged deployment.[167]

The need to protect the deployed forces' depth, echelons, and layouts could become compromised because of battle conditions. Here too an effort had to be made to use the terrain to the best advantage for defense, even at the cost of retreat in certain limited areas. Layouts are generally chosen because of their suitability to renewing the attack rather than perpetuating the defense. It is difficult, if not impossible, to set up a protective screen in this defense area. Even if such an echelon was established, it would be much shallower than in an organized defense layout.

Protection and use of the reserves is one of the basic features of the hastily set up defense layout. The reserves will be based mainly on mobile forces prepared to carry out many tasks, such as reinforcing the layouts, intercepting the enemy, counterattacking, and defending the rear.

Obstacles and minefields set up on the front and in the depth will be relatively limited in scope. The use of mobile obstacle-dispersing forces is critical, and maximum use will be made of them along with antitank defenses. These are the key elements in the defense layout, especially when employed in conjunction with mobile antitank reserves.

The defense will have support and assistance layouts integrated into it. The artillery will be ready to assist the static defense and counterattack, shelling the enemy's artillery as a preparatory move. Artillery will also protect the main forces in the layout, employing static and mobile fire screens and concentrating firepower on selected targets. Air defense will be integrated into the defensive force; combat engineers will strengthen positions, put up obstacles, prepare roads, and carry out acts of deception. Chemical and electronic warfare layouts, and support alignments for command-and-control centers will be integrated into the defense layout. Logistical assistance will remain mainly in an offensive formation. An all-out effort will be made to prepare these units for an offensive.

The Egyptians established a hasty defense layout at the bridgeheads that answered almost all of the needs foreseen in the warfare doctrine. The transfer of the layout to the east side of the canal enabled the Egyptians to quickly organize (and accomplish) all of the tasks. Moreover, the Egyptians' near-total success in destroying the IDF's counterattack in the initial stages of the Yom Kippur War resulted in their consolidation in western rim of Sinai — an achievement that would eventually be translated into political gains on the negotiating table.

Figure 12: The Antitank Plan in the Second Infantry Brigade's (Nineteenth Division) Frontline Layouts First-Echelon Brigade Deployment — Battalion Layout

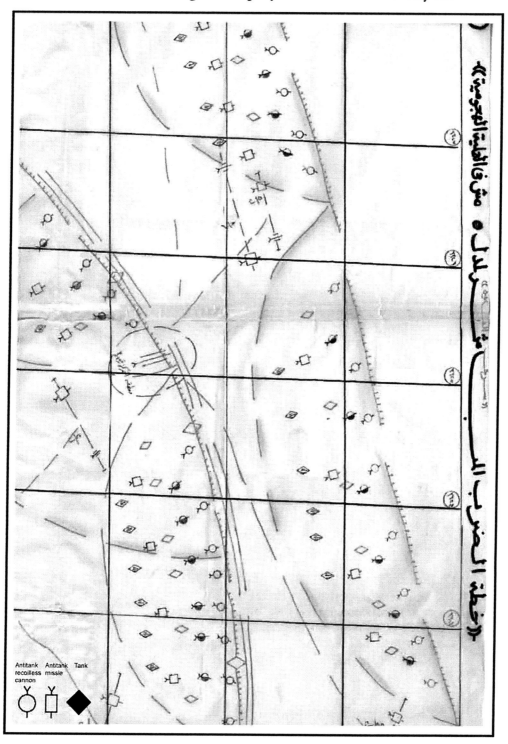

The Antitank Layout — The Answer to Israel's Armor Superiority

The use of antitank weapons by the Arabs — especially the Egyptians — is regarded as one of the main innovations of the Yom Kippur War. In an article on the Soviet argument in favor of antitank warfare, the British historian Phillip Karber compares the infantry's employment of antitank missiles for knocking out tanks to the fourteenth-century tactical innovation in the Battle of Laufen. In 1339, a small group of Swiss soldiers, armed only with bayonets, outfought armor-clad knights by pulling them off their horses. This tactic opened a new period in the history of warfare.[168]

The two aggressor armies in Yom Kippur War — Egypt and Syria — acted according to the Soviet warfare doctrine. Defense in general and antitank defense in particular were planned down to the last detail. Since armor was the main tactic that Israel was expected to throw against an attack, antitank weapons became the Arab assault forces' — especially the Egyptians,' basic defense at the bridgeheads, and in their deployment against the Israeli counterattack. The Soviet doctrine held that antitank warfare should be based on secondary layouts that included static and mobile alignments. Well aware of their inferior maneuverability, the Egyptians developed their antitank defense mostly on a static layout. Over the years they had reinforced the layout, according to doctrinal recommendations, with troop concentrations and task-oriented weapons in strongholds, localities, and the dominating terrain inside infantry layouts. These layouts were made up primarily of antitank weapons. The Egyptians cleverly responded to the Israeli threat by dispersing the concentrations in almost equal proportion along the defense lines.

Nevertheless, according to the Soviet doctrine, antitank reserves also had to be set up at the brigade, divisional, and field-army levels. These were mobile infantry units employed to defend the flanks, block counterattacks during the offensive, and reduce the enemy's ability to wage a defensive battle.

The Arabs' solution to Israel's armored superiority was to develop and train on a massive scale highly sophisticated antitank forces on both fronts (in addition to the relatively large number of Egyptian and Syrian tanks).[169]

These formations were made of various units: antitank commando teams, battalion-level antitank batteries, brigade-level antitank companies, and divisional, field-army, and GHQ antitank battalions. The assault units also included numerous antitank formations from other units. Most of the task-oriented units were equipped with antitank missiles (usually "Sagers," or, as NATO termed them, AT-3s) carried on foot or transported by special vehicle[170]; personal rocket launchers — especially RPG-7s; antitank cannons (usually 85- or 100-millimeter dual-purpose guns); recoilless cannons; and even obsolete assault cannons used for reinforcing the western canal front.

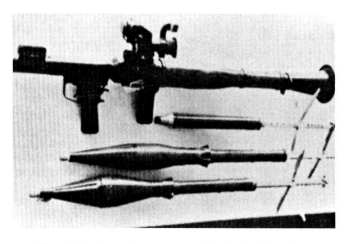

The R.P.G.-7, used very successfully by the Egyptian commandos and infantry on the front of their bridgeheads, on the east side of the Suez Canal.

During and after the war — and especially on the canal front —

the antitank Sager missile was used massively on the forward contact line. This was Egyptian knockout punch against Israel's armor superiority.[171]

Although the missiles caught Israel totally by surprise, they should not have surprised anyone. According to Lt. Col. Zvi Lanir, an Israeli military historian, immediately after the Six-Day War the Egyptians began looking for an answer to Israeli armor's superior maneuverability and firepower which had inflicted so bitter a defeat on the Egyptians. The solution was to equip infantry units with a preponderance of antitank missiles and adapt the combat doctrine to their capabilities. Before the Six-Day War, Egypt obtained antiquated "Shmel" antitank missiles. During the War of Attrition it procured the newer, more effective Sager missiles (in Russian: "Malyutka") and, like the Syrians, employed them on a number of occasions at the end of the War of Attrition in 1970. Lanir claims that the IDF intelligence branch kept close tabs on this development and issued warnings about the new antitank missile. Its technical profile was collected, its operating system analyzed, and IDF units received an updated report that included the missile's technical details, methods of operation, and estimated quantity. To the best of my knowledge, and I concur with the Agranat Commission's conclusion, these reports failed to present the battlefield implications of Arab antitank weapons in a major war. At any rate, if such an assessment existed, it did not filter down to the units.

East of the Suez Canal, where the Egyptian defense was based mainly on Sager missiles, the weapon is perceived by both the combatants and students of the war as the biggest surprise of the Yom Kippur War.[172]

RPG-7 rocket launchers were also used massively by infantry (regular and mechanized) units, and SF (commandos and paratroopers). The missiles were an integral part of the antitank screen that was generally deployed in forward positions, and they succeeded in crippling IDF tanks and halting their advance.

The Egyptians realized that Israel's armor superiority posed a major problem for the bridgeheads on the east bank. Therefore they viewed their antitank layout — its organization, training, and deployment — as a key element in their war plan.[173]

Defense Against Tanks — The Doctrine

The Soviet warfare doctrine that the Egyptian and Syrian armies adopted considered the destruction of enemy tanks to be of crucial importance in a defensive battle.[174] Since the tanks are the main fighting force in a modern offensive, meeting their challenge became one of defense's main goals. Since the optimal solution to the tank threat was an antitank defense, antitank units became an organic part of all defensive formations.

The relative growth of armor in the ground forces allowed for the dispersion of antitank units among all defense branches. This tactic altered the traditional concept of the antitank forces as the main element in the defense layouts — a concept prevalent in Soviet thinking in the sixties — excluding a few cases. Antitank defense became an organic part of the entire defense layout. According to the *Dictionary of Military Terms* (1966 edition), antitank defense is the essence of defense, therefore it forms the basis of the defense layout in all units and formations.[175] In other words, modern defense can only succeed if it is capable of blocking the enemy's armored punch.[176] Doing away with independent antitank defense layouts (and the doctrinal demand that every stronghold and defense locality is capable of withstanding an armored attack) are the outstanding signs of this change.

Instead of a defense in which all of the weapons are classified according to two basic categories (static weapons and antitank missiles),[177] they were divided up among the defense layouts, with some of them remaining as antitank reserves if the battlefield development required their involvement, while the tank units played the main tactical role and generally functioned as reinforcements under the command of a brigade, division, or field army. They were planned for use in the entire defense area and, according to their echelon, for strengthening the layouts and counterattacking between the echelon layouts beneath them. The idea behind this was that while antitank and tank reserve activity in the defense was planned, it could also be used for battlefield contingencies.

In addition to preserving flexibility in the use of mobile forces, the Egyptians also wanted to prepare an infrastructure that would provide them with advantages during encounters with the enemy. This infrastructure was made up mostly of "lines of fire" — a network of positions for a tank company or battalion, or for a platoon or battery of antitank missiles. The lines were usually dug in dominating areas so as to allow fire superiority at relatively long ranges.

The time and place for employing the reserves would be decided by the commander, depending on the enemy's offensive moves. The reserves' main function was to take part in the counterattack which was designed to block the enemy's advance and enable the level of command in charge of the attack to destroy the enemy.

The doctrine also recommended the density of antitank fire relative to the defended area — in order to guarantee the destruction of at least half of the attacking armored forces, on the assumption that inflicting heavy losses would halt the offensive. It was of prime importance that fire intensity be attained in the defense layout's front facing the expected routes of the enemy's attack.

Along with the doctrinal changes, there was also technological development. The Red Army discovered the inherent hidden potential of antitank missiles,[178] and was actually one of the first armies in the world to develop and use missiles mounted on armored combat vehicles in such large quantities.[179]

After the relatively poor showing of antitank missiles in the Six-Day War, Russian military correspondents noted that an improved method for fighting tanks emerged. They reported witnessing "serious changes" based on technological developments that allowed a guided shell to destroy any tank at a range of several kilometers.

In 1972 the Soviet Union published the classic work, *Antitank Fighting*, which included a chapter on antitank missiles.[180] It noted the missile's especially long range and ability to penetrate armor even greater than that of tanks.[181] They also discussed the missile's high chances of scoring a hit. However the authors also stated that because of its limitations the missile will not replace other antitank weapons, but by being added to the antitank arsenal, it would create a complete antitank layout.[182] The antitank missile doctrine developed at the same time as the missiles' entrance into the combat layout and absorption into the units.[183]

The Egyptians gave the guided antitank missile units[184] a major role in the war plan, and gathered all the information they could from Soviet doctrinal material, adapting them to the needs and reorganization of Egypt's missile units. In 1971, the Egyptian army's military research branch published a manual on the principles and tactical use of an antitank guided missile battalion and its ancillary units.[185] The manual dealt primarily with Sager missiles[186] that had been absorbed in large quantities.

Two types of antitank battalions are discussed in the manual: one battalion of two to four companies equipped with man-portable missiles; another battalion, made up of four companies, based on missile-carrying armored vehicles.

The manual states that missile units and other elements in the antitank layout will be used in two main ways: the majority under the command of (or provided as support to) battalions or even companies; the rest as an antitank reserve at the brigade, divisional, or field army level.

The unit allotted will usually be a platoon of portable antitank missiles and as such will either be attached to a company or under the direct control of a battalion commander. The antitank platoon in the company layout will serve in a defensive capacity, operating from firing positions in the perimeter of the company stronghold (most of which will be deployed in forward infantry trenches). A concentrated missile force will deploy in firing positions between the battalion's first and second echelons, or in the gaps between first-echelon companies. Another possibility: the entire platoon will act as a reserve force, whether as the battalion's or as a separate antitank reserve.

Antitank units functioning as a reserve force will be used for either defensive or offensive purposes, and will operate alongside other antitank weapons or as a separate missile reserve. Companies in brigade reserves, and battalions in divisional antitank reserves, will not be placed in firing positions but will be concentrated in assembly areas. When the enemy's armor efforts are located, these reserves will be deployed in "firing lines" on the routes of penetration. The selection of the waiting position close to the firing lines will provide concealment and cover until the moment the unit enters its position. This position will also be used for storing and supplying additional missiles.

The manual also refers to nighttime operations, and includes several ideas of how to provide assistance with illumination shells from organic platoons, with 82-millimeter mortars[187] or from artillery batteries. A separate chapter discusses battle in movement, encounters, and antitank ambushes. The appendix also contains a large number of examples, with Soviet tactical signs, detailing the recommended deployment in various types of battles and the procedures for coping with the supply and replenishment of ammunition.

The manual clearly illustrates the path taken by the Egyptian planners. The development of military thinking in conjunction with technological innovations[188] in tank fighting had a significant influence on Egypt's war preparations and the fighting and its results. The Egyptians were well aware of the dangers that awaited the crossing force and the troops building and consolidating the bridgeheads, therefore they seriously studied the doctrinal manual. They learned from the experience of others and achieved extraordinary results in the development and application of the doctrine to their particular abilities and needs.

Egypt's Antitank Layout[189]

The Egyptians expended enormous energy in searching for an answer to Israel's armor superiority. They finally came up with the solution of amassing huge quantities of antitank weapons on the front where their forces were crossing and building bridgeheads. Shazli claims that "by pulling back from the bridgeheads and reducing their depth we were able to concentrate greater defensive firepower, increase the number of antitank weapons on every kilometer of the front, and provide the bridgeheads with artillery and antitank support from the western bank."[190] The distribution of antitank units, and missile units in particular, as the war approached, differed from the standard ORBAT. Various levels were reinforced with antitank weapons so that they could be used in broad contiguous sectors.

The Egyptian plan envisioned each crossing sector reinforced with fifty-four to fifty-seven antitank weapons (recoilless cannon and or more powerful weapons) or launchers on each kilometer of the front (crossing sectors were four kilometers long).[191] The plan called for nineteen to twenty-two guns or launchers per kilometer on the front for the defense of the divisional bridgeheads.

At the start of the campaign, each infantry division crossing the Suez Canal was equipped with hundreds of antitank weapons. Every unit was generously stocked with recoilless anti-tank weapons (RPG-7 s). Each regular or mechanized infantry battalion had twenty-seven launchers; an infantry division had 450. The organic units of each armored division went to battle with 324 launchers, while a mechanized division was equipped with 406 of them.[192] In addition, each division was supplied with thirty-six rifle-propelled RPG-7s and a commando battalion.[193]

Each mechanized infantry battalion incorporated an antitank company with ten B-10 or B-11 recoilless cannons; ninety recoilless cannons were in a division. The tank brigade attached to the infantry division contained a mechanized battalion. Some battalions were given an additional company of recoilless cannons as part of the divisional ORBAT.

Each regular or mechanized infantry brigade in the infantry division had a battery of six antitank cannons. A first-echelon field army infantry division crossed the canal with thirty-six 85-millimeter antitank cannons (dual-purpose guns that functioned as indirect fire-laying artillery). The mechanized and armored divisions in the field army's second echelon had a mechanized battalion equipped with six SU-100 tank destroyers (instead of antitank cannons).

Before the war the mechanized battalions that had been issued new APCs (BMP-1s) were without an antitank company, but, as stated, at the outset of hostilities they received Sager missiles and 73-millimeter antitank cannons mounted on the APCs.

As previously noted, antitank missiles were the main weapon at the bridgeheads.[194] The troops had seventy-two portable Sager (AT-3) missile launchers: a company of twelve launchers in each brigade and thirty-six launchers in an antitank battalion).[195] Other divisions were supplied with thirty-two launchers mounted on BMP-1s.

The best guarantee for the success of the crossing and construction of the bridgeheads in the first stage of the offensive was to take the antitank missile units from the mechanized and armored divisions — that were not in the first waves — and perhaps from paratroop brigades attached to the infantry forces leading the assault. This reinforcement provided an additional twelve to twenty launchers to each of the divisions making the crossing. According to Sha-zli, "We reinforced the lead infantry units with portable, antitank guided weapons. This required using our emergency stockpiles and taking the missiles from every unit and layout not connected with the first waves.... This was the only way to supply our vanguard with an armor-busting capability."[196]

A commando battalion that was engaged in ambushes and antitank blocking in order to isolate the battlefield would be reinforced with companies employing Sager antitank missile launchers taken from units of the SF headquarters.[197]

Each infantry division directly involved in the crossing was reinforced with a tank brigade equipped, in addition to its tanks, with six armored vehicles (BRDM-2s)[198] carrying Sager missiles (altogether fourteen missiles and six missile launchers per vehicle). Each of the divisions was provided with thirty-six BMP-1s capable of launching Sagers. These vehicles were requisitioned from the tank and mechanized divisions not involved in the crossing stage.[199] Each of the crossing divisions was also given one battalion of thirty-six 100-millimeter dual-purpose cannons capable of functioning as regular field artillery or being integrated into the antitank battle.

Along with organic antitank units, or those attached to divisions, additional field army and GHQ antitank forces operated in the battle zone. Each field army was made of the following antitank forces:

— One battalion of mobile 100-millimeter antitank cannons (eighteen guns), mounted on the hulls of T-34 tanks. (These weapons — like 100-millimeter field artillery pieces — generally carried out standard artillery assignments).

— One antitank missile group made up of twelve Sager-carrying BRDM-2 armored vehicles and twelve antiquated "Shmel" (AT-1) missile launchers.

BRDM-2 APC carrying Sager antitank missiles, an A.T. system that was not very effective during the 1973 War.

— One battalion of light tank-destroyers[200] and another unit of heavy tank-busters — altogether thirty SU-100 cannons and thirty JSU-152s (heavy assault guns) that served less as antitank weapons and more as direct-line-of-fire sources for pounding the fortifications.

— Additional antitank missile battalions, from the GHQ level, were appended to the field armies. Each battalion was made up of eighteen BRDM-2s. The Second Army had such a battalion, and the Third Army was apparently assigned one also.

Tasks and Deployment

The massive quantity of antitank weapons and the way they were deployed turned the entire layout into a kind of antitank defense position.[201] The infantry and mechanized forces were provided with short-range antitank weapons, and long-range missiles and cannon. The layout was reinforced with tanks and tank-busters[202] — some in forward positions, but most of them in concentrations on stand-by for an Israeli counterattack.

At the same time that antitank weapons were deployed in massive formations close to the forces at the bridgeheads, huge quantities of antitank weapons were deployed at the ramps and positions on the western side of the canal in the first stages of the campaign. The antitank weapons were intended for defense against IDF counterattacks and for strikes against Israeli strongholds on the "Bar-Lev Line." On the first and second days of the fighting, the Sager missiles in these positions were effectively used against IDF forces on the way to the elevated dirt embankment, and against IDF counterattacks and attempts to link up with the strongholds.

Two tasks of highest priority were the stabilization of the defense line and the reinforcement of Egyptian units on the east side of the canal with antitank forces. A close look at Egyptian plans for crossing the canal and transferring antitank weapons to the east reveals the following[203]:

• The first wave carried across RPG-7 antitank launchers.

• In the second wave, each battalion had a platoon of Sager missiles (two missiles per launch team).

• Recoilless cannons were transferred to the eastern bank in the third wave. All of these weapons were deployed, and according to the progress at the bridgeheads, sent to the antitank lines on front, and even used in antitank ambushes in front of the Israeli strongholds.

• The fourth wave brought across ammunition carriages for the battalions which provided each launcher with another four antitank missiles.

• The succeeding waves — the fifth to the eighth — transferred additional antitank missile units for reinforcing the battalions and brigade reserves.

Once the ferries started operating — and after the bridges were constructed — tanks, armored vehicles (BRDM-2s) carrying Sager missiles, and towed antitank weapons were sent across. These weapons had priority in the crossing. Antitank equipment that went across in later stages of the war — dual-purpose artillery, assault cannon, and other antitank missiles — were added to the antitank reserves. One reserve unit operated in each brigade sector.

The divisions had two, sometimes three antitank reserves (although according to the warfare doctrine only one antitank reserve was required). Each field army was given two or sometimes more antitank reserve forces. These included various types of assault cannons, dual-purpose antitank artillery battalions, and one or two companies of antitank missiles.

The field army's reserves were generally used as a support force at the divisional level and were responsible for setting up and securing the bridgeheads. A number of alternative fire lines (operational bases from which forces would emerge as situations arose) were established at the brigade and divisional levels.

Antitank missiles were an integral part of the battle, joining in infantry attacks during and after the crossing, but mainly defending the divisional layouts at the bridgeheads in prepared positions. The reserves at the different echelons — including the field army echelon — were sent across the canal to reinforce the front at the bridgeheads.

The commando forces in the first echelon divisions crossed in the first waves,[204] setting up antitank ambushes for protecting the bridgeheads. Other antitank forces appended to the field army and GHQ isolated the battlefield at greater depths. The Egyptian plan called for a heliborne commando battalion to operate deep in Sinai along the entire length of the front, up to the mountain passes. Eventually the commandos operated only on the littoral axis, in the Rumani sector, and on the Ras Jundi axis in the southern fighting zone.

Operating the Sager System

Two types of antitank missiles were used in the fighting: those carried by the infantry and launched from the ground, and those mounted on and operated from the back of an APC or armored vehicle.[205] The Sager missile systems, especially man-portable ones, were generally found in infantry units.

The Soviet warfare doctrine asserted that Sager units should strengthen the defense lines and operate as a traditional antitank defense. This was an important stratum in each defense layout that was built according to Soviet guidelines.[206] In the Yom Kippur War, because of the importance of antitank defense, the Egyptians positioned most of the Sager launchers 100 to 200 meters from the front-line defense layout — ahead of the forward line (in ambush) or in the defense layout (as part of the antitank reserve). This was done in order to achieve maximum missile range. An Egyptian analysis comparing the relative advantages and disadvantages of an Egyptian and Israeli mechanized infantry brigade noted that by reinforcing the Egyptian brigade with antitank missiles, its ability to deal with Israeli tanks at distance of three kilometers was improved, which significantly compensated for Egyptian tanks' inferior firing range. The antitank weapons also assisted in destroying Israel's superior number of APCs in its brigades.[207]

Most of the Sager companies were deployed one and a half to two kilometers along the front-line defense layouts. Sager-carrying BRDM-2s were also spread out along a similar length. Three Sager companies were planned for each of the brigade layouts at the bridgehead fronts. Sager units were generally deployed in platoons, but in the advanced stages of the fighting the platoons came under command of a company commander.

Missile teams were stationed opposite possible areas of an Israeli armor breakthrough, generally on the flanks or the spaces between the Egyptian forces. The teams usually operated in platoon forma-

Sager missile system, the main A.T. system used by the Egyptians on the front of their bridgeheads, on the east side of the Suez Canal.

tion consisting of two squads, each containing two teams. As required by the Soviet doctrine, positions were taken in relatively high spots, a few hundred meters from the layout front, to compensate for the missile's limited range — approximately 500 meters. Depth was also created in the antitank layout by deploying missile launchers in battalion layouts at a distance of up to two kilometers from the front.

Portable-missile teams consisted of three soldiers: a navigator and two missile carriers, each with two missiles. Each team had an extra two missiles in the platoon arsenal located behind the squads' positions. Missiles were generally launched from behind an observation post which maintained a visual line with the target.

Missile-carrying vehicles were employed mainly in defensive roles in the mobile antitank reserves. The vehicles moved into prearranged firing positions overlooking possible routes of the enemy's breakthrough. The weapons were supposed to be in the deployment areas in the center of the layout, in a place that allowed for the speedy entry into firing positions. The missile could be guided from a forward position; the APC launcher was tucked away further back. Sometimes the Sagers were released in pairs or threesomes in order to intensify the effectiveness of the fire.

Each division was provided with a massive quantity of Sagers — sometime as many as 1,250 missiles for the first three days of the fighting (460 on the first day alone). Each launch team was allocated twenty missiles[208] and each infantry division twenty-four carriages for toting them.[209] Each carriage carried an additional eight missiles, which meant that each team could be reinforced with some of the carriage's 192 missiles (plus four additional ones), besides the two that the teams had with them at the outset.

While they were being deployed at the bridgeheads, the teams carried eight missiles per launcher which were kept in dumps. The rest of the missiles were transported by a vehicle which supplied them to the teams.[210]

In the belly of each BRDM-2 were eight missiles. Six more were positioned on its external launchers. Vehicles from the echelons reinforcing the batteries and battalions carried additional missiles.

This concentrated use of antitank missiles at the bridgeheads' improvised defense layouts in the first stages of the war — and in the organized layouts in the later stages — was the

Figure 13: Part of the Plan for Targeting Objectives on the Canal Line (Captured Document)

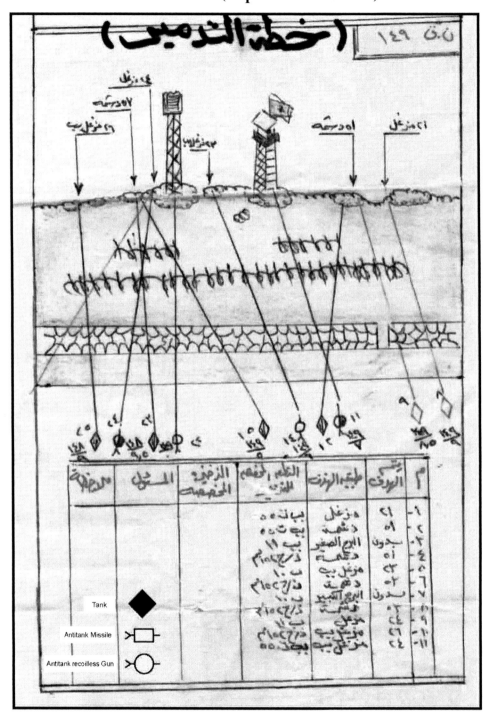

first-ever attempt to use these weapons on such a wide scale. The war's final results — and the severe damage that the missiles caused to IDF armor — proved their effectiveness.

The Use of Forces with RPG-7 Antitank Missile Launchers

As stated, the RPG-7 was the main antitank weapon at short ranges. Many IDF tank and APC commanders reported encountering them and being hit.

The grenade launcher was the basic weapon in every Egyptian infantry and commando team. An RPG team consisted of two soldiers carrying five rockets. For special tasks — especially ambushes — a team numbered three soldiers: operator, rocket carrier, and rifleman who carried ten rockets.

Tank units placed in front of the strongholds' forward line were also equipped with RPGs for use at ranges between one and two kilometers in front of the layout, along roads, and on the defense line itself. We can learn about the theoretical use of tank-hunter groups from Egyptian doctrinal material dealing with "wartime use of tank-hunter groups and training methods[211]:

"Tank hunting is considered one of the most important battlefield activities that complement the use of other weapons. In our war zone, the desert, tank hunting is crucial — especially at nighttime (this is why night-vision devices based on starlight amplification are appended to the launchers) and especially after the establishment of the bridgeheads. In order to guarantee the infantry's consolidation at the bridgeheads, tank-hunter groups will be sent as far forward as possible. Each seven- to nine-man group will be armed mainly with RPG-7s. The groups will be dispersed over as wide an area land as possible at the expected routes of the enemy's armored advance."

The publication lists the tasks that the tank-hunter group had to accomplish:
- Destruction of enemy tanks trying to disrupt our forces during the crossing;
- Incapacitating enemy tanks' ability to advance from their defense positions;
- Paralyzing enemy tank reserves attempting to counterattack; destroying the majority of the targets;
- Hitting the enemy's retreating tanks;
- Knocking out enemy tanks that managed to penetrate the defense line front and flanks;
- Wiping out enemy armor ambushes.

Regarding the tank-hunters' superb modus operandi, the doctrinal material noted that "tank-hunter groups will cross the canal in the first wave and take up positions on the hills overlooking the enemy armor's approach roads. The tank hunters will protect the main forces during the crossing. Tank hunters will proceed in front of and on the flanks of the main crossing force. When reaching the outer limits of bridgeheads, they will take up positions in the front and flanks, concentrating on the expected routes of the enemy's armored advance. They will become part of the defense effort to block enemy armor counterattacks, generally deploying on the rear slope of a hill in order to gain the element of surprise."

This technique was practiced in training for the war. Tank-hunting instruction manuals[212] state that the teams must not be clustered in areas where an enemy tank can easily destroy them. They must be spread out in a way that guarantees their safety and at the same time allows them to coordinate their moves. The teams must not enter the firing zones of other tank hunters lest they interfere with their comrades' freedom of action.

Regarding the use of antitank weapons: the team must use both antitank rockets and grenades but always the rocket launcher before the grenades. The furthest tank, the one providing cover, must be hit first; in this way it will be easier to destroy the tanks closer to it.

Figure 14: An Infantry Battalion Crossing the Canal from Its Positions and Deploying at the Bridgeheads (Captured Document)

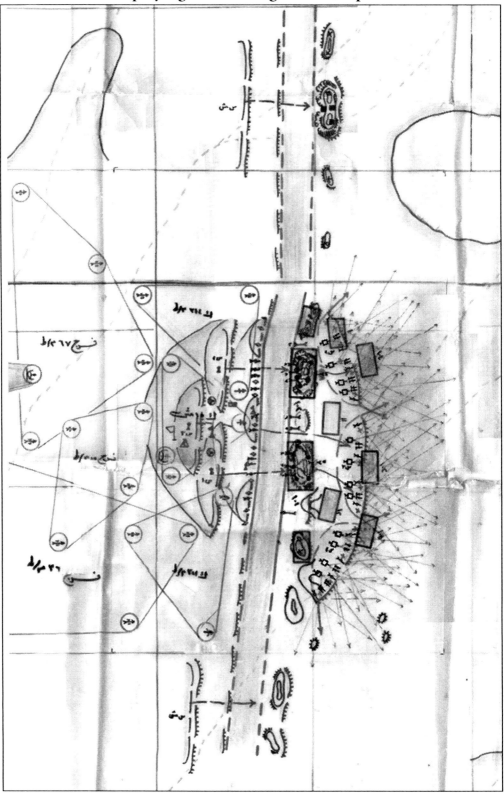

Although the antitank rocket launchers in the Yom Kippur War received less glory than the antitank missiles, they were the more successful of the two weapons. Their application was studied by many armies and is still applied today.

Conclusion

The Egyptians fully understood that Israel's armor superiority posed a critical challenge to the assault force and bridgeheads on the eastern bank. The solution to this problem lay in meticulously planning and establishing an antitank layout, with special emphasis on antitank rockets.

Gamasi, the Egyptian chief of staff in the Yom Kippur War, recalls the achievements of the antitank weapons on the first day of the war[213]: "Infantry battling tanks is an unorthodox tactic that demands expertise and courage. On the opening day of the war we faced three hundred Israeli tanks. Egyptian intelligence estimated that the Israelis would make a quick counterattack. Our infantry had crossed the canal with antitank rockets, in addition to their standard antitank weapons. Infantry and commando units destroyed a hundred tanks — one-third of the enemy's force deployed on the forward line — thus foiling the counterattack and enabling the completion of the crossing."

A study by an American colonel, T. N. Depuy, based on Egyptian sources, notes that over 70 percent of the Israeli tanks were hit by antitank rockets or rocket launchers.[214]

General Tal claims[215] that in the first day of fighting in the south, the Egyptians were armed with only light antitank weapons but managed to knock out 80 of Israel's 150 attacking tanks. Tal also notes that the Egyptians found their defense capability sufficient to allow the antitank units to dig in and force Israel to wage a static war and squander its armor in the process.[216]

The Arab military commentary, Hitham al-Ayubi, summed up his view of the war by stating that many task-oriented antitank units completely surprised the enemy, inflicting unexpectedly heavy losses, to the point where Israeli observers began to ask: has the tank become obsolete?[217]

After the war, the Soviet Union held a series of conferences and symposiums on the lessons to be gained from the Yom Kippur War. Defense Minister Marshal Grechko wrote that "in the Middle East fighting, modern defense achieved greater stability when the defenders were armed with powerful weapons mainly because the primary instrument of the attacker — the tank — became vulnerable and its advantages on the battlefield compromised."[218]

The Egyptians' view of the rocket system was analyzed in the Egyptian newspaper *al-Ahram*[219]: "Indeed, non-armor troops forced the world to rethink its methods for using tanks. The [Egyptian soldiers] and their rockets are now a legend in Egyptian and world military history. They destroyed scores of enemy attacks in the first hours of the fighting."

The effective use of various antitank weapons — especially rockets, their integration into different layouts, and concentration at the bridgehead fronts, produced excellent results against the IDF's tanks in the Yom Kippur War. The Egyptian solution in countering enemy armor forces is still studied in military academies and will remain a tactic worth emulating in the future.

The Attack from the Bridgehead

Throughout the planning, preparatory, and training stages of the war, the Egyptians examined both the doctrine and their ability to launch an attack from the bridgeheads, and realized that several factors influence the organization and command of the attack: the number and size of bridgeheads, the time needed to defend them, the terrain, and the depth of the enemy's defense lines.

A field army begins an attack from one or more bridgeheads (the length of time depends on various factors). The attack may take place immediately after the canal crossing and consolidation of the bridgeheads. However, if the forces are held up at the bridgeheads, the attack will lose the key element of surprise. In order to avoid this situation, the army's largest force must be sent into battle while in movement, without deploying on the contact line. The Egyptian planner sees no need to call a pause — a halt that the Israelis previously termed an "operative pause" — but conditions may force the troops to linger at the bridgeheads.[220]

An attack from the bridgeheads may occur while in contact with the enemy. In that case, all the troops and their equipment must be concentrated at the bridgeheads a night or two before D-Day.

An attack from the bridgeheads calls for first-echelon tanks because of their mobility, strength, and great firepower. Antitank reserves and moveable obstacles play an important role in the attack by reducing the maneuverability of the enemy's tanks (the IDF's main defense weapon). The attack also requires the massive, concentrated use of artillery against enemy targets. The time needed for pre-attack preparations should be three or four hours.[221] The advancing forces will direct support fire mainly against select targets. SF will land deep behind enemy lines to secure the layouts; air strikes will also be integrated into the attack.[222] Once the enemy's forward defense lines are captured, second-echelon forces will develop an in-depth attack, securing and taking over secondary defense lines.

Divisional and brigade missions will attack from the bridgeheads, penetrating deeper than missions in a battle involving a water crossing. The division's direct mission depends on the depth of the enemy's defense layout and may extend up to eight or ten kilometers. The following mission will be the same as the daily mission and reach twenty or even thirty kilometers. By remaining at the bridgeheads, the Egyptians will give the IDF's defense layout the opportunity to stabilize. As the attack proceeds, a main effort will be launched for breaking through the stronger sectors in the enemy's defense layout, which will give the Egyptians the opportunity to develop the attack at a later time. What happened in reality is that instead of pursuing the attack from the bridgeheads, the Egyptians botched their October 14 offensive.[223]

The "Operative Pause" — Mission Depth and the Reduction of the Dimensions of the Attack

One of the key questions surrounding Egypt's moves in the initial days of the Yom Kippur War relates to mission depth.

The argument still rages among Egyptian political and military leaders, between them and their Syrian counterparts, and between Israeli commanders and Israeli war analysts, over why the Egyptian army, after crossing the canal, failed to pursue a deep attack into Sinai.

Did the Egyptian commander and war planners intend to push ahead and capture vital areas in the mountain passes and Refidim Opening or establish a defensive line eight to twelve kilometers east of the canal?

Egypt's "reduced" plan and the extent to which the war objectives were diminished have been discussed in this book in the section entitled "The Egyptians' Application of the Crossing Doctrine: The Plan." The Egyptians turned to a "theoretical base" to justify their "non-development" of the attack, terming it an "operative pause." Various explanations tried to assuage their Syrian ally who was displeased over the change in original plans.[224] The Egyptians concealed the possibility from them that the war might be fought with limited objectives. According to Shazli, in all of the meetings with the Syrians, the Egyptians brought up the broad plan (that the attack would develop to east of the Straits of Tiran) but kept silent about the limited plan.[225]

Arab military analysts have debated the October War's "*al-wakfa al-ta'abuya*" (operative pause) at length.[226] Like President Sadat, Chief of Staff Shazli and Gamasi (the head of the Operations Branch) also had to state their opinion on the issue in order to rebuff the Syrian claim that the pause was supposed to be taken only in the later stages of the war after Syrian troops reached the Jordan River and Egyptian forces captured the mountain passes.

Already in the first version of Egypt's "official history" Heykal explains that the Egyptian attack plan was based on a concept different from that in the Soviet warfare doctrine.[227] In the Egyptian commentators' description of the initial stage, it is pointed out that "this was not a period of quiet vigilance, but one of active operations and continuous Israeli counterattacks, during which Egyptian forces strengthened their position on the east bank." Furthermore, the operative pause "cost the enemy heavy losses ... and created excellent conditions for the [Egyptians] to develop an in-depth attack."[228]

Indeed, after the crossing Egypt's static layout at the bridgeheads served as bulwark against the IDF reserves' counterattack. The Egyptians put off their in-depth attack, and when it was launched, it came as a whimper.

The Egyptian generals hastened to sum up the war, stressing the achievements of the "operative pause" in repelling the Israeli counterstrike, stabilizing the bridgeheads, buying time, organizing the administrative apparatus, establishing the air defense layout on the eastern bank, and exhausting the Israeli air force.[229]

I believe that the Egyptian planner wanted to lengthen this effective stage as much as a possible, and if politically feasible, proceed no further.

Israeli military analysts describe the "operative pause" as a preplanned stage in Egypt's war strategy in the Yom Kippur War. Israeli scholars, whose versions became the "official history," perceive that this stage in the campaign (between the canal crossing and capture of the bridgeheads and the drive toward the mountain passes and the Refidin Opening[230]) was supposed to enable first-echelon Egyptian forces[231] to deploy in strength and secure a tight hold on the bridgeheads in order to block the enemy's reserve forces' counterattack and inflict maximum losses. When this stage ended (no mention of its continuation appears in captured Egyptian war plans), the second phase of the offensive would commence.[232]

In an article written eleven years after the war by Lt. Col. Yona Bandman, the head of Egyptian research in Israeli MI and later a senior analyst in the GHQ's history branch,[233] the operative pause and the reasons why the successful breach and crossing were not actively pursued are attributed to the paralysis and astonishment that swept through the Egyptian troops (perhaps the officers too). According to Bandman, "the successful crossing and accomplishments of the first stage of the operative plan with was carried out with losses far lower than the original estimates, and this may have worked to the [Egyptians'] detriment, creating paralysis and stupor. It may also have led to an overcautious attitude and tendency to attempt only what was certain."[234]

Anyone searching for the answer to the question as to why the Egyptians halted and whether a connection exists between what happened in the Third Army sector and the Second

Army's failure to exploit its success, and looks for technical miscalculations, blunders, or other excuses, will come away empty-handed.

Lt. Col. Bandman notes that on the night of October 6 the Second Army already managed to transfer the bulk of the first-echelon fighting forces to the western bank. However, only limited forces remained at the bridgeheads the next day, in the direction of the army's main effort: the Refidim Opening (according to Bandman's assessment of Egyptian intentions). This time, as before, he based his estimate on Hanoch Bartov, the author of a best-selling biography on Chief of Staff David Elazar,[235] who claimed that the reasons for the Egyptians' failure to advance began with the difficulties and delays in bridging the canal and the transfer of troops to the Third Army sector.[236]

To the best of my knowledge, the search for a convincing explanation for Egypt's modus operandi — crossing the canal, capturing a narrow strip of land on the eastern bank, and going over to the defense — was the main factor in Israel's keen interest in the issue. Israeli intelligence's prewar estimate of Egypt's modus operandi did not correspond with events on the battlefield. Israeli intelligence analysts, as well as military commanders and political leaders, expected the Egyptian army to race forward at full speed after the crossing, thus enabling the IDF to make maximum use of its superior maneuverability and firepower. The Egyptians, as stated, devised an entirely different plan of action.

Regarding the degree of Israeli miscalculation, Zvi Lanir wrote that five days after the war broke out, Dayan sat in a closed meeting with newspaper editors and could still claim: "If Sadat doesn't reach the mountain passes in this attack, he'll not only fail to conquer Israel but he'll also fail to recapture Sinai and liberate the occupied areas.... After six years of preparing for the great war, he won't even attain his limited goal of twenty kilometers."[237]

Why didn't Egypt throw its second-echelon troops[238]into the campaign on the heels of the crossing forces, and exploit the initial success in order to capture the mountain passes? This was the question that Israeli intelligence officers, who saw their estimates go down the drain, wanted to answer.[239]

The "operative pause" was designed to reduce the number of missions in the attack. In the Soviet combat doctrine, the term "operative halt" is a historical term dating from the 1930s when it appeared in military plans for a "deep campaign."[240] The term received practical application in the Soviet advance from the Dnieper to Berlin in the last phase of World War II. The Russians realized that the systems level might be pervaded with a slackening in momentum. When the attacking force is advancing in enemy territory, the closer it approaches its goal the more frequent the phenomenon of "culmination" appears, that is, the force becomes exhausted by the burden of the effort. The deeper the penetration into enemy territory, the more the force weakens and the entire campaign momentum slackens.[241]

Basically, the "operative pause" describes a predictable situation in an offensive. The planner recognizes the geographical features in the campaign when the offense can be transformed into the defense. The idea behind the tactical shift is to cause the enemy to commence attacking and by doing so to renew the mass, and close the gap between the spearhead or shock divisions (the fast-moving armored and mechanized units) and the infantry divisions. At some point the renewal of the mass enables the attack momentum to be renewed.[242] Doctrinal literature defines the "operative pause" as occurring between two successive operations and as necessary for replenishing and replacing personnel, weapons, and equipment, realigning the forces, advancing the logistical layouts, and bringing up supplies and technical material. The term also connotes temporary inactivity in a particular stage of the campaign when both sides cease offensive operations.

According to the Soviet warfare doctrine (that served Egypt before and during the Yom Kippur War) the attack at the field army level should proceed uninterruptedly, that is, without any operative pauses. The armies' missions at the front's first echelon were to break through the enemy's tactical defense area, destroy his first-echelon forces, and accomplish the first operative mission, usually by capturing a clearly defined systems objective.

The Soviet warfare doctrine (which was still in practice in this period) prohibits static operational conditions, such as halting after crossing an obstacle and reorganizing at the bridgehead or after the breakthrough. In other words, an obstacle is perceived as one link in a complex defense system that must be continuously and rigorously dealt with.[243]

The overall commander of the armed forces defines the operational goal for each field army and its offensive assignments. The goal consists of specific missions for destroying the enemy's forces and capturing objectives and areas of key importance to both the defending and attacking forces.

The goal of the army attack[244] is generally accomplished by carrying out the direct mission and following mission, while the depth and substance of these missions are liable to change according to operational and strategic circumstances.

The field army's direct mission is assigned to the first echelon operating on the main axis of the effort. For example, the Egyptian field armies are generally tasked with breaking through the enemy's defense layout, destroying his forces deployed in the tactical defense zone and local operative depth, and taking over an area (or the line) in order to secure the operation's successful continuation. According to the Soviet doctrine, the direct mission's depth may reach seventy to one hundred kilometers over a three to five day period.

The field army's first echelon's following assignment in the main effort is usually developing the attack to an operative depth, destroying the enemy's operational and deep (or strategic) reserves, and capturing vital areas in order to carry out the operation's goals. The following mission's depth may reach 80 to 110 kilometers (and sometimes greater, depending on the nature of the theater and the needs of the attacking army). When the field army operates as the only echelon on the front, the following mission will become part of the final mission, as in the final stages of the strategic attack operation.

The depth of the field army's attack, according to the Soviet warfare doctrine (in conventional war conditions) is 100–250 kilometers. This is the depth reached when a field army carries out its direct and following missions.

The doctrine that was taught in the Nasser Higher Military Academy by Soviet instructors in the early 1970s referred to field army operations at a depth of 190–240 kilometers. These distances seem to have been adapted to the needs of Egyptian military strategy, that is, from the Suez Canal to the international border with Israel — the Green Line. The ranges correspond exactly to the needs of the Egyptian planner, who worked under the command of Nasser and War Minister Fawzi in planning the recapture of Sinai and perhaps the Gaza Strip. In this case, the depth of the field army's offensive operation is exactly that of the strategic offensive operation.

In lectures and study programs in Egypt's military academies, much of the material comes from the Soviet warfare doctrine. One of the lectures, adapted to the Egyptian theater of operations and a full-scale offensive developing from the crossing,[245] states that the depth of a field army attack in Sinai must be identical to the depth of the strategic operation. Another series of lectures (translated from Russian into English for the Egyptian cadets at the Nasser Academy)[246] makes no mention of the specific needs of the theater, but notes that the strategic offensive may take place in two or more field army moves with a "operative pause" between them. This was based on the Red Army's combat experience in the European Theater of Operations in World War II.[247]

After the Yom Kippur War, Israeli military analysts who examined the planning of Egyptian army mission depths were unanimous in their opinion regarding the depth of the direct mission. The depth of the field armies' bridgeheads, like those of the divisional bridgeheads, was ten to twelve kilometers.[248]

Analysts assert that the Egyptians' following mission in the war had to be the pursuit of the in-depth attack, that is, the seizure of the Gidi and Mitle mountain passes, Wadi Sudar in the canal's southern, the Refidim Opening (in the vicinity of Bir Gafgafa) along the central axis, and the area of Matzfaq (Nachal Yam) on the northern coastal axis.[249] When the attacking force arrived in these areas, it had to prepare their defense (according to the warfare doctrine) in a seven-day "operative pause" (with an additional three or four days' leeway for its completion).

To the best of my knowledge, Israel has almost no information from or before the war regarding the length of the halt (if such a plan ever existed).[250] Information on the army's final objectives comes mostly from later sources[251] — doctrinal material written in the planning period for the all-out war (1970–1971), before the "Granit 2" plan was truncated (or improved).[252]

Two viewpoints emerge in the disputes among military analysts in Egypt and the Arab world.[253] The first, faithfully espoused by Chief of Staff Shazli, states that the pause at the conclusion of the direct mission fulfilled the war aim and was adapted to the Egyptian army's needs and abilities. The "race for the passes," the second stage just before the following mission, was conditional and was planned solely as an option — an option that the army was far from prepared for.[254]

The second — Heykal's critical perspective — apparently influenced by the Syrian version, claims that the "operational pause" was intended for implementation at the end of the following mission, after the Syrians reached the Jordan on the Golan front and the Egyptians arrived at the western mountain passes in Sinai. According to Heykal, the original Egyptian plan envisioned pressing the attack up to the defiles in the first stage, but it was decided to implement the operative pause at an earlier stage because of the Egyptian leadership's vacillation and uncertainty about the army's capabilities.[255]

The Syrian version appears in an article entitled "The Results and Strategies of the October War" that was published in the Syrian military journal *Tishrin*, in which several Syrian officers are quoted. Col. (Akid) Fuad Lahwi claims that in retrospect, the Egyptians had their own goals in the war: liberating the Suez Canal and gaining a foothold in Sinai — goals that were attained. Maj. Gen. Jibril Batar asserts that the Egyptian army was ordered to halt at an earlier point than in the original plan, and this allowed Israel to carry out what the Syrians and Egyptians had decided to prevent it from doing. Maj. Gen. Adiv Alamor notes that Egypt's plans were different from Syria's in that a final victory was not achieved. The article also quotes President Sadat as saying that he declared on numerous occasions, "Give me ten kilometers on the east bank and I'll settle for that."[256]

The idea of the "operative pause," at least as Shazli conceived it, meant "halting until conditions changed that had caused the halt ... [this] could last weeks, months, or longer." Shazli explained that he realized from an earlier situation estimate that the army was capable of carrying out only a "war of limited dimensions," and that the launching of the next stage — the capture of the passes — required other types of weapons and training methods. He also states that he made it explicitly clear to his officers that the crossing and advance to the defiles were two completely different phases of the campaign, adding that he did not expect "the army to be ordered to carry out the second stage." His field army commanders, and even the war minister, shared his feelings.

Indeed, Shazli admits that it was the war minister, Ahmad Ismail Ali, who ordered him to plan the following mission, fearing that the Syrians would not go to war if they believed that Egypt had no intention of attacking the mountain passes.[257]

Shazli's meticulous descriptions, which conform to the vast majority of war documents captured by Israel, reveal that the army's performance on the battlefield in the first stage of the war — the construction and securing of the bridgeheads — fulfilled the plans of Egypt's top military leaders and the political goals of the government. Another version of events, closer to the truth than Heykal's, regarding the original Egyptian plan, claims that the first stage of the war would continue the momentum of the attack up to the defiles.

Gamasi devotes an entire chapter in his memoirs to the debate over the raison d'être of the first stage — "The Long Wait: A Tactical Time-Out." This term (and title of his chapter) is the only reference to the prewar orders that Israel possesses. Gamasi uses the expression "tactical time-out" when referring to what was later termed the "operative pause." He relates that in his October 9 meeting with the war minister, he reminded Shazli that "the war plan specifically stated that following a successful assault and breakthrough from the canal, the attack would gather momentum and proceed to capture the passes, with or without a tactical pause." In other words, the principle of expanding the attack eastward to the passes had already been decided. End of argument! Gamasi, in opposition to Shazli, asserts that the plan envisioned attaining the strategic objective of the mountain passes. It was inconceivable that the chief of staff had claimed in the planning stage that he was against an expansion of the attack and capture of the passes.[258]

An analysis of Egyptian activity in the first days of the war points to a plan "based on stages." The "race to the passes" was would only be carried out if special conditions prevailed. Field armies' second-echelon troops — the armored and mechanized divisions — which were supposed to spearhead the advance, not only remained on the western bank throughout the entire war, but many of them were annexed to the infantry divisions that made the first crossing and came under their command. Against expectations, which the apologetic Egyptians nurtured and Israeli military analysts were convinced of, the Egyptians transferred only one headquarters (that of the Twenty-first Armored Division) to the eastern bank. The headquarters of the Fourth Armored Division, like those of the Twenty-third and Sixth Mechanized Divisions, remained on the western bank throughout the war.

Also the "dash to the east" — the Egyptian armored attack that began on October 14 — slowed down because the units were exhausted and only three armored brigades were added for reinforcements.

For years, the debate over the move's timing, like the debate over the move itself, absorbed Egypt's political and military figures and news analysts. The goals of this stage were not purely military. Shazli, who claims to have opposed the "dash to the east" in the planning stage, avows that the decision to carry out the October 14 attack was the first major mistake made by the Egyptian leadership.[259] The halfhearted attack cost Egypt's armored units dearly. It gave the IDF the opportunity to cross over to the western shore, seize Egyptian territory, advance one hundred kilometers from Cairo, and surround the Third Army on the east back.

Egypt's real intention in planning the various stages of the war, especially the "operative pause" and the following attack, continue to generate controversy among the Egyptians. It seems to me that the difficulty in understanding Egypt's moves during the first week of the fighting[260] still persists among the Israelis.

The October 14 Armored Attack

The only Egyptian military activity during the Yom Kippur War that may have been intended as an offensive with operative objectives beyond the front's eight to twelve kilometer perimeter — the depth of the divisional bridgeheads — was the armored attack on October 14. The fact that this attack was a hesitating attempt to deviate from the original mission is the most evincing proof that the Egyptians planned an all-out war of limited dimensions.

The Egyptians would have been satisfied with limited-range gains at the bridgeheads on the eastern bank, but it seems that the only way they could instill a sense of solidarity and credibility in their northern ally was by jolting the static military situation in Sinai that up to now had fulfilled all of their expectations.

President Sadat realized the military advantages that defensive deployment on the bridgeheads provided and understood the thinking of the Israeli commanders "who expect us to plunge headfirst into Sinai."[261] He ordered the October 14 attack — as he and Egyptian military commentators insist — for the sole reason of easing the pressure on the Syrian front. Referring to Sadat's decision, Shazli declared: "Even today, six years after the war, I haven't the foggiest notion why the attack was made.... It was pure folly."[262]

The Israeli counterattack on the Golan Heights reversed the Syrian advance, and returned the situation to what it had been on October 10. The Syrians had managed to penetrate deep into the Israeli-held heights and reach a point overlooking the Sea of Galilee in the southern sector, practically completing their objectives. But the Israeli counterstrike forced them to retreat to their starting positions, while they incurred heavy losses on the way. On October 11 Israel's Northern Command launched a determined attack, smashing through the Syrians' fortified layouts and penetrating deep into Syrian territory in the northern sector of the Golan Heights.

The Syrian war plan became totally disarranged, and the Syrians felt themselves under tremendous pressure as their troops were too exhausted to stem the Israeli juggernaut. The roads leading to the heart of the Syrian layout — the strategic area located in the Damascus basin — were practically left wide open to the enemy advance. The first troops of the Iraqi expeditionary force arrived on October 12 and were immediately dispatched to check the IDF push to the east. Jordanian tank brigades that were supposed to come to Syria's assistance in just such circumstances were delayed in their movement north and entered the battlefield only on October 16. The Syrians' sole alternative was to turn to their Egyptian allies and urge them to honor their earlier commitment and develop their attack east toward the vital territory that opened the way into the heart of Sinai — the Gidi and Mitle mountain passes and the Mlaz area between Bir Gafgafa and Bir Tmada.

The Syrians hoped that massive Egyptian pressure would lighten Israeli pressure on the northern front. Syria's demands and expectation for Egypt's pursuit of the attack were based on the assessment that pressure in the southern front would force Israel to switch its main effort from the Golan Heights to Sinai. A determined Egyptian offensive would compel the Israeli air force to concentrate on the southern front, thus reducing the pressure on the Arab armies in the north and stemming the IDF advance to the east.

The Egyptians' main tactic was to limit the war aims. Naturally they were very reluctant to go beyond their well-organized defense layouts at the bridgeheads. They heavily reinforced their defense line with minefields and antitank layouts, making it relatively secure under a thick umbrella of antiaircraft missiles based on the western bank. Egyptian troops successfully performed their missions, repulsing IDF armored counterattacks and frustrating

Israeli warplanes. At this point the Egyptians felt that they had accomplished the war's aims, and could put the limited ability of their soldiers — and their army as a war machine — to the best possible use. The Egyptians reached the stage where they were capable of retaining areas vital for the static defense of the Suez Canal, without involving the army in mobile battles, complex combat maneuvers, and risky operations. The Egyptians wanted to end the war and continue the fight in the political arena.

As the Syrians implored their southern ally to pursue an in-depth attack, the Egyptians continued to diddle. On October 12 the IDF expected a renewed attack. While the Egyptians drew up a hasty battle plan, the chief of staff, who commanded the officers preparing the general attack, opposed expanding the war's dimensions. Despite his opposition, the field units received marching orders. But something went amiss, and the Seventh Infantry Division ordered the Twenty-fifth Armor Brigade to attack the IDF forces defending the Gidi Road–Artillery Road junction. In the rest of the sectors, static exchanges of fire continued.[263]

The Egyptian attack was not planned as an additional stage in the general war, but was a sluggish maneuver slightly based on earlier operational plans prior to the decision to embark upon a war of limited dimensions.

The Egyptian October 14 advance encompassed most of the combat theater in Sinai. But, after the operative pause, was this operation supposed to capture systems objectives deep in Sinai — as the official Israeli history and several Egyptian publications present it? The Third Army's battle diary — the only authentic document that Israel captured that gives details of Egyptian military activity at the systems level during the war — leaves us in the dark.[264] Nor does the rest of the captured material shed light on plans for this stage — the forces, missions, or method of a "field army attack." The divisions only seem to have been required to carry out local moves in each sector with reduced brigades. The forces were neither planned nor used as an integral part of a "divisional offensive."

For the attack, the Egyptians employed armored forces that had been engaged in the fighting and defense of the bridgeheads. They were reinforced with only two tank brigades (the Third Armored Brigade from the Fourth Division and the First Armored Brigade from the Twenty-first Division) that were transferred from second-echelon forces on the western bank.[265]

The sluggish attack failed to proceed according to clear objectives. The Egyptians probably had no intention of reaching the final lines in the sectors and routes where the attack was being made.[266] The units were ordered to engage only in local tactical, "attainable" missions, that is, "to make a show of doing something." They advanced hesitantly, halted in each sector after a few kilometers or wherever they encountered enemy fire (whose source was usually static defense positions).

It is hard to describe the Egyptian advance in generalized terms since each brigade tended to move along one axis in a limited brigade-level operation, apparently without a divisional (let alone field army) envelope.

In the Eighteenth Infantry Division's sector, the attack began with the Fifteenth Independent Armored Brigade (T-62 tanks), which had been annexed to the division. The brigade rumbled onto the Kantara-Baluza axis and was stopped after about four kilometers before the Artillery Road.

In the Second Infantry Division's sector, the Twenty-fourth Armored Brigade of the Twenty-third Mechanized Division went into action. The brigade, which had been annexed to the Second Infantry, made to a wide sweep in the Firdan sector but was blocked every time it tried to break out of the defensive areas at the division's bridgeheads.

Diagram 15: Master Plan of the Attack on October 14, 1973

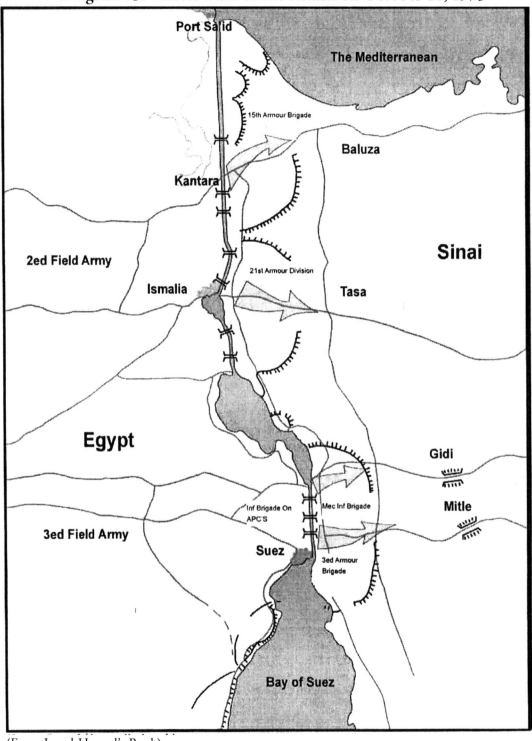

(From Jamal Hamad's Book)

At the Sixteenth Infantry Division's bridgehead, in the area between Ismalia and Deversoir, two tank brigades (the First and Fourteenth, both from the Twenty-first Mechanized Division) commenced operations. The Fourteenth had been active here since the beginning of the war as part the infantry division's reinforcements. The First Brigade was one of only three tank brigades that had crossed the canal to strengthen the attack. This was the only sector in which two armored brigades from the same division operated. Could their halfhearted advance be considered a coordinated divisional attack? The brigades proceeded in two flanks along the bridgehead. No attempt at coordination or concerted effort was visible. In this sector, too, where both sides employed huge numbers of tanks, one intelligence officer in Arik Sharon's division recalls that the Egyptian offensive was hardly a full-scale armored division thrust; it was more like a piecemeal approach to the east[267] that was repulsed by IDF tank fire every time it came in range.

The Egyptian armored forces, at the Third Army's infantry divisions' bridgeheads, also advanced east into Sinai. The independent armored brigade that had been part the Seventh Infantry Division's ORBAT, was again sent east (like the previous day), and again the daylight maneuver was blocked by IDF tanks which didn't budge from their fixed positions on the Artillery Road.

A fresh armored force in the Nineteenth Infantry Division (Third Army) sector, the Third Armored Brigade (the only element of the Fourth Armored Division to make the crossing), was sent to the east bank. The brigade operated in a cul-de-sac — Wadi Mabuk — an area where no major armor battles had taken place till now. The relatively deep advance, to the outer limit of the narrow areas at the divisional bridgehead, came up against the IDF infantry's forward defense perimeter and was forced back by Israeli infantry fire which immediately received armor and air support.[268] Additional forces from the Twenty-second Armored Brigade (Sixth Mechanized Division, which operated as part of the Nineteenth Infantry Division) made a parallel flanking move south of the Twenty-second. However, IDF infantry, defensively deployed in the area, impeded this effort too.

The relative advantage of the IDF's armored forces came to full expression in this stage of the war, destroying a large number of enemy tanks,[269] quickly seizing the initiative, crossing the canal into Egypt proper, and advancing to within 101 kilometers of Cairo. In addition, the Israelis managed to encircle the Egyptian Third Army on the east bank, cutting off their medical supplies, as well as food and water.

The Egyptians may have intended to give Israeli commanders the impression that it was finally facing the armored attack it had been expecting since the outbreak of war: a full-scale tank thrust along the entire length of the front. After most of the Egyptian armor had been hit earlier by IDF tank fire, it now proceeded gingerly. The tanks that escaped the Israeli firewall retreated and were reabsorbed in their organized defense layouts at the divisional bridgeheads; there they came under the protection of infantry and antitank weapons.

Special Forces (SF) (Commandos) and Their Use in Combat

Egyptian SF in general and especially the commando forces were an integral part of the operational plan and the events that developed during the fighting.

Commandos took part in all phases of the fighting, mostly according to the warfare doctrine which called for their maximum use in the opening stages of the war: the canal crossing and capture of the bridgeheads on the eastern bank. This activity was carefully planned and organized.

In the later stages of the war, the fighting, and especially the commando operations that tried to thwart the IDF crossing and breakthrough to the western bank, was hastily carried out and repeatedly changed. The Egyptian units were thrown haphazardly into unplanned missions.

Since the commandos and their officers operated as a light-armed mobile force, they fought without complex operational orders. Israel has almost no material on them. Also, the Israelis captured no commando headquarters or installations during the war. Nevertheless, in every order at the divisional level and higher, a commando force was integrated into the battle plan and their missions outlined. The material in this chapter is based on Egyptian and Soviet doctrinal material, captured documents (mostly from the Third Army), and a retrospective analysis of commando and other SF operations during the war.

The Commando Forces — The Combat Doctrine

Egyptian commando units can be identified by two types of missions. First, as an elite infantry unit, they are used at the tactical level for carrying out special assignments or serving as a reserve force for battlefield contingencies. Second, as highly skilled troops alongside paratroop battalions and brigades, they are sent on airborne missions far behind enemy lines.

An elite infantry force, the commandos are subject to all of the doctrinal principles and rules of engagement. As an airborne force, they are likely to take part in operations deep in enemy territory. They assist the field units on their tactical or operational assignments, and can also be employed on special reconnaissance and sabotage operations deep in the enemy's rear, like the Russian SF (Spetznatz).

A deep-penetration SF landing can be made in daylight or nighttime by air, sea, or a combined air-sea operation. Small commando units can infiltrate the enemy rear by several means: parachute, helicopter, naval vessel, land vehicle, or on foot.

At the operative level, SF strength will be a battalion or brigade that will operate in conjunction with the field army's mission. According to the combat doctrine, GHQ will have command over the force during the preparatory and initial stages until the force links up with the forward troops; later the force will be transferred to the field army's command.

Forces landed at the tactical level will be taken from commando units or second-echelon infantry units. These forces will generally be in the strength of a company or as far as a battalion, and will come under the command of the field army during all phases of the operation, until it joins up with the forward troops. Only in exceptional circumstances will the landing be carried out under divisional command, and only after the necessary equipment has been supplied.

The Soviet warfare doctrine recommends preparing and training companies of regular and even mechanized infantry units for missions entailing landing operations. In July 1972 the Egyptian chief of staff ordered all divisions to train a reinforced infantry company or a special-task company for landing operations. But, because of the large number of fully operational commando battalions, there was no need to train regular infantry troops for special assignments.

The mission of the tactical forces landed in enemy territory is likely to entail securing vital areas in the enemy's defense layout; neutralizing command-and-control facilities; attacking artillery batteries; disrupting command and maintenance systems; capturing mountain passes; and so forth. For attack operations in coastal areas, seaborne landings are planned. Seaborne forces' missions might include isolating the battlefield in order to hamper the arrival of enemy reserves, raiding military installations, recon patrols, and sabotage.

Organizing and Preparing the Commandos for Combat

The Egyptian commandos were (and still are) part of the SF layout that also includes paratroopers and marines. The supreme commando headquarters is responsible, like the headquarters of all the other branches in the Egyptian army, for the force's instruction and training, and maintenance of its strength and operational level. The supreme commando headquarters also deals with operational planning, especially its technical aspects, while the use of the force in the field usually comes under the command of the divisional or field army headquarters that the commando force is assigned to.

When the Yom Kippur War broke out there were twenty-four commando battalions in the Egyptian army, organized in six groups (*majmu'ot*)—each of which consisted of three to five battalions. Support units included one battalion of Sager antitank missiles[270] and a group of BM-21s (122 millimeter rocket launchers)—for long-range assistance to the force operating deep in the fighting zone.

The commander of the commando group assigned to the field army or divisional headquarters is responsible for the group's operations. When a battalion-sized (or smaller) commando force is attached to a division or field army, command of the force is given to the commander under whose jurisdiction the force has been assigned.

The structure of a commando battalion enables the flexible use of its troops. It may be divided into company teams reinforced with support weapons, and even smaller teams, such as tank-hunter parties. The operational function of the commando units creates a structure suitable for carrying out such missions.

The commandos' warfare doctrine calls for a high degree of mobility on land and in the air (generally coordinated with helicopters). Commando units are also trained for naval operations on the high seas, in lakes, and Egypt's canals. For this purpose the units practiced using rubber boats. Another SF unit is the "marine brigade"—a mechanized infantry brigade that uses amphibious vehicles. The 130th Amphibious Brigade—built on the same structure as the commando battalions—was transferred from its base in Alexandria to the Third Army's northern sector.[271] The unit was trained in independent antitank fighting, given the necessary equipment, and instructed in defense procedures and antiaircraft combat. Night fighting was of special importance, a skill that was acquired through intensive training and sophisticated night-vision equipment that provided the Egyptian commandos with tactical superiority over the enemy.

A commando battalion, the basic SF formation, consisted of three combat companies, one support company, and a company-sized headquarters. Each combat company had three platoons and one squad of special antitank troops equipped with six RPG-7 antitank rockets. Each commando platoon was made up of two eight-man teams, including an extra two-man antitank team (shooter and loader).[272]

A commando company numbering roughly seventy men was smaller than a regular infantry company but had relatively greater firepower to enable it to engage in independent fighting. The support company, too, was stronger than a regular infantry support company, and provided the commando battalion with independent support capability. The support company contained one platoon of light (60-millimeter) mortars; one eighteen-man sniper platoon of nine two-man teams; and one engineering platoon of twenty-three sappers equipped with mines, explosives, and mine detectors.

The basic commando force—the battalion—generally received nonorganic support units to assist in the missions. The battalion was also given a platoon or company of man-portable

Sager antitank missiles, as well as a platoon of personal SA-7 antiaircraft missiles (that the Egyptians called *al-Haya*, more commonly known as "Strela" missiles). The battalion was also provided with fire support from the unit whose area it was operating in. The battalion further received organic support from the SF group in the form of a company or battery armed with long-range, B-21 rocket launchers.

The commandos were chosen from recruits, generally high-school grads, who were in excellent physical condition. Commando candidates underwent rigorous training to prepare them for special operations in challenging combat conditions. In addition to basic military skills, their training included physical exercises, and especially intensive practice in navigation and evasion.

The company was the basic commando training framework for practicing raids and ambushes. Commando battalions went through regular infantry offensive and defensive exercises, as well as special training that approximated live combat conditions.

Special task training included helicopter drills, daytime and nighttime navigation, amphibious exercises, combat in a coastal environment, day and night antitank ambushes (with or without missiles), destroying tank parks, and survival in enemy territory. The war planner found practical application for all of these skills.

Commando Missions in the War

The Egyptians put great stock in their commando force, building the units with top-notch soldiers and supplying them with first-rate equipment and instruction. The intensive use of commando units in the War of Attrition — in raids, ambushes, and strikes against strongholds — taught lessons that the entire army benefited from. Chief of Staff Shazli regarded the commando force as "his baby,"[273] and men of the SF were held in high esteem in the army.

Commando missions were carried out deep inside the Israeli layout. The commandos were a reserve force specially designed for troubleshooting. In-depth missions (the majority of which were not carried out) included isolating the battlefield in order to block enemy reserves from entering the combat zone; protecting the ground forces' advance by capturing vital areas deep in the enemy's territory; and sabotaging command and control installations.[274]

The first two missions in the war that commandos undertook were combat operations and seizing the enemy's layouts in the mountain terrain of the Gidi and Mitle ridges. The subject had been taught and practiced in 1972 when the Third Army prepared a doctrinal study on "seizing and securing the mountain passes in an offensive operation."[275] The study found that sealing off the entrance and exit to the passes could be accomplished by parachuted or helicopter-landed troops who would capture the passes, defend their entranceways, and link up with the advancing ground forces. A company- to battalion-sized commando force would land on each flank of the passes. The plan's impressive details characterized, as stated, Egyptian military thinking in 1972. When the plan for a limited offensive operation was adopted, most of the long-range commando missions were canceled.

The third mission was disrupting enemy headquarters, communications and radar bases, water and phone lines, and supply depots. According to 1972 doctrinal studies, this was supposed to be accomplished by highly trained and well-equipped commando groups that would infiltrate enemy territory two or three days before the offensive and sabotage command centers. To the best of my knowledge, this was a copy of Soviet Spetznatz missions.[276] There is no proof that Egyptian commandos carried out such raids before the war.

At the tactical level, the commando units were part of the initial stage of the war: seizing and securing the waterline, attacking special strongholds (such as "Mezah" fortress in the Nineteenth Division's sector), carrying out raids, and setting up antitank ambushes. They were also ordered to protect the attacking force's flanks and secure the gaps between the bridgeheads.

Three commando formations (six groups) were planned to engage in operations during the war[277]: two groups — under the command of the chief of staff— for isolating the battlefield and cutting off the in-depth axes; two — with the support of the field armies — to assist in establishing the bridgeheads; and two — under the command of the officer in charge of the Red Sea Command — to take over the bay's eastern coast and the Sharm e-Sheikh area.[278] The groups under the command of the General Staff were tasked with protecting deep areas of the battle zone by setting up ambushes and blocking axes in order to prevent the advance of IDF reserves.[279] The commando groups would operate in coordination with each of the field armies' sectors in sealing off the mountain passes at their western egresses, thus enabling the field armies to establish bridgeheads in their particular sectors. The commandos would continue this activity until they linked up with the field armies' forward units.

The commando groups' mission, which was an essential element in the plan to capture the entire area up to the passes, was worked out to the last detail. Be that as it may, it was canceled when the plan was jettisoned and its objectives reduced.[280]

According to the aforementioned 1972 doctrinal study, "the takeover and securing of the mountain passes" meant capturing and holding the Mitle defile. This would require one or two airborne commando battalions, reinforced with mortars and antitank weapons, supported by planes and artillery, and at least one additional motorized infantry battalion that would link up with them. According to the author of the study, the capture of the Gidi could be accomplished by a smaller force.

The Seventh Division's battle order for Operation "Granite 2 Improved" — Battle Order No. 1— which was probably issued in early 1973 before the cutback in missions, envisioned a commando battalion landing in the western entrance to the Gidi defile, "in order to detain the enemy's reserves and prevent their advance as early as possible."

The electronic warfare orders for Operation "Granite 2 Improved," issued by the Third Army on September 28, 1973, also mentions the commando group's missions operating under the field army's command. The document states that the three commando battalions would assist in developing the attack in the enemy's depth. They would move out of the Third Army's front line, penetrate east of the defiles in Wadi Sudar, Mitle, and Gidi in order to disrupt the IDF's retreat, assist the Egyptian units breaching the enemy's second defense line, and prevent the enemy from reinforcing his defensive positions.

In reality, neither in the opening or later stages of the war were the commando battalions helicoptered to the passes' western and eastern openings. To the best of my knowledge, no commando landing occurred in the areas facing the main combat zone — the Refidim Opening and Gidi and Mitle Passes.

A seaborne and airborne landing was made on the margins of the Second Army's area — in northern sector's marshy region near Rumani — but no serious activity was detected on the main axis from Tasa and the Refidim Opening.

Israeli Air Force (IAF) sources note helicopter activity on the first evening of the war: a commando battalion was airlifted in the Katib e-Sabha area (between Tasa and Refidim). According to the IAF, most of the helicopters were shot down in flight. Whatever happened, no commando activity was located in the area. If such a landing was attempted on the first evening, why was it not carried out in more important and convenient areas for SF operations, such as the Mitle and Gidi Passes?

A force (about the size of a commando battalion) did land at Wadi Sudar, on the southern fringe of the Third Army's combat zone.[281] Despite the field army's efforts on the axes leading to the Mitle and Gidi Passes, or at the passes themselves, no commando activity was detected in the area.

According to the official Egyptian version (that Israeli military historians also adopted), the change in H-Hour for the opening shot of the war was the reason why the missions were canceled.[282] Some people (wishing to justify their decision) claim that moving the H-Hour forward from the evening hours to 14:00 made a commando landing impossible because of the danger of detection parallel with the launching of the canal crossing.[283] I believe that the campaign's limited dimensions and the size of the bridgeheads not only put the commando operations in harm's way, but also made it imperative that they be canceled. On the one hand, it was impossible for the crossing units to link up with the commando forces; on the other hand the commandos would be hard-pressed to pull back and reach bridgeheads of reduced scope.

Some observers see another reason for the commandos remaining on the sidelines: a landing just before evening would not leave them enough time to block the IDF counterattack.[284] It would have taken the IDF armor reserves approximately four hours from the time the war broke out to organize and reach the fighting zone on the canal. In my assessment, only at that point could the Egyptian commandos carry out their main task of isolating the battlefield from the enemy's main forces — the reservists' divisions. The IDF's regular (conscript) divisions in Sinai, that were supposed to meet the challenge of the initial attack, were much smaller than the reservist units that would soon enter the fray.

The Egyptians adopted many elements in the Soviet SF warfare doctrine. The Spetznatz was trained for long-range operation behind enemy lines. In the European theater, they were expected to reach their objectives a few days before the offensive opened. In the unique environment of an open desert, and in the Egyptians' plan for a surprise attack, there was practically no room for pre-strike commando operations.

Two commando groups were planned to go into action. One managed to carry out seaborne and airborne landings deep in Israeli-held Sinai. Both groups were dispatched to the Red Sea Command to capture the eastern shore of the Bay of Suez. Their goal was to gain control of the "oil corridor" (whose center was the town of Abu Rhodeis) and assist as much as possible in the capture of the "Solomon vicinity" (whose capital was Sharm e-Sheikh). Another goal was to employ the commandos in this remote sector as a kind of diversionary force that would demoralize the IDF while the troops were engaged in the main combat theater on the canal.[285]

Operations were supposed to take place in two stages. The commando group operating on the first evening of the war was supposed to land on the coast between Ras Malab and Ras Shargiv (where the Sixth Mechanized Division's First Motorized Brigade would pass on its way from the city of Suez to Ras Sudar) and proceed south to Sharm e-Sheikh. The commando group had to protect the brigade's movement, and then proceed with it on its assignment.

The second group was planned to be seaborne and airborne into Sinai and would capture part of the Sharm e-Sheikh area. This stage depended on the success of the ground moves and the motorized brigade's advance along the Bay of Suez coast.

Although some of the first group's battalions reached their destinations, things soon went amiss. The motorized brigade failed to arrive,[286] and after a few days of taking intense evasion action, the exhausted commandos were wiped out or taken prisoner. Other units from the group were shot down while in flight or during the landing by ground fire and Israeli warplanes. Gamasi relates that a number of helicopters were destroyed by Israeli aircraft while the commandos were deplaning, and before the helicopters had time to take off.[287] Most of the forces crossing in rubber boats were annihilated from the air.

Some observers blame the nonuse of Egyptian commandos in the Bay of Suez on the forces' failure to accomplish their missions. I see it as another example of the limited attack, and the senior political level's strategy of gaining limited objectives on the canal front. Since the fighting in the secondary sectors would have only negligibly contributed to the main effort, it was abandoned. We should note that the Egyptian force that was supposed to link up with the commandos at the Bay of Suez and proceed with them on their mission, was used falteringly for limited operations and was easily crushed by an Israeli paratroop brigade.

Two other commando groups were more active. Operating under the command of the field armies, the commandos were used mainly for infantry assignments in coordination with the crossing forces or in the relatively deep sections of their front — missions that were successfully accomplished. These missions included helping set up and securing bridgeheads; laying ambushes and raiding headquarters, artillery batteries, and tank concentrations in the enemy's tactical depth; sabotaging communications and water lines; attacking special strongholds (such as the Mezah stronghold in Port Ibrahim), and guarding the "seams" between friendly units.[288] In reality, the maximum depth the commandos operated did not go beyond twenty-five kilometers from the canal — to the vicinity of Rumani and Ras Sudar (on the flanks of the main effort).[289]

Six commando battalions were used in the initial crossing wave and two in later operations. Each infantry division that made the crossing was reinforced with a commando battalion.[290] The Nineteenth Division received a battalion whose mission was to capture the Mezah stronghold. Infantry units were given antitank teams from infantry divisions that were scheduled to land by helicopter behind the canal road during the artillery softening up (in the first thirty minutes of the war), and operate as an antitank, rear defense line and tank hunters on the routes of advance that the Egyptian planners assumed would be taken by Israel's tactical reserves deployed in the strongholds.[291] This type of mission, recommended in the warfare doctrine, appeared in one of the early attack orders.[292] But no such missions appear to have been carried out during the war. Each commando group seems to have kept one battalion on the eastern bank as a field army reserve.[293]

The commando battalions that reinforced the infantry divisions were planned for special missions: crossing the canal in rubber boats in the first waves; assisting in the erection of the bridgeheads; and sporadically attacking key targets in enemy territory.

Although the use of commando forces appears in the basic plan — to the tactical depth of thirty kilometers from the bridgeheads, the SF were not sent on missions except in the northern sector of the combat zone, the Rumani area, where they landed deep in enemy territory and set up ambushes to block the northern axis. The use of commandos in the later stages of the fighting, after the securing of the bridgeheads, was uncharacteristic of deep operations. The only place where Egyptian commandos operated with some degree of success was, again, in the northern sector, where they gained hold of a sandbank close to the coast and in the marsh area, and carried out raids and ambushes. In later stages of the fighting (especially after the IDF crossed the canal into Egypt proper), the commandos were used as light, mobile forces to stop the gaps in the rear of the Egyptian layout and block and harass advancing enemy forces.

The 130th Amphibious Marine Brigade

The basic plan for using SF in the war called for the integration of an additional force — the 130th Amphibious Marine Brigade. This unit was built along the lines of the Soviet Naval Infantry Regiment. When the brigade was set up, the Egyptians applied what they learned from IDF amphibious landings in the Abu al-Daraj and al-Zafrana area on September 23, 1969.[294] The brigade was made up of two battalions, each with three companies of APCs and a company of light tanks (as well as logistical and administrative units).[295]

The brigade was established in 1972 with some structural differences from the Soviet naval infantry regiment. The main difference was the reduction of the tank battalion to two tank companies, each of which reinforced a motorized infantry battalion. Also, there were no administrative or support units, nor even an air defense battery, missile battery, or ABC (atomic, biological, and chemical) unit. The brigade's structure was adapted to Egyptian needs. Two amphibious missions were carried out in the combat theater, one in the lakes area and the other north of the Bay of Suez. Thus, two parallel frameworks seem to have been set up.[296]

In his memoirs, Shazli discusses the creation of the amphibious brigade and its mission training. He recalls that on June 15, 1972, with the brigade's completion, he prepared and circulated Order No. 15: "The Amphibious Battalion Operating as the Spearhead in Negotiating a Water Obstacle." On August 28 trial runs for a landing were carried out, and the brigade's first serious exercise was held on the night of October 22–23. The brigade participated in another practice drill in the presence of the chief of staff on the night of July 18–19, 1973, in which it underwent night naval operations, sailing almost thirty kilometers, landing at a predetermined site, and advancing deep into the enemy's layout to attack his positions and isolate the battlefield. One of the battalions accomplished its mission, but the other lost its way in the water, landed in the wrong place, and made a series of blunders: two vessels with ten soldiers capsized, and three of the men drowned.

Prior to the war, the brigade, under the command of Col. Mahmud Shueibi, numbered approximately one thousand men. Two of the battalions were reinforced with APCs and light amphibious tanks,[297] a mechanized infantry company and antitank company of BRDM-2s (armored scout cars) bearing Sager rockets.[298] These sophisticated defensive weapons were added in order to improve the battalions' ability to counter IDF armor. A commando company whose objective was to knock out Israeli mortar batteries was also planned to take part in the landing.[299]

The brigade came under Third Army command. In the original offense plan, the brigade was supposed to make an amphibious crossing north of the Bay of Suez and Little Bitter Lake and join up with and strengthen commando forces in the western openings of the Mile and Gidi passes.

Seventh Division's Operational Order No. 1 defined the amphibious battalion's mission in the following manner: "At the start of the opening artillery barrage, a battalion team will set out from the abandoned Camp Shalufa and make a seaborne landing on the shore of the Little Bitter Lakes (in the direction of Gidi) where it will proceed as a task force and quickly link up with commando forces already operating at the western entrance of the Gidi Pass. It will block the pass so as to prevent the enemy's reserves from going through it."[300] The operational plan called for breaking through the IDF's defense layout (on the assumption that only token IDF forces had been left to defend the lakes and Bay of Suez region).

In addition to amphibious brigade activity in the Third Army sector, similar operations took place on a smaller scale in the Second Army sector. A force of ten amphibious APCs floated across the Great Bitter Lake, landed on the eastern shore under the command of the Sixteenth Division, and immediately began to seal off the axis road east of canal.[301]

The plan's reduced dimensions naturally resulted in a cutback in the brigade's missions. Maj. General Wasal, Third Army commander, canceled the southern mission and kept the two battalions in Camp Shalufa in the vicinity of Kabrit (on the western shore of the Little Bitter Lake). Some brigade units crossed the lake and reached objectives east of the canal. The cancellation of the commando landings also had a diminishing effect on the brigade's missions. A ground force was no longer available to link up with and reinforce the units in a blocking position at the entranceways to the mountain passes.[302]

The brigade[303] embarked upon its assignment at the beginning of the artillery softening-up, about a half hour before the canal crossing. Brigade troops crossed the eight kilometers of the Little Bitter Lake, landing on the opposite shore without any losses.[304] The Third Army's battle diary notes that the brigade's first forces hit the beaches at 14:36 (approximately forty minutes after starting time). The brigade continued its eastward advance, perhaps in an attempt to reach the Gidi defiles. The Egyptians claim that a small brigade force headed east, raided a radar station at Mitle on October 7, and attacked the Bir Tmada airfield on October 8. Nothing in the Israeli sources corroborates these claims.[305]

The result of the clashes with the IDF, deep in enemy territory (on the Great Bitter Lake coast and Artillery Road in the "Mitzva" stronghold), was heavy destruction to the lightly protected amphibious force. The survivors linked up with units in Seventh Division's defense layouts at the bridgeheads, and the force split into two battalions: one to protect the bridgehead's northern flank and mainly defend the besieged "Botzer" stronghold on the eastern shore between the two lakes; the other battalion reorganized on the western bank.

On October 17, the Twenty-fifth Independent Tank Brigade moved out from the bridgehead south of the lakes, and attacked northward along the eastern shores in an attempt to seal off the IDF's crossing corridor in the Deversoir area. The Egyptian failure had repercussions: some of their forces had to withdraw from the Botzer stronghold and return to the western bank.

The Twenty-fifth and 130th Brigades, dug in on the western shore of the Great Bitter Lake, engaged in a defense battle against Israeli units that had crossed the canal and were pushing south to the city of Suez.[306] The remaining Egyptian forces held the stronghold until the cease-fire went into effect.

Summary

It will be recalled that the Egyptians established a formidable SF (commando) ORBIT. SF units were planned and trained to carry out various operations (most of which had been performed with relative success in the War of Attrition) and were supposed to provide an excellent addition in the Yom Kippur War.

In the 1973 War the commandos were planned to take part in a wide range of missions at the operative level. However the majority of these missions were canceled when the war plan itself was reduced. SF units that were sent far behind enemy lines achieved very minimal results. One of the reasons for their failure was the extreme vulnerability of the Egyptian helicopters ferrying the troops to their destinations. The IAF made mincemeat out of them.

Twenty of the fifty helicopters used on the first day of the war were shot down in flight or when landing in the target area. Undoubtedly, such high losses in aircraft and commandos made flying a very risky operation and detracted from the willingness of the commanders and troops to embark on further operations.

The Egyptian commandos who remained deep in enemy territory had to engage in evasive maneuvers and try to join up with their advancing forces (which did not take place and, apparently was not even planned to take place in any of the sectors). The commandos' attempts to carry out their missions — for example, the ambush in Wadi Sudar — failed disastrously at a heavy cost in lives. Some slightly more successful attempts, such as blocking the northern axis in the Rumani area or setting ambushes on the Mediterranean coast near the "Budapest" stronghold, were quickly eliminated.

The SF's contribution in tactical combat was significant. When commandos fought alongside regular infantry units at the bridgeheads, the level of fighting improved. The commandos displayed greatest skill when operating as tank hunters close to the lines, and were relatively successful in blocking the penetration of Israeli units on the western bank of the Suez Canal.

In sum, the Egyptians apparently believed that by constructing a formidable SF layout, the commandos would carry out daring missions deep in enemy territory. In the end, SF units were used too close to the front lines and in too small of a number. Under these conditions their effect was minimal.

Egyptian Artillery Before and During the War

As stated, the Arabs suffered from air inferiority in the Yom Kippur War. In order to overcome this problem they concentrated on applying artillery, especially in the preparatory stages of the war. The Syrians had nearly 500 artillery pieces on the Golan Heights front (less than seventy kilometers long), and the Egyptians made exemplary use of their 1,500 barrels on the canal front (almost 170 kilometers long, though the guns were not employed in certain sections, such as the marshes north and south of the lakes).[307] The Egyptians applied support fire against a wide range of targets in the opening stages of the war.

The massive concentration of firepower assisted the infantry during the construction of the bridgeheads and reduced to a minimum the need to make complex maneuvers in the combat zone.

The IDF proved its superior maneuverability (especially in the Six-Day War) and knew how to make the most of its mobile troops during an attack, but the Egyptians limited their use of armor and motorized forces in the Yom Kippur War, a tactic which offset the advantages of Israeli ground troops.

Captured maps and documents, and statements from Egyptian POWs (and Israeli soldiers who were on the receiving end) all provide a valuable understanding of Egypt's prewar artillery planning and its application in the first stages of the war.

The Artillery Doctrine

According to the Soviet concept, artillery is not only a support weapon but also a key element in the success of a mission. The idea that artillery is a weapon of destruction stands at the base of artillery's organizational structure, application, and the support frameworks that it requires.[308]

Artillery and rockets furnish tremendous firepower, and pave the way on the battlefield, both physically and psychologically, for infantrymen, mobile troops, and tanks. For hundreds of years the Russian army has put the artillery to better use than any other army in the world.[309]

The Soviets internalized the lessons of the "Great Patriotic War" (World War II), the largest land conflict in human history in terms of men and weapons. Soviet artillery reached its acme when it employed "breaching divisions" for offensive operations. The Soviets concentrated a massive density of guns, sometimes 200 to 250 per kilometer in a sector planned for an attack. In the advance on Berlin the density at the front exceeded 500 guns (cannons and mortars) per kilometer.[310]

The Russians estimate that field artillery alone caused the Germans about 70 percent of their damages and losses in World War II. These statistics dramatically illustrate the reason for artillery's priority in Soviet military thinking.[311]

World War II taught Soviet military planners that the concentration of artillery fire in a conventional war[312] greatly assisted the advance of armored and motorized forces. The Egyptians deployed their artillery in the Yom Kippur War on the basis of the Soviet doctrine,[313] generally using it as support for the infantry which carried out the main tasks in the campaign: crossing the canal and defending the bridgeheads.

The Soviet military encyclopedia has a number of definitions for "artillery": a military branch; a type of weapon; and the production of artillery weapons and their use on the battlefield. This broad definition includes tactics and the art of application.[314] The following section discusses the theory of artillery application in offensive moves at the field army, divisional, and brigade levels — the levels that the Egyptian artillery was employed in during the Yom Kippur War. Almost all of the material is based on captured documents that deal at length with the doctrine of artillery usage. Nearly all of the material was translated from Soviet doctrinal sources.[315]

As stated, artillery is the land army's main weapon of firepower. It is used for incapacitating and demolishing enemy forces and their weapons (cannons, mortars, tanks, headquarters, and command-and-control systems).

In order to paralyze the enemy's defenses and protect one's maneuvering forces (infantry and tanks), artillery must lay down a preparatory barrage before the attack and during the breaching of the defense layouts. The barrage accompanies the operation into its tactical depth, continuously pounding away at key targets. In the nineteenth century, the use of artillery in an offensive was characterized by three stages: the initial softening-up, support fire, and accompanying fire that reaches the enemy's tactical depth.[316] We will add a fourth stage: the preliminary stage (*ha'amna'a* in Arabic) — covering fire for the forces advancing to the attack. Two stages, the preliminary and accompanying fire stages, were irrelevant for the Egyptian plan.

As a rule, in preparatory fire (and support fire at a later stage) the artillery is integrated from the first-echelon brigades, divisions, and field army. If necessary, second-echelon divisional artillery will reinforce the first-echelon artillery and be integrated into it to increase firepower. Direct trajectory fire by tanks, tank destroyers, and other antitank weapons may also take part in the preparatory stage.

Artillery will be regrouped at the completion of the first stage of the operation (in the Egyptian case, after crossing the canal and securing the bridgeheads) or while the second echelon is maneuvering to repulse counterattacks. The reinforcement and regrouping of the artillery at the divisional level will be altered during an operation according to each division's location and assignments. A division engaged in the main effort will receive three or four extra battalions.

When two or more divisions are used on a main-effort axis, a field army artillery group of four to five battalions will be created. The group will be employed as anti-battery fire against enemy artillery and be used to destroy vital targets. It will also assist the field army's second echelon and help to beat back enemy counterattacks. This artillery group may be divided into subgroups according to the number of divisions (usually two), as in the Egyptian case.

The scope of softening-up fire depends on the nature of the enemy's defenses, its vulnerability, and the number of weapons in the attacker's arsenal. Direct or indirect fire will be used to paralyze the enemy's troops and neutralize his weapons.[317] The softening-up stage should take place in daylight so that accurate adjustments can be made. The time span for the preparatory fire is between forty and sixty minutes (sometimes longer),[318] in three to five barrages lasting five to twenty minutes.

The Soviet doctrine recommends preparatory fire on the enemy's first layout, his artillery and mortar positions, headquarters, and logistical facilities. The second barrage should be deeper, enabling direct trajectory fire to hit front-line targets. Another barrage will pound the enemy's forward layout, during which time assault forces, under the cover of friendly fire, will approach their objectives. The barrage will cease a few minutes before the assault so that the attacking force can proceed safely.

Support fire must continue throughout the operation, pounding at the enemy's defense layout, installations, weapons, and any other position that obstructs the forces' progress. Support fire against the enemy's defense layout calls for a "rolling fire curtain" to paralyze the enemy's troops and weapons. The curtain will be at a two- or three-kilometer depth and is generally delivered only in the sector where the main effort is taking place because it requires a dense concentration of artillery pieces and enormous supply of ammunition.[319]

When the defense layout is based on unconnected strongholds, like those on the "Bar-Lev Line," firepower will consist of concentrations of successive fire or massive fire on select targets. Each target will receive a successive concentration of fire from one artillery battery. The timespan for each line of fire delivery depends on the distance between the lines and the attacking force's rate of advance.

The doctrine discusses in detail fire support for the second echelon. The second echelon's mission was to seize and secure the line, then deploy on it and proceed to advance. When the Egyptian planners decided to limit the war's tactical objectives, the second echelon no longer had to develop the attack. Some of the second-echelon artillery units were sent to the bridgeheads where they continued target fire while defending the bridgeheads.

According to the warfare doctrine, the artillery's missions in the transition to a defense position are: employing long-range fire concentrations to disrupt approaching enemy columns; employing massive firepower to neutralize enemy forces on their deployment line; and helping repulse tank and infantry attacks in front of and inside the contact line using static smoke screens and concentrated direct fire.

According to the doctrine, the air force — especially fighter aircraft — will be used for ground support and integrated into the softening-up fire, especially against enemy installations and reserves. Later in the operation, the air force will carry out strikes against targets and provide air defense to cover the attacking forces.

Egyptian Artillery Just Prior to the Outbreak of the Yom Kippur War

The reader will recall that the Egyptian artillery was organized and positioned before and during the Yom Kippur War according to the Soviet warfare doctrine, which had been adapted to Egypt's unique operational needs in Sinai.

Besides cannons, mortars, and rocket launchers, the Egyptian artillery layout also included surface-to-surface Frog and Scud missiles, as well as locally manufactured inferior quality missiles. The artillery branch was in charge of the antitank layout,[320] which was based primarily on Sager antitank missiles, as well as antitank rocket launchers and dual-purpose cannons that were used for indirect artillery fire.

The Egyptians gained valuable artillery experience in the War of Attrition.[321] The branch became an organic part of the field formation from the brigade and division level to the field army level.

Every Egyptian brigade had an organic field artillery and antiaircraft missile battery attached to it. Infantry brigades had portable missiles, and armored brigades had BRDM-2s for transporting the missiles. Motorized and infantry brigades also had a 120-millimeter mortar battery and antitank cannon battery attached to it.

At the division level, the artillery was generally based on a three- to four-battalion artillery group, an antitank missile battalion and antitank cannon battalion. Two armored divisions received a battalion of BM-21 rocket launchers (relatively long-ranged modern weapons) and an antitank cannon battalion. The motorized divisions were reinforced with a battalion of older rocket launchers taken from the armored divisions.

The field army (the Egyptians employed two field armies on the canal front) concentrated its artillery forces in a field-artillery brigade, along with a regiment of heavy assault cannon,[322] a battalion of light assault cannons,[323] a battalion of self-propelled antitank weapons,[324] and a battalion that carried out patrols and target acquisition for the artillery.

Before the war the general staff organized another artillery force, most of which was reinforcement for the artillery ORBAT at the field formation level. Part of this layout was assigned other (usually long-range) missions and came under the direct command of the general staff.

This force was made up of two mixed artillery brigades containing 122-millimeter long-barreled cannons, 130- or 152-millimeter cannons, a number of 180-millimeter cannons, a few 155-millimeter cannons, a brigade of rocket launchers consisting of a number of battalions furnished with new BM-21 rocket launchers, a brigade of 160- and 240-millimeter heavy mortars, a Frog surface-to-surface rocket brigade, and a brigade of surface-to-surface Scud missiles.[325]

The Egyptians also employed a brigade-sized force of surface-to-surface, Egypt-made Tin and Zeitun rockets.

Command and Control at the Artillery Layout

According to Egypt's warfare doctrine, the field army and general staff has command of the artillery, and tries to centralize control over it as much as possible. Still, there is a tendency to give the contact forces direct control. At all levels, from the general staff to the brigade, an organic artillery unit exists for independent use as needs arise.

As the war approached the Egyptians sought to create an artillery group at the army, divisional, and brigade level, as doctrine recommended. Because of the problem of providing the entire front with a single artillery group, the group was divided into two subgroups.

The general staff's artillery was allotted to the field armies. This artillery and the field army and second-echelon division artillery were supposed to become an artillery task-force group for the field army and first-echelon divisions.

Some divisions assigned battalions from their organic artillery to reinforce or establish artillery groups for the brigades making the crossing. In order to guarantee nonstop, quick-response artillery support for the armored units, the artillery was not transferred from the tank brigades to the infantry brigades. Each level was left without reserve artillery units. Those that were not integrated into the first-echelon divisions' artillery groups remained to support the level that was making the crossing.

Two field army artillery groups were set up in the Third Army sector[326]: one had two battalions, the other four. These groups were established by annexing to the field army units (e.g. 180-millimeter cannons) from the GHQ's mixed artillery brigades. There is less information regarding Second Army sector. Here three artillery groups were apparently built at the field army level in order to support each of the divisional sector crossings.

The establishment of artillery groups created a problem of control. The Egyptians had to decide who the commander of the brigade group and the organic battalion was. Was it the senior battalion commander or the commander of the artillery brigade whose battalions were annexed to the units?

In addition to the artillery groups, the Egyptians organized antitank reserves which included self-propelled assault cannons and dual-purpose (field and antitank) towed guns. At the field army level there were generally two or more antitank reserves made up of various weapons from SU-100 tank-destroyer battalions, a battery of antitank cannons, and a battery or two of antitank missiles. At the divisional level, two and sometimes three antitank reserves were organized instead of the one reserve that the doctrine recommended. Each of the brigades also set up antitank reserves. As stated, the increase in the number of reserves demanded reinforcements with antitank weapons from the higher echelons.

In the first stages of the fighting the Egyptian fire plan was designed according to fixed calculations of the number of guns needed for a specific assignment; the amount of ammunition to be distributed was decided according to the number of barrels needed for each assignment, the required units, and the rate of delivery.

The commanders of the battalions and batteries generally worked alongside the commander of the assault force. According to the doctrine's recommendation, the fire units remained under the command of a gun position officer or deputy battalion commander — lower-level officers in the chain of command.

Acquisition[327] of Targets[328]

The Egyptians employ all the known systems for target acquisition. The theoretical literature emphasizes air photography and reconnaissance as the main sources of target acquisition.[329] The Egyptians do not seem to have regarded them as important elements in the war.

Each artillery headquarters in the field armies had a spotting battalion that employed various devices for target acquisition: sound detection of enemy batteries, muzzle-fire detection, communications, patrols, meteorology, and even a special battery for ground photography. At the divisional level, the artillery had reconnaissance and observation batteries, a platoon that specialized in sound detection, and ground radars for locating cannon and mortar fire.

Each artillery group was allotted technical gear for target acquisition. There were also electronic warfare units at the field army level, capable of locating enemy ground radar. The SNAR self-propelled battlefield surveillance radar was operated by field army artillery subgroups and used most effectively in night conditions because of its special viewing features.

Range Adjustment and Fire Control

Forward observation officers attached to the operational forces at the company level and higher were often responsible for range adjustment. Battery and artillery battalion commanders served as observation and fire control officers in forward positions — serving in forward artillery observation posts and in forward positions of the assault forces' commanders. Optical range finders and binoculars were the most common means for calculating target range.

The Egyptians' dream was to have an artillery battalion commander next to every assault battalion commander, and a battery commander alongside every company commander. Artillery commanders chose the type of ammunition and number of shells, etc., that would be used. Gun position officers in the field army sector generally made the range adjustments.[330]

Forward observation officers were also planned to operate deep in enemy territory, when they were attached to reconnaissance and commando units. The subject was planned by the two field armies but it proved inoperable because of communications problems in reaching the forward observation officers in the Third Army sector.

The registration and collection of grid coordinates for the targets was done manually; computers were practically nonexistent. Aircraft-dropped smoke bombs were used to mark targets in the field.

The Deployment of Egyptian Artillery

According to defense plan "Amalia 200," most of the Egyptian artillery batteries were placed in a deliberate deployment — well-entrenched fighting positions — on the west bank of the canal.

The warfare doctrine called for gradated battalion deployment, that is, one or two batteries forward and one or two further back, in areas 800–1,000 meters in length and 400–600 meters in depth. When an artillery battalion found itself in a narrow space or near the canal it was sometimes positioned in a straight line. Artillery deployment was made in brigade and divisional groupings and field army subgroups. Deployment on the western bank was planned to extend over a wide area, while on the east bank it would be confined to a narrow area, mostly across from the main axes of advance.

Just before the opening barrage, several artillery units leapfrogged to alternate positions, but the majority remained in the emplacements they had been deployed from the last few preceding months. Reinforced artillery units moved forward and entered positions where they had been previously deployed or would be deployed in a defensive battle. Just before the war, a number of GHQ units moved into their forward battle positions.

Brigade artillery groupings deployed two to four kilometers from the canal; heavy mortars five kilometers from the waterline; and long-range weapons — especially 130-millimeter cannons — remained six to seven kilometers in the rear. All of this movement proceeded according to the Soviet warfare doctrine.

Fire Plan

According to the fire plan, the operation should open with a massive artillery barrage lasting fifty-three minutes, scheduled to commence fifteen minutes before H-Hour — that is, before the first forces entered the water.[331]

The first volley (fifteen minutes): The plan called for the shelling of enemy strongholds, fire sources, and radar stations. Under the cover of artillery fire, direct fire-laying units would secure their positions.

The second volley (twenty-two minutes): Shelling would continue on the strongholds and the inflammable device ("Or Yikarot"), as well as targets deeper in the rear.

The third volley (five minutes): Shelling would continue on the front-line strongholds and rearward headquarters.

The fourth volley (six minutes): The preparatory fire against the strongholds on the waterline would cease in order to allow Egyptian troops to assault them.[332] Artillery fire would be directed in-depth and against new targets. The cessation of fire on the front would enable the first wave to secure a toehold on the east bank.

The fifth volley (five minutes): Shelling would last until H-Hour plus thirty-eight minutes against new targets (close to the front and deeper inland).

Heavy 240-millimeter mortars were used against the Bar-Lev Line strongholds. The Egyptian plan called for two 240-millimeter mortars to fire sixty shells apiece in order to raze the stronghold. The plan also called for Egyptian-made, surface-to-surface Zeitun rockets to destroy the strongholds' compounds, communications trenches, observation posts, and obstacles at the entrances.

According to the doctrine, the breakthrough and crossing required more than seventy artillery pieces for each kilometer of front. This number was almost attained. The Egyptians discerned the difference between the "general density" of artillery in each attack sector, and the "specific density"—that is, the density needed only for the breakthrough. The concentration of Egyptian artillery in the softening-up barrage in the crossing stage was seventy-four guns per kilometer the entire length of the Seventh Division front on the Gidi axis, and sixty-nine guns in the Nineteenth Division breakthrough sector on the Mitle axis. All of this was in an area four kilometers deep. Together with the artillery in the secondary sectors, the artillery density in the entire sector of the divisional attack was twenty to thirty guns per kilometer of front.

The Third Army sector of attack — not including the gaps between the bridgeheads and flanks — was roughly twenty-eight kilometers (approximately sixteen kilometers for one division and twelve for the other). According to doctrinal recommendations, the length of the crossing and breakthrough sector for each division was about four kilometers, and the Third Army breakthrough front was eight kilometers.

The Third Army[333] received approximately thirty artillery battalions and fifteen batteries which were divided equally among the crossing divisions.[334] Each field army sector had about six hundred guns (120-millimeter mortars and heavier equipment, including dual-purpose cannons).[335] Each kilometer in the breaching sector was allotted seventy-five guns.[336] In addition to artillery, there were antitank cannons of various calibers, as well as antitank missiles. The breakthrough sectors had at least fifty antitank weapons (twenty per kilometer). The Second Army's situation was very similar.

The plan for transferring indirect fire-laying weapons[337] to the eastern bank called for the passage of 82-millimeter mortars in the third wave, that is, about fifty minutes after the crossing began. The 120-millimeter mortars were the first artillery pieces to make the crossing. Their transfer was planned for seven to nine hours from the start of the crossing (most of the other artillery pieces making the crossing would be deployed two to three kilometers from the east bank). The 180-millimeter long-range cannons, 240-millimeter heavy mortars, and one battalion of 130-millimeter cannon would remain on the west bank.

In my estimate, artillery preparatory fire would include surface-to-surface Frog rockets that would be launched in the opening and later stages of the war against quality targets, such as the Refidim airfield and fortified command posts far behind the lines. The Sixty-fourth Frog Missile Brigade's targets included the electronic warfare center at Um Hasiba (H-Hour minus five minutes); the Israeli backup headquarters at Um Mahatza (H-Hour minus three hours); the Bir Tmada airfield and control center at Um Rajm (H-Hour minus six hours). The fire plan called for six rockets against each of the targets.[338]

The Distribution and Supply of Artillery Ammunition

The ammunition for the towed artillery was carried by trucks and unloaded next to the artillery positions. The supply of ammunition concentrations was planned and prepared at the divisional and field army levels. Trucks would transport some of the ammunition directly from the ammunition depots to the frontline cannons. Ammunition supplies would generally be brought in at night.

The following is the Egyptian plan for ammunition distribution in various stages of the war:
- One quota of ammunition in the softening-up stage prior to the crossing;
- 1.45 quotas for the first day of combat;
- 1.9 to 2.2 quotas on the second day of combat (enemy counterattacks expected);
- One to 2.15 quotas to be distributed in the fighting sectors on the third day.

Total: three to five allotments will be distributed during the first three days of fighting, and in the following days, two to three additional quotas of ammunition.

The Egyptian army's plan for ammunition quotas in the war: Roughly sixty shells per medium-sized gun (long-barreled 122 millimeter guns, 130 millimeter guns); roughly eighty shells for field artillery (short-barreled 122 millimeter guns and D-30s — Russian-made towed howitzers); approximately forty shells for heavy mortars. The main ammunition planned: high explosive shells tipped with impact fuses. In addition, there would be (exploding smoke) phosphorous shells and a small number of illumination shells.

Employing Fire

The Egyptians planned to use all of the various types of ammunition and weapons against a wide assortment of targets.[339]

Destructive fire required the massive concentration of fire mainly against the strongholds along the canal. This fire was intended to demoralize the enemy and neutralize his fighting ability. Main weapons in the barrage were160- and 240-millimeter mortars.

Neutralization fire would temporarily incapacitate the enemy's fighting ability, maneuverability, and control over his forces. It would be used mainly as counterbattery fire,[340]and against armor concentrations, and strongholds on the second defense line. Neutralization fire had to effectively integrate all of the artillery weapons in the Egyptian arsenal, especially the various rocket launchers. Counterbattery fire was generally carried out by an eighteen-cannon battalion, with fire dispersion over a 100 by 400-meter area. Israeli reports reveal that nearly all of the IDF's artillery batteries that were within range of Egyptian artillery were hit with counterbattery fire, even though most of this fire was delivered blindly against recognized, alternate, or spotted positions that usually escaped under Egyptian observation or range adjustment.

Harassing fire was used against transportation axes, tank parks, supply concentrations, and rear headquarters. Long-range cannons were employed to prevent Israeli forces from performing organizational tasks and routine activity.

The Egyptians generally concentrated their artillery fire at the battalion level in order to achieve the best results against targets and in order to change the fire system from static fire curtains, along the length of a fixed line, or from "rolling fire curtains" that leapfrogged ahead of the forces and assisted them in their forward movement.

After the preparatory fire, artillery support was used in the breakthrough sectors, in two or three consecutive concentrations of line fire. These concentrations were designed to continuously paralyze enemy troop concentrations in the sector and prevent IDF armored forces from reaching the strongholds. Later, as the opportunity arose, these fire concentrations were used against targets. Similar fire screens, thinner in dimension, preceded the advance of the armored forces in the October 14 offensive.

The Fire Units' Order of Crossing

The Egyptians' concept of a limited war — crossing the Suez Canal and capturing the bridgeheads in an area extending eight to twelve kilometers from the waterline, was based on securing the bridgeheads and immediately shifting to a defensive layout. This tactic was the rationale of Egyptian artillery. When hostilities broke out, the artillery fired from fixed positions on the western bank. Artillery support of the forces at the bridgeheads in the later stages of the war also came from these positions. Be this as it may, the Egyptians planned to transfer large sections of their artillery layout to the eastern bank. In each case priority was given to short-range artillery and the organic artillery units of the forces already deployed on the east bank.

During the crossing, the priority for transferring the artillery was based on the details outlined in Order No. 41 that Chief of Staff Shazli issued in March 1973. Further details regarding the artillery appear in a document entitled: "Organizing the Transfer of Artillery Units of the Reinforced Infantry Division."[341] The Egyptians' planned a meticulous crossing operation in the document: "More Weapons and Ammunition, Less Administrative Demands."

Seven crossing waves were planned for the first operational echelon. Ammunition and antitank weapons would also be transferred. A forward layout that included liaison and observation officers, spotting devices, communications systems would land on the eastern shore.

The first wave included forward observation officers from the artillery and mortar batteries that were attached to the infantry commanders.

The second wave: the artillery battalions' headquarters and observation centers, and the battalion commanders' assault command posts would make this crossing. Joining them would be the observation centers of the batteries and battalions that formed the assault brigades' artillery groups.

In the fifth wave, the commander of the brigade's artillery group and his advanced team would make the crossing, along with the divisional group's observation centers and artillery linemen who would set up communications links. This crossing also included the battery commanders of field army artillery subgroups and optical (flash-detector) positioning platoons.

The seventh wave: divisional artillery headquarters, especially the technical fire direction elements, would cross in this wave, followed by more linemen and the forward command posts of the divisional group and field army battalions.

Additional artillery elements would cross with the second-echelon forces only after the support tanks carrying the infantry reached the eastern bank. Some artillery units received priority in the seventh wave:

• First priority: the transfer of communications and cable vehicles for laying the artillery's communications lines, artillery battalions and 120-millimeter mortar units (the 82-millimeter mortars would have already crossed in the first waves).

• Second priority: the transfer of field artillery and organic intermediate units (minus the administrative elements). Ammunition trucks would also make the crossing over the bridges or by boat.

• Third priority: the transfer of the organic battalions' administrative elements, especially command, supply, medevac, and maintenance vehicles for one day of combat.

• Fourth priority: the transfer of all vehicles needed for the logistics of the combat units. Priority would be given to maintenance and evacuation vehicles, and to ammunition trucks for a one-day supply of food and water.

• Fifth priority: no artillery element would cross the canal. The rest of the artillery's administrative vehicles would be transferred in the sixth and last priority.

Summary

Summing up Egypt's artillery activity, we must note that it contributed to the Egyptians' relative success in attaining the war's goals and objectives. The massive use of firepower within the framework of the maneuvering forces' limited objectives enabled effective artillery support in all stages of the campaign. The Egyptian army's short-range objectives led to the effective use of artillery (mostly towed). The large scope of deployment on the western bank contributed to the securing of the bridgeheads. The short-range artillery's leapfrog to the eastern bank allowed it to exploit its advantage and continue most successfully throughout almost the entire war. The effectiveness of artillery, mainly as an organic part of the forward echelon force, compensated for the meager use of tactical air support.

The scientific approach that the Egyptians adopted for all aspects of their artillery corresponded to the Soviet warfare doctrine. The experience from the War of Attrition proved invaluable. The artillery units' enormous ORBAT was organized according to the required command and control layouts. The artillery units' deployment was coordinated with the distribution of ammunition, target acquisition, and fire control range adjustment. When all of these elements worked smoothly, almost the whole fire plan could be carried out. The Egyptians' employment of artillery fire according to the doctrinal code enhanced its effectiveness on the battlefield.

Maj. Gen. Israel Tal summed up the impact of artillery fire on IDF activity[342]:

During the Yom Kippur War, the Egyptian and Syrian artillery made it very difficult going for the IDF. The artillery power balance was to Israel's disadvantage,[343] while the importance of artillery in deciding the nature and results of the war was significant.

The enemy's artillery fire impeded the operational functioning of IDF tank and artillery units.... One artillery battalion failed to carry out 50 percent of its mission because of counterbattery fire.

Massive artillery fire often fell on tank units for hours at a time and the tanks had to maneuver into new positions, and even there they came under heavy artillery fire.... One tank battalion was shelled for a solid three hours with artillery fire during the holding defense battle, sustaining twenty casualties and three tanks totally destroyed.

Diagram 16: Artillery Deployment in the Seventh Division Sector Prior to the Attack and after Securing the Bridgeheads (Captured War Document)

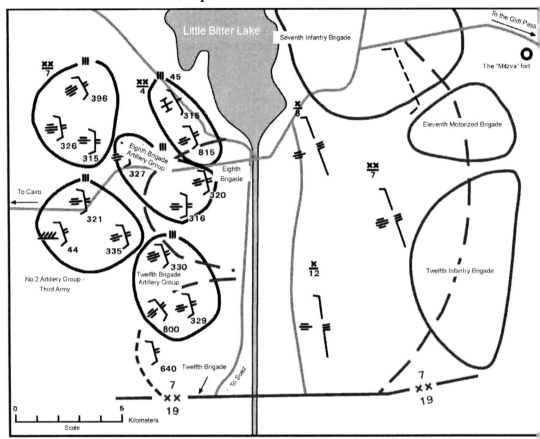

Artillery in the Seventh Division Sector at the Outbreak of the War (Eighteen Artillery and Missile Battalions)344

• The organic ORBAT of the brigades and the Forty-ninth Divisional Group, with seven battalions: two 100-millimeter battalions, four long-barreled 122-millimeter battalions, and one short-barreled 122-millimeter battalion.
• The Forty-fifth Artillery Group (Fourth Armored Division).
• The 810th Organic Artillery Battalion (Twenty-fifth Independent Armored Brigade).
• The Second Artillery Subgroup (Third Field Army — three battalions).
• The Sixty-fourth Missile (Rocket) Brigade (less one battalion).

Seventh Division Artillery on October 15 (Mainly Deployed on the Eastern Bank)345

• The Forty-ninth Artillery Group: the 396th Medium Battalion, the Forty-fourth Rocket Launcher Battalion, the 315th Field Artillery Battalion (from the Forty-fifth Brigade).

• The Twelfth Brigade Artillery Group: the 330th Medium Battalion, the 800th Field Artillery Battalion.

• The Eighth Brigade Artillery Group: the 320th Field Artillery Battalion, the 326th Medium Battalion.

• The Eleventh Brigade Artillery Group: the 329th Field Artillery Battalion, the 327th Field Artillery Battalion.

• Second Army Artillery Subgroup: the 337th Medium Battalion, the 397th Medium Battalion, the 823rd Medium Battalion.

Logistical Layout and Combat Support

The use of troops in wartime requires logistical support in all stages of combat.[346] The general principles of logistical support in the Soviet warfare doctrine are similar to those in other doctrines. The following are a few of these principles:

• Planning the concentrations at each level in order to achieve efficiency, economizing, and flexibility;

• Uniformity of weapons and equipment systems in order to simplify the maintenance and supply of spare parts;

• The supply of "urgent" material from the highest to the lowest echelons occasionally requiring circumventing intermediate-level echelons in order to speed up delivery;

• The forward deployment of supplies, maintenance equipment, and medevac units in order to guarantee quick and efficient use of them;

• Top priority for all matters related to supplies and their distribution, especially ammunition, weapons, and oil, afterward followed by food and medical supplies.

At the national level, the headquarters of the various branches were responsible for their branches' supplies. For example, missile and artillery headquarters were responsible for the supply, storage, and repair of all artillery, missile, and antitank weapons. The headquarters were also in charge of ammunition and care of task-oriented equipment. The armor corps was responsible for the maintenance of armored combat vehicles: tanks, APCs, and armored cars.

In addition to the branches, there were other bodies, too, that were responsible for maintenance, supply, and storage in professional areas. These bodies included various administrations: vehicle, transportation, communications, chemical, and home-front services (e.g., food and clothing, fuel, lubricants, and medical services).

During wartime, responsibility for logistical matters passes from the ministry of defense and military zones to the frontline headquarters and field armies[347] whose logistical responsibilities include supplies, the preparation and maintenance of supply lines, repair and removal of damaged equipment, medical treatment and evacuation, POWs, and captured weapons and other materials.[348]

The logistical organization at the front and field army levels is identical to that at the national level: the headquarters in the rear have overall responsibility. At the divisional and brigade levels, maintenance is administered through the branches, with branch deputy commanders being in charge of technical matters.

At the battalion level, the commander is responsible for the maintenance. Several officers assist him: the headquarters OC, who organizes the battalion's home-front services; a technical officer, responsible for the maintenance of weapons; and the commander of the supply unit, whose responsibility includes ordering, storing, and distributing equipment and supplies to the battalion.[349]

The minimal level of supplies in each unit's quartermaster stores is detailed in the "allotment norms" regulations. These norms change according to the unit's tasks, which determine the level of the needs and supplies. The amount of equipment and supplies that are finally determined are received by the units via regular supply pipes.[350] This task is the responsibility of the home-front headquarters.[351] A complete supply of goods at the divisional level has to be sufficient for four or five days. At the field army level a complete supply has to be enough for six to eight additional days of combat.[352]

Maintenance — Supply, Storage, and Battlefield Medical Aid

Naturally, the logistical chain was built to serve the needs of the units on the battlefield. It will be recalled that various types of supplies were moved forward from the front level to the company level and even to the individual soldier.[353]

The maintenance and repairs layout was based on the concept of forward deployment so that it would be of greatest assistance to the frontline units. The task of the tactical medical teams was to treat the wounded as close to the contact line as possible and evacuate them to an area where they could receive proper medical care.

The supply layout was the most important feature in the front's supply base. This main base included separate depots for various kinds of equipment and supplies as determined by branch headquarters and professional units. This base would be set up near the supply lines, 150–200 kilometers from the front. The field army's supply base was of similar structure but smaller, and would be set up 100 kilometers from the frontlines. If necessary, supply bases would be set up in more forward positions for the field armies.

The supply bases at the formation level would be mobile and under the command of a logistics officer at the unit's rear headquarters. Truck supply would be maintained in a divisional concentration twenty-five to forty kilometers behind the forward forces. The brigade's mobile supply point for the battalions would be established ten to thirty kilometers behind the front.[354]

Before the attack, the units' stock would be examined and replenished if necessary, and mobile secondary bases set up. Supplies would be filled to the maximum at divisional level in order to ensure a five-day independent fighting capability. Ammunition, especially for light arms, was of special importance. A huge quantity of ammunition would be transferred with the crossing forces[355] or on ammunition wagons, and a large quantity of ammunition positioned in advance in firing emplacements on the western bank.

Supply facilities would be moved forward during the attack as circumstances dictated. Mobile supply avenues would accompany the fighting forces, with refueling and restocking taking place every day before or after the fighting, and, when necessary, emergency supplying would be carried out.

The limited ability to stock supplies in the forward combat zone created dependency on senior echelon supply and repair units. Battalion-level repair and removal groups carried out routine maintenance and light repairs, and the brigade's repair company performed intermediate-level repairs.

The division's maintenance and repair battalion had two ordnance companies: one for dealing with tanks; and the other for light vehicles. In addition, there were special vehicles for repairs and towing damaged equipment. The combat companies would establish collection and repair points for wrecked vehicles.

The field army's maintenance units can move forward and reinforce layouts on the forward lines, while most of the units from the motor pools and stationary facilities at the front level carry out more difficult repairs. The front will also be built to reinforce the forward troops with mobile forces.

A special point to the rear of the battalion would be set up during the fighting to assess damage and decide whether a vehicle could be fixed on the spot or had to be removed for more serious repairs. Vehicles that could be fixed within five hours would undergo immediate repair; vehicles more seriously damaged would have to be sent to the brigade park; and vehicles needing complicated repair work would be transferred to divisional collection points or field army and front facilities. Vehicles that could not be evacuated would be repaired by senior-echelon mobile teams so that the crews could advance with their units.[356] The evacuation points set up near the crossings and bridges were of special importance in the initial operation, since their role was to remove damaged vehicles from the transportation axes.[357]

Medical and Evacuation Layout

The medical and evacuation layout would be set up as close as possible to the fighting forces. The battalion medical station would be erected two to three kilometers to the rear of the forward forces. The wounded from the battalion companies would arrive there for first aid and then be sent further to the rear for continued treatment.

The brigade medical stations would treat, classify, and transfer the wounded to the appropriate medical facilities, including rear-based hospitals. These stations would be set up ten kilometers to the rear of the forward line.

A divisional medical battalion would organize a field hospital twelve to twenty-two kilometers from the front, where approximately 400 wounded soldiers could be triaged, operated on, and given further treatment. From here the wounded would be sent to permanent field hospitals and facilities of the field army and front,[358] which would be located, according to the doctrine, fifty to seventy kilometers from the front lines.[359]

Divisional medical battalions were planned to reinforce the forward forces during the crossing. Medical evacuation centers would be set up near the bridges, and collection and evacuation centers would be established for each of the battalions making the crossing. A dirt mound would be erected on the eastern bank to protect the center. All of the fording equipment would be used for ferrying the wounded across canal for treatment in rear-based medical centers.[360]

The Egyptians' Logistical Preparations for the Yom Kippur War

During the preparations for the Yom Kippur War, the Egyptians developed a logistical layout to allow the fighting units to be as independent as possible and to reduce the threat of damage to the stockpiles. In order to reduce dependency and defense construction, the layouts and maintenance areas for the various echelons had to be scattered.

Until the Six-Day War the Egyptian logistical layout was based on three echelons: the forward echelon in Sinai, the rearward echelon in the camps along the Suez Canal, and the GHQ echelon in the vicinity of Cairo. Once the IDF was entrenched along the Suez Canal, the Egyptians constructed a new layout about seventy kilometers west of the canal.

The structure deviated only slightly from the doctrine's seventy-kilometer recommendation by making use of previous facilities that were closer to the front. The logistical layout was mainly taken from abandoned British camps and deployed on the new front, and later used in the Yom Kippur War. The Egyptians invested little in new facilities and structures. Most of the equipment was stored in field revetments.

While the GHQ facilities[361] remained in place, field army storage depots in the rear were set up according to the doctrine, fifty to seventy kilometers from the frontline. Half the quota of the field army's supplies was stocked in these warehouses: ammunition piles, oil dumps, general equipment, medical and engineering supplies, food stores, technical workshops, spare parts, tank trailers, and field hospitals.

Forward extensions of the army storerooms were set up near the transportation axes twenty-five to forty kilometers from the front. The storerooms, two for each field army, were built close to the forces but beyond the range of enemy artillery. Half the field army's supply was located here.

The divisions also had rearward storerooms set up on the main maintenance axis about twenty-five kilometers from the canal. This distance enabled the transfer of supplies to the fighting force without fear of being hit by enemy artillery. The division's transportation battalion, medical company, motor pool, ammunition piles, and oil dumps were housed in these storerooms.

The brigades' storerooms were also set up according to the warfare doctrine, fifteen kilometers from the front line on the brigade's main axis. The storerooms, which held a quarter of the brigade's supply quota, would leapfrog ahead, just behind the attacking forces. Oil dumps and food stocks, the transportation company, the brigade motor pool, and medical unit were all concentrated here.

Logistics were handled from the rear headquarters of each formation, which was generally located at the force's warehouses and stockpiles, and overseen by the unit's administration apparatus.

In preparing for the Yom Kippur War, the Egyptians deployed logistical layouts over wide areas, making sure that fresh water reached the troops. The water network, whose sources were the Nile Delta and freshwater canal that reached the Canal Zone, went through renovations. Pipelines were laid up to the banks of the canal, and during the war floating lines brought the water to the eastern bank, where temporary depots were built for the forces at the bridgeheads.

The food stores at the field army and lower levels were filled to capacity. The civilian oil layout was used to provide all of the army's needs. Fuel was transferred to the dumps and stored in the front and rear in formation reservoirs.[362]

The transportation system was reinforced. The field armies' transportation layout depended on both the organic transportation units and the GHQ layout which made maximum use of civilian resources.

The ordnance layout was also reinforced. The motor pools for armored combat vehicles, artillery, and other vehicles were set up in each unit's logistical rear. The medical care and evacuation layout was prepared for battlefield situations. In addition to the civilian hospitals near the canal that would be diverted to military needs, a number of field hospitals were set up on the western bank (mainly for emergency surgery).

Egyptian maintenance at the assault level was also based on the Soviet doctrine. It was taught in the military academies[363] and in various courses, and absorbed into the units through training and operational planning.

The logistical layout of a first-echelon attack division in a crossing operation would be similar to that in a regular attack. Brigade-level logistical units would be deployed two to three kilometers from the bank and reinforced from the division located three to five kilometers further back.[364] According to the warfare doctrine, reserve echelons would be deployed ten kilometers from the water obstacle; the division's first echelon eight to ten kilometers from it, and the second echelon fifteen kilometers from it.[365]

Battalion echelons would cross only after their units had been transferred to the eastern bank; brigade echelons would be split into two: half would follow the first-echelon and half the second echelon. Divisional echelons would also be divided; some would advance after first-echelon forces and others after the second echelon. The second echelon would cross only after the bridgeheads had been expanded to a depth of twelve to fifteen kilometers.[366]

The Application of the Fighting Layout

The Egyptian army's logistical plan was to leapfrog the layout as close as possible to the advancing forces. According to the combat doctrine, the system has to always keep "one foot on the ground." The advancing formation opens a forward extension near the fighting forces that it gradually fills with rear-based, prewar-prepared stockpiles. As the extension advances, it becomes the main supply base and spawns another forward extension with the advancing troops. This procedure repeats itself throughout the campaign.

The war plan called for a number of logistical stages that corresponded to the operational plan. For example, in the preparatory stage, the field army's forward extensions would be reinforced, and first-echelon divisional warehouses would be opened. Once the crossing and construction of the bridgeheads were completed the field army would bring up the ordnance motor pools to the canal and begin setting up forward extension supply depots on the eastern bank. Divisional supply depots would be leapfrogged in this stage. The logistical layouts at the brigade and battalion levels — motor pools, evacuation units, collection and medevac platoons, and supply echelons — would also function according to the guidelines in the doctrine, but would also improvise as conditions necessitated.

The plan to pursue the attack into Sinai envisioned the establishment of a field army "forward foot" on the eastern bank so that the distance between the supply camps and fighting forces would not exceed thirty-five kilometers. This did not take place in all stages of the fighting (which in itself testifies to the Egyptians' "limited plan"). The lack of a determined effort to advance eastward beyond the rims of the field armies' bridgeheads meant that there was no need to bring the logistical centers across to the eastern bank.

Conclusion

The Egyptians decided to launch the Yom Kippur War (or the "October War" as the Arabs refer to it) in order to break the diplomatic stalemate and reach a political arrangement. They believed that such an arrangement would be attainable only if the political wheels began to turn. If the war's basic aim was to overcome the impasse, then the Egyptian-Israeli struggle, as Sadat defined it, would be "a head-on clash with Israel's security doctrine." The strategic concept chosen by the Egyptians for achieving victory on the battlefield was the offensive. In light of the Egyptians' lessons from the past and their awareness of their relative weakness, they decided to restrict the confrontation to an "all-out war of limited dimensions." According to this concept — that was based on the Egyptian leaders' experience and their assessment of the best way to get the political process rolling — the first stage in the overall strategic plan would be an offensive of limited proportions and objectives.

Based on this strategy and the political level's definition of the war aim, the military was assigned the following missions: breaking the stalemate on the front; inflicting the heaviest possible losses on the IDF; and liberating the "occupied lands" in stages, according to Egyptian army's capabilities and battlefield opportunities. These were the senior military level's marching orders. The army drew up the war plan, developed a combat doctrine for the operation, and trained the troops for the missions.

While the Egyptian planners formulated operational plans, they located the problems that the Israeli military prepared for them: air and armored superiority, and a ground defense line that included the Suez Canal itself. These obstacles contributed to "the conception" that took root in Israel's security establishment that Egyptian army was incapable of embarking upon war. Egypt's military's response was to come up with the appropriate answers to enable it to go to war.

In their search for a suitable answer to these problems, the Egyptian military planners turned to the Soviet combat doctrine. This doctrine was born on the battlefields of Europe in World War II, and, as a model for emulation, was adopted by nearly half of the world's armies in the postwar period, that selected relevant sections — generally those dealing with subversion and guerilla activities — and adapted them to their needs. The Egyptian army, too, selectively adopted and adapted the Soviet military doctrine — especially the parts relating to an all-out war — to the Egyptian army's needs on its eastern front. Soviet military advisors stationed in Egypt played an important role in helping the Egyptians modify the doctrine. Despite the Egyptians' discomfort with these advisors, the Soviets made a great effort, at various levels of command, to transform, revamp, and assimilate their doctrine into the Egyptian army and have it serve as the basis of the operational plan for the Yom Kippur War.

The main focus of this study has been the examination of the Egyptian offensive doctrine and its comparison with the Soviet model. The study reveals a near-parallel correlation between the Egyptian and Russian databases used in Egyptian operational planning. Soviet doctrinal literature (in translation) and the sections adapted to the needs of Egyptian cadets and commanders served the Egyptian planners at the general staff, field army, divisional, and brigade levels, as well as the field commanders in charge of operations.

These officers adapted it, in the first stages of its absorption, to the Egyptian army's needs and abilities, and to theater conditions. Later, when the main operational plan for the Yom Kippur War was being worked out, the Egyptians reconstructed the doctrine into a kind of cocktail. They modified doctrinal solutions to fit operational plans based on their war aim and the tasks the military commanders would be assigned.

In addition to strategy-related questions that the war was supposed to solve, the Egyptian planners had to devise answers for problems at the operational level that the Israeli defense system had created. These included strategic depth; air superiority; the advantage of armored maneuverability; a ground defense array based on a powerful reserve in the rear; and the need to remain alert and fully prepared to throw off an Israeli counterattack.

The Egyptian army's—especially its ground forces'—weakness and unreadiness convinced the operational level of the need to narrow the missions and fit them to the limited abilities of the main fighting force—the infantry. The Egyptians' air inferiority forced the planners to forgo an initial in-depth air strike of the type recommended by Soviet military doctrine. As an alternative, they set up a strong air defense system, based mainly on antiaircraft missiles operating west of the canal that would create a short-range air umbrella sufficient to protect the invasion forces at the bridgeheads. The minimal air participation in the opening gambit of the war required, as stated, an initial artillery barrage with the minimal use of surface-to-surface long-range Frog rockets so as not to over-escalate events and trigger an Israeli counterstrike. (Also the Egyptians' supply of FROGs was limited.) The use of intense artillery fire was one of the Egyptians' crowning achievements in the war.

On the tactical and technical level the Egyptians had to overcome complex obstacles such as the water barrier; the dirt embankment on the eastern side; the inflammable liquid facilities that could be ignited by remote control, turning sections of the canal into a pool of fire; strongholds; and the IDF's quantitative and qualitative superiority in its tank force (strength, mobility, and firepower).

The lengthy planning finally produced an extremely detailed blueprint that concentrated mainly on solutions at the tactical and even technical-tactical level. The Egyptian military planners worked on key military issues: attack, crossing a wide water obstacle, establishment and defense of bridgeheads, and construction of a massive defense antitank layout.

In order to prepare their army in a relatively short time for a quick and effective implementation of combat missions, they made full use of the Soviets' doctrinal recommendations and relied on Soviet experience, equipment, and practical knowledge. The Egyptians modified Soviet techniques and recommendations to their needs and applied them to the specific conditions in which they would be operating at the Suez Canal front.

At the operational level, the key ingredient in the Egyptian was simplicity. The different stages in the plan are still a matter of dispute, not only among scholars and journalists but also among the planners themselves and the officers who led the Egyptian army during the war. One of the most controversial issues deals with the war's objectives. What was the forces' actual mission? Did the Egyptians launch a major offensive in the Yom Kippur War or was it only a thrust across the canal and establishment of bridgeheads, after which the Egyptians went on the defensive by bringing their defense array to the eastern bank in order to crush the IDF's ground and air counterstrike?

The cocktail that was devised in the final planning stages was not solely an attack plan. Although its opening moves were based on the offensive doctrine, they quickly transformed into defensive measures. Once the crossing was completed and the bridgeheads secured, the Egyptians preferred (in their planning, as well as performance) the defense concept. This concept, ironically, ran counter to Israeli expectations and assumptions (which are still prevalent among the majority of scholars today).

The Egyptian plan abstained from an advance in stages and an in-depth attack. Bridgeheads were constructed relatively quickly, but expanded slowly. Their job was to block the IDF counterattack — especially the armored offensive — that the Egyptians feared. According to the warfare doctrine, second-echelon units were planned to break through and advance across the bridgeheads, but they were weakened almost to the point of being neutralized. Their transfer to the first echelon included not only their fire layout, with its entire artillery ORBAT and most of its antiaircraft layout, but also their armored brigades which were key elements in their organic units. Thus, the Egyptian planners willingly sacrificed their ability to use the second echelon in a concentrated fashion on the east bank for breaking out of the bridgeheads and pursuing the momentum of the attack.

The political goal at the basis of the war plan did not call for an in-depth offensive in Sinai. Contrary to Israeli intelligence estimates, the Egyptians' modus operandi and mission dimensions eschewed the capture of in-depth objectives. However, by conceding this element, the Egyptian planners in effect lost sight of the basic doctrinal principles in the art of operational warfare. Instead of an offensive move that required operations management, striking power, coordination of the forces' activities, and the adroit handling of command and control, the Egyptian move's main aim was to break the stalemate and wear down the enemy's fighting force. Since the Egyptian planner limited the depth of the offensive and size of the missions, he no longer had to order the second-echelon forces to protect the steamroller offensive. He called off nearly all the missions of the leading ground forces — airborne and amphibious — that were involved in rapidly advancing and seizing vital objectives deep inside the Israeli defense layout.

In effect, this was an abrupt volte-face from an offensive battle to a defensive one designed in order to stem the counterattack and shatter the Israeli armor's overwhelming superiority. Thus, by dictating the combat environment, the Egyptians avoided battle conditions that the Israelis wanted. The Duke of Wellington combined such a strategic offense with a tactical defense when fighting Napoleon's forces in Spain (1808–1814).

In the initial stage of the war, the Egyptians relinquished the recommended type of attack according to Soviet doctrine — "an attack while in movement." Instead they chose the "attack with contact" — but here too they limited the size of the attack with regard to almost all aspects of in-depth missions. The Egyptians maintained an unbroken fortified defense array along most of the canal for two years. It was from this position that they went on the offensive, embarking on a contact attack contrary to the advice from the European theater of battle, where only a small portion of the forces, mostly reinforcements, would have made the crossing. By fording the canal on a wide front at almost all the gaps between the Israeli strongholds, the Egyptians were later able to expand the bridgeheads.

Each infantry division assaulted from its defense array west of the canal, traversed the water barrier, and quickly redeployed at limited-sized bridgeheads and new defense lines that were reinforced with infantry and commando units, reserves, and antitank and antiaircraft systems.

The Egyptians devoted their main effort to the opening stage of the fighting — the canal crossing. This stage, defined as the key to success, was planned in minute detail. They worked out timetables, distribution of equipment, positions of units, and order of priorities. Everything was planned to enable the crossing to take place under the watchful eye of the Israeli defenders. The Egyptians successfully trained all the operational levels in a relatively short time, instilling in them the essence of the war plans. Their triumphant fulfillment of the mission at this stage was way beyond their expectations.

During the "technical-operational" maneuver of crossing the canal, and capturing and constructing bridgeheads, the Egyptians superbly integrated the army's support elements: engineers, antitank units, antiaircraft batteries, artillery, and logistics layout.

According to the Soviet doctrine, large elements of the armored and mechanized forces were supposed to reinforce, maneuver, and push forward the attack. Instead, the Egyptians used them to strengthen the infantry divisions' layouts on the bridgeheads. But, here too, the depth remained in bridgeheads' defense layout rather than in the attack array of the division or army. The Soviet doctrine recommended developing an attack from the bridgeheads as soon as possible. The Egyptians, however, chose to wait, and in effect establish a static defense position that eventually provided them with a relative advantage over the IDF's mobile counterattack. The Egyptian army's defensive build-up of the bridgeheads was not only a tactical solution to battlefield contingencies, but also a systems solution — even a strategic one — that afforded it an advantage and enabled it to carry out almost all of the missions ordered by the political level.

The Egyptians kept the rest of their armored and mechanized forces west of the canal in reserve, perhaps in order to continue the attack at a later stage, but first and foremost to serve as a second echelon in the defense layout. The forces west of the canal were deployed one line forward, but their main mission was to bolster the layouts in the second defense strip west of the canal.

The transfer of a small part of the force remaining in the second-echelon divisions — two tank brigades and possibly an additional mechanized brigade — to the east bank, in the later stages of the war, and their integration into the sporadic, desultory armor attack of October 14, is a bone of contention that still chafes Egyptian planners. This deviation from the original plan weakened the depth of the entire Egyptian defense alignment — especially west of the canal. The transfer of the brigades to the east "generously" enabled the IDF forces to bridge the canal, penetrate deeply into the Egyptian territory, capture areas on the western bank, and surround the bridgeheads leading to Egypt's Third Army on the eastern bank. Although the Israeli action contributed to the IDF troops' sense of victory, it had only a marginal effect on the Egyptian army's overall accomplishments.

The extensive research that has been carried out on Egypt's activity and war preparations proves that they assessed the situation correctly by thoroughly familiarizing themselves with the canal sector and learning to exploit it to their advantage on the battlefield. They located the obstacles that Israeli planners and the IDF had prepared for them on the front. They recognized their own strong points — and especially their weaknesses — and wisely adapted them to the plan for a general war that put the entire Egyptian war machine on an ambitious, but limited, course of action. It was the plan's limited dimension that enabled the Egyptians to overcome the Israeli defender's advantages.

Unlike in the past, this time the Egyptian decision makers employed the proper strategy for winning a full-scale war with limited objectives on the land, air, and sea. The Egyptians learned the lessons of the Six-Day War and War of Attrition, and correctly evaluated their own strengths and weaknesses, and those of their enemy. They studied the lay of the land, followed the enemy's moves, analyzed each side's abilities, drew the necessary conclusions, and came up with a realistic plan based on short-range missions. In their situation estimate and war planning, Egyptian strategists also took into account the possibility of military defeat. Nevertheless, they reckoned that even in such an eventuality, most of their goals would be gained.

In the first stages of the war, the Egyptian army worked like a well-oiled machine, according to a systematic doctrinal formula. When the baptism of fire came, the "Egyptian doctrine" enabled the troops on the battlefield to demolish the foundations of the Israeli concept that had rejected the likelihood of Egypt initiating a war. The Egyptian doctrine, and its application to military planning and performance, gave a fitting answer to most of the problems that the Israeli defense layout had positioned on the Sinai front on the eve of the Yom Kippur War. In the end, the Egyptian army accomplished the majority of its missions and contributed to the attainment of the goal that the president had defined. The Egyptians' limited moves resulted in military achievements, and later political ones, both during and after the war.

Problems and Solutions: A Comparison of the Soviet Warfare Doctrine with Its Egyptian Application on the Sinai Front

The strategic level

Need/Problem	Soviet Doctrinal Solution	Egyptian Solution	Comments
The need to regain territory of the homeland. The need to break the détente (the political stalemate) and the status quo created by Israel's hold on Arab lands in general, and Sinai in particular.	Continued attempts at negotiations at the highest political level. • Inciting subversion/a people's war to topple the enemy's regime. • Launching a general war.	Adopting a military solution (war) as a catalyst for jump-starting a political process that would culminate in a political arrangement.	Egypt's failed attempts (1967–1971) to find a political solution to Israel's control of Sinai. • Sinai's sparse population, unsupportive of Egypt's efforts, and the Palestinian population's physical distance from Sinai precluded a people's war.
The need to cooperate with all the Arab states and solve problems related to them.	Employing satellite/vassal states, in cooperation — and especially under the same flag — for realizing the common goal.	Launching an operation in Egypt's interest with only minimal regard for general Arab goals.	A conceptual metamorphosis that led to a change in — and limitation of— the war's aims.
Deciding on the strategy; defining the war aims.	Exploiting the enemy's weaknesses.	Breaking the stalemate, dealing directly with Israel's defense doctrine.	The following missions were ordered by the political directive based on the overall strategy and definition of objectives: breaking the stalemate, wreaking heavy losses on the enemy, and liberating the occupied lands in stages and according to capabilities and opportunities.

Need/Problem	Soviet Doctrinal Solution	Egyptian Solution	Comments
Choosing the military course of action.	Battlefield victories are won by a full-scale offensive.	"An all-out war of limited dimensions."	A general war based on the dictum: "to return by force what was taken by force," was beyond the Egyptian army's capability. The limited dimensions of the "War of Attrition" failed to bring the desired solution.

The operational level

Need/Problem	Soviet Doctrinal Solution	Egyptian Solution	Comments
Inability and unreadiness on the part of the military establishment in general, and ground forces in particular.	Expanding formations; increasing military strength.	Adapting and limiting tasks to the Egyptian force's abilities (principally the infantry).	The infantry makes up most of the ground forces. Their assignments correspond to their limited abilities.
Combat under conditions of enemy air superiority.	• Opening the war with a preemptive strike that cripples the enemy's air potential while still on the ground, by employing long-range aircraft and missiles. • Creating an "umbrella" by integrating missiles, antiaircraft weapons, and other air defense systems to protect the attacking ground forces.	• Forgoing an opening strike deep inside enemy territory because of limited resources. • Massive use of air defense systems, with an emphasis on short-range antiaircraft missiles west of the canal and creating a short-range umbrella sufficient only to protect the forces at the bridgeheads.	The use of the air force against targets in order to gain air superiority. This was carried out meagerly and only against airfields and command centers in western and southern Sinai. The Egyptians also planned to leapfrog their missile batteries east of the canal in the early stages of the war, but in practice only a small number of them were advanced.
The IDF's superior maneuverability of ground and armored forces will probably come to expression in its attacks, counterattacks, and in its mobile counterattack deep in the Egypt's defense layouts.	Establishing a defense layout with a strong antiaircraft base. Advancing from this position to "movement to contact" with large armored and mechanized forces.	Establishing a defense layout based almost entirely on various types of antitank arrays, with an emphasis on antiaircraft missiles throughout the length and depth of the layout. The use of armored and mechanized forces solely as reinforcements and as a secondary echelon —*not* as an advanced force engaging the enemy.	The only deviation is the erratic, short-range Egyptian armored attack on October 14.

Need/Problem	Soviet Doctrinal Solution	Egyptian Solution	Comments
Superior IDF firepower in all aspects of aerial combat.	Stipulating the opening attack on a preemptive air strike.	Minimal aerial participation in the opening stage of the war. Laying down an artillery barrage in the opening stages. Limited use of surface-to-surface rockets.	The Israeli air force functioned as "flying artillery" in the War of Attrition. The phenomenon was studied, and solutions found that generally called for its neutralization by a missile-based air defense network.
Deploying for an attack while remaining prepared for defense.	The forces exploit the depth for "an attack in movement," while leaving part of the force on the line to deal with the enemy on the front.	Using infantry divisions that had been positioned in defense layouts for "an attack with contact." Releasing forces in the defense array (except for the main force of second echelon close by these layouts).	This method, intended to simplify Egyptian activity, in the realization that it would obstruct the IDF from going over to an offensive on the western bank of the Suez Canal.
A broad front, 170 kilometers long in the canal front, and 200 kilometers in length in the secondary sectors — the coastlines of the Gulf of Suez and Red Sea.	Focusing an attack on a particular sector using troops from the maneuvering forces, and concentrated fire.	Attacking with infantry on "a broad front" (almost the entire length of the canal sector), and with commandos in large areas of the gulf.	The method intended to divide the efforts of the IDF's defensive force, while using the Egyptians' main ORBAT — the ground forces — to the greatest advantage.
A large and powerful reserve force (IDF armored reserves) deep in the enemy rear.	• Concentrating armored and mechanized forces as a second echelon for action in the advanced stages of the attack. • Concentrating air power and missiles for dealing with enemy reserve forces deployed in depth. • Isolating the battlefield by special forces landed in-depth to block enemy reserve from reaching the front.	• Leaving the second echelon's main forces outside the battle zone, west of Suez. • Minimal use of the air force — mainly for strikes near the fighting area. • Employing special forces for blocking axes only in the front's flanks. • Establishment of bridgeheads, reinforced with antitank weapons for breaking the counterattack and the IDF's armored reserves.	The Egyptians' plan of action is based on a sober awareness of its army's strengths and weaknesses.
Continuous movement for taking advantage of the crossing and capturing vital areas deep in Sinai, in the face of superior Israeli armored forces.	Exploiting the breakthrough of the defense layout on the front; rapid penetration deep into the enemy's layout of armored and mechanized formations.	Freezing the situation on the front; stabilizing the defense layout; halting the attack momentum into the enemy's depth.	Opinion is divided on this issue. Some regard the stalemate as an intermediate situation — an "operational halt" to be followed by the continued movement of forces.

Need/Problem	Soviet Doctrinal Solution	Egyptian Solution	Comments
The surprise element.	• Wide-scale use, at various levels, of deception and subterfuge, concealment and protection. • Entering the war from a military exercise.	• Deception mainly at the strategic level. Negligible deception and feinting at the operational and tactical levels. • Activity consisting mainly of concealment and field security at all echelons. • Launching the attack under the pretext of the military exercise "Liberation 41."	No comprehensive deception plan was prepared for anything connected with "another operational plan."

The tactical level

Need/Problem	Soviet Doctrinal Answer	Egyptian Path	Comments
The canal obstacle. A wide and difficult water barrier.	A detailed doctrine for crossing a water barrier, mainly designed for river crossings.	Detailed planning and precise steps for crossing the Suez Canal provide an answer to all the problems that the obstacle placed before the Egyptians.	The Egyptian General Staff detailed the main points of the plan in Order 41.
A high dirt embankment (approximately twenty meters) on the eastern bank of the Suez Canal.	Standard solutions provided by military engineers.	An original solution: blasting the embankment away with jet sprays from high-powered water hoses.	
The "Or Yikarot" oil storage facilities that could be ignited, turning the surface of the canal into a burning death-trap.	Problem unknown.	Intelligence gathering, and knowledge that most of the system was made up of inactive units. Neutralizing the system by blocking the pipe with cement.	The Egyptians exaggerated the issue and depicted their handling of it as a heroic deed, even though they were aware that the system was a sham and posed little threat.
Reinforcement of the Israeli defense layout on the front: the strongholds.	Flanking and encirclement, and destroying the enemy in later stages of the breakthrough. Neutralizing and overwhelming the enemy with direct and indirect fire.	Bypassing the strongholds, encircling them, and capturing them from the rear only in the advanced stages of the war. Dealing with most of the strongholds only with covering fire in the early stages of the war.	In most cases, the front's width enabled the enemy's strongholds to be flanked. Their location and small numbers rendered them insignificant obstacles for the canal crossing.

Need/Problem	Soviet Doctrinal Answer	Egyptian Path	Comments
The IDF's quantitative and qualitative advantage; and the superiority of its tank doctrine.	Increasing the number of tanks on the front involved in combat; integrating antitank units on the front and flanks of the contact line.	Strengthening the front with tanks and antitank weapons (mostly missiles and launchers) used on the front line of contact and even ahead of it (as tank hunters).	

Appendix A

The Soviet Warfare Doctrine—The Attack at the Divisional and Field Army Levels

A field army is an operative formation of ground forces. When it implements an attack, it is part of the general military layout, and acts in conjunction with adjacent field armies, the air force, airborne troops, air defense units, and sometimes marine and naval forces.[1]

A field army attack is based on the front's overall plan, that is, operations and battles working for the same goal within the same time-space framework. Field army operations are carried out according to a single idea, in cooperation with the air force, air defense, and missile and artillery—all engaged in destroying the enemy's operational forces and gaining control of tactically (or strategically) vital territory in order to fulfill the campaign's goal.

A field army's role and position in the overall strategic layout is based on the operation's basic idea. A field army may attack the enemy's first echelon—in the primary or secondary effort,[2] or, as stated, operate in the front's secondary effort. A field army may be active in the center of the front's sector or its flanks.[3] Under certain circumstances a field army may attack in an independent effort.

A field army's operational aims are derived from the strategic operation's goals. These goals may change but generally they include repulsing an enemy attack; transferring the fighting to enemy territory; destroying the enemy's defense forces and capturing vital territories; coming to the aid of allies under attack; and so forth.[4] During an attack, the supreme commander at the front decides the field army's operational goals and missions. The missions are defined according to the particular enemy forces that have to be destroyed and the objectives and key areas that must be captured.[5]

A first-echelon field army operating in the main effort is responsible for breaking through the enemy's tactical defense area, overpowering his first-echelon forces, and completing the primary mission. A field army on the primary effort axis is larger than the other field armies since it has been reinforced with tanks, artillery, air defense, combat engineers, and chemical units from the front's or GHQ's reserves. The air force's main efforts are concentrated in the field army's sector, and airborne troops are also integrated into it.

The mission of a field army on the secondary effort is to destroy the enemy's secondary force, and assist the formations attacking on the primary-effort axis. A second-echelon field army is generally required to exploit the primary-effort axis in order to destroy the enemy's more distant reserves or develop an attack on a new axis. Sometimes second-echelon field army

187

forces will be used for mopping-up operations in the first echelon's rear, for countering airborne or seaborne enemy troops that have made in-depth landings, or for additional missions.

The field army's tasks and location in the battle layout may change in the course of the attack. A second-echelon field army may be transferred to the first-echelon field army that has begun attacking a secondary effort. Later it may be transferred to the primary-effort sector.[6]

The goal of the field army attack is obtained by carrying out the direct mission and following mission.[7] The depth and essence of these missions are subject to change.

The direct mission of a first-echelon field army operating on the primary-effort axis generally consists of breeching the enemy defense layout, destroying the enemy's forces in the tactical defense area and the nearest operative depth, and gaining control of an area that enables the successful continuation of the operation. The direct mission's depth may reach seventy to a hundred kilometers and may take three to five days.[8] A first-echelon field army's following mission on the primary-effort axis usually consists of developing the attack to an operative depth, destroying the enemy's tactical or strategic reserves, and gaining control of the lines that demarcate the completion of the operation's goals. The depth of the following mission may reach 80 to 110 (and sometimes even 150) kilometers over a four- to seven-day period.[9]

Mission depth and the rate of advance of a field army operating on the secondary-effort axis may be less than on the primary effort. The primary mission will be between thirty and fifty kilometers, and the following mission will not exceed seventy to ninety kilometers.

A second-echelon field army in a strategic attack is responsible for developing the primary attack or a new attack effort. Its direct mission will be to complete the destruction of the opposing enemy group and its distant strategic reserves, and capture those areas that provide suitable conditions for completing the attack. In this case, the field army's following mission will be to gain control of an area that enables the successful attainment of the GHQ's objectives in the attack.[10]

The scope of the attack is determined by its length, depth, rate of advance and time requirement.

The length of the front in an attack depends on the number of operative efforts, the size of each axis, and the amount of first-echelon formations. The length of the field army's frontal attack (according to the Soviet warfare doctrine) with three or four first-echelon divisions is forty to sixty kilometers.[11]

The field army depth in the attack (according to the doctrine) in conventional warfare is 150 to 250 kilometers. This includes the direct mission depth (70 to 100 kilometers) and the following mission depth (80 to 150 kilometers).[12] A field army mission on the European battlefield in modern times (in conventional warfare) may increase to 250 to 350 kilometers and take six to nine days to complete.[13]

The rate of advance in an attack in the European theater (according to the Soviet doctrine) is greater than in the Middle East. The doctrine states that in modern operations, effective firepower and mobility lead to a rapid breakthrough of the enemy's defenses.[14]

In the direct mission stage when the enemy's tactical defense area is being breeched, the attacking forces will advance at a rate of fifteen (sometimes thirty) kilometers a day. While the deep attack is being implemented, the rate of the field army's following or final mission increases to thirty-five, forty, or even fifty kilometers a day depending on the nature and organization of the enemy's defenses. Soviet sources published after the Yom Kippur War mention a thirty- to fifty-kilometer advance a day under favorable conditions in a European theater.[15]

When the attack involves the crossing of a water barrier the rate of advance is slower. The organized crossing of a wide, heavily-defended water barrier will take one day. The rate of crossing and capture of the bridgehead is twelve to twenty kilometers a day and in difficult conditions is less than eight to ten (and in extreme cases, five or six) kilometers in one day of combat.[16]

In conclusion, the average rate of advance of a field army attacking to the maximum depth will be six to twelve days.

The Field Army's ORBAT and Battle Formation

The ORBAT of the field army making the attack is not fixed but is determined by the supreme commander depending on the operation's priority in the field army's overall mission, the nature of the enemy's defenses, forces, and weapons, the terrain, and, most importantly, the troops and weapons that implement the attack.[17]

A first-echelon field army operating on the primary-axis effort will usually consist of three to four infantry or mechanized divisions, one armored division, one or two independent armored brigades, and one or two independent infantry or mechanized brigades.[18]

The field army will also be reinforced with special forces (SF): one or two commando groups or an airborne, paratroop, or marine brigade.[19]

The field army will be provided with three to five artillery brigades of medium-sized cannons, heavy mortars, and rocket launchers, and also receive in various stages of the operation a battalion or brigade of rockets or surface-to-surface missiles. In addition, it will operate independent units: battalions and groups of tank destroyers, cannons, and antitank missiles.

A field army will be provided with air defenses: one or two surface-to-air mobile missile brigades and one or two brigades of light and medium antiaircraft cannon, as well as a number of independent antiaircraft battalions, and a battalion of man-portable antiaircraft missiles.

A combat engineer battalion will be attached to the field army. When operations include a water crossing, the force is supported with a bridging brigade and task-oriented engineering battalions for road construction, fortification building, and obstacle laying.

In addition, chemical units protect the field army in nonconventional warfare. Smoke and flamethrower units, recon teams, military intelligence, electronic warfare and communications units also join the field army. During various stages in the attack, a field army will be provided with fighters, bombers, as well as planes and helicopters for battle control, medevac, equipment transportation, and ferrying troops to their destinations.[20]

During the attack, the field army will be grouped in an operative layout made up of the following forces: several levels of assault troops, reserves from all branches (including task-oriented reserves), artillery, air defense units, and airborne or seaborne forces.[21] Combat groups and teams will be set up according to the modus operandi selected for the attack and the enemy's destruction, the method and direction of attack, the nature of the terrain, the enemy's defense system and fortifications, the attacker's ORBAT, his quality and type of troops, and his artillery and air layouts and their methods of operation.[22] The structure of the echelons and reserves will be designed to guarantee the attack's ongoing momentum. The forces' size, strength, and equipment at the various levels may change since they are dependent, as stated, on the operational idea, attack depth, volume of the main axes, enemy strength and estimated modus operandi, and the nature of his defense layout.[23]

In general, when the enemy's defense layout is prepared or organized in-depth,[24] the attacking force is grouped in two echelons with a reserve force. When the defense layout is deeper and more heavily fortified, the attacking force will be made up three echelons. The operative layout of one of the echelons will be used against a weak or hastily prepared defense layout, or when the enemy lacks reserves in his depth.[25]

The first echelon is the main attack force. It includes most of the attacking force — about one half to two-thirds of it — and most of the tanks and artillery support. Its task is to breech the enemy's defense in the tactical depth, wipe out enemy troops in their layouts and the tactical and operative reserves, and develop the attack to the depth of the field army's direct mission. The force includes most (two or three) of the field army's infantry or mechanized divisions,[26] and is reinforced with one or two independent tank divisions or brigades from the mechanized or armor divisions that are planned to operate in the second echelon.[27]

The second echelon maintains the attack momentum, especially on the primary-effort axis, while reinforcing the first echelon's efforts (unless ordered to develop an attack in a new direction). The second echelon's missions include completing the breakthrough in the enemy's tactical defense area; developing a tactical breakthrough for an operative breech; capturing the intermediate layouts; and gaining control of vital objectives in the operative depth. The second echelon will surround and destroy enemy forces that it encounters, repulse any counterattacks, destroy enemy forces that have landed in depth, and replace exhausted first-echelon forces. The second echelon has up to two armored or mechanized divisions reinforced with a number of independent infantry or tank brigades.[28]

Fully-staffed reserves are generally be established when second-echelon forces are absent. Its main assignment is to carry out unplanned assignments. This reserve force usually consists of a single division or one or two independent brigades. It is sometimes formed when the field army operates in two echelons, in which case it is smaller (one independent brigade or a single commando group).

The field army artillery group's[29] task is to provide fire support to the main force in its primary effort. The artillery group usually includes three to four long-range guns battalions.[30] The doctrine states that it may be split into two groups for assisting two efforts at the field army front, with each group containing two to four cannon or missile battalions.

The field army's air defense is made up of antiaircraft gun groups and surface-to-air missile brigades.[31] The gun groups consist of light and medium cannons and units (platoon and company sized) of personal antiaircraft missiles. The mobile SA-6 missile brigades attached to the field army operate on the primary-effort axis, providing air defense cover to the armored and motorized units breaking through the enemy's deep layouts.

The field army's antitank reserves usually include units made up of cannons and antitank missiles, tank-destroyer teams, and sometimes flamethrowers. Two of these reserve groups are generally in operation, and may have airborne troops or tank-destroying helicopter units attached to them.[32] The antitank reserve's mission is to repulse armored counterstrikes, protect exposed flanks, and reinforce the defense layouts where the field army is deployed during or at the conclusion of the operation.

Mobile mine-laying reserves are intended to quickly set up obstacles — generally antitank minefields. Two mobile mine-laying forces — each battalion size -usually operate at the field army level in coordination with the field army's antitank units.

Engineering and chemical reserves are also attached to the field army. Their primary mission is to provide protection against chemical warfare. They reinforce the efforts and replace task-oriented forces that have been damaged during the fighting. Other task-oriented forces include tactical airborne forces, paratroopers,[33] and marines. All of these forces are battalion size and have the key task of capturing key objectives.

The Operational Maneuver

The success of an attack in conventional warfare depends on a number of factors — the most important being a preemptive air strike that destroys the enemy's forces and installations. A parallel attack should be made by the attacker's ally. Of equal importance is the aggressive attack made by all the maneuvering units.[34]

One of the foremost elements for a successful attack is the correct choice of an operational maneuver. This depends on the operational idea at the assigned level, the field army's missions and ORBAT, the enemy's defensive strength and nature of his defense layout, and last but not least — the terrain and weather.[35]

The two basic operational maneuvers are an attack in concentrated efforts and an attack in separate efforts. The concentrated attack is used against an enemy who lacks strong reserves and that has amassed his forces in the depth of the near defense layout. By making a concentrated division of his layout, the attacker can encircle and destroy the enemy. A separate attack will be made against a contiguous and homogenous defense layout, when the enemy's reserves are divided in the depth. A separate attack on a number of efforts will split the defense, allowing the attacker to divide and destroy the enemy in piecemeal fashion.

Other maneuvers, such as circumventing the defense layout and attacking from the rear, are carried out only when the conditions of the terrain and defense layouts permit a flanking movement or a rapid breeching of the weak flank and reaching the enemy's rear.

To recall: maneuvers are chosen according to battlefield conditions and the field army's needs. During the operation various maneuvers may be integrated, such as carrying out a direct mission on one route and proceeding with a following mission on another route.

The field army attack usually takes place in two or three efforts, one of them being the primary effort.[36] The primary-effort axis will be where the field army's efforts have been concentrated for completing its missions and fulfilling the attack's objectives. The choice of axis is based on a situation estimate of the effectiveness of the forces and weapons being employed for the missions. The main consideration in the choice of axes is the force's ability to accomplish a quick breakthrough in the enemy's defense layout and create conditions for developing the attack on the flanks and in depth. Another consideration is the ability to commit the troops — especially the armored force — along the length of the axis. Deciding which axis to take is a process that will accompany the entire operation, but is liable to change at any point if certain conditions develop that lead to selection change.

The primary effort will be directed as much as possible to the weak points in the enemy layout. The selected axes and areas are located on the margins of the sector or in the exposed flanks or are thinly defended by inferior forces. An attack in the enemy's strongest sector is made only when this is the quickest and easiest way to attain objectives and when the field army has sufficient means to neutralize the enemy. The attacker will build up the necessary forces (including tanks, air defense, and other support systems — especially air support) on the primary-effort axis. This sector will be assigned to the strongest formations, with most of the second echelon and reserves being directed to it.

Afterwards a secondary effort will be made on the axis in order to strengthen the success of the main effort by encircling and destroying the enemy, protecting the field army's flanks, preventing enemy detection, maneuvering against the main effort, and finally capturing the objectives that enable the completion of the mission at as early a date as possible.

The Soviet authors of the doctrine regard the overall fire dimension, which includes airpower, artillery, missiles and rockets, as being of exceptional importance on the modern battlefield. The importance of the attack's opening moves and successive moves are emphasized in modern military literature[37] more than in Soviet or Egyptian literature before the Yom Kippur War.

The maneuvering forces are provided with an accompanying fire layout (especially artillery) and air layout. As the main fire source for the ground forces, the artillery is used to paralyze and destroy the enemy's forces, artillery, and mortars. The artillery is integrated into antitank fighting and is also employed to destroy select targets, such as headquarters and command-and-control installations. Air units are used mainly for in-depth strikes in the enemy's battle zone.

Fire is delivered in two main stages: preparatory fire — before and during the breakthrough of the defense layouts; and support fire — for continuing the attack.

The weapons of all field army units (including the GHQ and front reinforcements) contribute to the softening-up fire. Antitank weapons and even tanks employ indirect trajectory fire against in-depth targets. The fire is delivered simultaneously against the enemy's tactical depth and targets of tactical and operative importance. Aircraft will attack targets, such as enemy headquarters, supply depots, and in-depth reserves, and provide air cover for the attackers.

As the main fire support during the attack, the artillery will leapfrog in the wake of the advancing forces in order to maintain concentrated effectiveness ("rolling" fire screens).

Paratroopers and other airborne forces will be employed at the operational and tactical levels[38] to isolate the battlefield or hit targets deep in the enemy's rear.[39] When the attack is made close to a shoreline, marines may be used to isolate the battlefield, capture vital areas, and carry out reconnaissance and sabotage. The forces will be of battalion size for a tactical seaborne operation, and the size of a reinforced brigade (or larger) for an operative seaborne operation that is landed at a depth that depends on changing circumstances and its ability to link up with the advancing overland force.[40]

Attack Preparations

Preparing for the attack is the most important stage for the field army commander and his staff. This is the stage where operational plans are formulated, missions assigned, and coordination between the different forces and support units worked out. During the preparations stage the forces taking part in the operation will be reorganized and assigned to their appropriate deployment areas. Command-and-control centers[41] are set up and support operations carried out: patrols, engineering works, defensive measures against nonconventional and electronic warfare, camouflage and deception, maintenance — these activities are necessary to create the best conditions for a successful operation.

Camouflage and deception activity, for example, is vital for concealing the preparations for the operation and preserving the element of surprise at the time of the opening blow. This can be achieved only by duping the enemy as to the attacker's true intentions. Camouflage and deception are done mainly in the preparations stage, but also during the operation itself:[42] the field army embarks upon a bogus additional effort; second echelon forces create a phony advance; attack preparations are made on the wrong axes.[43] The warfare doctrine also recommends setting up decoys, especially dummy headquarters.

Before and during the attack the field army's logistics are extremely complex. They are mainly concerned with organizing and stockpiling supplies, such as ammunition, fuel, food, water, and equipment. Maintenance of weapons and equipment — especially for armored combat vehicles and medevac units — is crucial.

Part of the preparations for the attack requires the reorganization of the field army and consolidation of deployment areas. The concentrated forces are aligned in a more favorable state for carrying out the operative plan, advancing from the rear to the frontlines, the rear of the front, or the length of the front.[44] This activity is carried out as quickly as possible, while remaining on a high state of alert and carefully concealing the moves.

When the attack proceeds from direct contact with the enemy,[45] a few days are needed to make a new formation. As a rule, the moves are carried out at night under the cover of reinforcing or fresh troops. Artillery, antiaircraft, and antitank forces are deployed two or three nights before the attack. The divisions' first-echelon brigades enter deployment areas in the first and second defense layouts two nights before the attack. Second-echelon brigades and support units wait in the assembly areas or deploy in or behind the third defense layout[46] on the night before the attack.[47] The units take up positions in canals and trenches with their weapons carefully concealed.

When an attack in movement is made, the forces are deployed on the night preceding the attack in forward assembly areas twenty to forty kilometers from the contact line.[48] The second echelon, followed by the reserves or GHQ echelons, assumes positions in these areas and are responsible for protecting the areas while deployed in them.

Implementing an Attack at the Field Army Level

The first-echelon field army breaks through the enemy's defenses to the depth of his defense layout. All of the attacker's fire elements — including aircraft and electronic warfare units — open the operation with preparatory fire.[49]

In this initial stage SF may also be employed in the enemy's deep layout in order to isolate the battlefield or take over key objectives.

Under the cover of preparatory fire, first-echelon forces advance to the assault lines and firing positions. When the assault commences, shelling continues in the form of concentrated successive fire and rolling fire curtains. This firewall helps the attackers obtain their objectives. The infantry, which bears the main brunt of the assault, is supported with tanks and APCs.

The advance to the heart of the enemy's layout is made in a coordinated armor-infantry maneuver while exploiting the gaps in the enemy's defense layout. However, the annihilation of the defending troops is only carried out in the later stages by second-echelon or mopping-up units arriving from the rear.[50] In principle, first-echelon forces avoid tangling with pockets of resistance. They cannot allow themselves to linger in large urban areas, for example.[51] During the attack, each of the support layouts performs its assigned mission.

When breeching the enemy's tactical defense zone, a wide-scale fire maneuver is made against the enemy's flanks and rear. First-echelon divisions send their forward troops to gain control of vital in-depth objectives and hold them until the main force arrives. The same use will be made of tactical heliborne troops who overtake the enemy's control system.[52]

The attacking forces expand the breakthrough sectors in order to impede the defense's counterattacks. By deploying in force on a number of axes, congestion is prevented and the armored advance is able to push forward, especially when second-echelon forces join battle.

The deep defense layouts are generally breeched in an attack in movement or outflanked while exploiting the breakthroughs and gaps, and attacked from the rear. If the breakthrough from the in-depth layouts fails, the forces will redeploy for defense after a brief halt, quickly reorganize, and make another assault against the layouts. From the Soviets' experience in

World War II, twelve hours are needed to prepare for a renewed attack. Later, three to four hours were found to be sufficient for renewing the attack.[53] Second- and first-echelon artillery of sufficient range or that have leapfrogged ahead will lay down the softening-up fire.[54]

During the attack, the field army must be prepared to repulse the enemy's counterstrikes. It is assumed that that the enemy may carry out one or more counterattacks on a number of axes in an effort to thwart the attack and restore the situation to its previous condition. The ability to repulse the enemy's counterattack is of great importance in modern warfare since it is easier than in the past to command mobile reserves. Countering the enemy's reserves must be based, inter alia, on the coordinated and concentrated use of the air force.[55]

The counterattack is checked while waging a battle of encounters against the attacking force, or by shifting part of the field army to the defense, and simultaneously pursuing the attack on other axes while hitting the enemy in his flanks and rear. An encounter battle is fought when the enemy's counterattack intentions are discovered and the field army preempts it with air strikes and artillery barrages, and sends forces to attack him on the flanks and in the rear. The shift to defense enables the attacker to meet the counterattack from a static position and halt the attack's momentum.

The second-echelon field army is planned to reinforce the first echelon's efforts and open the attack in the operative depths of the enemy defense line. Priority on the main effort axis is preserved by using the second echelon. The second echelon may be sent into battle in order to complete the direct mission and accomplish the following mission.

The second echelon's missions focus on developing the attack in the direction of the main effort.[56] The missions may include completing the breakthrough of the tactical layout; developing a tactical breech into an operative one[57]; reinforcing intermediate layouts and, while in movement, gaining control of vital objectives in the depth; turning back enemy reserves; and encircling and destroying the enemy's reserves during the attack.

The second echelon may include up to two (generally armored or mechanized) divisions. A force of this strength can reinforce the first-echelon effort and gain superiority over the enemy. The entire echelon may be sent into battle or divided into one or more efforts after brief preparations or while engaged in an attack in movement.

The overall plan is to have the entire second echelon make a single effort through the gaps between the first echelon divisions and reach the flanks of the field army's primary effort.[58] This maneuver will gain the attacker superiority over the enemy so that he can be defeated with decisive blows within a short time.

The second echelon is provided with artillery and air support and the advancing forces of the first-echelon divisions. Its exposed flanks are protected by antitank reserves and the field army's mobile obstacle laying units. It is also reinforced with first-echelon reserves.

The second echelon is protected by aircraft, ground-based air defense measures and the field army, and is reinforced with first-echelon formations.[59]

In addressing a field army attack, the warfare doctrine discusses the advanced stages of the operation. The advance into the operative depth requires adequate preparation for a number of encounter battles. The enemy's in-depth retreat allows the attacker to embark upon another battle form — the pursuit.[60] While these chapters in the Soviet doctrine are of general relevancy, the Egyptians had no need of them for their war plans in 1973.

The field army attack is completed when the objectives have been obtained. When enemy strongholds are located on the field army's operative axis, they are overcome by two or more successive field army attacks.

According to the modern Soviet warfare doctrine, the field army shift to — and completion of—the following operation are made without a halt. A halt between successive operations is termed an "operative halt." In World War II it was sometimes necessary in order to redeploy forces that had been severely reduced in manpower and weapons. In the Yom Kippur War the Egyptians had no need of an operative halt. Therefore, their stopping seems to have been the result of having obtained a sufficient amount of the war's aims.[61]

The main mission facing the field army headquarters and troops at the end of the attack is to establish themselves in areas that have just been captured and remain on alert for enemy counterattacks and air strikes. If no further attack is planned, the force will regroup and realign for defense in order to consolidate its gains.

The Attack at the Divisional Level

The division is responsible for planning the attack and applying the doctrinal principles to the tactical moves. The enemy's defeat will be achieved by employing firepower from all available weapons, and making a decisive assault while developing an in-depth attack that divides and destroys the enemy. The basic elements in the attack—firepower, shock, and maneuverability—come to expression.[62]

Tactical operations at various stages include movement to the attack line; assault with concentrated fire; locating and repulsing counterattacks; and exploiting the success in order to reach the front's depth.

Soviet tactics call for exploiting massive firepower to paralyze key targets on the front and in the depth of the enemy's defense layout. Firepower will also be used as a cover for the attacking forces' determined movement. While advancing, the forces will try to bypass and outflank the enemy's heavily defended layouts.[63]

The nature of the attack changes according to battlefield conditions: the type of enemy defenses (hastily prepared, organized, or fortified); whether the battlefield is situated on or close to a water obstacle; the nature of the terrain; the time of the year; day or nighttime operations.[64]

The shape of the attack maneuver also changes according to circumstances—from a frontal attack to a close lateral movement or deeper outflanking. The attackers will try to take advantage of the gaps in the enemy's defenses and maneuver against his flanks and rear.

The attack may be carried out while in movement, as the attacker flows through friendly units that are in contact with the enemy. Another possibility is to attack from positions already established while in contact with enemy. Speed is a central factor in the attack, and is of great advantage in an attack while in movement.[65]

The element of surprise is of paramount importance in the attack and should be meticulously applied. Deception and feinting are also key features in the ground forces' attack.

A division carrying out an attack under the command of a fully staffed field army may serve as a first-echelon unit, a second-echelon unit on the primary- or secondary-axis effort, or a reserve force.[66] The role and location of the division in the field army's battle layout depends on its combat capability and battlefield conditions.[67]

The use of a first-echelon division on the primary-axis effort depends on its ability to break through and destroy the enemy's main forces. This stage is crucial for the success of the battle. The success of the division in the secondary effort may result in shifting it to the main effort. An infantry division is usually employed at this echelon.

A second echelon or reserve division is used to increase the strength of the attack and exploit its success. The division will take the lead in developing the attack on the main-axis effort and be the decisive force used in destroying the enemy's reserves.[68] Mobile (armored and mechanized) divisions are generally used at this level.[69] They are used at the first echelon and on the main-axis effort during a breakthrough of hastily prepared defense layouts.

The Division's Mission

The division's missions are determined according to the following considerations: the main battle concept, enemy strength, the nature and method of enemy defenses, the combat ability of the designated division, air support, the terrain, and weather conditions.

The operative plan directs the attack at the tactical level. According to the plan, the axis of attack is part of a wide-scale maneuver. The plan also determines operational moves such as dividing the defense layout, destroying select enemy forces, and the targets to be captured (how and when).[70]

The division is usually assigned a twenty-four-hour combat mission[71]— taking control of an area up to a certain line and destroying the enemy in it. The battle mission consists of a series of missions. This is planned in order to create a more effective use of troops and weapons for annihilating the enemy, enable an effective organization of the participating forces (and cooperation between them) in the battle and greater control over them.

The division's combat mission is divided into the direct mission, the following mission, and the daily mission. At the brigade level, instead of the daily mission, there is a continuous move in the direction of the attack.[72]

This system allows the capture of a particular line and destruction of part of the enemy's force, and establishes conditions for pursuing the attack. It enables operation to be carried out, while safeguarding the battle layout and organization of cooperation. At the same time, mission depth is coordinated with the division's operational strength.

The missions are determined according to their depth and objectives[73]:

• The direct mission: the breakthrough of the first defense layout and destruction of the enemy brigade at its first defense echelon.[74] Mission depth depends on the brigade's deployment at a distance of approximately eight to ten kilometers.

• The following mission: breeching the enemy's division's second defense layout and destroying its second-echelon or reserve forces. Mission depth will be about twenty kilometers. If the defense strip is deeper, then the breakthrough becomes the division's daily mission.

• The daily mission: the development of the in-depth attack, coordination with neighboring forces in order to destroy the enemy's operative reserves and gain control of a line favorable for defense or the development of the attack (roughly to a thirty kilometer depth).

A brigade carrying out its direct mission at the division's first-echelon will break through to a depth of three or four kilometers and destroy the enemy's first echelon brigade's battalions. The following mission is identical to the division's direct mission and completes the breakthrough to a depth of eight to ten kilometers. Once this is accomplished the brigade attacks on a predetermined axis. The daily mission of a brigade operating on an independent axis advances about twenty kilometers.

The doctrine states that the direct mission is expected to secure a line fifteen to seventeen kilometers from the canal. The mission calls for crossing the canal, destroying the enemy's covering troops, breaking through the first strip while in movement, destroying the first-echelon brigade's main forces, and gaining control of a deployment area for the artillery.[75]

The following mission develops the in-depth attack, and completes the breakthrough and destruction of the first echelon brigade, capturing a line approximately twenty-five kilometers from the canal. The daily mission gains control of a line thirty to thirty-five kilometers from the canal.[76]

The rate of advance also influences mission depth. The rate of advance of infantry units struggling to overcome the enemy's defense layouts is less than one kilometer an hour. An infantry brigade needs three to four hours to advance three kilometers (the direct mission's depth). Once the main defense layout is breeched, the rate of advance is approximately one and half kilometers an hour. At this stage the division will complete the in-depth breakthrough and block the counterattack. A ten- to fifteen-kilometer mission will be completed in eight or nine hours (sometimes even as much as twelve hours).[77]

In the course of the fighting until the daily mission is completed, the rate of advance is two to three (or more) kilometers an hour. At this rate the division needs fifteen to twenty hours to complete its mission. The first day is the slowest and toughest; afterward the rate of advance increases.[78]

The command level determines the division's attack sector length, depending on the operational concept and combat mission, the nature of the defenses, and the terrain. The sector's length should provide the attacking troops with battlefield superiority, especially in the breakthrough sector, favorable maneuvering conditions, control over the forces, and the possibility of deploying and dispersing them.[79] An infantry division generally attacks on an eight- to ten-kilometer-long front. This length increases to ten to twelve kilometers when a mechanized or armored division is involved.[80] The sector's length is designed for a division making an attack with two first-echelon brigades. The length of an infantry brigade's sector with two forward but separate battalions is four kilometers. This is the case when each battalion carries out its attack on a line one and a half to two kilometers long.

When the enemy is organized or deployed on a fortified defense line, the length of the breakthrough sector is reduced so that the first-echelon division (or brigade) attains a 3:1 superiority (in troops and weapons) over the enemy. This reduction also enables a sufficient number of weapons to concentrate on paralyzing the enemy.[81] The length of a division's breakthrough sector may reach four kilometers,[82] and a brigade's sector two.

The Divisional Battle Layout

On the eve of the battle, troops and equipment will be grouped in a layout that guarantees numerical superiority over the enemy on the main-axis effort. The layout also has to guarantee maximum use of firepower, the possibility of implementing a wide-scale maneuver, and the continued expansion of the force as the battle develops. Furthermore, it has to provide effective control and cooperation among the forces, the ability to impede a counterattack, the use of troops according to their ability, and the effective exploitation of the terrain in the battle zone.[83]

The battle layout is based on fully staffed units in the echelons. In almost every offensive operation, a division will attack a two-echelon layout, in which the defense layouts are organized and gradated in depth on the primary-axis effort. The force's build-up will be made on one echelon when the division operates on the secondary axis and the layout has been hastily prepared. When attacking one echelon, a division will also build a reserve force the size of one or two battalions.

In addition to the echelons, the battle layout includes an artillery group, antiaircraft units, antitank reserves, a mobile obstacle laying force, and chemicals and engineering reserves.

Sometimes the layout also has reserve SF units for operations against enemy troops landed in-depth behind the lines.

The first echelon, whose mission is to attack and breech the main layouts, includes leading assault echelons whose mission is to complete the initial stages of the attack. These forces will be reinforced with tanks, artillery, and engineering and antiaircraft units. If the first echelon is a tank force, it will be reinforced with infantry and other units.

The first echelon in an infantry or motorized division generally includes two reinforced brigades. A brigade's first echelon will be made up of two battalions reinforced with tanks. When the mission calls for hastily prepared layouts[84] to be breeched, a division's mechanized or tank brigades will be integrated into the first echelon.[85] An Egyptian infantry division was organized on the eve of the war with two infantry brigades reinforced with additional forces, which served as the division's first echelon.

The second-echelon mission is to augment the first echelon's strike and exploit the success. In addition, it must be prepared to block enemy counterattacks, protect the flanks, and replace first-echelon units that have incurred heavy losses. During the attack, the division's echelons are separated by fifteen to twenty kilometers. In brigade echelons the distance are five to fifteen kilometers.[86]

The second echelon may be larger than the first echelon when the defending enemy has deployed most of his forces in depth.[87] A tank battalion from the infantry division may be included in the second echelon, but the combat doctrine recommends leaving it in the division's reserves. Its role is to add momentum to the first-echelon attack, develop the attack to the depth, and carry out contingency missions. Sometimes it also acts as an advanced force in pursuit of the enemy and gains control of vital lines in the depth of the combat zone.

The echelon is made up of a brigade from the division and a battalion from the brigade. In Egyptian infantry divisions, as they were organized on the eve of the war, a mechanized infantry brigade was formed that served as a divisional second echelon.[88] In addition, each infantry division was reinforced with an independent tank brigade or from a second-echelon division. These were also used as the second echelon in a first division making the attack.

Organic artillery units and those temporarily attached under a single command are grouped in the first-echelon divisions making an attack. The divisional grouping is deployed five kilometers from the forward line and is made up of two or more battalions. A brigade grouping of two or three battalions is positioned two to four kilometers from the forward line.[89]

A divisional antiaircraft group may consist of two regiments: the division's organic regiment and another regiment attached for operational needs.

The divisional antitank reserve is made up of a battalion of antitank cannons and one or two companies of antitank missiles and assault cannons. The brigade has a reserve of one or two batteries of antitank cannons. These are accompanied by a force of mobile obstacles from an engineering company. The brigade is provided with one or two platoons of sappers.[90]

In certain cases, the attacking division's battle layout may include additional task-oriented forces. An advanced force the size of a reinforced battalion or brigade is established in the division, and includes a tank company, artillery battalion, antiaircraft battery, an engineering force, and chemical recon unit. If the force is made up of a single tank battalion, it is reinforced with an infantry company and other elements. The force's mission is to assist in developing the deep attack, while capturing and consolidating vital objectives deep in the enemy's layout.

The advanced force will complete the breakthrough of the first defense strip. While proceeding to its mission it will avoid contact with enemy and detour pockets of resistance. Its moves will be coordinated with those of other forces operating in the area.[91]

Another force operating in similar fashion is the circumventing force. This force moves at the beginning of the breakthrough operations or on the margins of the defense layout in an attempt to reach the depth without engaging the enemy in direct contact. It is also planned to isolate the enemy forces. Its size and composition are similar to those of the advanced force.[92]

A division spearheading an attack may employ an airborne force the size of an infantry company or battalion. Its missions are to take over vital objectives deep in the enemy's rear, isolate the combat theater, and block the enemy's operative reserves.[93] The division may also employ small commando forces to harass and disrupt the enemy, sabotage communications lines, and strike vital targets. Airborne forces at the divisional level operate at a depth not greater than twenty-five to thirty kilometers — the depth of the division's daily mission.[94]

Divisional Level Support Layouts and Their Application in an Attack Battle

The attacking divisions are provided with support layouts. These include the fire layout (artillery and air force), air defense layout teams, and security and combat support layouts: reconnaissance, chemical-biological and inflammable materials, camouflage, electronic warfare, engineering, and logistical units.

The artillery has a central role in fire assistance. Its missions in the attack battle are neutralizing enemy forces, weapons, and command-and-control posts; providing countermeasures against electronic warfare; destroying enemy positions and tanks with direct fire; and demolishing strongholds. The artillery can blind the enemy, illuminate areas, and sometimes forge openings in obstacles.

The attacking forces employ artillery in the softening-up and fire-support stages.[95] The division's organic artillery group is reinforced with additional artillery from the second-echelon divisions and higher levels.[96] The field army commander determines the number and type of reinforcement allotted to the division according to the calculations made in the field army's artillery headquarters. These calculations are based on the dimensions of the fire mission, the division's strength, its missions, the nature and strength of the enemy's defense layouts, the missions that air and naval forces are carrying out in the sector, and finally the amount of artillery that the field army can muster.

Based on the doctrine, the planners try to reach a high density of artillery pieces on each kilometer at the front. At least a hundred artillery pieces are needed to breech the enemy's organized layout on a main-axis effort; eighty barrels on a hastily prepared layout; and at least forty guns in secondary-effort attack.[97]

The calculation of number of artillery pieces that an attacking division needs is made in the first stage when the general dimensions of "preparatory fire" are determined.

On the basis of these calculations, the division needs ten to eleven battalions, in addition to its organic ORBAT, in order to simultaneously attack and lay down preparatory fire.[98]

These battalions are grouped in two brigade groups, each consisting of two or three battalions, to assist the first-echelon brigades, and a divisional grouping of three or four battalions. The division participating in the main axis effort is also assisted by a field army artillery group and an artillery group from a second-echelon division. A division on the secondary axis effort attacks using its organic units or it may be reinforced with two or three artillery battalions.

Artillery fire is used in maximum density in the preparatory-fire stage (several barrages continuing until the assault forces arrive at their objectives). In the following stage, the support-fire stage, barrages are carried out in successive concentrations and "rolling fire curtains," according to the earlier plan and the needs of the attackers.[99]

Air support during the softening-up fire is mainly concentrated in the attacking division's sector on the primary-effort axis. The targets of the air strike include airfields, surface-to-surface missile batteries, artillery and mortar positions, second-echelon reserves, and the enemy's defensive division's command strongholds. The air force may also operate against select enemy strongholds.[100]

At the preparatory fire stage, and according to the predetermined plan, the division is provided with fifty fighter-bombers, used as close as possible toward the end of the artillery softening-up and commencement of the main assault. The attack is allotted another forty to sixty air strikes for the daily twenty-four-hour mission.[101]

The division's antiaircraft defense is based on organic and other elements that have been assigned to it. Each division has an antiaircraft regiment, and each brigade an antiaircraft battalion. The division operating on the main-axis effort is reinforced with an additional antiaircraft regiment, as well as portable antiaircraft missiles and mobile antiaircraft cannon. Surface-to-air missiles from the field army and national air defense forces are deployed in the division's sector.

Light antiaircraft batteries are positioned near the advanced forces and two kilometers from the contact line; medium antiaircraft weapons are placed in brigade layouts two or three kilometers from the line; mobile antiaircraft guns are deployed 400–500 meters from the forward contact line. Platoons of personal missiles are put in the first-echelon battalion's layouts.

Acquisition of air targets is carried out by field army and air defense radar stations deployed in the area. In addition, antiaircraft observation posts are set up at all levels. Command-and-control posts over the entire layout are concentrated in divisional or field army headquarters and are responsible for maintaining close cooperation among all of the air defense elements.[102]

"Multi-sided protection" and support are a vital part of the overall operations in order to assist the units in their missions and prevent the enemy from interfering with the attackers.

Intelligence reconnaissance during the attack carries out observation, raids, ambushes, prisoner-seizing, and covert patrols. The ongoing aggressive patrol activity before the attack is designed to supply fresh information that will be of great assistance in preparing and planning the attack. Patrols operating in the attack may be as large as a company and integrated into the lead elements in the division's forward guards. They will form the patrol groups in the divisions and brigades and be used for reconnoitering in the lead battalions.[103]

Defense against chemical and biological weapons consists of the following measures: detection and warning, protective equipment and engineering preparations, means for countering the effects of an attack.[104]

Camouflage and deception are an integral part of the effort at concealing the operation and heightening the element of surprise. The main methods used are dispersal and concealment of the forces' movement and location; communications security — especially radio silence; muffling noise and maintaining blackouts; concealing friendly radar and disrupting enemy radar; decoys; feints; and smoke.[105]

The aim of electronic warfare is to disrupt the enemy's control layouts and protect the division's equipment from enemy disturbances. Counter-activity is carried out by task-oriented units attached to the field army.[106] A blocking company may be used in the division's sector. Blocking units move along the division's flanks and operate while halting. The use of various measures to physically destroy the enemy's electronic targets is the best way to paralyze him.

Engineering support includes engineering patrols to obtain information on the enemy and the terrain in the theater of action. Engineering forces pave roads and assist in removing (or setting up) obstacles.[107]

Logistical support in a division and brigade includes medical, ordnance and quartermaster units that operate on two levels: the first is the mobile level that remains close to the rear of the first combat echelon or on the same line as the second echelon; the second level is deployed twenty to twenty-five kilometers to the rear of a division and only ten kilometers behind a brigade.

The maintenance units leapfrog in unison with progress of the fighting so as to guarantee a continuous flow of supplies to the troops.[108] The brigade medical company leapfrogs toward the fighting when the wounded have to be evacuated more than ten or fifteen kilometers. The division's medical battalion and mobile field army hospital leapfrog every thirty-five or forty kilometers. The light vehicle and armored vehicle motor pools give part of their equipment to repair groups operating just behind the assault forces. The brigade's ordnance company leapfrogs every eight or ten kilometers, and the divisional motor pool leapfrogs at the end of a day's combat as far as necessary. A brigade's second-echelon maintenance units leapfrog two or three times in a day of combat as necessary. At the divisional level they leapfrog only once a day.

Mobile stockpiles and reserves of supplies and equipment follow close behind the forces. Replenishing is carried out with priority given to the most essential missions. Units take supplies directly from the storerooms when the divisions are without means of transportation. Responsibility for supplying and purifying water and making maximum use of water sources in the captured areas falls on special engineering units.

Command and Control

The commander has direct control over the troops, or controls them through his staff officers and their branches. Command at the divisional and brigade levels is done through three headquarters:[109] the main headquarters (command post);[110] the rear headquarters (the rear command post); and the forward commander stronghold (C.P., observation stronghold). During the fighting the commander and headquarters leapfrog according to developments on the battlefield.[111]

Appendix B

The Development of Deception in the Soviet Warfare Doctrine

The Soviet warfare doctrine developed the art of deception long before World War II. In the 1920s Soviet military theorists viewed operational deception as a key means of achieving surprise. The czarist legacy and hard-earned experiences in World War I and the Civil War led Russian military thinkers — Tukhachevsky, Svetzin, Verkhovsky, and others — to formulate the basic principles for organizing and implementing deception in future wars.

An article published in 1924 entitled "The High Command" stated that the primary method of attaining surprise is through operational deception, which had to be based on the principles of activism (*activnost*), credibility, routine behavior, and operational moves.[112]

Before the outbreak of World War II, Soviet military planners applied these principles in fighting the Japanese in Khalkin-Gol (1939) and scored an overwhelming victory. However, the fundamentals of the doctrine were based on the experience acquired in deceptive operations during World War II. This hard-won knowledge proved that the correct application of deception could keep the enemy in the dark about operational intentions, deployment areas, ORBAT, alert levels and operational readiness — thus allowing the attacker to achieve total surprise and increase the operational forces' chances of survival. Diverse operational situations, combat missions, ORBAT, and changing weapons required various deception tactics: concealment, simulation, decoys, feints, and disinformation.

The Soviets' development of operational deception in World War II may be divided into three stages:

The first period focused on strategic defense from June 1941 to the encirclement of German forces in Stalingrad. The lack of operational experience, shortage of troops and weapons, and retreat to the outskirts of Moscow left the Soviets with almost no card to play except for the concealment of their forces and battle plans. The forces designated for the main effort were concentrated a great distance from the front and attack axis. They generally moved, assembled, and deployed under cover of darkness. Secrecy was strictly maintained, troop concentrations hidden, and the main-effort units concealed from air surveillance. The attack was frequently carried out for the first time as a mechanized offensive by forces dispatched from assembly areas located in the front's depth. Decoys were used and simulated troop concentrations appeared in nonessential sectors. In 1942 frontline field army staffs began devising separate deception plans as the basis for guaranteeing the operation.

Also in this period the Soviets became aware of the critical importance of operational deception, taking the first steps in acquiring practical experience. They developed methods of concealing their main defense layouts, gaining enormous experience in simulating attack preparations in areas where a weak defense was deployed in depth. Troop concentrations remained hidden during the attack, and large-scale feints were carried out in the direction of secondary efforts. Radio networks spread misleading information.

In the middle of the war, from 1943 until early 1944, during the Russian counterattacks in Moscow, Stalingrad, and Kursk, a more sophisticated use of deception was made on a wide scale in strategic operations. The Armed Forces General Command (Stavka) and other top-level headquarters formulated the concept and goals of deception only in the planning stage. However, during operations, deception tactics for fooling the enemy were not implemented. Prior to the attack, the front and field army headquarters drew up plans for operational deception that included its overall concept and modus operandi, as well as the troops and weapons to be used in its implementation.[113]

An example of a deception plan is the Thirty-eighth Army's operational plan on the Belgorod-Kharkov front in the summer of 1943 (after turning back the German counterattack against the Kursk arc). The plan set aside a number of areas for simulating troop concentrations, the absorption of reinforcements and assembly lines of reserves, and an attack by divisions deployed in the defense.

Concealment received much attention. Deception activity included reducing the number of people with knowledge of operational plans; giving the mission a green light only a day or few hours before it was scheduled to take place; building up assembly areas and carrying out troop movements only at nighttime; and adjusting artillery ranges with single guns only one or two days before the operation. A special effort was made to conceal troop and weapon concentrations carried by rail — men and equipment were unloaded at night and left immediately for carefully camouflaged assembly areas. Soviet forces gained invaluable experience in smoke screens, methods of blinding enemy positions, and covering up armored and infantry forces as they moved into assembly areas and later when they engaged in the attack. The smoke screen was also used to conceal the crossing sectors and simulate crossing efforts.[114] Impressive progress was also made in the use of decoys for simulating large troop concentrations and attack preparations. Forces the size of a reinforced division took part in deception tactics when a field army operation was planned.[115]

The period witnessed the transformation of deception activity into an overall operational framework — a comprehensive method expanded and refined the concept of deception and staff level supervisory mechanisms. The element of surprise became an essential part of every operational move.

The third period of World War II, which was characterized by vigorous attacks on numerous axes in the direction of Berlin, maintained the range and variety of deceptive activity. The boldness and scope of deception operations was based on the Red Army's new standards that were published in 1943, and especially in a 1944 regulation: "The Assumed Lines of the Breakthrough in the Organized Defense Layout." The large battles in 1944 employed concealment tactics that were an integral part of the primary effort and its preparations. Frontline headquarters was charged with the main responsibility for planning operational deception. The headquarters had to allocate troops and plan the organization and supervision of the deception moves. Much activity was devoted to concealment — especially against enemy aerial patrols and ground observation. Less attention was given to providing disinformation to German listening systems. The operations' security efforts were improved and strengthened, and emphasis was placed on field security.

Redeployment, concentration, and activation of the operational forces were carried out far from the contact line and mainly at nighttime. According to the deployment plan prepared by the first echelon, the reinforced troops were amassed far from the contact line and a number of possibilities were drafted for sending them into battle. Artillery groups were kept in reserve in the rear and moved to the front just prior to the commencement of fire. The idea was to do everything possible to conceal the assault force so as to reduce the enemy's ability to locate the direction of the main strike.

Together with concealment activity, along the entire length of the front the field army took steps to confuse the enemy regarding the time and place of the main effort. Beginning in 1944, deception activity received a new momentum with the introduction of decoys and feints that included contact with the enemy and purposely leaving various units visible.[116] Deception operations improved and included fake layouts, decoys, and simulated troop activity. Entire units carried out feints with skeletal forces performing simulated crossing attempts. Deception called for the use of large numbers of real units, such as armored and mechanized assault forces, engineers, artillery batteries, aircraft, and chemical units that created smoke screens.[117] At this stage the involvement of infantry units (whose whereabouts enemy intelligence had little knowledge of) diminished.

By the end of World War II the doctrinal formulation of operational deception was of key importance for concealing the operational concept and nature of the ORBAT and for achieving surprise on the battlefield. Combat experience proved that a deception plan had to be adapted to the operational concept of a given campaign and the capabilities and strength of the forces involved in an operation.

To sum up: experience in deceptive tactics in World War II taught the Soviets that the element of surprise was the most important factor in a battle. Successful deception came at a low price, but its benefits were invaluable. It enabled combat missions to be carried out with a minimum number of forces and means and accomplish operational goals with minimum casualties and weapon losses.[118]

Appendix C

The Infantry Division Crossing a Water Obstacle

ORDER NO. 41 FROM THE COMMANDER-IN-CHIEF OF THE ARMED FORCES[119]

Introduction

1. This order and the information contained herein is top secret. It is absolutely forbidden for it to fall into anyone's hands whose name does not appear on the circulation list, including officers of the armed forces.

2. Parts of this order may be extracted and given to secondary units who are interested parties, but this order must not be circulated in its entirety to any level lower than an infantry brigade.

   Seven detailed colored plates have been added — "5" to "20" — relating to special issues on the first day of the crossing.

   The plates:

   Plate 5 — Time needed for an infantry battalion to cross a footbridge.

   Plate 6 — Time needed for an infantry division to cross with boats.

   Plate 7 — Stages in building a bridgehead for a reinforced division. The first *majmu'a* (boat crossing):

   The first stage — from H-Hour to H-Hour plus 1.

   Plate 8 — Stages in building a bridgehead for a reinforced division. The first *majmu'a* (boat crossing):

   The second stage.

   Plate 9 — Stages in building a bridgehead for a reinforced division. The first *majmu'a* (boat crossing):

   The third stage.

   Plate 10 — Stages in building a bridgehead for a reinforced division. The first *majmu'a* (boat crossing):

   The fourth stage.

   Plate 20 — Stages in building a bridgehead for a reinforced infantry division. The reinforced infantry division's deployment at the divisional bridgehead: from H-Hour plus 18 to H-Hour plus 24.

Sa'ad al Shazli

Chief of Staff, Armed Forces • War Ministry • 20 March 1973

Order No. 41—Armed Forces Chief of Staff: The Infantry Division Crossing a Water Obstacle

1. General
- Since the development of amphibious weapons, vehicles, and tanks, water obstacles have become less formidable, especially with the tanks' ability to use snorkels and travel submerged across the floor of the obstacle.
- The ground forces can cross a water obstacle from movement and along a wide front. All the assault forces' necessary information can be obtained via observation (patrols). This includes information on the coast's suitability for amphibious vehicles to descend and ascend both banks. Further information is needed regarding the floor of the water obstacle and the practicality of driving submerged tanks across the floor.
- Given the economic limitations and wartime production problems, the country will be unable to supply each armed forces unit with amphibious vehicles, therefore those vehicles that we possess will be used to transfer only some of the combat echelons whose main task will be to secure the distant shore and later to establish bridges across the water obstacle for the transfer of the rest of the combat and administrative levels. Given the development of bridges, a 200-meter-long bridge can be set up in thirty minutes.
- If, in addition to the abovementioned factors, airborne forces are landed on the distant shore, then crossing the water obstacle is no longer as difficult a task as it was in the past.

2. The Suez Canal as a water obstacle
- The Suez Canal is a singular water obstacle unlike any natural river or fresh water or artificial canal. This is true for the following reasons:
  1) The banks have a gradated structure and their edge is composed of rock—both features prevent amphibious vehicles from descending or ascending the water barrier unless engineering preparations have been carried out.
  2) The dirt embankment (ten to twenty meters high) that the enemy built directly on the rim of the eastern bank prevents amphibious weapons from crossing the canal until the embankment has been breached.
  3) The defense line (the Bar-Lev Line) consisting of heavily fortified strongholds and tank parks along the eastern shore and local rear.
  4) Napalm and inflammable materials containers on the eastern shore enable the enemy to ignite the canal area, turning it into an inferno designed to repulse the assault force crossing.
- This order [Order No. 41] is applicable to an Egyptian reinforced infantry division crossing of the canal.

3. Troop assembly and crossing
- In view of what has been said:
  1) The infantry will cross the Suez Canal with all the weapons, ammunition, and equipment that it can carry in the boats. Afterward the material can be brought up the dirt embankment.
  2) Amphibious vehicles will be able to cross only after the dirt embankment has been broken through and landing docks have been prepared on the local and distant shores. This may take seven to nine hours to complete from the start of the attack.
  3) After the dirt embankment has been breached and landing docks prepared on the local shore, pontoons can be used to transfer the infantry, but ascents do not have to

be built on the distant shore. The breaching preparations can commence approximately two hours from the start of the attack.

4) After the breaching has been made on the distant shore, pontoons can transfer vehicles and heavy artillery. This may take five to seven hours from the start of the attack.

5) Every type of vehicle and tank will be able to cross after the bridges have been built and the dirt embankment broken through. This will take seven to nine hours from the start of the attack.

• Given all of the above mentioned limitations, the infantry division will have to be reorganized before the crossing and divided into two main groups:

6) The first group will be made up of the infantry and all that they can transport — weapons, ammunition, technical equipment, but minimal administrative gear.

7) The second group will consist of tanks, all types of amphibious and non-amphibious vehicles, and all types of heavy weapons (mobile and towed).

• In order to complete the first wave's crossing and economize on boats and pontoons, the infantry division will cross in successive waves according to the following arrangement:

The first wave will include first-echelon companies from first-echelon battalions, first-echelon brigades from a first-echelon division, artillery batteries, and observation officers from 82-millimeter mortar batteries.

The second wave will include second-echelon companies from first-echelon brigades (from a first-echelon division), one battalion headquarters with Sager antitank missiles (two missiles per launcher).

The third wave will include light support weapons from first-echelon battalions from the division's first-echelon brigades. The following weapons are either reinforcements or organically part of the battalion:

B-10 recoilless cannon with nine rockets;

B-11 recoilless cannon with five rockets;

12.7-millimeter machine guns with three boxes of ammunition (150 bullets per box);

One 82 millimeter mortar with the twelve rockets.

The fourth wave will include a large supply of ammunition for all of the weapons needed to reinforce an infantry battalion. The ammunition will be loaded on infantry wagons towed by three men from the infantry group. The group will be made up of no less than seven men. Each weapon will be provided with the following ammunition:

Sager launchers — four rockets per launcher (one infantry wagon carries eight rockets per two-man team);

B-10 recoilless cannon — twenty rockets carried on the infantry wagon;

B-11 recoilless cannon — eight rockets carried on the infantry wagon;

12.7-millimeter machine guns — seven ammunition boxes with belts (350 bullets per belt) carried on the ammunition wagon;

An additional ammunition box (179 bullets) carried on the ammunition wagon;

82-millimeter mortar — thirty rockets.

The fifth wave: second-echelon battalions from the division's first-echelon brigades.

The sixth wave: the completion of the crossing of the first-echelon command post.

The seventh wave: the completion of the crossing of the divisional command post in the fifth wave, first echelon brigades' antitank reserves and Sager antitank missile reserves in the sixth wave.

The eighth wave: the completion of the crossing of the divisional command post in the seventh and eighth waves.

The ninth wave: the completion of the crossing (across the infantry's bridges) of first-echelon battalions from the division's second-echelon brigades in the ninth and tenth waves.

The tenth wave: the completion of the crossing of the division's command post in the seventh and eighth waves.

The eleventh and twelfth waves: the completion of the crossing of second-echelon battalions from the division's second-echelon brigade.

Regarding the second division,[120] strict priorities must be determined for the crossing according to the troops' needs. In general, the following crossing priorities will have to be determined:

Crossing Priorities on the Pontoons and Bridges

First priority:

1. Tanks (all types for infantry support) without the armored units' administrative vehicles.
2. Combat vehicles carrying or towing antitank weapons, plus the maximum amount of ammunition (without administrative vehicles).
3. Armored vehicles (for laying phone lines) at full capacity (without administrative vehicles).
4. Jeeps mounted with B-11 recoilless cannon (plus seventeen rockets).
5. One 1.5-ton truck for every two 12.7-millimeter machine guns (plus sixteen ammunition boxes); 1,360 bullets per machine gun.
6. One 1.5-ton truck for each company of flamethrowers (to complete the stock).
7. 120-millimeter mortar units (without administrative elements).

Second priority:

1. Ammunition vehicles for completing the supply to all of the units' vehicles that crossed in the boats or that will be crossing on the bridges, until completing the supply of the entire quota of light weapons and artillery ammunition.
2. The rest of the vehicle: two 1.5-ton trucks for each infantry battalion. Each truck will carry twenty-five boxes of 12.7-millimeter ammunition. Total — 2,140 bullets per machine gun.
3. Field artillery and medium artillery units with one fire quota (without administrative elements).
4. Antitank units with two fire quotas (without administrative elements).

Third priority

1. The rest of the infantry battalion's vehicles (excluding troop transports).
2. Administrative elements of each battalion-level or parallel-level unit (and secondary units) that have crossed (without less essential elements such as motor pools and kitchens).

Fourth priority: brigade-level secondary administrative units.

Fifth priority: administrative units at the infantry division level and vehicles carrying additional mines (fifty tons) to the bridgeheads.

Sixth priority:

1. Trucks for transporting infantrymen, intended for transporting first-echelon troops, must remain west of the canal, unless it is decided to launch a divisional attack east of the canal, in which case the trucks will cross the canal.

2. Sometimes a limited number of trucks will have to be included in the second priority or in its rear so as to create a mobile reserve the size of an infantry battalion reinforced with a divisional second-echelon brigade, or the trucks will have to be divided among second-echelon battalions (of all the brigades) according to the division commander's orders.

4. The flexible crossing of an armored brigade

In the event that the division is reinforced with an armored brigade[121] and the division commander expects an imminent counterattack against one of his armored brigades, he may send an armored brigade across bridge immediately after the first priority vehicles. If he has reason to believe that the attack is not imminent, it is better to postpone the armored brigade's crossing (at least until after the transfer of the second-priority vehicles).

In other cases, the armored brigade's crossing may be postponed until after the fifth priority. Depending on the situation, if the armored brigade crosses immediately after the first priority, it will leave all of the administrative vehicles behind that will later be annexed to the second- or third-priority brigade according to the standard operating procedure in the division's brigades. If the brigade crosses after the second priority, the administrative elements at the battalion level will be attached to it (that is, they will leapfrog over the first, second, and third priorities). The rest of the brigade-level administrative elements will cross at the end of the fourth priority.

5. The commander's roles; coordinating movements

The infantry division's crossing demands a high level of command and control in order to ensure that the priority arrangements are adhered to and the vehicles reach the secondary units that crossed in boats. This demands first-rate performance on the part of the commander and clockwork coordination at all the levels — down to the individual soldier.

The commander's role and the operation's coordination will be based on the following principles:

1) Vehicles will be marked with colors according to the crossing priority. The marking will appear on the windshield next to the driver and will be identical for all levels. The marking will be printed at general headquarters and distributed to all crossing units. The following colors will be used in accordance with the instructions in this order:

    Red — first priority

    Green — second priority

    Blue — third priority

    Black — fourth priority

    Yellow — fifth priority

    White with a red "X" in it — sixth priority

2) The ordinal numbers will be marked in chalk on every tank and vehicle. Care must be taken so that number is not repeated. The numbers must be marked on vehicles according to the crossing priority.

3) Each division will add other markings that are characteristic of the unit or secondary unit. This marking — in the shape of an animal or geometrical pattern — will help the crossing monitors on the bridgeheads direct the vehicles to their units without excessive confusion.

4) The routes and junctions that the vehicles will be encountering after the crossing will also have to be marked. At nighttime the markings will consist of colored illumination (red, green, yellow, etc.), and in daylight various shapes according to the division commander's standing instructions.

5) There will also be markings in white (oil paint) on the helmet of each soldier (infantry and mechanized infantry) according to the following arrangement:

A. The rank will be drawn in front according to the natural size of the officers' shoulder insignia. The insignia will be marked so the length of two bars will not exceed six centimeters (three centimeters in each direction).

B. An animal figure will be drawn on the right side of the helmet to identify the infantry brigade or divisional unit.

C. Geometrical shapes will be drawn on the left side of the helmet to identify the battalion or parallel unit.

D. The rear of the helmet will be marked with symbols of the secondary unit (the size of an infantry company).

E. The markings of the reinforcing units will be identical to those of the units or secondary units that they are attached to.

6) Each crew-operated weapon attached to the infantry will be given a number. The numbers will be arranged according to bridgehead. An identical number will be given to the accompanying towed vehicle so the crew can be recognized and identified. The weapons of the units will be listed as follows:

A first-echelon battalion or brigade on the right — numbers 1–26.

A first-echelon battalion on the left/first-echelon brigade on the right — numbers 27–52.

A first-echelon battalion on the right/first-echelon brigade on the left — numbers 53–78.

A first-echelon battalion on the left/first-echelon brigade on the left — numbers 79–98.

A second-echelon battalion/first-echelon brigade on the right — numbers 99–118.

A second-echelon battalion/first-echelon brigade on the left —119–138.

7) A second-echelon divisional brigade — numbers 139–198.

The boats will be given ordinal numbers at the bridgehead. For example, they will be numbered from right to left with the numbers 1 to 144. Four battalion-crossing sectors will have thirty-six boats in each sector. Each battalion-crossing sector will consist of two company crossing points, each with eighteen boats. The company crossing point will be about 400 meters long at the front and no less than 100 meters deep at each of the bridge or pontoon openings. The company boats will have a twenty-five-meter space between them.

8) Each infantry battalion will be reinforced with a three-man weapons crew (excluding medium machine-guns) to assist in towing the infantry wagon carrying the ammunition for each weapon. These troops will be concentrated in the infantry units (according to standard operating procedure) so that the group consists of no less than seven men. After the battalion's ammunition point across the bridge is reached, the infantrymen will return to their organic units.

9) B-10 recoilless cannons will support the crossing battalions. Each cannon will consist of a crew of seven whose organic unit is responsible for reinforcing each crew with three soldiers above the standard number.

10) Before the start of the battle, each infantryman must learn the following information:

A. His wave and boat number; his crossing time; the names and description of the soldiers on his right and left; the direction of the attack after the crossing; what to do in case he loses directions and is cut off from his unit.

B. Infantrymen will be supplied with food and water for a 24-hour period. Later they will receive extra food and water rations.

C. The soldiers will have a quantity of ammunition some of which they are forbidden to use. They will receive specific instructions on the amount of ammunition to be used during the assault, the amount needed for repelling local counterattacks, and the amount needed for firing on low-flying aircraft, etc. It will take an hour to replenish the ammunition.

D. What to do in case they are wounded and unable to continue with their unit.

E. The expected time of arrival and distribution of the rest of the weapons and ammunition, and how to recognize them.

11) Every driver must know:

A. His crossing priority.

B. The expected time for crossing over the bridge; the crossing priority within his unit; the number marked on his vehicle; the names and numbers of the drivers in the cars in front and back of him.

C. The time for leaving the dug-out and starting to move toward the bridgehead, the route leading to the bridgehead and the signs on the route.

D. The route to take after the crossing, its nighttime colors and daytime signs.

E. His unit's approximate location.

F. The need to preserve the rate of flow through the obstacle. Every reduction in speed will delay our forces' crossing and reduce our combat ability for repulsing the enemy's attack. On the other hand, increasing speed beyond that specified in the orders may result in accidents or breakdowns on the bridge which would pejoratively influence the rate of flow.

G. The flow to and beyond the bridge will continue even during an enemy air attack on the bridge and in the vicinity of its bases. It is forbidden to increase or reduce speed because of the air attack during the aircraft's approach or flight away from the bridge. Soldiers must allow the air defense units and land forces to deal with the enemy planes.

H. The driver must be fully aware that once he proceeds to the bridge, he must carry out his commander's orders to the letter and not the orders from any other source until he reaches his unit on the distant shore, unless the unit commander permits the vehicle loading officer to override his orders, or unless orders come from the military police who are organizing traffic to the bridge and at the bridgehead crossing.

12) A loading officer will be appointed for each vehicle who will be responsible for vehicles that get lost and cut off from their units. The loading officer will have two or three deputies in the event that he is killed.

13) For details on the organization of the officer's convoys, see Appendix A.

6. For information on the division's infantry group during the canal crossing, its arrangement in the boats and wave priority, see Appendix B.

7. For information on the infantry division's vehicle group during the canal crossing and its crossing priorities, see Appendix C.

8. For a detailed table of the loadings of the division's reinforced infantry units according to the crossing priorities, see Appendix D.

9. The means of crossing (excluding boats).

A. Pontoons

1) The Egyptian army has several types of pontoons:

Flow/hour		*Speed on the bridges (kms per hour)*		Vehicles
Vehicles	*tank*	*Vehicles*	*tank*	*bridges*
200	120	10	6	TPP
220	120	10	6	Uniflot
300–400	240	15–20	10–12	PMP

2) Density during crossing:
  Twenty-five tanks per kilometer.
  Twenty-five vehicles per kilometer.

3) A time interval will be kept between the secondary units (every thirty or fifty tanks — sixty vehicles) that equals a quarter of the time needed for a secondary unit to cross. This will guarantee a time interval equal to the length of the unit's line in order overcome unexpected delays in the units, increase control on the bridges, and prevent congestion at the bridgeheads.

4) The enemy may carry out air strikes and artillery barrages while our forces are crossing the bridges. We may assume that the bridge will not be operational more than sixteen hour a day, that is, after every four hours of movement across the bridge, we can expect a two-hour halt for bridge repairs.

  B. The Uniflot pontoons (96-type) crossing point
    1) This is the point through which one unit is capable of transporting two tanks, or four 4-ton trucks or two artillery pieces plus their towing equipment, or eight jeeps.
    2) Two pontoons will be operational at the crossing point.
    3) One crossing point is capable of handling three roundtrips per hour. If a breakdown occurs, each unit will make only two roundtrips per hour. Therefore, the total flow per hour at a crossing point will be eight tanks, or eighteen trucks, or sixteen ZIL trucks, or eight cannons with their towing gear, or thirty-two jeeps.
  C. The crossing point for fifty-ton pontoons
  The crossing flow of fifty-ton pontoons is half that of the ninety-six-ton ones but employs the same method of operation.
  D. The crossing point for lightweight 2x12 pontoons
    1) The crossing point with one 2x12 pontoon is capable of handling a roundtrip with a total weight of twenty-five tons. This is equal to two artillery pieces plus their towing equipment, or two trucks with a three-ton load (fully loaded), or four empty trucks, or six jeeps.
    2) Two pontoons will operate at one crossing point.
    3) The rate per hour at the crossing point per hour (taking breakdowns into account) is eight artillery pieces plus their towing gear, or eight fully loaded trucks, etc.
  E. The crossing point for amphibious trucks
    1) P.T.S. amphibious trucks and one or two K-61 amphibious vehicles will use this crossing point.
    2) The load strength of the P.T.S. truck is equal to that of a fully loaded GAZ-63 truck or an empty ZIL truck (total load: seven tons on land, ten tons in the water).

3) The load strength of a K-61 truck is equal to that of an empty GAZ-63 truck or loaded jeep (total load: three tons land, five tons in the water).

4) Each truck is capable of making three roundtrips per hour (taking breakdowns into account).

5) Total flow per hour at the crossing point is three fully loaded GAZ-63 trucks or six jeep-69s.

F. The amphibious crossing point

1) The crossing point enables amphibious vehicles to descend into and climb out of the water.

2) The vehicle's speed in the canal is 100 meters per minute. The vehicles will cross at a density of twenty vehicles per kilometer, that is, with a fifty-meter (approximately) interval between vehicles. The traffic rate at a crossing point is 120 vehicles, given the possibility of breakdown. This rate is based on eighty vehicles per hour.

G. The infantry bridges

1) Two bridges will be allocated to each infantry division that must be ready by H-Hour plus 2 at the latest.

2) These bridges will be used as support elements for accelerating the battalion/the division's second-echelon brigade crossing.

H. Four-ton bridges

1) One four-ton bridge will be used in each infantry division's crossing sector.

2) This bridge functions principally as a decoy but can be used for lightweight vehicles that cross at a rate of sixty vehicles per hour (taking breakdowns into account). It can also be used for evacuating light vehicles.

I. The boat battalions

1) The establishment of the boat battalions has been completed. Each infantry division will have one boat battalion attached to it. The battalion's role is to assist in setting up a bridgehead. The battalion will operate 144 boats simultaneously.

2) The boat battalion is made up of three companies; each company has four platoons, and in each platoon — three squads. Each squad consists of a commander and twelve soldiers.

3) Each company can operate seventy-two boats (with two soldiers per boat). It will supply an infantry brigade's crossing needs at two echelons where the first echelon is made up of two battalions.

4) Each platoon can operate eighteen boats (with two soldiers per boat). It can transfer one infantry company per roundtrip.

5) Taking into account that the division's main effort consists of twelve waves over a three hour period, the boat battalion will split into two companies and leave the third company as a reserve force to replace the company operating in the direction of the main effort, thus the soldiers will not operate the boat for more than six roundtrips throughout the division's crossing.

6) The boat battalions are responsible for guarding and maintaining the boats and ensuring that their instructional markings are kept intact, the rope ladders are in place, etc. The battalions are not administratively independent, that is, they are subordinate to the infantry divisions' engineering battalions.

7) After an infantry division completes the crossing, the boat battalion can be used for one of the following operations:

a) Transferring additional mines and ammunition in infantry wagons to secondary units at the bridgeheads.

b) Replacing losses in the engineering units.

c) Replacing the infantry soldiers towing the infantry wagon alongside the weapons until the infantrymen return to their original groups.

d) Carrying out whatever assignments the division commander decides.

8) Commanders at all levels must be fully aware that the creation of the boat battalions does not mean that they [the commanders] have less responsibility for transporting the boats, getting them into the water, and rowing them to the distant shore. The main purpose in creating these battalions is to have soldiers who will return the boats from the eastern bank to the western side after crossing to the east.

10. Crossing requirements

A. Each reinforced infantry division designated to cross the Suez Canal will be provided with the following crossing equipment:

144 NDL-10 boats (at least seventy-four will be equipped with ramps).

1 TPP bridge.

1 PMP bridge.

3 pontoon crossing points capable of bearing a fifty-ton load.

1 crossing point for amphibious trucks.

1 four-ton bridge.

1 infantry bridge.

288 rope ladders.

288 towropes (fifteen to twenty meters in length).

288 steel angle poles (1.20 meters in length).

144 hammers.

288 identification markings with the numbers 1–144, two of each number and equipped with night illumination.

436 hand-pulled infantry wagons (twenty-four for carrying Sager missiles; 198 for ammunition; 171 for mines; 33 for communications lines; ten for identification numbers).

B. The bridges and pontoons that are designed for the infantry division according to these standards will enable approximately 700 vehicles (or one hundred tanks and 550 vehicles) to cross per hour. Total time of transferring an infantry division's tanks and vehicles will be four to five hours.

11. Breaching the enemy's dirt embankment.

A. Prior to H-Hour plus 7, eleven breaches will be made in the dirt embankment in the infantry division's crossing sector. The allocation will be as follows:

Number of breaches	Designation (allotment)
2	One for each heavy bridge
3	One for the pontoon with the fifty-ton load capacity
4	One for each amphibious trucks crossing
1	For a four-ton bridge
1	Reserves
11	Total number of breaches in the infantry division's crossing sector

B. The breaches will be separated one from the other by 600 meters.

C. From H-Hour plus 7 to H-Hour plus, 14 more breaches will be made, two on each flank (side) of the division's assault sector in order to create reserve openings and enable one of them to be used in the near future for transferring amphibious vehicles. The opening of these breaches depends on the tactical situation, that is, the division's bridgehead must extend at least ten kilometers from the breaches.

D. If one heavy bridge is allotted to the division and the second bridge is replaced by a number of pontoons, then the number of breaches (openings) will have to be increased so that all of the pontoons will begin operations at H-Hour plus 7 at the latest.

E. The breaches must be made on the flanks of the companies' crossing points.

12. Guarding the bridges and pontoons

A. The crew chiefs are responsible for guarding the engineers while they set up and operate the bridges and pontoons.

B. The enemy may use laser-guided bombs to knock out the bridges from distances greater than the range of antiaircraft missiles. The best way to disrupt laser action is by churning up dust and smoke, therefore if the canal crossing is made during a sand storm this will reduce the chances of the bridges being hit by aerial bombs.

13. For the timetable of the infantry division's boat crossing, see Appendix E.

14. For details on the time table for an infantry battalion crossing a bridge on foot, see Appendix F.

15. The time needed for the crossing of an infantry division.

A. An infantry group (*majmu'a*) will make the crossing if the crossing gear (as it appears in this order) is prepared within three hours. The first stage in setting up a bridgehead will be completed by H-Hour plus 4 (approximately).

B. The vehicle crossing of an infantry division reinforced with crossing gear (as mentioned in Section 10) will be carried out in the following manner: (provided that the enemy has not destroyed one of the bridges):

Total number of infantry divisions reinforced with an armored brigade			Armored brigade		Infantry division		Priorities
total	vehicles	tanks	vehicles	tanks	vehicles	tanks	
633	505	128			505	128	first
700	700				700		second
330	233	97	233	97			armored brigade
601	601				601		third
439	439		66		373		fourth
219	219		101		727		fifth
828	828		101		727		sixth

Appendix 2 explains the following:

1) The rate of flow of the infantry division in the main effort.

2) The rate of flow of the infantry division in the secondary effort in which an armored brigade crosses after second priority vehicles has completed its crossing.

3) The rate of flow of an infantry division in a secondary effort in which an armored

brigade crosses immediately after the first priority vehicles has completed its crossing.

C. A division will be assigned fifteen crossing points for heavy pontoons (thirty 96-ton pontoons) as a substitute for one of the bridges. The pontoons' capacity is equal to that of a heavy bridge (as previously mentioned). The pontoons are generally considered better than bridges because they are less vulnerable from the air. Their drawback is that they require fifteen breaches in the dirt embankment on the eastern side of the canal instead of three openings that a bridge requires (one main opening and two alternates). A pontoon also requires fifteen breaches on our (the western) side of the canal.

16. Choosing a crossing sector

A. Determining a bridgehead means that the division has to reach the bridgehead in an allotted time. This is the responsibility of the field army commander. It will be the division's final mission. The base of the division's bridgehead is usually sixteen to twenty kilometers long, and eight to ten kilometers deep.

B. The bridgehead will be set up in two stages:
   1) In the first stage a small bridgehead will established by the light infantry with man-portable or towable weapons. In this case, the bridgehead base will be eight kilometers long and five kilometers deep. This is considered the division's direct mission.
   2) In the second stage the bridgehead will be immediately expanded once the tanks, vehicles, and weapons arrive. At this point the bridgehead will take its final shape.

C. When deciding the division's crossing sector, the following points have to be considered (even though they are sometimes contradictory).
   1) The site where the division's two heavy bridges will be set up and the need to guard them while the engineering forces are working on them.
   2) A bridgehead in the first stage.
   3) A bridgehead in the second stage.
   4) Expected enemy activity.

   This means that in the first stage the division's two (main) bridges will not necessarily be located in the middle of the bridgehead, but the bridges should be in the middle of the bridgehead in the second stage.

17. The establishment of the bridgehead

A. A divisional crossing sector of six or seven kilometers.

B. When the first wave reaches the western shore it will set up a defensive layout on the dirt embankment until the arrival of the second wave.

C. When the last troops of the second wave reach the top of the dirt embankment, the first wave will advance about 200 meters from the embankment under covering fire from the second wave.

D. The first wave and second forces will remain where they are until the third and fourth waves arrive, after which they will rejoin their secondary units. This stage will be over at H-Hour plus 1 (Appendix G).

E. After the support forces (reinforcements) arrive, a first-echelon battalion will advance as far as two kilometers east of the canal at H-Hour plus 2 (Appendix H).

F. The bridgehead depth will extend up to 3.5 kilometers east of the canal at H-Hour plus 3 (Appendix I).

G. At approximately H-Hour plus 4 the length of the bridgehead will reach approximately eight kilometers and its depth five kilometers. This will be the situation when the tanks and towed artillery arrive (Appendix J).

H. The second stage will commence at H-Hour plus 15 with the expansion of the bridgehead. At approximately H-Hour plus 18 it will reach a depth of eight kilometers and the bridgehead's base will be sixteen kilometers. The forces at the bridgehead will be prepared to repulse the enemy's counterattack (if it does not commence earlier). (Appendix K)

18. Evacuation to the rear

A. There will be no retreat to the main bridge (over the bridge) before H-Hour plus 36 from the time of the attack. Evacuation to the rear will be carried out according to the division commander's orders.

B. A 4-ton bridge may be used to remove light vehicles to the rear. This will require a high-degree of command and control on the part of the division so that the vehicles heading east and the vehicles returning from the west will not clog the bridge.

C. Evacuation of the wounded will receive first priority.

19. Minefields

A. In general no minefields will be laid while the bridgeheads are being established so that the mines will not interfere with our forces' advance and maneuverability.

B. In certain cases minefields may be planted when the enemy is expected to mount a counterattack against the divisional bridgehead with one or more armored brigades.

If at H-Hour plus 4 to 6 the engineers have not succeeded in setting up the bridges and pontoons (before H-Hour plus 2 at the latest), it is advisable to plant minefields in front of the infantry forces that are engaged in turning back the counterattack on the line detailed in the enclosed Appendix I.

C. Transferring the mines across the canal and dirt embankment to the holding defense line is one of the infantry division commander's main tasks when setting up the bridgehead. Using infantrymen is the only way to carry the mines across and this naturally limits the number of mines that can be employed. Therefore it is imperative to minimize their use and plant them only in the most critical places.

D. While the infantry is carrying the mines, the following matters must be taken into serious consideration:

   1) First-echelon companies (from the brigade's first-echelon battalion) must not be ordered to carry any mines so as to keep their movement swift and light.

   2) Every infantry squad from every infantry element remaining in the division will carry fourteen mines — an average of two mines per man plus one infantry wagon per squad. This will guarantee the transfer of an average of 630 mines per first-echelon brigade; 1,134 mines per second-echelon brigade; total: 2,394 mines per division.

   3) With the completion of the crossing at every unit and secondary unit level, the commanders will distribute the mines according to their plans or intelligence reports of the enemy's activity so that the second-echelon mines can be concentrated in the direction of the enemy's main strike. We recommend an alternative plan, one that is not based on knowledge of soil or the direction of the enemy's counterattack, that is based on the following redistribution of the division's infantry wagons after the crossing is completed:

   72 hand wagons (1,008 mines) to the first-echelon division's first brigade.
   72 hand wagons (1,008 mines) to the first-echelon division's second brigade.
   27 hand wagons (378 mines) to the second-echelon division's third brigade.

4) Secondary units will carry their mines to other secondary units according to their commanders' instructions. This will include the infantry tow-wagon and its contents to the designated unit, after which the men will rejoin their original units and hand over the mines to the new unit that has just received responsibility for towing and laying them. For example, an infantry squad can tow three infantry wagons. This means an average of two men for each wagon. The commander will make sure to concentrate all of the wagons in one secondary unit. In this way, a battalion on the right/divisional second-echelon brigade can be ordered to carry its mines (27 infantry wagons) to a battalion on the left/divisional first-echelon brigade. A battalion on the left/second-echelon brigade will transfer its mines (27 infantry wagons) to a battalion on the right/first-echelon brigade. In this way, while the bridgehead crossing is being made, there will be a total of 1,008 mines on the division's first-echelon brigade front. According to these figures, there will be thirty-six infantry wagons containing 504 mines, twenty-seven wagons with 378 mines, nine wagons with 126 mines.

E. While the bridgehead is being set up (before the arrival of the tanks, vehicles, and towed artillery) mines will be placed on the ground. Sometimes they will be planted in the ground. But in all cases the mines must be classified and marked so our vehicles will not accidentally detonate them when they cross toward the bridgehead. Because of battlefield developments, we may have to leave the mines on the ground as the advance to the east continues, and be satisfied with making breaches for the passage of tanks and vehicles.

F. After the bridgehead has been completed and our forces have shifted to the defense, the mines will be planted defensively. Those that were earlier scattered in the rear, at the end of the first stage of the bridgehead, must now be planted. We have to guarantee that all the mines (including those that were detonated) are accounted for.

G. When an infantry division is setting up a bridgehead, this is the stage in which the defense line is consolidated for the mechanized and armored units, and minefields must not be planted in front of the bridgehead so that the flow of forces toward the enemy will be maintained. This generally depends on the nature of the soil, the location of our forces and the enemy's forces, etc.

20. Keeping to the timetable

A. The timetable must be strictly kept to.

B. Some waves — the second, third, fourth, etc. — will not be coming across in boats in their entirety — but this does not mean that the following waves will cross quickly in the boats that they received before the designated time, since this may lead to a loss of control and unnecessary complications.

C. Everyone must be fully aware that the lines our forces reach are the result of considerable study and coordination among the following (contradictory) elements:

1) The boats' crossing speed.
2) The speed needed to climb the dirt embankment.
3) The speed in getting support weapons to the infantry.
4) Our forces' ability to advance.
5) Our forces' ability to repulse enemy counterattacks.
6) Troop and vehicular congestion at the bridgehead.
7) Time needed for tanks and heavy weapons to reach infantry units.
8) Artillery's ability to provide fire support to the advancing forces.

D. Adjustments in the crossing timetable will be made personally by the division commander after he has taken the abovementioned contradictory factors into consideration.

21. The enemy's destructive capability

Assuming that the infantry division sets up the bridgehead on a wide front in accordance with the general attack plan, then the enemy's ability to destroy it will require hitting many targets, and this will significantly reduce the enemy's ability to damage the division's crossing points. The enemy's ability to concentrate a destructive force against one bridgehead is not to be underestimated, but this will be instead of other bridgeheads. We have taken into account the limit of the enemy's ability to concentrate his firepower against a divisional bridgehead according to his ability as of January 1973.

A) Regarding a possible enemy aerial attack:

1) Eighty strikes on the first day. Strikes will be carried out by two aircraft at night and four-plane formations in daylight.

2) The enemy may hit the divisional bridgehead according to the following table:

Load tonnage	Bomb load Bomb load tonnage	Number of attack planes	Estimated time from	to
20	5	4	H	H+6
20	5	4	H+6	H+12
360	5	72	H+12	H+24
400				

B. Regarding the enemy's overall artillery fire:

1) Enemy concentrations can be expected to bomb our forces with 130 tons of explosives.

2) The field divisions' ammunition is calculated on the basis of one firing quota for each division.

    Tank brigade — 67 tons.
    Field artillery battalion (estimated reinforcements) —15 tons.
    Medium artillery battalion (estimated reinforcements) —15 tons.
    Total — 97 tons.
    Mechanized infantry brigade — 40 tons.
    Field artillery battalion (estimated reinforcements) —15 tons.
    Medium artillery battalion (estimated reinforcements) —15 tons.
    Tank battalion (estimated reinforcements) —18 tons.
    Total — 88 tons.
    Total reinforced armored brigade + reinforced mechanized infantry brigade —185 tons.
    Total artillery fire on the bridgehead — 315 tons.

C. This table indicates that the enemy's maximum shelling on the divisional bridgehead will be 715 tons on the first day of the fighting:

From	To	Aerial attack	Artillery shelling	total
H- Hour	H+6	20	100	120
H+6	H+12	20	100	120
H+12	H+24	360	115	475
		400	315	715 tons

D. Every antitank missile and shell (excluding bazookas) that the enemy has will be calculated in the attempt to counter his infantry division attack while the bridgehead is being
established. According to our figures the enemy has 192 antitank missiles and 5,436 antitank shells.

22. Our firepower:

A. Assuming that the division has been reinforced with the following:
   1 tank brigade.
   5 field artillery battalions.
   6 medium artillery battalions.
B. The division's firepower will be reinforced on the basis of one fire quota:
   3 infantry brigades (each of 60 tons)—184.2 tons.
   1 armored brigade—68.8 tons.
   1 field artillery brigade/division (2 field artillery battalions)—33.5 tons.
   1 divisional antitank battalion—6.8 tons.
   1 divisional tank battalion—(no data)
   11 field artillery battalions as support fire—361.7 tons.
   Total—665 tons.
C. Our forces will be able to shell the enemy with approximately 1,500 tons per infantry division bridgehead in the first twenty-four hours, according to the following:
   400 tons of artillery softening-up.
   250 tons until H-Hour plus 6.
   850 tons until H-Hour plus 24 (650 tons for repulsing the enemy's counterattack).
D. All antitank missiles and shells (excluding RPG-7s) in the reinforced infantry division
   and all antitank weapons come to the following numbers:
   552 antitank rockets.
   12,719 antitank shells.
E. One fire quota of light weapons with the reinforced infantry division guarantees us the
   following quantities of ammunition:

	Infantry at the bridgehead	Other elements that traversed the bridges with their equipment	Total
Automatic rifles	391,440	2,303,160	2,748,000
Semi-automatic Rifles	2,940	99,060	102,000
Light machine guns	138,400	444,600	583,000
Sniper rifles	5,940	3,960	9,900
Medium machine guns	162,000	415,500	577,500
Submachine guns	218,640	1,042,620	1,261,260
total	919,360	4,362,900	5,282,260

23. Replacing losses [reinforcements]

• The estimated losses for an infantry division in the battle at the bridgehead as of H-Hour
  plus 48 will be ten percent of its men, weapons, and equipment. This percentage may be
  higher for the infantry and armored forces breaking through the enemy's fortified strongholds or repulsing counterattacks, but the rise in losses will be in place of a decrease in
  losses in other secondary units.
• The units engaged in the battle on the bridgehead will be reinforced in the following manner:

- When the infantry division is ordered to establish a bridgehead, it must be reinforced before the battle with approximately ten percent of the force. The reinforcements will be distributed as follows:
    1. Five percent will be divided among secondary units at the infantry battalion (or parallel unit) level.
    2. Five percent will remain at the divisional level under the command of the division commander and under the direct supervision of the commanders of the division's branches.
    3. Units will not be reinforced prior to H-Hour plus 24.
    4. In the event that weapons, equipment, or fighting material and crews are rendered inoperable, units will not be reinforced at the bridgehead with crew members unless they come replenished with the weapons, equipment, or fighting material that were destroyed, so as to forestall unnecessary congestion at the bridgehead. If weapons and equipment are lost but the crews remain intact, the crew members will stay at the bridgehead to reinforce other crews.

24. Conclusion

A. An infantry division is able to cross the Suez Canal despite the dirt embankment and other obstacles.

B. The success of the division's crossing depends on efficient organization and the detailed instructions that each soldier receives regarding his assignments and what is expected of him.

C. The catchword for the crossing should be: carry the maximum amount of weapons and ammunition, and the minimum amount of administrative paraphernalia. This means that officers and enlisted men are expected to make an all-out effort especially in the first twenty-four hours of the campaign.

D. Ammunition and mines will be taken out of their crates and loaded on portable wagons in order to reduce excess weight. However certain ammunition will remain in its boxes lest it be damaged. On the whole, light loads and sacks, etc. are the best packing means. Special care should be taken to avoid inflammable material.

E. Ammunition consumption must be kept to a minimum in the event that bridges and trucks are destroyed.

F. The faster infantrymen, tanks, and vehicles get to the other side, the greater our chances of succeeding in battle.

G. The infantry's rate of advance at the bridgeheads must be coordinated with the construction of the bridgeheads so that the size of the bridgeheads will be suited to the volume of traffic flowing across them.

H. Human congestion at the bridgehead will not exceed 300 men per kilometer in the first stage.

I. Vehicular density at the bridgehead in the second stage will not exceed forty vehicles per kilometer. Foxholes must be dug as quickly and as deeply as possible in all stages of the operation in order to guarantee maximum defense for the troops. At the end of the first stage in setting up the bridgehead, construction on the defensive layout will be accelerated in order to repulse the enemy with trenches and minefields.

J. A TPP or Bailey bridge's capacity is equal to fifteen 96-ton ferries. A PMP bridge's capacity is 1.5 to 2 times that of a TPP or Uniflot bridge.

K. The crossing plan is the responsibility of commanders at all levels. Every commander must be familiar with the crossing plan and make sure that it is implemented. The plan must not be left to the corps of engineers. The engineers are responsible for carrying out the commanders' instructions and operating the crossing equipment according to the plan that the commanders have approved.

Organizing Command and Control Headquarters and Supervising the Crossing

1. The purpose of organizing the commanders' and headquarters' activity

The goal of organizing the activity and control of the forces is to make sure that the following missions are carried out:

A. Moving the infantry (on foot) from the starting areas to the crossing points at fixed times.

B. The boat battalion's operation — transferring the waves of infantry according to fixed times and priorities.

C. Breaching the dirt embankment at fixed times.

D. Completing the use of crossing equipment (bridges and ferries) at fixed times.

E. Transferring tanks and vehicles from their assembly areas to the bridges and ferries designated for them according to fixed times and speeds.

F. Moving tanks and vehicles to the distant shore (after the crossing) and to their units and sectors as planned, on routes and dirt tracks, at speeds and intervals as designated in the instructions for organizing coordination.

2. Headquarters activity

A. Carrying out these six (abovementioned) tasks demands a vigorous command that can expertly organize them. A delay or breakdown in one will have a pejorative impact on the rest. In such an event the headquarters has to immediately choose one of the following solutions:

  1) Sticking to the original crossing plan: each unit will traverse its designated crossing point according to necessary adjustments in the timetable or by advancing and retreating according to battlefield developments or delays in the timetable.

  2) A correction in the crossing plan will be made while some of the units or secondary units or vehicles are in the process of crossing from the bridges or ferries assigned to them to other bridges or ferries. The plan for moving to a crossing point and the plan for moving after the crossing will be corrected as necessary.

  3) The transfer of fording (amphibious) equipment from one crossing point to another in case of destruction or breakdown requires readjusting the traffic flow at and access routes to the two crossing points.

B. The commander in charge must realize that success is not measured by speed of crossing to the distant shore but by the speed by which the vehicles and troops reach their designated positions in the battle formation in the shortest time possible and under full control.

3. The sector commander and divisional crossing point

From all that has been discussed so far it is clear that the commander of the division's crossing sector must be the division's chief of staff who will remain in the sector headquarters (at the crossing point) until the transfer of the fifth priority is completed. He must be equipped with:

A. A crossing plan for the division and for reinforcement units (boat and ferries).

B. A reliable communications network that keeps him in contact with the commanders of the crossing areas and the bridge commanders.

C. A reliable communications network that keeps him in contact with the division commander on the distant shore.

D. A reliable communications network that keeps him in contact with the field army's chief of staff.

4. The sector commander at the brigade crossing point

In order to facilitate the workload of the division's chief of staff, two brigade crossing sectors will be set up where first-echelon brigades' chiefs of staff will be stationed, and who will remain in the headquarters of the sector crossing until the transfer of the fifth priority is completed. The division's chief of staff must be equipped with:

i. The crossing plan for the entire division and its reinforcement units moving through this sector, even if the forces do not belong to the brigade, because this role makes him the division's acting deputy chief of staff rather than brigade commander (his regular role).

ii. A reliable communications network that puts him in contact with the battalions' control points and the commanders at the crossing points and the bridges in his sector (four to five bridges/ferries plus two battalion control points).

iii. A reliable communications network that keeps him in contact with the units crossing in his sector during every stage in the operation, beginning with their stay in the assembly or starting areas up to their arrival at their designated places in the bridgehead's battle formation.

iv. A reliable communications network that puts him in contact with the division's chief of staff.

5. The control point for the battalion crossing

A. Two control points for the crossing battalion will be set up in each brigade's crossing sector. Each control point is responsible for reporting when the infantrymen arrive and pass.

B. The divisional commander will determine the men to be stationed at these points. They should be officers from brigade headquarters.

C. The commander of the control crossing point will be in direct contact with the company crossing points. Boat concentrations and reserves will be positioned 1,500 meters from the shore in a central point in the battalion crossing sector.

D. In the event that some of the assault boats from one of the companies are destroyed, the commander of the control point crossing will dispatch reserves to a designated area to replace the boats or troop losses.

6. The commander of the bridging point or pontoon crossing point

An officer of special bridge engineers will be stationed at each bridge or pontoon. He will be equipped with:

A. A detailed crossing plan for all tanks and vehicles passing over his crossing point, according to their priority, identification marks, timetable, etc.

B. A reliable communications network that keeps him in contact with the divisional area's crossing commander.

C. A reliable communications network that keeps him in contact with the commander of the brigade's crossing sector.

7. Control point of the battalion crossing

A. An officer will be stationed (preferably a boat battalion officer) at every company crossing point.

B. The commander of the company control crossing point will have a detailed plan that includes all of the men who will be going over in the boats, their priority, and the schedules for their waves.

C. The point commander will be in direct contact with the commander of the battalion control crossing point and will follow his instructions.

8. The shore commander

A. The commander on the western bank must have control over traffic in the assembly areas and the division's defense sector, and must prepare for the attack. This will be accomplished by organizing the crossing and by devising an effective communications plan, both of which actions will guarantee speed of movement and the flow of secondary units to the crossing points on the eastern bank, and will leave open the possibility of maneuvering.

B. The longitudinal and latitudinal routes in the division's attack sectors will be organized according in the following manner:

    1. The division will be allotted three latitudinal routes, each marked with a letter of the alphabet in the following way:

        a) The division's latitudinal route at a distance of four to six kilometers will be marked with the letter A.

        b) The brigade's latitudinal route at a distance of two to three kilometers will be marked with the letter B.

        c) A latitudinal route at a distance of approximately one kilometer will be marked with the letter C.

    2. The division will be allotted ten longitudinal routes (this number is equal to the number of crossing points). The routes will be numbered one to ten from right to left. Each route will be given an identifying number. If there is a shortage of color, the main routes (at least) can be painted with identical numbers, and allocated to units and secondary units according to their place in the assemble areas for the attack and the crossing points allocated to them.

    3. Companies (organic and reinforced) of military police will organize the movement in the assembly areas up until the control point crossings.

9. The bridgehead commander

A. The bridgehead commander will control the traffic across the bridge so that the bridgehead can be set up in two stages, each one completing the other. This will require the following operations:

    1. The establishment of five routes at the bridgehead.

        a) A service route for the division's units and second echelon brigades.

        b) Two routes for a first-echelon brigade/on the right.

        c) Two routes for a first echelon brigade/on the left.

        d) Scatter points designated for the battalions and companies at the bridgehead according to their locations, as clarified in the enclosed A/1.

        e) These routes will be considered the continuation of the routes set up on the local (western) bank and will be given numbers and markings identical to those on the routes of the local bank.

    2. The establishment of two latitudinal routes on the eastern bank of the canal (to make maximum use of existing routes) with alphabet markings in the following manner:

        a) A latitudinal route up to a distance of 1.5 kilometers will be marked with the letter D.

> b) A latitudinal route up to a distance of three to four kilometers will be marked with the letter E.

B. A company of military police from the division and the brigade's defense and vehicle companies will be responsible for organizing the movement at the bridgehead. The routes must be marked and equipped with phone lines and radio communications before H-Hour plus 6.

C. The organization of the commander's activity on the eastern bank has been made clear in the enclosed A/1.

10. The communications network in the commander's service

A. The communications network must be in good working condition. This can be achieved by basing it mainly on phone lines, with wireless radio kept as an alternative.

B. The following equipment will be needed to set up the division's communications network:

1) 110 kilometers of line cable (fifty kilometers of it at the bridgehead for the headquarters, commander, and control of operations).
2) Seventy-five radio sets from divisional sources and its reinforcements and the bridge units.
3) The communications line in the defense area will guarantee communications in the area west of the canal.
4) The plan for the phone line and wireless system has been made clear in the enclosed A/1.

11. Conclusion:

A. Responsibility for setting up and directing the crossing and crossing points must be transferred from the secondary units engaged in crossing to an independent mechanism that will be established and be responsible for all aspects of control and supervision of the crossing operations.

B. The (combat) elements making the crossing: the infantry, tanks or vehicles may be likened to a train or plane passenger who receives instructions at the beginning of his journey from headquarters.

C. The officers and enlisted men must follow the instructions of the crossing sector and control point commanders.

D. Each infantry division will organize a commander's service plan for the crossing throughout the month of April 1973.

> Sa'ad al Shazli
> Commander in Chief, Armed Forces

Appendix D

The Second Infantry Division's Attack Order in the Yom Kippur War[122]

1. The Enemy:

No change since last intelligence account.

2. The Division's Assignment:

The Second Infantry Division reinforced with the Twenty-fourth Tank Brigade from the Twenty-third Mechanized Infantry Division and additional reinforcements in conjunction with air defense units, the adjacent Sixteenth and Eighteenth Infantry Divisions, air support, tank fire, and a twenty-four hour artillery barrage will attack the Suez Canal front on D-Day from Sector No. 735 to Kilometer 62 on the canal and neutralize and destroy enemy forces on the front.

3. Forces and Assignments:

The first-echelon forces in the five infantry battalion formation will cross the canal, destroy enemy forces and weapons on the front, gain control of the enemy's dirt embankment on the eastern side of the canal, and capture and consolidate the tank positions on the enemy's second line (6.5 kilometers east of the canal).

The 508th Infantry Battalion (from the 120th Infantry Brigade) will capture the strongholds at Firdan.

Support weapons units will be part of the attacking force, and a second-echelon brigade will cross the Suez Canal.

The division will take control of its direct mission line, reinforce it, and prepare to block and destroy the counterattack being carried out by the enemy's second-echelon forces from his armor and mechanized infantry brigades. This counterattack will commence either six to eight hours from the start of the war or on the morning of the second day of the war. With the addition of tanks, support weapons, antitank units, and towed artillery to the division's forces east of the canal on the second day of the war, the division will complete the destruction of the enemy's second-echelon forces involved in the counterattack.

The division will exploit its success, depending on the circumstances, in order to develop the attack eastward, maneuvering between the second echelon of the 117th Mechanized Infantry Brigade (less one battalion) from the forward line (line no. 1) or rear line (line no. 2) together with the Sixteenth Infantry Division, and will take control of the division's following mission line (the Tabat el-Shajra-Beit el-Huda line).

The division will prepare to block and destroy the counterattack on the morning of the third day of the war. The enemy's force can be expected to include an armored brigade, mechanized infantry brigade, and perhaps another armored brigade.

When the tanks arrive and link up with the forces, the capture and destruction of the strongholds[123] will be completed by a battalion from the 117th Brigade attacking from the east.

The division will finish off the destruction of enemy's reserve forces that perpetrated the counterattack on the morning of the third day of the war. The division's first echelon brigades will take over the line of Kathib Abu Kathira- Height Spot 89 on the division's final mission line, in cooperation with the Sixteenth Division to the south of it. At the end of the third day of the war, when division arrives at its final mission line it will join up with the Sixteenth Division at the field army's bridgehead.

On the division's left flank, to the east of al-Balah Island, a reinforced infantry company from the 120th Brigade will take over Bir Abu al-Aruch.

At the end of the third day of fighting, the division and the Sixteenth Division will deploy and prepare to block the enemy's counterattack.

The Twenty-fourth Tank Brigade will cross the Suez Canal from the assembly areas on two axes and deploy in defense positions at the division's bridgehead and serve as the division's second echelon, after the mechanized infantry brigade has completed its advance. The tank brigade (supported with reserves and weapons) will prepare to break through from the division's bridgehead in a series of counterattacks. The brigade will be sent to one of two possible destinations: to Kathib Abu Kathira or in the direction Height Spot 89.

After blocking and destroying the enemy's counterattack, the division will prepare to launch an attack in the direction of Tasa with a force of division strength (minus one brigade) on two axes in conjunction with the Sixteenth Division and according to Second Army's instructions.

4. The Division's Primary Effort:
During the attack: on its left flank.
In defense of the bridgehead: it will hold onto the following areas: Height Spot 66, coordinates 22863386; Kathib Abu Kathira-Height Spot 100—al Shajara 132.

5. The Battle's Development:
During the attack: two echelons and reserves.
The first echelon — from the right (with the Fourth Infantry Brigade).
From the left: the 120th Infantry Brigade.
The second echelon will consist of the 117th Mechanized Infantry Brigade (minus one battalion).
Reserves — the Twenty-fourth Tank Brigade from the Twenty-third Mechanized Infantry Division.
During the reinforcement of the bridgehead: two echelons and two reserve forces.
The first echelon — from the right: the Fourth Infantry Brigade.
From the left: the 120th Infantry Brigade.
In the middle: the 117th Mechanized Infantry Brigade (minus one battalion).
The second echelon — a Tank brigade from the Twenty-third Mechanized Infantry Division.
Reserve No. 2: the 239th Tank Battalion.
Neighboring forces:
In front — the 129th Commando Group.
On the right — the Sixteenth Infantry Division.
On the left — the Eighteenth Infantry Division.
In the rear — the Twenty-third Mechanized Infantry Division.

Appendix E

Battle Order No. 1 for Operation "Granite 2 Improved"

ISSUED BY THE COMMANDER OF THE SEVENTH DIVISION[124]

Seventh Division Headquarters
Operations Branch
Date: 1973

1. The enemy

A. Total enemy forces on the Third Army Front:

Twelve brigades (eight motorized infantry and paratrooper brigades and four armored brigades).

Two independent tank battalions and two infantry (Nachal) companies.

Fourteen artillery battalions (including four antitank missile battalions).

B. Total enemy strength on the Seventh Division front: A maximum of three infantry and two armored brigades and ten artillery battalions (including two antitank missile battalions).

C. Enemy formation:

The enemy's forces are built on two levels: a tactical reserve and a strategic reserve.

D. The enemy's modus operandi:

1) If the enemy discovers our intentions prior to the operation, he may launch counteractions in an attempt to gain air superiority and bomb us from the air, and he may carry out special operations against our forces in the starting area and depth or seize prearranged tank positions on the canal's dirt embankment and in the near depth. He may also reinforce his strongholds with some of his local and adjacent reserves. He will strengthen the fortifications at the entrances adjacent to the straits and at the same time tactically deploy reserves in suitable adjacent assembly areas while counterattacking our troops.

2) The directions of the main strike:

The Kabrit airfield — south of the lakes — toward the Nineteenth Infantry Division.

3) Defense stages and timetable:

A. The attempt to prevent our forces from crossing by raking with them with fire from the strongholds and dirt embankments, plus using artillery fire, air strikes, and inflammable devices on the canal, and holding battles in the strongholds while completing the siege.

B. Counterattacking with the support of local reserves on H-Hour plus ten minutes.

C. Counterattacking with the support of adjacent reserves the size of a mechanized infantry battalion (minus two companies) plus one or two tank companies in addition to the forces that retreated when our units crossed the canal at H-Hour (or H-Hour plus one or two hours). Hopefully these measures will provide our tactical second-echelon forces with favorable conditions for carrying out a counterstrike.

D. Within six to eight hours the enemy's second-echelon tactical forces will be prepared to counterattack at the bridgehead in order to return the canal situation to its previous state, using a force the size of a mechanized infantry company plus armored brigade, in addition to the forces that retreated. This blow can be expected twelve hours later.

E. If the enemy fails to destroy some or all of the bridgeheads, his forces will withdraw and take up suitable lines while maintaining contact with our forces and continuing the effort to destroy the bridgeheads. At the same time he will send his strategic reserves forward to prepare a counterstrike to prevent our forces from leaving the bridgeheads or reaching the straits.

F. Whatever the case, the enemy will carry out his battle moves with tactical air support, while using gas and flammable materials, and waging wide-scale electronic (radio and radar) warfare.

2. Forces and missions

A. The Seventh Division will be reinforced with the Independent Twenty-fifth Armored Division, the 127th Commando Battalion, artillery and antitank battalions, and additional bridging teams according to the following composite: the Sixtieth Heavy Assault Bridges Battalion; the Sixty-fourth Rapid Assault Battalion; one company from the Third Battalion — heavy assault bridges; plus engineering units. [The order also gave details of the artillery, antitank, and engineers ORBAT.]

B. The method:

1) After a massive, thirty-eight-minute artillery softening-up, the division will attack the Suez Canal in the last light of the first day in along the canal's 133.5–144 kilometer sector, with the Twelfth and Eighth Infantry Brigades, whose mission is to block the enemy's local and adjacent reserves from impeding our forces, and to destroy the enemy's forces — troops, weapons and concentrated fire sources in the strongholds and dirt embankment on the eastern bank.

2) The division main effort will be concentrated on the left flank.

3) The division's battle formation will be in the two echelons.

C. The division's direct mission:

The division will destroy the enemy forces on the dirt embankment of the east bank, block the enemy's local and adjacent reserves, and capture the area on kilometers 8/142–17/114 on the el-Shat-Ismalia road — two hundred meters from the coordinates 03063334 and 33 (?) 03053337 — fifty meters west of the railroad kilometer 90 signpost — and block the enemy's tactical second echelon from H-Hour plus six until the morning of the second day.

D. The attack mission

The second echelon will be dispatched with the *majmu'at* commandos. The division will launch the attack to the east and destroy the enemy's forces engaged in the counter-attack and take over a line on kilometer 144 — kilometer 15/116 el-Shat-Ismalia, triangulation number 43 (03073330) and point 74 (03103334). From triangulation no. 84 (03103341), five hundred meters west of the 33/97 kilometer sign on the el-Shat-Ismalia Road, its daily mission will entail establishing a bridgehead to a depth of eight to ten kilometers. On the morning of the third day of the attack, it will reinforce the line and prepare its reserves for blocking an enemy counterattack.

E. In order to block the enemy's counterattacks, the division will expand the bridgehead together with the Nineteenth Division, and build the field army's bridgehead in the depth of its sector.

F. The division will assist and protect the Fourth Division's advance from the line at point 91 (03123341) and point 47 (03073344). Afterward, in conjunction with the Nineteenth Division, it will develop the attack along with the western openings of the Gidi Pass.[125]

G. In order to confuse the enemy and cause him to lose control of his forces, it has been decided that the 127th *majamu'at* commando battalion will exit the first ring of the attack and operate in groups near the enemy command centers, artillery positions, and communications lines. It will also set ambushes and mine the dirt embankment in the near depth and on the routes of the enemy reserves' expected advance.

H. In order to delay the enemy reserves' advance through the passes and prevent him from passing through them too early, a *majmu'at* commando battalion will be airlifted and landed on the first and second days of the war at the western entranceways of the Gidi Passes.[126] With the onset of the artillery softening-up, a battalion team from the 130th Amphibious Brigade[127] will cross from the vicinity of the abandoned camp — Camp Shalufa — on the Little Bitter Lake in the direction of the Gidi. There it will function as a task force to create rapid a link-up with the commando forces that were landed at the western entrance to the Gidi Pass, and will close the pass and prevent the enemy's reserves from moving through it.

I. The Seventh Division will send an advanced *majmu'at* of mechanized infantry to the 130th Independent Amphibious Brigade's rear headquarters to the Little Bitter Lake where it will function as an antitank line protecting the division's operations.

J. The commander of the division will send out heavily equipped teams to destroy the enemy forces east of the Little and Big Bitter Lakes in the vicinity of Kabrit. This move will be done in conjunction with Second Army troops.

K. The division commander is responsible for covering the connection points with the Nineteenth Division with artillery fire and covering the army's left flank with fire from an artillery battalion.

L. The division's left border will be the field army's left border.

3. My plan

A. Following thirty-eight minutes of artillery fire, tank fire and direct line fire from the western embankments, the forces of the Seventh Division's forces will assault the Suez Canal in the sector between kilometer 144 and kilometer 133.5. An assault will be made by the division's first echelon forces (the Eighth and Twelfth Brigades) in the weakly defended sectors of the embankment. Tank hunters and ambushes will enable us to quickly capture and consolidate the eastern dirt embankments and the close depth.

B. Following sabotage operations and direct-line fire on the stronghold south of the lakes) the Forty-sixth Infantry Battalion team (Eighth Brigade) will attack and isolate the stronghold south of the lakes at H-Hour plus thirty minutes. With the support of combat engineers, who will cross to the dirt embankment on the east bank, an attack will be made against the stronghold to the south of the lakes, neutralizing enemy troops, weapons, and equipment, and seizing the stronghold.

C. In using the division's second-echelon units, antitank weapons, and light antitank armored vehicles in conjunction with the tanks' direct line weapons fired from the dirt embankment on the western bank, I will give orders to annihilate the enemy beginning at H-Hour plus one or two hours.

D. Until H-Hour plus three to four hours I will implement the division's direct mission to a depth of three kilometers and construct a bridgehead with infantry support. At H-Hour plus six hours I will be prepared to dispatch the tactical second echelon.

E. When the first-echelon brigade tank crossing and vehicle advance is completed at H-Hour plus ten or eleven hours, I will continue to advance and launch an attack with the division's second-echelon Eleventh Mechanized Infantry Brigade, while operating in conjunction with first-echelon Eighth and Twelfth Brigades, and will consolidate the divisional bridgehead to a depth of eight kilometers.

F. On the night of the first day and throughout the second day, all of the division's brigade forces and weapons will cross the canal and, in order to consolidate the division's bridgehead, the Twenty-fifth Independent Armored Brigade will seize defense positions at the division's bridgeheads at H-Hour plus eleven hours.

G. The division's success crossing in blocking the enemy's tactical second-echelon counterattack and operative moves of the first-echelon brigades, in conjunction with the Nineteenth Division, will enable the bridgehead to be expanded to a depth of eight to ten kilometers, while the division completes its combat mission.

> On the third day the division will prepare to repulse a counterattack by the enemy's tactical reserves. When the division succeeds in blocking the enemy's counterattack I will expand the bridgehead, in conjunction with the Nineteenth Infantry Division, and establish the field army's bridgehead.

H. The following steps will be taken to protect the first-echelon units' combat operations and isolate the strongholds and adjacent local reserves:

1. The success of the 130th Independent Brigade's will be exploited by transferring an infantry company from the Eleventh Mechanized Infantry Brigade, reinforced with the Leopard Company, at the start of the artillery softening-up in order to seize the antitank missile line in the vicinity of the Gidi and el-Shat Crossroads.

2. A commando battalion (less one company from the 127th command *majmu'at*) will be sent with the first assault waves in order to spread confusion in the enemy's ranks and cause him to lose control of his forces. The battalion will operate in groups, hitting the enemy's headquarters, artillery positions, and communication lines, and will set ambushes and plant minefields along the enemy reserves' routes of advance.

I. The divisions will concentrate its primary efforts:

1) During the attack in the direction of kilometer 118 — point 26 (03063339), point 83 (03093343).

2) Reinforcing point 104 (03123340) on kilometer 33/98 on the el-Shat-Ismalia Road at kilometer 136 (according to the reckoning from the canal).

J. Battle Formation:

1) In the attack up to the completion of the division's direct mission will be at two levels:

The first level: the Eighth and Twelfth Infantry Brigades.

The second level: the Eleventh Mechanized Infantry Brigade.

2) After completing the battle mission, the bridgehead will be reinforced at two levels:

The first level: the Eighth, Eleventh, and Twelfth Brigades.

The second level: The Twenty-fifth Independent Armored Brigade.

K. The flanks

1) On the right — the Fifth Infantry Brigade (Nineteenth Division) will be deployed in the starting area in the vicinity of el-Shat at kilometer 144 and the Shalufa Airfield.

2) On the left: the Sixteenth Infantry Brigade (Second Army).

4. Positioning the headquarters staffs:

The division's field Army H.Q. will be located at point 32 (03013335).

The field Army H.Q at point 83 (02893337).

The staff of the rear supervision at point (02893337).

The field staff's direction of movement will be triangulation point 20 (03043336) and point (03083342).

5. Reports:

Reports will be sent:

A. At the beginning of the Suez Canal assault.

B. During the seizure of the strongholds' embankments.

C. Battle reports every two hours.

D. Urgent reports — immediately.

Signed:

Brigadier General (Amid) staff officer

Kouri Uthman Badr Ahmad

Chief of Staff— Seventh Infantry Division

Signed:

Brigadier General (Amid) staff officer

Badri Sid Ahmad

Commander — Seventh Division

Appendix F

The IDF's Defense System on the Suez Canal and Its Capture by the Attacking Forces[128]

Document contents:
1. Learning about the strongholds.
2. Defending the canal front from outside the strongholds.
3. Attack concepts and methods.
4. Requisite weapons.
5. Requisite training.

Study material:
- Studying the enemy's defense methods east of the canal, opposite the Second Army's confrontation line.
- The enemy's positions opposite the Second Army's front.
- The organization of the enemy's defense opposite the Second Army's frontline.
- Aerial photographs of the strongholds.
- Map 1:100,000.
- Training instructions 1/71, 6/71, training a reinforced infantry battalion to attack the enemy's strongholds across a water obstacle. Training a reinforced infantry battalion to attack and capture the fortified obstacle (the strongholds).

Studying the strongholds:
1. Details on the strongholds:
   Length of front facing the canal: 120–200 meters (average 160 meters).
   Depth: 100–140 meters (average 120 meters).
   Height: 15–20 meters, angle inclination: 35–45 degrees.
   Width of the external embankment: 15–20 meters.
   Internal perimeter: 250 meters (on the average).
2. Firepower
   The stronghold is defended on all sides by a network of fortifications, minefields, and flammable devices. The position's location creates a fusillade of 14–23 bullets per meter of front, and allows grenades to be thrown a great density. The stronghold's force is made up of 1–2 infantry platoons.
   The stronghold is supported with:
   - 5–10 medium artillery pieces.
   - 2–4 mortars.

- 4–8 antiaircraft machine guns (0.5 inch).
- 1–3 tanks.

3. Engineering structure:
   - The stronghold has 6–10 bunkers, and is surrounded by firing positions and communications trenches that are hidden from the front.
   - The stronghold is surrounded with 8–15 layers of barbed wire that provide it with a great width.
   - A belt of mines encircles the stronghold at a depth of 70–100 meters.
   - Containers filled [with fuel?] are placed at a distance of 50–100 meters, and their burning range[129] will be 10–50 meters.
   - The stronghold has one or two entrances facing east.

4. The stronghold had a communications network and radio lines that enable communications links inside the bunkers and contact with patrols.

5. The stronghold can be self-sustaining for 3–5 days.

6. A number of strongholds were built at the main junctions: four at Kantara, two at Firdan, and two at Ismalia.

7. The role of the strongholds:
   - The strongholds' construction, done mostly after the cease-fire, in key areas, and their munitions and equipment clearly reflect the vital role they are intended to serve: an obstacle prevent a water barrier crossing, and a target that will weather the first blow and absorb the brunt of the attacking forces' fire.
   - The strongholds' fire sources are concentrated on the western front, and will be employed against our forces deployed on the western bank and preparing for the attack.
   - The correct choice of manpower in the stronghold will reduce the injury to the defending force, strengthen its endurance under the devastating conditions of a barrage and increase its ability to hold out. The stronghold will become a thorn in our side to any force that tries to breach its defenses or attack it from the rear.
   - The stronghold serves as a base for patrols and for securing the length of the contact line.
   - Doubt exists as to the effectiveness of the flammable devices,[130] and the strongholds' ability to repulse the breeching forces while they are in the water.

8. Advantages and disadvantages
   Advantages:
   - The defensive measures strengthen the stronghold's ability to withstand a barrage and to continue fighting even after it is neutralized[131] by our forces.
   - The stronghold's planning renders a direct attack into a costly operation that incurs heavy casualties and enormous losses of equipment and ammunition.
   - The surrounding defenses allow a high density of fire.
   Disadvantages:
   - Direct intervention against the forces the water is limited to the range of the inflammable device [?].[132]
   - The strongholds can be neutralized at some stage with sophisticated methods, totally paralyzing them, especially when the enemy troops are seeking shelter in the bunkers.
   - After the stronghold's assault and capture, it can be used as a convenient place for our forces to gain control over flat areas east of the canal.

- When the enemy exits the hidden bunkers, he will be vulnerable to air strikes whose effectiveness cannot be overstated.
- There is a deep dug-out in the middle of the strongholds. By detonating large explosive charges in it, the ensuing pressure will kill the soldiers in the bunkers.

9. The strongholds modus operandi

General:

It will be of utmost importance to isolate and neutralize the strongholds, that is, to neutralize their advantages for as long as possible by minimal means, which will eventually lead to their encirclement and destruction.

Any attempt to attack them and destroy their weapons and equipment in the initial stages of the attack will be a fatal mistake, one that the enemy wants us to make.[133]

Up to the attack:

- A diversionary move against the observation posts; destruction of the enemy's weapons in his exposed positions with 82-millimeter mortar and cannon fire and air strikes.
- Limited operations designed to block or reduce the strength of the networks and preventative measures.[134]
- Disrupting the enemy's range-finding operations.
- A major effort will be made to destroy/breech openings in the obstacles on the strongholds' flanks.

At the start of the attack:

- Neutralizing the stronghold by detonating large quantities of explosives (missiles and napalm) in its center for one to two hours. This will allow our forces to surround the stronghold from the rear, and rely on only limited artillery fire.
- Employing direct-line fire from short-range weapons (B-10 and B-11 rocket launchers) to destroy all of the exposed targets.
- Allocating elements from the attacking forces to complete the encirclement and carry out diversionary operations (one reinforced infantry team on each side).

While attacking and developing it from the rear: completing the stronghold's isolation and assaulting it with a second-echelon company [from a battalion from a second-echelon brigade?].

Defending the canal outside the strongholds

1. The plan:
   - The dirt embankment — must be studied thoroughly, especially its reverse inclination and soil (to a distance of 100 meters).
   - Intelligence reports on the minefields in the main sectors and their flanks must be acquired.
2. Tank positions on the canal banks: (the first line 30–100 meters from the canal)
   - A main position and one or more alternate positions for each tank.
   - Protective fire from our forces on the western bank or in the water.
   - Most of the recently built positions have a side protection[135] against flanking fire (this facilitates isolating the position during the attack).
   - Elongated tank positions allow Israeli tanks to move on them and make it difficult for our forces to destroy them with direct-line fire.
   - The elongated positions protect the stronghold's flanks.

3. Firing position in the near depth: one to three kilometers from the canal.
   - The second line lying 200–300 meters from the canal and the third line at 500 meters are the near depth of the strongholds and the first line. These lines protect the stronghold from encirclement by forces that manage to break through.
   - The enemy also has a fourth line at the junctions located two kilometers from the canal.
   - The firing positions can be transformed into defense lines for tanks in the vicinity.
   - Minefields may be protecting the flanks or roads leading to the near depth lines.
   - These lines are considered the main defense lines in the security layout, and lie one to three kilometers from the canal. Other units the size of an infantry or mechanized squad or company may be employed to destroy enemy forces that succeed in the breaking through.
4. The defense system on the security layout:
   The enemy's layout is based on two mainstays: firepower and high mobility, in other words — speed and rapid response.
   - The longer our forces are held up at on forward front (the first line of positions), the greater the enemy's advantage.
   - Therefore, the main obstacle facing our forces in the attack will be the enemy's tanks in their positions outside the strongholds.

The main lessons to be learned:

1. The strongholds present:
   - A solid barrier for receiving the attacking forces' first blow plus massive enemy artillery fire.
   - An observation point, warning line, plus fire control position.
   - A source of fire against our forces deployed on the western bank.
   - The stronghold will not be a source of fire on our forces in the water.
   - In certain cases, the enemy's sources of fire can be neutralized during the attack.
   - A frontal attack, especially in the initial stage of the breakthrough, will be a costly operation in terms of equipment and wearing down of a large part of our troops.
   - Assuming that we allocate reinforced infantry company (a modest estimate) to each stronghold, we will need about twenty first-echelon companies to attack all of the strongholds (or seventeen to open the main axes in the attack).
   - Assuming that about the twenty companies (from the field army's first echelon) take part in the attack,[136] then two-thirds of the field army's first echelon will be engaged in attacking the strongholds (two first-echelon brigades in each of the three divisions x 2.5 battalions x two first-echelon companies in each battalion). Taking into account the strength and ability needed to neutralize the strongholds the entire length of the sector, this will require over eighty percent of the artillery force, in addition to the effort required to open the barriers and clear the minefields.
2. The openings between the strongholds were prepared as first line of tank positions. They will be are relatively easy to break through. Their capture requires:
   - Neutralizing the strongholds for a length of time.
   - Preventing enemy tanks from seizing these positions or neutralizing their advantage.
3. The forces' main goal in the initial stage of the attack is to break through and quickly gain control of the forward positions. Once this layout has fallen the enemy will be unable to use his prepared line as a base for launching his armored reserves' counterattacks. This will result in the main battle taking place beyond the forward positions in open territory.

4. A way must be found to continue neutralizing the strongholds so that they can be destroyed at a later stage, after the end of the main battle against enemy armor.

5. The main battle must be waged against the enemy's armored forces. We cannot allow ourselves to become bogged down at the strongholds[137]—but deny them the advantages that their defense system is based on: high mobility and enormous firepower.

6. Denying the enemy his high mobility requires:
   - Isolating the battlefield from the rear and dealing with it with aircraft, artillery, ambushes, shelling, and SF operations.
   - Disrupting the enemy's command and control networks.
   - Simultaneous attacks on a broad front (from Suez to Port Sa'id).
   - Employing deception (feints and diversions against the enemy from the rear).
   - Using smoke screens.
   - Employing the surprise factor.
   - Having a maximum number of units take part in the attack and continuing with the rest of the operations along the entire length front.
   - Causing the enemy's armor heavy losses in the initial stages of the attack.
   - Securing roads and junctions at as early a stage as possible.

7. Denying the enemy the advantage of firepower (especially from his artillery) requires:
   - Not exposing large concentrations of our forces to enemy fire without a reason. In the initial stages of the attack, basing operations on small units (companies) combined with breeching and antitank forces. And finally, not exposing the main attack forces in the initial stages or concentrating and deploying them prior to the attack only in the rear of the second echelon.
   - Making a surprise attacking simultaneously on a wide front; employing deceptive tactics and smoke screens continuously and determinedly; causing the enemy's armor maximum losses.
   - Gaining control of enemy artillery positions and other sources of fire.

Neutralizing weaponry
1. Missiles of no less than 500 kilograms.
2. Delayed action aerial bombs.
3. Explosive/napalm charges.
4. Artillery, aerial bombs — after enemy soldiers have exited the bunkers.
5. Heavy artillery or anti-battery fire against enemy guns in the strongholds.[138]
6. Direct-line weapons; no more that one or two units (to be allocated from direct trajectory forces) for each stronghold for destroying enemy tanks.
7. Forcing the troops in the strongholds to fire their weapons and use up their ammunition. The best means of causing this are: artillery barrages, air strikes, and fire from 60-millimeter or 82-millimeter mortars.

Operations against the strongholds (second-echelon or battalion)
A reinforced flamethrower team will be allocated for the attack on each stronghold. The team will be made up of two light flamethrowers, hand-grenades, a light antitank flamethrower, and smoke-screen canisters.

In sum: We must not allow ourselves to be held up more than necessary. It is imperative to avoid wearing down the forces in the fighting at the strongholds or in the battle zone three kilometers east of the canal. We must open the main routes and junctions where the enemy has established his defenses.[139]

Modus operandi and the idea behind the attack

The basic idea:

1. To neutralize simultaneously all of the strongholds along the length of the field army line and cause the enemy maximum loss of equipment and manpower. By making minimum use of our troops and efficient use of weapons we will neutralize the enemy's strongholds for one or two hours (first with maximum strength, then gradually reducing it). This amount of time is needed in order to gain control of the enemy's tank positions either by capturing them or neutralizing them while causing him maximum losses in every possible way which will result in the destruction of his tanks (by sniper teams[140] and antitank fire). Sabotage operations such as mine laying will precede this activity order so as to deny the enemy the possibility of maneuvering and pulling out his tanks. Diversionary and deception tactics will also be employed.

2. Once this mission is accomplished, the right conditions will be created for expanding the attack with the main forces, and expanding the attack from the enemy's rear, while taking control of his first-line positions, and finally destroying the enemy in his strongholds and establishing the bridgeheads.

Required weapons

- Short-range missiles — up to 1,000 meters in range and weighing no more than 500 kilograms.
- Napalm charges with ranges of 500–600 meters. Medium-size charges of steady strength are preferable.[141]
- Aerial bombs and artillery shells.
- Sixty-millimeter mortars.

Requirements for additional training

1. The idea of attacking the stronghold (in a frontal assault) was rejected outright as were the training systems. The doctrinal material is useless because it is based on the idea of breeching the strongholds at the start of the attack (Circular 72).

2. The need may arise for training special units/battalions for making a frontal attack on the strongholds (despite the risk that this entails).

3. There will be no additional training until the egregious mistakes in Plan No. 2 have been corrected.

Enemy simulation

- Training models of the strongholds were too small (seventy meters for the front line). They have three entrances. The density of the surrounding barbed wire fences was too weak. It must be remembered that the firing positions in the original strongholds will be facing on our forces during the crossing.
- Obviously there is no use in using these models in training exercises, especially since the plan is based on a model of the enemy's strongholds as they were before the cease-fire and does not take into account the major improvements in them after the cease-fire.

5. Our forces

An attack against two strongholds are allocated one infantry battalion reinforced with a tank company, one battery of 100-millimeter guns, one artillery battalion, one battery of 120-millimeter mortars, a platoon of engineers, one battery of 85-millimeter cannons, two antitank companies, 142 and one platoon of light flamethrowers, plus support teams and forces. The reinforcements of this size are inoperable under any conditions. An estimate of the amount of Second Army forced needed to attack the strongholds comes to twelve reinforced infantry battalions (this figure refers to the strongholds on the main routes of advance). The method requires a division-sized force for attacking the stronghold (without blocking operations) and expanding the attack into the depth while these forces are left vulnerable to the intense and determined activity of the enemy's tanks.

Added: A sketch of the stronghold.

Chapter Notes

All titles are presented in English though the sources were published in Hebrew unless otherwise noted.

Preface

1. For a description and analysis of Egyptian policy on the domestic, inter–Arab, and international fronts, and especially its attitude toward the superpowers — the Soviet Union and United States — I have found Yoram Meital's research and published works invaluable. See: Yoram Meital, "The Political Development of Egypt in the Conflict with Israel: 1967–1977," PhD dissertation, Haifa University, July 1991; and *Egypt's Struggle for Peace, Continuity, and Change, 1967–1977*, University of Florida Press, 1997. These studies are based on Egyptian publications and other sources, and deal with Egyptian policy in the period that my work relates to — 1967 to 1973. Meital's work has provided me with an indispensable working tool and freed me from the necessity of undertaking parallel research on the subject's political aspects, which are an integral part of any attempt to describe the military's strategic considerations. Nevertheless, I have tried to make use of other sources relating to this period, especially material that directly touches upon developments in Egyptian military thinking. The books by Yehoshafat Harkabi and Fuad Ajami supplied me with a lucid understanding of the background, mind frame, and temperament in Egypt and the Arab world.

2. Published material on the war, such as the works of Efraim Kam, Michael Handel, Uri Bar Yosef, Aharon Zeevi (Farkash), and others that focus mainly on surprise attack, deception and intelligence failure, helped me clarify terms and understand the military background.

3. For a comprehensive study on this subject, see: Shmuel Bar, *The Yom Kippur War in Arab Eyes*, Tel Aviv: Ma'arachot, 1986. The work details various aspects of the political and military systems involved in the war. As the title indicates, the book contains statements by various elements, and later publications, most of which reflect the Arab perspective.

4. Most of the key documents — those dealing with doctrinal issues, operational orders at various levels, and training plans — were translated into Hebrew, circulated, and given the title "Captured Egyptian Documents." There are whole volumes of translated captured documents available for perusal at the IDF Center for Special Studies (CSS).

5. A wealth of maps and charts can be found at the IDF Command and Staff College.

6. The "Great Soviet Encyclopedia," for example, has many volumes devoted to military topics.

7. The first Soviet work on the art of operational warfare that reached the West was Maj. Gen. V. A. Samanov's *A Short Article on the Development of the Art of Soviet Operations* (Moscow, 1960).

8. Marshal of the Soviet Union Sokolovsky's book, *Military Strategy* (1962), provided the West with its first opportunity to study and comprehend Soviet military views (the previous Soviet military "bible" was *Strategy*, by Gen. A. A. Suachin, published in 1926). Following Sokolovsky's work, which elicited enormous interest in the West, scores of articles, commentaries, and books came out, reflecting the need, especially in the United States, for as much information as possible on Soviet military plans and theory. For more on this book see: Walter Darnel Jacobs, "Strategy According to Sokolovsky," *Cyclone*, 11, Ma'arachot Kana, 155, 6–11, and the article by A. G. "Military Strategy in Soviet Eyes," Ma'arachot Kana, 156, 9–10.

9. The most conspicuous of these is the officers' monthly *Viani Vastnik* (The Military Announcer). A systematic reading of this and similar publications, such as *The Red Star*, (a Soviet Defense Ministry newspaper), affords a partial tracking of developments in Soviet tactical thinking.

10. Between 1962 and 1966, Ma'arachot, the Israeli Defense Ministry's publishing house, collected, translated, and published Soviet doctrinal material. A key figure in this effort was Maj. (later Lt. Col.) L. Merchav, who translated, edited, and published several articles on this subject.

11. See: Dr. Shimon Naveh, *In Pursuit of Military Excellence, the Evolution of Operational Art*, London, 1997 (Hebrew edition, Tel Aviv, 2001). The book discusses Soviet doctrinal development in detail, and contains a comprehensive bibliography of publications and studies by Soviet and western writers, including P. A. Karber, Baxter, and C. N. Donnely.

12. A special publication of the U.S. Army Instruction Department dealing with the warfare doctrine of land forces in the Soviet army was translated into Hebrew by Hatzav Publishers under the title: *The Use of Land Forces in the Soviet Warfare Doctrine*, October 1981.

13. Graham Hall Turbiville, Jr. (ed.), *The Voroshilov Lectures, Issues of Operational Art* (Material from the Soviet General Staff Academy), Vol. III, 1992, Washington, D.C.: National Defense University Press, 1992 [hereafter: *Voroshilov Lectures*].

Introduction

1. Anwar Sadat, *My Life*, Jerusalem: Idanim & Yediot Achronot, 1978, 250.

2. Rafi Yisraeli, "President Sadat: The Image of the Leader," in *Sadat, War and Peace* (IDF Education Branch, September 1979), 8.

3. Ibid.

4. Lt. Col. Avi Shai, "Egypt Prior to the Yom Kippur War: War Aims and the Offensive Plan," *Ma'arachot 250*, 20.

5. Soviet military thinking, based primarily on experience from the "Great Patriotic War" (World War II), was updated in the 1960s and adapted to the nuclear age. The new type of warfare shunned the conventional warfare doctrine. See: L. Merchav, (ed.), *Soviet Military Doctrine in the Nuclear Age,* Tel Aviv: Ma'arachot, 1969.

6. Avi Shai, "Egypt Prior to the Yom Kippur War: War Aims and the Offensive Plan," *Ma'arachot 250*, 20.

Chapter 1

1. Yehoshafat Harkabi, *The Arab-Israeli Conflict* (Dvir Publishers, 1967), 86–88.

2. Yoram Meital, *Egypt's Political Development in the Conflict with Israel: 1967–1977*, PhD diss., University of Haifa, July 1991, 27.

3. Chaim Raviv, "The Pressure of the War of Attrition, an Expression of Public Disaffection," in *The Waning of Nasserism, 1965–1970, The Decline of a Messianic Movement,* Shimon Shamir, ed., (Tel Aviv University, 1979), 335.

4. Fuad Ajami, *Arabism and Arabs since 1967* (Tel Aviv: Yediot Ahronot Publishers, 2001), 154.

5. Yehoshafat Harkabi, *The Arabs' Lessons from their Defeat* (Am Oved Publishers, 1972), 10.

6. *The Six-Day War—The Campaign in the Egyptian Theater* (IDF History Unit, December 1971), 29–30.

7. The better-known improvised forces were "Force Shazli" and "Force Yakut," the armored, infantry and artillery groups — regular army and reserves — that were formed to fill in the gaps in the defense plan.

8. Mushir Abd al-Ghany Gamasi, *Gamasi, Mizkarat al-Gamasi, Harb Oktober 1973 (Gamasi's Memoirs, The October 1973 War)* (Paris, 1990), 120 [Arabic] [hereafter: Gamasi].

9. According to Gamasi, 123, the Egyptians suffered 9,800 dead and missing.

10. *The Six-Day War—The Campaign in the Egyptian Theater*, 419.

11. Gamasi, 123.

12. Uri Ben-Yosef, *The Watchman Fell Asleep: The Surprise of the Yom Kippur War, Source Material* (Lod: Zemora-Bitan, 2001), 80.

13. Emanual Gloska, "The Road to the Six-Day War: Israel's Military Command and the Political Leadership in Light of the Security Problems (1963–1967)," PhD diss., Hebrew University, 2000, 151.

14. Ibid., 152–153.

15. For a discussion on this issue, see Dan Shiftan, "From the Six-Day War to the War of Attrition" in *The Waning of Nasserism, 1965–1970, The Decline of a Messianic Movement,* Shimon Shamir, ed., (Tel Aviv University, 1979) 319–321.

16. Gloska, 153.

17. Nasser's speech appears as Document No. 12 in *Israel and World Politics of the Third Arab-Israeli War* (New York: Viking Press, 1968).

18. Gamasi, 33.

19. See, for example, the book by the commander of the Second Armored Brigade, a brigade of the Fourth Division, general staff reserves, Kamal Hasan Ali, *Fighters and Peacemakers* (Ma'arachot, 1993), 39. The high command's desultoriness can be seen in the way it assigned fourteen different missions to the Second Brigade when it was dispatched to Sinai (and, adding insult to injury, not one of them had been part of the original "Kahar" plan — the defense plan for Sinai). Later, all of the assignments were revised.

20. "Strategic balance" was a concept that referred to the correct distribution of forces in Sinai whereby one-third of the force went to the principal defense layout at the front, one-third to the army's second echelon or reserve forces, and one-third (or slightly less) to the quality force — especially the Fourth Armored Division — as GHQ (strategic) reserves near the canal. (According to the original defense plan, the Fourth Division apparently should have been deployed west of the canal.)

21. This was the only official plan, but the Egyptians, like all armies, must have had additional plans, including offensive ones.

22. According to Gamasi (69) during the GHQ meeting on May 25, 1967, that Nasser himself chaired, additional tasks were assigned.

23. Ibid.

24. According to Mahmud Fawzi, the Egyptian chief of staff in the Six-Day War and War of Attrition, in his book *Harb Al thalath Sanuat 1967–1970—Mithkarat al Fariq-Awal Mahmud Fawzi Wazir al Harabiya al Asbak (The Three-Year War, Memoirs of Mahmud Fawzi the former Minister of War)* (Cairo: Dar al Mistakabal el-Arabi, 1984), 174 [Arabic] [hereafter: Fawzi].

25. After the war Nasser frequently blamed the military echelon under the command of Field Marshal (Mushir) Amar for the defeat, claiming that for many years, when Amar was in command, the army had not been under the political leadership's control and that this was the root of the 1967 debacle. Despite this, he did not manage to completely clear his part in the responsibility for the defeat. See Yoram Meital, *Egypt's Struggle for Peace Continuity and Change, 1967–1977*, 13 [English], and Yoram Meital, *Egypt's Policy in the Conflict with Israel, 1967–1977*, 42. Today Arab writers point to Nasser's role in pushing Egypt headlong into this disastrous campaign. See Fuad Ajami, *Arabism and Arabs since 1967*, 217.

26. In order to judge Field Marshal (Mushir) Amar's military proficiency, one should recall that he "skyrocketed" from the rank of major to chief of staff in 1952. The exact circumstances surrounding his death are still disputed. See Gamasi, 53.

27. Gamasi, 58.

28. The fortification was prepared before the war at the eastern entrance to the Gidi axis, not far from the Bir Tmada airfield.

29. Yehoshafat Harkabi, "The Weak Spots in Nasser's Army, Social Shortcomings," in *The Waning of Nasserism, 1965–1970, The Decline of a Messianic Movement,* Shimon Shamir, ed., (Tel Aviv University, 1979), 201–205.

30. Yehoshafat Harkabi, *The Arabs Lessons from their Defeat*, 12–15.

31. Gamasi, 62–63.

32. The following is based on *Egyptian Captured Documents,* according to "Views of the Potential Enemy: Organization and Conduct of the Offensive," Lesson No. AK — 241 (Nasser Higher Military Academy, no date).

33. Shefi Gabai, "Gamasi: I was the Architect of the Yom Kippur War," *Ma'ariv*, June 29, 1987.

34. Gamasi, 10.

35. On the changes that the Egyptian army went through, see the chapters on the War of Attrition and the preparations for the Yom Kippur War.

36. In addition to dealing with the Egyptian-Israeli conflict as the main objective in Egypt's foreign relations and the main focus of its military activity, Egypt was also

active on the domestic front and in other areas. After the 1967 defeat the government made great efforts to attain domestic goals. Besides rehabilitating the army, it strove to restore its own legitimacy and regain public support (especially after the antigovernment demonstrations in February 1968). Its endeavors to stabilize the domestic scene should be seen against the background of the demand for wide-scale reforms (like those expressed in Nasser's March 30, 1968, declaration and his guarantee to bring democratization to Egypt). See Meital, *Egypt's Struggle for Peace*, 25.

37. For a comprehensive article on this subject see Yoram Meital, "The Khartoum Conference and Egyptian Policy after the 1967 War: A Reexamination," *Middle East Journal* 54, no. 1 (Winter 2000), 64–82.

On the conference and its decisions, especially regarding Egypt, see Meital, *Egypt's Struggle for Peace*, 41–46. A matter-of-fact description of the Khartoum Conference and its decisions can be found in Yehoshafat Harkabi's anthology, *Arab and Israel: Anthology of Translations from the Arabic*, 1 (1975) 93. Evidence of Nasser's trend toward a political—rather than a military—solution to the crisis appears in a memo that Nasser sent to Johnson, "United Arab Republic: Internal Situation," Memo, 2.1.68 in The Lyndon Johnson National Security Files: The Middle East 1963–1969.

38. In addition to "the three noes," the conference also decided that military units from other Arab states would be sent to the canal front. Only Algeria honored all of its commitments and dispatched a fully equipped infantry and artillery battalion. Sudan and Kuwait each sent one infantry battalion. In the final analysis, these foreign forces were a minor contribution. See Mustafa Cabha, *Harb al-Istanzaf, The War of Attrition According to Egyptian Sources* (Tel Aviv University, 1996), 69–71 [hereafter: Cabha].

39. See Meital, *Egypt's Struggle for Peace*, 11.

40. According to Yehoshafat Harkabi in his work *Changes in the Arab-Israeli Conflict* (Tel Aviv: Dvir Publishers, 1978), changes and innovations were made in Egypt after the Six-Day War. Harkabi mentions Egyptian circles that advocated peace with Israel.

41. Meital, *The Development of Egypt's Policy in the Conflict with Israel, 1967–1977*, 34.

42. See ibid., 48–50, and also Meital, *Egypt's Struggle for Peace*, 15–19.

43. Fawzi, 202–204.

44. Magdub, al-Badri, and Zahari, *Harb Ramadan*, 52–56. All three defined the last stage as that of "no war–no peace." Gamasi presents it (149–151) as a preliminary stage to the 1973 October War.

45. Gamasi, 135.

46. This is how it was according to Fawzi.

47. For a discussion on Egypt's goals and priorities, see Meital, *Egypt's Struggle for Peace*, 25–29.

48. According to Nasser in different forums. In his speech at the Kremlin he declared: "Today our main goal is to eradicate the results of Israeli aggression on June 5. This must include punishing the aggressors." See Cabha, 50.

49. According to Taha Magdub, see Cabha, 48.

50. Gamasi, 135. According to Taha Magdub, "force" in this case refers not only to military force but to "force" in all its political, economic, and moral senses, in addition, of course, to the military sense. See Cabha, 48.

51. See Dan Shiftan, "From the Six-Day War to the War of Attrition," *Ma'arachot* 257 (August 1977), 11.

52. Meital, *Egypt's Struggle for Peace*, 29.

53. The decision called for Israel's withdrawal from "territories," and the question was raised whether this implied "all the occupied territories." For a detailed discussion on

the preliminary activity, Egypt's position, and its views of and responses to the decision, see Meital, *Egypt's Struggle for Peace*, 46–54.

54. Nasser's November 23, 1967 speech, ibid.

55. Some of the activity was directed to Gunnar Jarring, the UN secretary-general's special envoy to the Middle East, who studied the parties' positions and the ways of implementing Resolution 242. The Jarring Mission began in December 1967 and ended on January 4, 1971, when the special envoy presented his conclusions to the UN secretary-general and Security Council. For details on the Jarring Mission and especially its contacts with the Egyptians and Israelis, see Meital, *Egypt's Struggle for Peace*, 54–63.

56. Meital presents Egypt's political activity as nearly equal to its military activity in this period. See Meital, *Egypt's Struggle for Peace*, 32–33.

57. Fawzi presents Nasser's detailed plans for a three-year period of rehabilitation and training, after which a full-scale war of liberation would be launched. Fawzi, 190–198. Shiftan (*Attrition*) notes that Sadat's regime had to add, retrospectively, the War of Attrition as a preparatory stage in the glorious depiction of the Ramadan War (Yom Kippur War). Shiftan, 15.

58. Nasser sent Fawzi, the chief of staff since 1965, to Syria on a sensitive mission on the eve of the Six-Day War. On June 11 he was promoted to supreme commander of the Egyptian armed forces. On January 20, 1968 he was appointed minister of war (in addition to his role as chief of staff). On his appointment, see Fawzi, 167, 197–199, and Shiftan, 18–19.

59. Gamasi, 136.

60. According to Fawzi (11) reorganization of the armed forces was crucial—especially in the air force and air defense units; academically trained soldiers had to be recruited in order to place the armed forces on "scientific" foundations. Fawzi adds that the results of this qualitative improvement were realized in the Yom Kippur War.

61. Shortly after the Six-Day War, the Soviets supplied Egypt, by air and sea with 50,000 tons of brand-new military gear. The first arms shipment included 321 MiG-21s and 93 MiG-17s. In addition, MiG-17s were sent from East European states such as East Germany, Poland, and Yugoslavia. See Cabha, 54–55.

62. "Israeli arms Request," 3.1.68 in The Lyndon Johnson National Peace, Security Files, the Middle East 1963–1969 (University Publication of America); see also, Meital, *Egypt's Struggle for Peace*, 31.

63. On the Soviet military instructor, see a separate chapter in this book.

64. Cabha, 73–74.

65. Gamasi, 145–148

66. The discussion on the fronts is based mainly on Fawzi, 206–207; see also, Meital, *Egypt's Struggle for Peace*, 31–32.

67. On the inter-Arab contacts, the basic understandings between Egypt and Jordan on political activity and the Soviet Union, see Meital, *Egypt's Struggle for Peace*, 33–37 and "The Khartoum Conference and Egyptian Policy after the 1967 War": 62–82.

68. Fawzi, 227.

69. Gamasi, 149.

70. Some Israeli historians regard these incidents as the start of the three-year War of Attrition.

71. On the political standstill and its effect of Egypt, see Meital, *Egypt's Struggle for Peace*, 63–64.

72. The first-time success of sea-to-sea missiles against a live target boosted morale in Egypt and the Arab world. Egypt declared October 21 "Navy Day."

73. Parallel with the military escalation, Egyptian diplomatic activity reached its climax with the adoption of UN Security-Council Resolution 242 on November 22, 1967.

74. Gamasi, 161. On the Israeli layout, see Chapter 2 — "The Israeli Defense Concept on the Sinai Front."

75. Jamal Hamad, *Min Sina ela al-Julan (From Sinai to the Golan)* (Cairo: Al-Zahara Lilalam, 1988), 63.

76. An interview with Fawzi, Cabha, 80–81.

77. The Egyptians credit themselves with the initiative to open fire in response to IDF activity on the canal.

78. *Attrition*, 134. Ten of the victims were killed when their bunker was hit by an artillery shell.

79. Cabha, 82.

80. Fawzi, 228.

81. On Sisco's fourteen-point plan (June 1969) for a solution to the conflict, see Meital, *Egypt's Struggle for Peace*, 64–66.

82. Chaim Raviv, *The War of Attrition's Pressure*, 333–334.

83. On the "limited strategy" see a detailed discussion in B. H. Liddell Hart, *The Strategy of the Indirect Approach* (Ma'arachot, 1956), chapters 19–22. Avraham Zohar also dealt with this subject in "The War of Attrition," *Ma'arachot*, 257 (August 1977), 15. Yaacov Bar-Siman-Tov in his book, *The Israeli-Egyptian War of Attrition* (New York: Columbia University Press, 1980), 5–28, discusses the attempt to place the War of Attrition within the theoretical framework of a "limited local war." Harkabi, in *War and Strategy* (Ma'arachot, 1990), 127, defines "[l]imited war [as] a war that is limited in its objectives, its use of certain weapons, its degree of their application, its theater of operations, and the number of participants." A comprehensive look at the subject in the context of the Yom Kippur War also appears in the present work.

84. See Yehoshafat Harkabi, *War and Strategy*, 436.

85. Harkabi elaborates on the theory of a war of attrition in *War and Strategy* (433–434). He discusses Clausewitz, and examines Hans Delbruk (1848–1929) who interpreted Clausewitz as an attrition strategist. According to Delbruk, wars were waged according to two basic strategies: the conclusive strategy (crushing the enemy in a one-time event) and the attrition strategy (eroding the enemy's strength, exhausting him, and achieving victory in a gradual process). Attrition is employed when one party lacks the strength to subdue the other. See also Cabha, 17–29.

86. Gamasi, 163.

87. Chaim Raviv, *The War of Attrition's Pressure*, 333.

88. For a comprehensive discussion on the subject, see the chapter in this book on the Egyptian plan. Fawzi's memoirs repeatedly refer to the possibilities of this option. See Dan Shiftan, *Attrition* (Tel Aviv: Ma'arachot, 1989) 39, and also chapter 2 on whether Egypt had the military option to liberate Sinai, *Attrition*, 63–94.

89. Egypt's lack of long range-bombers was one of the pillars of the Israeli intelligence concept, according to which without these planes Egypt would not dare to embark upon an all-out war.

90. Despite the fact that in early 1969 three hundred Egyptian pilots returned from a training course in the Soviet Union. See Cabha, 86.

91. *Fawzi*, 289–290. According to Israeli sources, between March 1969 and August 1970 the Egyptians lost ninety-eight aircraft to Israel's fourteen. Shiftan, *Attrition*, 439.

92. Cabha, 94.

93. The reason for Ali's dismissal was his failure to carry out orders. When Nasser learned of the raid, he ordered Ali to rush to the scene and update him with details. When Nasser learned that his chief of staff had not gone as ordered, he relieved him of his duty. Cabha, 53, 87.

94. Captured Egyptian Document 431/1 from September 23, 1969 refers to the lessons from the debarkation operation in the Abu Aldarj and al-Za'afrana region. (Ministry of War Publications, Military Intelligence Authority, Information Branch.)

95. Cabha, 88.

96. Fawzi, 284.

97. Captured Egyptian Document 431/1, translated on January 4, 1974, an analysis of the IDF raid on the Egyptian radar company in areas under the Red Sea Command.

98. A ten-man squad was deployed at the defense station. When the assault began only two soldiers were guarding the facility, the rest were asleep. See Cabha, 91.

99. On the plan, its text, and the reasons for its rejection by the parties, see Meital, *Egypt's Struggle for Peace*, 66–67.

100. *Attrition*, 246.

101. See Meital, *Egypt's Struggle for Peace*, 67.

102. Jamal Hamad, *Min Sina ela al-Julan* (*From Sinai to the Golan*) 74–75.

103. On the in-depth bombing, its political impact on the Egyptian-Soviet system, and the American attitude to it, see Meital, *Egypt's Struggle for Peace*, 67–70.

104. See "The Text of the President's Message to the National Emergency Conference on Peace in the Middle East: 25.1.70," in *The Nixon Project*, White House Central Files.

105. Gamasi refers to this effort as "The Epopee of National Heroism." Gamasi, 103.

106. Yaacov Ro'i, *From Encroachment to Involvement, A Documentary Study of Soviet Policy in the Middle East, 1945–1973* (Jerusalem: Israeli University Press, 1974), 543 [English].

107. In early July 1970 five Phantoms and three Skyhawks were shot down.

108. *Attrition*, 264–265.

109. According to Meital, *Egypt's Struggle for Peace*, 71–72. Egyptian sources show that Nasser convinced the Soviets to take the initiative in order to complete the missile deployment, halt the supply of Phantoms from the United States to Israel, and give him (Nasser) a breathing spell in the War of Attrition and time to recoup his strength.

110. Gamasi, 186.

111. General (Liwa) Taha Magdub, *Al-Jish almisri baad Yuniu 67* (The Egyptian Army after June 1967); *Harb Yuniu 1967 baad 30 Sana* (The June War after 30 Years), (Cairo: The al-Ahram Center for Translations and Publications, 1998), 147.

112. In addition to the small-scale, cross-channel raids, the Egyptians used the canal's western arm (in the vicinity of al-Balah Island) for practicing the crossing of larger forces (even battalion-sized orders of battle).

113. "Low signature" is a modern military term that describes activity that is difficult to spot with standard methods of detection. Low-signature activity prevents the enemy from hitting the other side with weapons designed for larger targets.

114. On the Egyptians' methods in the Yom Kippur War, see the chapter in this book on the canal crossing and chapter 5 on the use of antitank weapons.

Chapter 2

1. Moshe Dayan, *Story of My Life* (Jerusalem, Tel Aviv: Idanim, 1976), 471.

2. Ibid., 523.

3. Golda Meir, *My Life* (Tel Aviv: Ma'ariv), 289.

4. Carmit Guy, *Bar-Lev* (Tel Aviv: Am Oved, Sifriat Hapoalim, 1998), 171.

5. On the periodization of the War of Attrition and the stages plan, see Mustafa Cabha's book: *Harb al-Istanzaf*, 35–42 [Arabic].

6. *Bar-Lev*, 174.

7. Ibid. 175.

8. Avraham Adan (Bren), *On Both Banks of the Canal*, (Jerusalem: Idanim), 44–45.

9. Ibid., 46.

10. Ibid., 47.

11. During the war, the distance and location of this road fit the Egyptians' needs for accomplishing their main task, which they determined, for the most part, as the target line for the bridgeheads' front.

12. Egyptian military research deals with the capture of the mountain passes during the army's offensive, *Egyptian War Booty Document 470/1*, printed at Nineteenth Division Headquarters.

13. Eli Zeira, 61.

14. According to Bren, 47–48.

15. Bar-Lev, 176.

16. Ibid., 178.

17. Regarding innovations, the chief of staff may have been referring to the "Or Yikarot" system — oil tanks with inflammable material that were supposed to exude a smear on the water's surface, in areas recognized as crossing points, and then set on fire. For more on this subject, see the chapter on Egyptian combat engineers operations. Another innovative idea was the elevation of the dirt embankment close to the waterline on the eastern bank in order to obstruct the Egyptian force from gaining a foothold. For more on this issue, see the chapter dealing with Egyptian solutions to engineering problems.

18. Bar-Lev, 179.

19. Bar-Lev, 177. The chief of staff seems to have erred and meant a third reinforced brigade, and not a second brigade that was already deployed in Sinai.

20. Yehuda Wallach, *Not on a Silver Platter*, (Carta, 2000) 95; Bar-Lev, 179.

21. Bar-Lev, 180.

22. Israel Tal, *Israel's National Security, Few against Many* (Tel Aviv: Dvir, 1996), 153.

23. Bren, 44.

24. Ibid., 48.

25. Fawzi, the Egyptian war minister, states this in his memoirs, 202–204. At this stage he called it *"al-tachidi wa-alrada'i."*

26. Avraham Zohar, "The War of Attrition," in *The Struggle for Israel's Security* (The Association for Military History, 1999), 160.

27. Israel Tal, 154.

28. Bar-Lev, 183.

29. Bren, 49.

30. General Tal claims that the failure of the stronghold system in the War of Attrition led to the use of the air force and in turn the establishment of a Soviet antiaircraft layout. During the Yom Kippur War the Soviet layout severely impeded the Israeli air force in fulfilling its missions and assisting the ground units. Israel Tal, 154–155.

31. By mid-July 1969, sixty-one troops had been killed and sixty-nine wounded, *The Struggle for Israel's Security*, 160.

32. Bren, 50.

33. Bar-Lev, 191.

34. Ibid.

35. Dayan, *Story of My Life*, 515.

36. Nine hundred sixty-eight Israelis were killed and 3,730 wounded in all of the sectors during the War of Attrition. *The Struggle of Israel's Security*, 167.

37. Bren, 50–52.

38. Zeev Eitan, "Shovach Yonim, Planning and Implementation under Fire," *Ma'arachot* 276–277 (October––November 1980), 38.

39. This testimony was presented to the Agranat Commission, *The Agranat Commission — Additional Partial Statement*, Vol. II, (Jerusalem, 1976), 193. On "Shovach Yonim," see the following material in *The Agranat Commission*. See also: Zeira, 64–65.

40. Hanoch Bartov, *Dado — 48 Years and Twenty More Days* (Tel Aviv: Sifriat Ma'ariv, 1978), Vol. I, 200–201.

41. Ibid., 201.

42. Ibid., 216–218.

43. At about this time the Egyptians realized that they lacked the strength to carry out such a plan.

44. Aviezer Golan, *Albert* (Tel Aviv: Major General Albert (Avraham) Mendler Memorial Foundation, Yidiot Achronot, 1977), 187.

45. Ibid., 185–186.

46. Zeev Eitan, "Shovach Yonim," 38.

47. Other fronts had other plans: "Sela" (Boulder) — a defense plan for the entire order of battle; and "Geer" (Chalk) — a defense plan based on regular army units that would hold the line until the reserves arrived.

48. *The Agranat Commission*, Vol. II, 192.

49. According to Uri Bar-Yosef, *Guard That Slept on His Watch: The Surprise of the Yom Kippur War and Its Sources* (Lod: Zmora-Bitan, 2001), 187, preparations for the plan began in 1970. I was unable to turn up evidence for this in any other sources.

50. The main principles of the "Shovach Yonim" plan are based on the description in Bren's book, 54.

51. This is the road that links Baluza, Tasa, Mitla, and Ras Sudar at a distance of thirty to forty kilometers east of the Suez Canal.

52. General Mendler's plans that were renewed in November 1972 discussed the possibility of a deep Egyptian penetration to "Lateral Road" and Israeli counterstrikes against this road. Albert, 186.

53. *The Agranat Commission*, Vol. II, 194.

54. In order to facilitate the call-up and arrival of the reservists in the battle zone, the emergency storerooms of the tank formations were transferred to points close to the combat sectors especially on the Golan Heights, but also in Sinai. Israel Tal, 186.

55. Therefore, based on the situation estimate from the summer of 1972, the GHQ decided to implement the emergency plan and establish a canal-crossing layout. This meant speeding up the development and production of fording equipment and training the forces designated for the crossing. Ibid.

56. From the GHQ's discussions and war games in 1972 and 1973, it turned out that in case of fighting on two fronts, the GHQ would be left without any reserve divisions; therefore the order of battle had to be increased. During a war the headquarters would be reinforced with only one hastily put together divisional headquarters.

57. Wallach, *Not on a Silver Platter*, 116.

58. Emanuel Valad, *The Curse of the Broken Vessels* (Tel Aviv: Schocken, 1987). 104. The criticism that was written after the war derives its strength mainly from the aftermath of the war.

59. According to the Agranat Commission, the committee that investigated the Yom Kippur War, *Agranat Report, An Additional Partial Account*, Vol. I (Jerusalem: Agranat Commission, 1974) 60.

60. Ibid. The second part of the conception was that

Syria would not make a large-scale attack on Israel unless it could do so simultaneously with Egypt.

61. According to Eli Zeira, *The October '73 War: Myth Versus Reality*, 91, this was not an estimate but was based on documented material that was found to be authentic and that told exactly what Egypt's objectives and preconditions were for embarking upon war.

62. The sections written with an "x number of" are missing from the published version of the report.

63. *Agranat Report*, 61.

64. Zeria, *Yom Kippur War: Myth Versus Reality*, 86.

65. General Zeira's code name for the intelligence source that supplied information on the conception.

66. *Agranat Report*, 62.

67. Ibid., 63.

68. Ibid., 64–65.

69. See also Zeria, *Yom Kippur War: Myth Versus Reality*, 88.

70. Brigadier General Yoel Ben-Porat, "The Yom Kippur War, a Mistake in May, a Surprise in October. New Facts on the Yom Kippur Surprise," *Ma'arachot* 299, (July-August, 1985) 3.

71. *Agranat Report*, 66.

72. Efraim Kam, *Surprise Attack* (Tel Aviv: Ma'arachot, 1990), 39.

73. Gamasi, 80.

74. Ibid., 99.

75. Mustafa Cabha, *Harb al Istanzaf*, 121.

76. The Agranat Commission did not receive captured documents for perusal, only information that reached Israeli intelligence before the war. The commission notes that the turning point in Sadat's and the Egyptian government's views began in the spring of 1973. *Agranat Report*, Vol. I, 85.

77. According to Gamasi, 225–227.

78. Dani Asher, "Antitank Fire as a Reply," *Ma'arachot*, 346.

79. See *Agranat Report, An Additional Partial Account*, 135, in which General Zeira asks, "What are Egypt's options in the event that hostilities break out?" And his reply that there are basically three possibilities:

A. Crossing the canal and reaching the straits.

B. Carrying out raids in Sinai and along the canal.

C. Commencing an artillery barrage.

He also mentions a fourth way — a combination of bombardment and raids. The quote is from a survey by the head of military intelligence during the October 5, 1973, ministerial meeting. On the same subject, see also: Yoel Ben-Porat, "The Yom Kippur War: A Mistake in May, A Surprise in October," *Ma'arachot* 299, 4, which presents the intelligence assessment from mid-May 1973 and discusses the enemy's most probable modus operandi.

80. See: *Egyptian Captured Document 766/4*, Order No. 41, the order issued by the Egyptian chief of staff, Shazli, concerning an infantry division crossing the water obstacle (the canal) — details and forces, and equipment and priorities for the crossing, March 20, 1973.

81. Zvi Lanir, *Fundamental Surprise — The National Intelligence Crisis*, 62.

82. *Agranat Report*, 85–86.

83. Yosi Melman, *Ha'aretz*, August 18, 1996.

84. Efraim Kam, 42.

85. The entire theory was developed by Yoel Ben-Porat. See his article, "The Yom Kippur War — Blunder in May, New Facts on the Yom Kippur Surprise."

86. *Agranat Report*, 80.

87. Ibid., 85.

88. Yoel Ben-Porat, *Enclosure*, 116.

89. Yoel Ben-Porat, "The Yom Kippur War — Blunder in May, New Facts on the Yom Kippur Surprise," 9.

90. Aryeh Arad, "Yom Kippur, the War That Launched the Missile Age, *Davar*, October 6, 1992.

91. In my opinion, Israeli military intelligence did not suffer from the lack of information; it suffered from the lack of properly analyzed information and from not internalizing the information. This shortcoming meant that the information was unable to influence or contribute to a change in the situation assessment.

92. Aryeh Arad, *Davar*, October 1992. According to the author, military intelligence had the information, but it failed to analyze its meaning and translate it into a glaring warning.

93. Ibid.

94. Yoel Ben-Porat, *Enclosure*, 123.

95. Brig. Gen. Aharon Levran, "Surprise and Warning — Studies on Basic Questions," *Ma'arachot* 276–277 (October-November 1980).

96. Shmuel Segev, *Sadat, the Road to Peace*, 34. The conversation took place during Sadat's visit to Jerusalem in November 1977.

97. Tal Bashan, "The 'Naif,' Not Everything Has to Fall on the Intelligence Branch," an interview with Lieut. Gen. (res.) Amnon Lipkin-Shachak, *Magazeen Yom Hakippurim shel Ma'ariv*, September 19, 1999, 26.

98. *Agranat Report*, 81. According to the commission, Israel's failure to foresee the Yom Kippur War was essentially a failure of logic and not a psychological or sociological failure.

99. Brig. Gen. Yitzhak Ben Israel in his article in *Davar*, September 24, 1993, "If I Could Only Discover the Truth as Easily as I Refute the Lie," summarized the main points in his book, *Dialogues on Information and Intelligence*, chapters 3 and 8.

100. Col. Sh., an Israeli intelligence officer, also wrote an article on why the conception collapsed. See: "The Conceptual Failures in the Warning of the Yom Kippur War and What Can be Learned from Them, *Ma'arachot* 338 (October–November 1994), 10–15.

Chapter 3

1. Shimon Naveh, *The Art of Battle* (Tel Aviv: Ma'arachot, 2001), 34.

2. Ibid., 35.

3. B. H. Liddell Hart, *Strategy* (New York: Praeger, 1954), 335–336.

4. Roger Ashley Leonard, *On War, a Short Guide to Clausewitz*, (Tel Aviv: Ma'arachot, 1967), 28; and also Liddell Hart, 334.

5. Andre Baufré, *An Introduction to Strategy* (New York: Praeger, 1965), 16.

6. Gavriel Ben Dor, "Thoughts on the Hebrew Strategy in the Yom Kippur War," in *In the Shadow of the Yom Kippur War* (University of Haifa, 1976), 200.

7. Avi Shai, "Egypt Prior to the Yom Kippur War: War Aims and Offensive Plan," 16.

8. Sadat in an interview with the Lebanese television, according to the Middle East News Agency, October 9, 1974.

9. Shimon Shamir, "The Formation of the Concept of the October Offensive," in *Egypt under Sadat's Leadership* (Tel Aviv: Dvir, 1978), 88.

10. Ibid., 89.

11. Meital, *Egypt's Political Development in the Conflict with Israel: 1967–1977*, 179.

12. According to Mahmud Fawzi's book on the October 1973 War, published in the Lebanese paper *al-Shara'a*, August–October 1988, Nasser issued this strategy as a di-

rective on June 11, 1967, and it became the basis of the operative plan for liberating Sinai — "Plan 200."

13. Mahmud Fawzi, *Harb el thalath Sanuwat 1967–1970 — Mithkarat al Fariq Awal Mahmud Fawzi Wazir al-Harabiya al Asbaq* (The Three Year War 1967–1970 — General Mahmud Fawzi the War Minister), 200 [Arabic].

14. According to Shamir, the term "the military solution" was eventually changed to refer to two solutions.

15. Nasser's speech on April 10, 1968, *al-Ahram*, April 11, 1968.

16. The army's assessment of its ability to liberate Sinai in this period is divided. Mahmud Fawzi, the minister of war during the War of Attrition, claimed that the Egyptians had the ability and operational plans, but due to Nasser's death the war was not launched. See Shiftan, *Attrition*, 62–81.

17. Meital, *Egypt's Political Development in the Conflict with Israel: 1967–1977*, 180.

18. Meital, *Egypt's Struggle for Peace*, 79–80.

19. Shamir, 92.

20. A synopsis (no date), published by the author, in Yoram Meital, *The Road to Peace: Egypt's Policy toward the Conflict with Israel, 1967–1977*, Working Paper No. 2 (University of Haifa, The Jewish–Arab Center, 1996), 2.

21. Shamir, 92.

22. Meital, *Egypt's Struggle for Peace*, 81.

23. One of Sadat's first decisions was to extend the cease-fire on the canal (that was supposed to end on November 8, 1970) for an additional three months (until February 7, 1971). Despite his announcement that 1971 would be the "Year of Decision" the cease-fire was extended several more times until the outbreak of the Yom Kippur War, mainly in order to buy time for preparing the military option.

24. Sadat went public with his initiative in a speech at the Egyptian National Council on February 14, 1971. See, Colonel Avraham, "Sadat's Reasons for the War," in *Sadat, War, and Peace*, IDF Education Branch, September 1979, 24.

25. Meital, *Egypt's Struggle for Peace*, 105–106. Professor Haggai Erlich, who examined the student demonstrations, notes that a wave of protest swept across Egypt because of Sadat's attitude toward the conflict and the failure of the "Year of Decision." See Haggai Erlich, *Students and the University in the 20ᵗʰ Century: Egyptian Politics* (London: Frank Cass, 1989), 65.

26. Speaking before the Northern Command on April 17, 1973, Moshe Dayan termed the decision "a return to the sword." See Aryeh Baron, *Moshe Dayan in the Yom Kippur War* (Jerusalem: Idanim/Yidiot Achronot, 1993), 21.

27. This was the background to Sadat's initiative in February 1971 for an intermediary Egyptian-Israeli settlement on the canal front and, following this, for U.S. and UN attempts at mediation. For details on the initiative, domestic and international responses to it and distrust of it, and Israel's rejection of it, see Meital, *Egypt's Struggle for Peace*, 86–96.

28. Baron, *Moshe Dayan in the Yom Kippur War*, 34.

29. Shamir, 96–97.

30. See ibid., 97; and also Heykal, *The Road to Ramadan* (Collins, 1977), 168.

31. According to Fawzi, chapter 3 (published in the Lebanese *al-Shara'a*, August–October 1988).

32. Shamir, 98; also chapter 2 in this book on "the conception."

33. Heykal, *The Road to Ramadan*, 115, and also Meital, *Egypt's Struggle for Peace*, 92.

34. Jamal Hamad, *Min Sina ala al-Julan* (*From Sinai to the Golan*), 223–224 [Arabic].

35. Ibid., 227–228.

36. Sadat increasingly realized that a political settlement with Israel would be possible only with U.S. intervention, therefore Egypt's multifaceted relationship with the Soviet Union had to be reduced. Meital, *Egypt's Struggle for Peace*, 108.

37. According to Shmuel Bar, *The Yom Kippur War in Arab Eyes*, 21, the official Egyptian version claimed that the formulation of the objectives and war concept began only after Soviet Union advisors were expelled.

38. Ahmad Ismail Ali, the Egyptian chief of staff, was dismissed in September 1969 following the Israeli raid at Zafrana. Ali had been appointed to the office six months earlier, after his predecessor, Abd al-Munam Riad, had been killed by an Israeli mortar shell. See the chapter in this book dealing with the War of Attrition. The dismissal took place following a sharp exchange of words in the "Supreme Council of the Armed Forces" on October 24, 1972. In addition to Sadaq, the deputy minister of war, Hassan al-Kader, and the commander of the Egyptian navy were also sacked. See Sadat, *My Life*, 179.

39. Shimon Golan, "The Army as an Instrument in the Egyptian Foreign Policy in the Yom Kippur War," *Ma'arachot* 338 (October–November 1994), 22.

40. Yona Bandman (Avi-Shai), "Egypt on the Eve of the Yom Kippur War: War Aims and Attack Plans," *Ma'arachot* 250 (July 1976), 16.

41. According to Field Marshal Ahmad Ismail Ali, who was serving as the war minister, in an interview with Mahmud Hassanein Heykal, *Al-Anwar*, November 18, 1973.

42. Avraham, *Sadat, War, and Peace*, 38.

43. A speech delivered on the fourth anniversary of Nasser's death, *Radio Cairo*, September 28, 1974.

44. Ahmad Ismail Ali, in an interview with Hassanein Heykal, *al-Anwar*, November 18, 1973.

45. Sadat, in an interview with Dr. Takla and Darwish Tawil, authors of the book *The Six-Hour War*, as it appears in the chapters that Fariq (Lieutenant General) al-Tawil published in the weekly *Achar Sa'a*, May 8, 1974.

46. Sadat, *My Life*, 250–252. [This is how it appears in the original.]

47. Avi-Shai, 17.

48. Ibid.

49. Sadat assumed that Syria would be integrated into Egypt's plans and that a two-front effort would be coordinated. According to Gamasi, 239–246, the Egyptian planners tried to get Jordan on the war wagon which would have opened a three-front war against Israel.

50. This is based on a lecture given by the Egyptian general and historian Jamal Hamad to the "Wafad" Party's public relations committee, published in the Egyptian paper, *al-Wafad*, November 11, 1987. See also, Sadat, *My Life*, 253. [This is how it appears in the original.]

51. Ariel Levita, *The Israeli Military Doctrine, Defense and Offense* (Jaffe Center of Strategic Studies, Tel Aviv University, 1988), 7.

52. On an "all-out war," see Harkabi, *War and Strategy* (Tel Aviv: Ma'arachot, 1990), 127. On "general war" as a term similar to "all-out war," see ibid., pp. 334–335.

53. Lieutenant-General Zoyalov, "The Soviet Military Doctrine," in "Soviet Military Thinking in the Nuclear Age," *Ma'arachot*, April 1969, p76.

54. Major General N. Soshko, "On War," in "Soviet Military Thinking in the Nuclear Age," *Ma'arachot*, April 1969, 19.

55. Colonel Professor N. Lomov, "On War and Weapons," in "Soviet Military Thinking in the Nuclear Age," *Ma'arachot*, April 1969, 30.

56. According to Marshal V. Sokolovsky and Major

General M. Cherdnichenko, "The Art of War in New Stages of Development," in "Soviet Military Thinking in the Nuclear Age," *Ma'arachot*, April 1969, 45, most Western European military thinkers believe that the art of war is a test of the commanding general's military skills. Proponents of this view contend that it has nothing to do with science.

57. Major General N. Soshko, "On War," 15.

58. According to Marshal V. Sokolovsky and Major General M. Cherdnichenko, "The Art of War in New Stages of Development," 46.

59. Ibid.

60. Ibid., 51–53.

61. Major General N. Soshko, "On War," 18.

62. In the 1960s the Soviets developed a comprehensive doctrine on all aspects of nuclear weapons in the battlefield, even at the tactical level. However, despite the thinking of military strategists, they continued to develop conventional weapons layouts and systems. See the anthology: *Soviet Military Thinking in the Modern Age*, where an article by Major General A. Rizansky (dotzent) appears as "The Revolution in the Art of Warfare and Units' Tactics, 63–74. The article discusses the changes that took place at the campaign and tactical levels following entry of nuclear weapons into the planned war zone. (Since the subject of nuclear weapons is not relevant to this research, I have dealt with it only minimally.)

63. Major General N. Soshko, "On War," 18.

64. Ibid., 21–22.

65. General Lieutenant Zoyalov, "The Soviet Military Doctrine," *Machshava Sovietit Bi'idan Hagarin*," 83–84.

66. The article also discusses nuclear weapons and their influence on the principles of warfare. I have chosen to ignore this aspect of the article and concentrate on principles relevant to the Egyptian army (that of course lacked a nuclear capability).

67. See Turbiville, Graham Hall, Jr., editor, *The Voroshilov Lectures*, the chapter dealing with offensive operations at the front, 51–129, and offensive operations at the army level, 61–363.

68. According to *Division (Brigade) Offensive Combat—Textbook*, 1971, Nasser Higher Military Academy — Advanced War College. The book on the Soviet doctrine was translated into English at the "Nasser" Academy. Its Hebrew translation, *The Division (Brigade) in an Offensive*, was published by the GHQ's Training Branch in June 1974, 9.

69. The list is from The Use of Ground Forces in the Soviet Military Doctrine, Hatzav Publications, 830/001, October 1981, 3–5. The translation of the book was published by the United States Army Training Branch. See also *The Soviet Army: Operation and Tactics*, 100–2-1 (Washington, D.C.: Department of the Army, 1984). The book, published in Hebrew after the Yom Kippur War, is based on the Soviet Union's lessons from the Yom Kippur War. The question of mobility and rapid pace of the fighting force that appears at the end of the list was discussed in Soviet military publications following the Yom Kippur War. See "The Pace of the Offensive as an Important Factor in the Soviet Combat Doctrine," Hatzav Publications, 832/03, July 20, 1978.

70. The Americans feared a Russian penetration into the heart of Western Europe. It was only natural, then, that they were also concerned over the Red Army's mobility and ability to break through and develop a "rolling" offensive. According to the Americans, the Soviets believed that the most important factor in a successful offensive in the European theater would be a rapid tactical and systems maneuver into the heart of the defensive layout. On this subject see David M. Glantz, *The Soviet Conduct of Tactical Maneuver Spearhead of the Offensive* (Frank Cass, 1991), 11.

71. For a comprehensive work on this subject, see Ariel (Alex) Vitan, "Soviet Involvement and Intervention in Egypt 1967–1972, The Military Aspect," MA Thesis, University of Tel Aviv, [no date]. Vitan published an article on this subject in *Ma'arachot* 289–290 (October 1983), 65–70.

72. Yoav Gelber, "*The History of Intelligence in Israel's Early Years*," IDF Intelligence Branch (internal publication) 1985.

73. Ibid.

74. Ibid.

75. On Soviet goals, methods, and involvement in the Middle East, see Bernard Lewis, "Israel, the Arabs, and the Blocs in the Middle East," *Ma'arachot 217–218* (September 1971), 10–15.

76. Mishel Solomon, *Red Star over the Mediterranean Sea* (Tel Aviv: Ma'arachot, 1972). See also Vitan, "Soviet Involvement," 6.

77. Vitan, "Soviet Involvement," 13–15.

78. Ibid., 19. The first squadron of the fleet's aircraft touched down in Egypt in December 1967.

79. *Al-Ahram*, June 22, 1967 [Arabic].

80. Dayan, *Story of My Life*, 512.

81. Vitan, "Soviet Involvement," 23–24.

82. According to the Soviet deputy chief of staff, Colonel General M. Greiv, and the commanding general of the air force, G. Dolnikov, over 8,000 Egyptian officers and NCOs (military experts) received training in the Soviet Union in this period. See A. Timofiev in *Novaya Vremya*, and in the Hebrew journal, *Bamachane*, May 3, 1989, 53.

83. Vitan, "Soviet Involvement," 25.

84. According to A. Timofiev (in *Novaya Vremya*), the Russian advisors took part in planning the early drafts of the Egyptian offense plan "Granite."

85. According to Vitan (*Ma'arachot*, 66), in some cases the Russian advisors demanded the removal of Egyptian officers of "upper class" backgrounds whom they believed endangered the regime. In their place, the Russians recommended promoting officers who had undergone military training and political indoctrination in the Soviet Union.

86. Captured Egyptian Document 474/005 (dated January 29, 1969) contains orders regarding the advisors' modus operandi in the Egyptian armed forces.

87. In a *Pravda* article published in October 1969, one "observer" notes that the Soviet Union will do everything necessary to eradicate the results of Israel's aggression. See Vitan, "Soviet Involvement," 28.

88. "Hassanein Heykal's Memoirs," *Ma'ariv*, April 30, 1975, 15.

89. Uri Bar Yosef, *The Guard That Slept on His Watch*, 48.

90. On the missiles based in Egypt, see Shimon Yiftach, *Ma'arachot 217–218* (September 1971), 19.

91. Moshe Dayan, *A New Map in New Relations*. See Vitan, "Soviet Involvement," 25.

92. Mati Meizel, "The Soviet Union's Aims in the War of Attrition," *Ma'arachot 335* (May 1994), 21.

93. Ibid., 23.

94. Ibid., 24.

95. The lack of these weapons was one of the reasons that Egypt developed its military concept. For a detailed analysis of the concept, see the chapter dealing with it.

96. The Soviet military doctrine was taught at various levels in Egyptian military academies. Many officers were sent to the Soviet Union to complete their military education.

97. According to Jan D. Glasman (*Arms for the Arabs*, 110–111), the strategic weapons that the Soviet Union refused Egypt were Tupolov-22 bombers, "Kitchen" air-to-surface missiles, and Scud SS-4 surface-to-surface missiles. All of these weapons were capable of hitting targets at ranges of hundreds of kilometers. In other words they could strike any area in Israel and provide an effective answer to Egypt's vulnerability. Just before the war, the Soviets supplied Egypt with twelve Scud-type missiles. See Victor Israelyan, *Inside the Kremlin during the Yom Kippur War* (Pennsylvania State University Press, 1995), 59.

98. On "the limited military path," see my chapter dealing with the plan.

99. Captured Egyptian Document 784/6 contains the Soviet advisors' work plan for 1973 instruction programs until December 1973. No mention is made of advisory work beyond the brigade level.

100. Vitan, *Ma'arachot*, 70.

101. Rubinstein, *Red Star on the Nile* (Princeton: Princeton University Press, 1977), 191, 200–201.

102. Mati Meizel, "The Soviet Union's Aims in the War of Attrition," *Ma'arachot* 335 (May 1994), 21.

103. Ibid., 17.

104. Shmuel Segev, *Sadat, The Road to Peace* (Givatayim, 1978), 33.

105. Ibid. Sadat stated that at some point he refused to receive Scud-type surface-to-surface missiles from the Soviet Union because of the proviso that their supervision would remain exclusively in the Russians' hands. Therefore he preferred missiles whose employment, in the event of war, would be independent of dictates from Moscow. The Scuds finally arrived in the spring of 1973, but were not used in the war, except perhaps in one instance toward the end of the fighting, when a missile was fired at an Israeli bridgehead on the east bank.

106. Israel Tal, *Israel's National Security, Few against Many*, discusses the effectiveness of the security doctrine in retrospect, 205.

Chapter 4

1. For a detailed description of Israel's defense layout, see Badri, et al., *The Ramadan War*, 30–31.

2. The Soviet doctrine mentions a fortified layout, in addition to the hasty and deliberate layouts. The relatively thin Bar-Lev Line was regarded as a deliberate layout — not a fortified one. According to the doctrine, the forts on the waterfront were security layouts that functioned as observation posts, deterrent points, and perhaps minor delaying obstacles.

3. *Captured Egyptian Document, 805/7*, "The IDF's Defense System on the Canal and its Capture by the Attacking Forces." The document states that, "it would be a mistake to attempt to overtake the fortresses in the initial stage of the war" since this is what the enemy hopes for (4). The document concludes: "Time should not be wasted in dealing with the fortresses [at this point]; and the troops strength should be preserved for the battle for the first three kilometers east of the canal" (10).

4. On the Soviet combat doctrine and the Soviet advisors in Egypt, see the following chapter.

5. On the need for this weapons system and its implications, see the section on the conception.

6. Order No. 37 (March 3, 1973), issued by Chief of Staff Shazli, dealt with "fighting in an area where the enemy has air superiority." This appears in *Captured Egyptian Document 27/10*, "The Supreme Command's Orders until August 18, 1973."

7. On the basic flaw in the Israeli concept regarding Egypt's ability to launch a war, see the section on the conception.

8. Since this book primarily deals with Egypt's army, I have not included a section on its air force and air defense branch prior to and during the war.

9. On Egyptian activity and the army's solution to overcoming IDF obstacles on the eastern bank, see the discussion of the plan, the canal crossing, artillery, and commando operations in chapters four and five.

10. See the section dealing with deception.

11. One of Shazli's first orders — Order No. 4 (September 25, 1971) — dealing with this issue was entitled "Defense Fortifications" and included a diagram of a reinforced infantry platoon defending a stronghold. This appears in *Captured Egyptian Document 27/10*, "The Supreme Command's Orders until August 18, 1973."

12. On the plan to overcome the canal obstacle and defending strongholds, see the section on the crossing and the appendixes. For an expanded discussion on the embankment and fuel-ignition facilities, see the section on engineering. The Egyptians' struggle with Israeli armor is interwoven throughout the entire work but the main points are discussed in the sections dealing with antitank warfare, commandos, and combat engineers.

13. Sa'ad al-Din Shazli, "An Interview with the Chief of Staff of the Yom Kippur War," in the weekly *al-Arabi*, October 2000.

14. Most of the captured material relates to the Third Army's staff, divisions, and brigades whose headquarters were captured when the IDF transferred to the western bank.

15. A comprehensive summary from various Arab sources on the Yom Kippur War includes official histories, memoirs, personal interviews, symposiums, panel discussions, and speeches, as well as books and articles. See Shmuel Bar's introduction to *The Yom Kippur War in the Arabs' Eyes*, 14–18 [Hebrew].

16. Mahmud Fawzi, *Harb al-Thalath Sanuwat 1967–1970 — Mithkarat al Fariq Awal Mahmud Fawzi Wazir al-Harabiya al Asbaq* (*The Three Year War 1967–1970 — The Memoirs of Lieutenant General Mahmud Fawzi, War Minister*), 190–199 [Arabic]; see also Mustafa Cabha, *Harb al-Istanzaf* (*The War of Attrition*), 36 [Hebrew].

17. Fawzi, 200.

18. According to Muhammad Hassanein Heykal, *The Road to Ramadan* (London, 1977) 50. The Soviet rehabilitation plan, rearmament and training of the Egyptian army should be attributed to Marshal Zacharov, who visited Egypt with Podgorny immediately after the Six-Day War and proposed rebuilding the Egyptian army from its foundations.

19. Ibid., 155. According to the source, Fawzi's offensive plan foresaw only the capture of the area up to the mountain passes.

20. Fawzi, *The Three Year War*, 201. See also Dan Shiftan, *Attrition* (Tel Aviv, 1989), 65. In the original "Al-Hata 200" and "Granite 1," as Heykal notes. We understand "Amalia 200" as a defensive plan that was still operational in 1973.

21. Fawzi, 190, 199.

22. Fawzi, *The Three Year War*, 230–231.

23. Ibid., 301.

24. Ibid., 210. See also *Harb al-Istanzaf*, 137.

25. Ibid., 211.

26. An article published in the Russian journal *Novaya Vremya* (New Time) entitled "The Russians Planned the Yom Kippur" (and cited in Israel's *Bamachaneh*, May 3, 1989, 53) states that Soviet experts — along with a handful

of Egyptian officers — prepared the first draft of "Granite" — Egypt's offensive plan. As various versions evolved, differences of opinion were voiced regarding the plan's chance of success.

27. Heykal, *The Road to Ramadan*, 155.

28. Ibid. "Tahrir 3" in December 1969 was an integrated-force exercise.

29. Fawzi, *The Three Year War*, 365.

30. Ibid., 366.

31. For details on the exercise during its various stages, see ibid., 369–374.

32. In *Attrition*, 78–95, Dan Shiftan discusses the plan's practicality. This issue is the subject for us, but it should be noted that the plan became a solid basis for subsequent offensive plans and a model for exercises at the Nasser Higher Military Academy. Israeli war booty included a map with the draft of an exercise describing Egyptian forces crossing the international border on their way into Israel.

33. Anwar Sadat, *My Life*.

34. Heykal, *The Road to Ramadan*, 135.

35. These reservations struck root in the Israeli intelligence establishment and developed into its "concept." It was this concept that failed to warn the IDF of the approaching war in October 1973.

36. Mahmud Riad, "Muzakarat" (Memoirs), in the Jordanian publication *al-Dastur* (November 1, 1989).

37. See the section on war aims.

38. Captured documents indicate January 14 as the earliest date for the offensive on the revised master plan. See Avi-Shai, "Egypt on the Eve of the Yom Kippur War," 35.

39. Abd al-Ghani Gamasi, *Muthkarat al-Gamasi, Harb October 1973* (*Al-Gamasi's Memoirs, The 1973 October War*), 200.

40. Gamasi (206) brings statements that he made at an international conference on the 1973 October War (held at Cairo University, 1975).

41. Ibid., 207–208.

42. See Fawzi's plan.

43. Gamasi, 201.

44. According to Gamasi, "This is How We Duped Israeli Intelligence," *Ma'ariv*, October 8, 1989 (Shefi Gabai's translation from the Egyptian weekly, *October*), the Egyptians estimated that first waves would amount to at least 85,000 casualties.

45. Gamasi, 201.

46. Ibid., 202.

47. To the best of my knowledge, the first exercise, "Tahrir 2," was carried out in April 1969. Prior to this there had only been staff exercises.

48. Sa'ad al-Din al-Shazli, *Crossing the Canal*, 11–12.

49. Ibid., 12–16.

50. Shazli claims that this was the only concept that could realize the Egyptian military option. See also Bar, *The Yom Kippur War in the Arabs' Eyes*, 27.

51. Ibid., 17. The "Tahrir" exercises were also held in the year prior to the war, and included "Tahrir 27" (November 1972) and "Tahrir 35" (May-June 1973).

52. Ibid., 17–19.

53. Ibid., 19.

54. Excluding Shazli's book, we have no other eyewitness accounts of internal discussions at Egyptian GHQ from this period.

55. Evidence of Egyptian plans to reach the mountain passes can be found in the military report "Gaining Control and Capturing the Mountain Passes during the Third Army's Offensive." *Captured Egyptian Document, 471/1 (8)* was prepared just prior to a meeting of the Nineteenth Division's brigade commanders (January 1972).

56. Heykal also states this (155). Gamasi (212) refers to

the plan as "Badar." This name appears in the sources and was later adopted as the name of the war.

57. Shazli, *Crossing the Canal*, 20.

58. Ibid., 20–21.

59. Gamasi, 212. The Egyptian order of battle makes no mention of the Third Army. Gamasi seems to continue dissimulation or minimizes the need to take Egyptian field security into consideration. According to captured documents from the Six-Day War, the First Army was recognized from the period of Egyptian-Syrian unification, and the Syrian army was called el-Jish al-Awal. Be this as it may, all of the units in the Egyptian army that were not part to the two field armies may be referred to as an additional army.

60. Gamasi mentions the standard depth for bridgeheads according to the warfare doctrine, and not the "limited depth" strategy that the Egyptians employed.

61. This is how it appears in the original. Gamasi uses the term that crops up in captured material, "operative halt," which was later coined by the Egyptians and "somehow" adopted by the authors of Israel's "official history." See the section in this chapter dealing with this subject.

62. Gamasi, 216.

63. Shazli, *Crossing the Canal*, 23.

64. Gamasi, 226.

65. Shazli, *Crossing the Canal*, 22. Shazli continues to refer to the plan as "High Towers."

66. Gamasi, 233.

67. Ibid., 235–236. Shazli states in *Crossing the Canal*, 23, that Ismail Ali informed him that the spring of 1973 (six months hence) was a possible date of the war.

68. Shazli, *Crossing the Canal*, 23. The division of the counterattacks into types and timeframes recalls the Soviet combat doctrine that Egypt adopted.

69. Sadat, *The Story of My Life*, 179.

70. See *Captured Egyptian Document, 766/4*, "The Egyptian Chief of Staff's Orders to Infantry Divisions Crossing the Water Obstacle (Canal) — Order No. 41" (March 20, 1973) and my article, "From Order No. 41 to Tahrir 41 — The Egyptian Combat Doctrine during the War," *Ma'arachot 332*, September–October 1993, 46–53. Parts of the original document appear in Shazli, *Crossing the Canal*, 24. Details of the plan are presented in the section on the crossing and in Appendix A.

71. For details on antitank planning, see the section dealing with antitank weapons in chapter 5 and my article "Antitank Weapons as an Answer — Egyptian Plans for Using Antitank Weapons in the Yom Kippur War," *Ma'arachot 346*, February 1996, 6–10.

72. The large-scale, in-depth landing of Egyptian commandos on the Israeli side of the canal was not carried out. The operation was apparently canceled in the later stages of the war when the Egyptians decided to limit the advance.

73. Limited depth is an example of doctrinal dimensions being modified and adapted to Egypt's needs on the canal front.

74. Shazli, *Crossing the Canal*, 24.

75. Ibid., 25.

76. Ibid., 25–26. The plan, as it appears in the book, is fully corroborated by the chief of staff's Order No. 41, *Captured Egyptian Document 766/4*, which details the crossing.

77. On the reinforcement of the divisions that were crossing the canal with artillery and antitank forces, see the section dealing with this matter in chapter 5.

78. From the article by Lieutenant Colonel Avi-Shai, "Egypt Prior to the Yom Kippur War — War Aims and Offensive Plan," *Ma'arachot 250*, July 1976. The map that ap-

pears in the article as the Egyptian offensive plan, "Operation Bader," appears in all of the official Israeli atlases, such as that of Yehuda Wallach, *Not on a Silver Platter*, (Carta, 2000), 112–113.

79. There is nothing in the plan about a deep landing of large numbers of forces in the area of the mountain passes, for example.

80. This is how it appears in the book. In the documents the order is known as "Granite 2 — Improved."

81. Shazli, *Crossing the Canal*, 27–28.

82. Ibid., 12.

83. Gamasi, 387.

84. "Egypt prior to the Yom Kippur War," 21–22.

85. Ibid., 22.

86. Mission depth was shallower than that recommended in the warfare doctrine, but it was suited to the abilities and needs of the Egyptian army. This depth would bring the troops up to Israel's Artillery Road.

87. Some captured documents imply that this stage was planned to take two days.

88. See the section on commando operations in chapter 5.

89. To the best of my knowledge, the Egyptians did not use this term. The only halt mentioned was the "tactical halt" (*Captured Egyptian Document 116/11*, "The Electronic Warfare Orders/Third Army Headquarters"). This was the term that Egyptian commentators later employed, and that was adopted by Israeli scholars retrospectively to explain the Egyptians' decision not to develop the armored offensive they had considered prior to and during the war.

90. Evidence of the planning of this stage appears in a handful of captured Egyptian documents and maps, all of which were printed before the end of January 1973. Later documents contain no details about the stage, only laconic mention of it. Scholars attribute the lack of details to the Soviet doctrine which holds that detailed planning is needed for the immediate task, and only general planning (objectives and routes) for the coming offensive.

91. Dani Asher, "From 'Order No. 41' to 'Tahrir 41' — from the Egyptian Warfare Doctrine to War." *Ma'arachot* 332 (September–October 1993), 48–49.

92. Sadat, *The Story of My Life*, 184.

93. Zeira, *The October '73 War: Myth against Reality*, 68–69.

94. "From Order 41 to Tahrir 41," 49, 53.

95. K. von Clausewitz, *Principles of War* (Tel Aviv, 1048) 198. See also Yehoshafat Harkabi, *War and Strategy* (Surprise, Deception, and Dissimilation), 493.

96. Barton Whaley, *Stratagem: Deception and Surprise in War* (Cambridge, 1969), 15.

97. Barton Whaley, *Codeword Barbarossa* (Cambridge, 1973) 173.

98. The terms were coined by Roberta Wohlstetter who analyzed the surprise attack at Pearl Harbor. Roberta Wohlstetter, *Pearl Harbor, Warning and Decision* (Stanford University Press, 1962) 2–3. A "signal" is a hint, a sign, or a fragment of evidence that describes a certain danger or the enemy's movements or intentions. "Noise" is a similar (or different) message from various information sources but is not helpful for understanding the expected event.

99. Dani Asher, "Deception in Allenby's Operations in the Conquest of Eretz-Israel," *Ma'arachot* 329, March–April 1993, 20.

100. Michael Hendel, "Intelligence and Deception," in *Intelligence and National Security* (Ma'arachot, 1987) 385. See also Michael Hendel, *Perception, Deception, and Surprise: The Case of the Yom Kippur War* (Jerusalem, 1976); and Charles Cruickshank's introduction to his *Deception in World War II* (Oxford University Press, 1981).

101. Michael Hendel, *Intelligence and Deception*, 387.

102. Ibid., 388–389.

103. Michael Hendel, *Intelligence and Deception*, 412–413. According to Barton Whaley, *Stratagem: Deception and Surprise in War*, 234, and according to the attempt to propose a methodology for assessing the cost-effectiveness of deception in *Thoughts on the Cost-Effectiveness and Related Tactics in the Air War 1939 to 1945* (Princeton and ORD/CIA Analytic, Methodology Research Division, March 1979).

104. Efraim Kam's comprehensive study, *Surprise Attack*, details this issue in the Yom Kippur War context. See pages 111, 137, and 138.

105. Voroshilov Lectures, 322.

106. Ibid.

107. On the use of institution and the modern Soviet perception, see V. Sevorov, *GUSM The Soviet Service of Strategic Deception*, I. D. R. Swiss, August 1985.

108. For more information on these incidents, see Jiri Valenta, *Deception Operation, Deception and Surprise in Soviet Interventions, Studies in the East–West Context* (UK, 1980). See also Jiri Valenta, "Perspectives on Soviet Intervention," *Survival* 24, no. 2 (1982), 51–61.

109. Aharon Zeevi, "Political Views in the Egyptian Plan for Deception in the Yom Kippur War," *Ma'arachot* 338, October–November 1994, 6.

110. Ibid., 6–7.

111. For an all-inclusive study of Egyptian preparations in strategic deception prior to the Yom Kippur War, see Janice Gross Stein, "Military Deception, Strategic Surprise and Conventional Deterrence: A Political Analysis of Egypt and Israel, 1971–1973," *Journal of Strategic Studies* 16/5/1 (March 1982), 95–120.

112. Aharon Zeevi, *Ma'arachot* 338, 8.

113. Ibid., 9.

114. *Captured Egyptian Document — Brochure No. 65*, "Operational Deception in an Offensive Crossing of the Suez Canal" (War Ministry, Military Studies Branch, October 17, 1970, 34) states that operational deception is based on four activities: camouflage, decoys, dissimulation, and disinformation.

115. Aharon Zeevi, *The Egyptian Deception Plan*, 39.

116. Aharon Zeevi, "The Egyptian Deception in the Yom Kippur War Plan" (M.A. Thesis, Tel Aviv University, September 1980) 30.

117. *Captured Egyptian Document 290/12* (September 30, 1973), "Organization Order for a Two-Echelon Strategic-Operational Headquarters Exercise — by Radio: Tahrir 41."

118. Since IDF intelligence estimated that the Egyptian army was incapable of attacking and subduing all of Sinai, it naturally assumed that this was only an exercise.

119. According to Aharon Zeevi, *The Egyptian Deception Plan*, 40–41.

120. According to Zeira, 115, the information that Egyptian reservists were being discharged convinced the Israeli intelligence officer beyond all doubt that a field exercise was taking place.

121. According to Zeira, 115, the IDF received information from its sophisticated intelligence-gathering methods that an Egyptian military exercise — the annual autumn exercise — was about to commence.

122. Zeira, 114.

123. Zeira, 116–119.

124. Muhammad Hassanein Heykal, *The Sphinx and the Commissar* (Tel Aviv, 1981) [Hebrew].

125. Zeira, 119–126.

126. The *Dictionary of Military Terms* defines deception as an act, or series of acts, generally of an offensive nature of relatively short duration, that are carried out by real

forces by means of decoys in order to conceal activity, and divert the enemy's attention from the main effort and lead him astray.

127. See the section on the October 14 plan for an armored attack.

128. According to the Soviet doctrine, the attacking force should designate a large portion of the order of battle to deception operations. *Captured Egyptian Document—Brochure No. 65* (39–40) states that for every infantry division on the offensive, two to three infantry battalions, one tank battalion, and other units should be set aside for deceptive feints.

129. Badri, *The Ramadan War*, 50.

130. Ibid., 51. The navy carried out similar acts, transferring vessels from one region to another, and even beyond Egypt's waters.

131. Ibid.

132. Various weapon decoys were found in the vicinity of the western bank, such as those deployed in the regular defense layout.

133. According to *Captured Egyptian Document 290/12* (September 30, 1973) "Order for Guaranteeing the Offensive Operation 'Granite 2 — Revised,'" the bridging forces had to "exploit the pauses in the crossing in order to trick the enemy by making real bridges appear as though they had destroyed. This was done with smoke and fire, and by dismantling parts of them."

134. A small number of decoy weapons were produced for each of the armies proximate to the opening of the war: bogus tanks, artillery pieces, mortars, recoilless cannons, and machine guns.

135. GHQ and divisional battalions used smoke screens extensively, mainly at the crossing areas, to conceal troop concentrations from aerial observation and Israeli air strikes, and to obstruct ground observation and low trajectory fire.

Chapter 5

1. General Lieutenant Zoeyalov, "The Soviet Warfare Doctrine," *Soviet Military Thinking in the Nuclear Age*, 81.

2. Other objectives could be added to the list of strategic targets: disrupting the enemy's system of mobilizing his reserves; removing or preventing the enemy's allies from joining the war; crippling the enemy's air, missile, and nuclear facilities. See *Voroshilov Lectures*, 55. The Soviet doctrinal work, *The Division (Brigade) in an Offensive*, 3, was translated by the Egyptians into Arabic and used as a basic guideline. It defines the offensive's goal as defeating the enemy, seizing his territory by inflicting powerful blows in coordination with all the forces taking part in the battle, breaking through his defense line, and advancing aggressively into his depth.

3. "The Use of Ground Forces in the Soviet Warfare Doctrine," Hatzav 830/001, October 1981, 7. In the Yom Kippur War, the Egyptian army attacked with two field armies on a single front under the GHQ's command, which functioned essentially like the Soviet one.

4. On the strategic offensive that was studied in Egyptian military academies, see "Strategic Offensive Operation," Lecture, A-163, Nasser High Military Academy, 1969 [Arabic].

5. *The Use of Ground Forces in the Soviet Warfare Doctrine*, 8.

6. On the use of artillery during the offensive, see the section on this in this chapter.

7. The Soviet army has two types of field armies: multi-branch and armored. In the Yom Kippur War, the Egyptian army had only two field armies. Soviet army headquarters on an offensive front might include four field armies and one armored army. *The Use of Ground Forces in the Soviet Warfare Doctrine*, 9–10.

8. On the Soviet field army in a World War II offensive, see *Army Offensive Operations in the Great Patriotic War,* Training Aid, A 171, Nasser High Military Academy, 1969.

9. According to *Voroshilov Lectures,* 58, an offensive's front may be 300–400 kilometers in length and 600–800 kilometers in depth after twelve to fifteen days of combat.

10. *Army Offensive Operations in Great Patriotic War,* 10.

11. According to *Voroshilov Lectures,* 68.

12. Ibid., 69.

13. Ibid., 119.

14. *The Division (Brigade) in an Offensive,* 3. In the introduction to the original version, Major General Pelekh, a professor of military science, and apparently a Russian general, discusses the combat training of the Egyptian armed forces, taking into account their formations, weapons, equipment and the geographical conditions of Sinai. According to the author, the book was written by a group of instructors at the Nasser Academy and was designed for officers at the brigade and divisional levels and cadets at Egyptian military colleges.

15. *The Use of Ground Forces in the Soviet Warfare Doctrine,* 43.

16. *The Division (Brigade) in an Offensive,* 3.

17. *The Use of Ground Forces in the Soviet Warfare Doctrine,* 44. Maximum priority will be given to speed in a battlefield when nuclear weapons might be employed.

18. According to "The Organization and Application of an Infantry, Mechanized Infantry, or Armored Division in Various Stages of the Battle," *Captured Egyptian Document* 1/511, 2, the attack (breaching the enemy's defenses) is the division's primary goal, and requires assistance from field army sources so that optimal conditions for the breakthrough can be attained.

19. Ibid., 9–10.

20. *Voroshilov Lectures,* 304. The division will move out of an assembly area forty to sixty kilometers behind first-level divisions.

21. On the division's role in advanced stages of the attack, see *Captured Egyptian Document,* 851/0005, "The Armored Division Advance and in an Encounter Battle," Armed Forces GHQ, Military Research Branch.

22. *The Use of Ground Forces in the Soviet Warfare Doctrine,* 45.

23. At the brigade level, it is unnecessary to determine a daily mission since it is prone to frequent change, inter alia, because of the changes in the enemy's layout.

24. *The Division (Brigade) on the Offensive,* 12–13.

25. On the depth of missions relative to the first-echelon division's missions in the Yom Kippur War, see the section in chapter 4 dealing with the narrowing of dimensions.

26. According to the Soviet doctrine, the enemy's layout will be analyzed as though it operated according to the same doctrine.

27. Soviet experts in Egypt attempting to adapt the doctrine to the Sinai theater regarded the Israeli defense layout on the eastern bank as though it were not next to the canal. The line of strongholds was considered a protective layout whose troops were covering a covering force.

28. *The Division (Brigade) in an Offensive,* 15.

29. Ibid., 16.

30. According to the doctrine, the rate of advance by an armored division in combat is twenty kilometers an hour in daylight and fifteen an hour at night. Its range of activ-

ity is between forty and sixty kilometers. It is capable of fighting continuously for three to five days on a front 250 kilometers in length. See *The Organization and Application of an Infantry, Mechanized Infantry, Armored Division in Various Stages of the Battle*, 8. These parameters apparently did not fit Egyptian needs and capabilities in the Yom Kippur War, nor were the Egyptian armored divisions used as such during the war.

31. *The Division (Brigade) in an Offensive*, 16–17.

32. According to *Voroshilov Lectures*, 302, the depth of the division's attack will also be between fifteen and twenty kilometers.

33. *The Division (Brigade) in an Offensive*, 18, 28. According to the doctrine's calculations and parameters, an attacking division will need a fortified layout for the deployment of approximately 300 artillery pieces in the breakthrough zone. This comes to 70 to 80 cannons for every kilometer of front (see page 29 in same source). Other figures for the density of artillery in the general attack and during the preparatory fire for the breakthrough reach a similar number. This comes to 85 cannons for every kilometer of front. On preparatory fire, see the section on artillery.

34. *Voroshilov Lectures*, 303.

35. On the doctrinal recommendations for crossing water obstacles and constructing bridgeheads, see the relevant section on the crossing.

36. On the Egyptian armored attack of October 14, see the relevant section in this chapter.

37. This was also the opinion of the former chief of staff, Shazli, who rejected an attempt to develop an attack from the bridgeheads. See Shazli, *Crossing the Canal*, 176–180.

38. While the Egyptians were studying this subject, the IDF, too, was keeping track of it. The need to understand the doctrine led the Israeli intelligence branch to publish an analysis in January 1970 of the Egyptian and Warsaw Pact armies' plans for a water crossing. Another study was published in July 1970 entitled "The Principles of Crossing a Water Obstacle, According to the Soviet Army's Warfare Doctrine." On August 28 the Lebanese paper *al-Anwar* printed an article based on a British intelligence document, entitled "Details on the Russians' Training, Arming, and Techniques for Crossing a Water Obstacle." The article was translated into Hebrew on September 7, 1970.

39. *Voroshilov Lectures*, 357–359. The section on water crossing focuses on rivers, especially the tactic of "crossing from movement," which suited Soviet needs in the European theater.

40. According to *Field Regulations* of the Soviet armed forces from 1962, and that was valid in the late 1960s and early 1970s. I obtained a copy in German translation—*Felddienstvorschrift der Streitkrafte der UdSSR*—Division Regiment, Militarverlag des Verteitgungs Ministeriums der UdSSR (Moscow, 1962).

41. Ibid., 186.

42. The Suez Canal was only 170 meters wide in 1973, but its importance was crucial.

43. The Soviet doctrine discerns three types of defense layouts, based on their strength: fortified, organized, and improvised defense layouts.

44. When this method is implemented in a short battle in a campaign, it is also termed an "improvised crossing." But since this method did not apply Egypt's needs, I will not discuss its finer details.

45. The "crossing from movement" also includes the advanced force in this stage.

46. Lieutenant Colonel Froika, "Equipment for Crossing a Water Obstacle," *Ma'arachot* 234–235 (January–February 1974). The article was also published in *Ma'arachot* 230 before the war, and describes in great detail the influencing factors on the crossing, the methods and kinds of equipment needed that were developed in the East Bloc, and some of which were acquired by Egypt before the war.

47. Under certain conditions tanks can cross by submerging. But this system was not adapted to the conditions at the Suez Canal.

48. On the system that the Egyptians chose to cross the Suez Canal, see Chief of Staff Order No. 41 in Appendix A.

49. *Field Regulations*, 189.

50. The subject was irrelevant to the conditions of the Yom Kippur War.

51. One of the first doctrinal reports, "Training Paper No. 68/2," was published by the armed forces instruction branch in 1968 and deals with the organization of tactical training for a reinforced infantry company in an attack while crossing a water obstacle.

52. Some exercises were carried out in broad daylight and observed by IDF soldiers on the eastern bank of al-Balah Island.

53. A concluding instruction manual, TK-50 of the Nasser Higher Military Academy, "The Requirements for Preparing and Implementing Special Preparations to Secure the Bridgeheads at the Suez Canal and Continue the Offensive from the Bridgeheads" (Captured Egyptian Document 851/0006), was published in 1972. A more general manual preceding this one was taught in the Nasser Higher Military Academy "Peculiarities of an Offensive Involving a Water Barrier Crossing," c.s.c. 122 (no date given) [Arabic].

54. Captured Egyptian Document, 766/44. "Egyptian Chief of Staff Order to Infantry Divisions Crossing a Water Obstacle (the canal) — Details of the Forces, Equipment, and Crossing Priority," Order No. 41. See Appendix A.

55. *Captured Egyptian Document*, 851/0006, 1.

56. The manual was supposed to deal with a wide-scale attack for liberating the Sinai Peninsula. The changes and reduction of the operation's scope were decided later.

57. See Captured War Document in Appendix A.

58. *Captured War Document*, 472/1, "Planning the Crossing of the Suez Canal." The document is anonymous, and no publisher or date is given. It was apparently written by the field army's artillery GHQ close to the outbreak of the war.

59. The Egyptians prepared most of the descents to the water under the observant eyes of the Israelis a long time before the war. According to Aryeh Brown, *Moshe Dayan in the Yom Kippur War*, 48, 62, from mid–September 1973 the Egyptians improved forty of the eighty-five descents to the water — after nearly a two-year halt — only in the Third Army's sector. On October 4 the Egyptians reported that an additional thirty descents in this sector had been completed.

60. Shazli, *Crossing the Canal*, 46.

61. Ibid., 2. The document emphasizes the details of the artillery weapons and equipment in each of the priorities. The number of the artillery pieces — according to Shazli, *Crossing the Canal*, 48.

62. Shazli, *Crossing the Canal*, 47.

63. *Captured Egyptian Document*, 275/12, "Timetable for the Attack and Crossing by the Various Echelons." Chief of Staff Shazli states that the timetables were twice as long as those obtained in training exercises and 50 percent as long as those obtained at night. See Shazli, *Crossing the Canal*, 50.

64. Yona Bandman, "The Third Army Crosses the Suez Canal, October 6–8, 1973," *Ma'arachot* 296 (December 1994), 27.

65. The Egyptians had to transfer 1,000 tanks and 13,500 support vehicles across the canal within six hours from breaching the embankment. Shazli, *Crossing the Canal*, 47.

66. According to Bandman's article, "The Third Army Crosses the Suez Canal," and based on Third Army Diaries, the establishment of the Third Army's bridges took much longer than planned, while the Second Army erected its bridges on schedule.

67. Shazli, *Crossing the Canal*, 51.

68. Most of the captured documents define H-Hour as the last light on the first day of the attack. Advancing the time of the attack to 14:05 was decided only a very short time before the war because of Egypt's need to reach a compromise with its Syrian allies.

69. *Captured Egyptian Document*, 851/0006.

70. Ibid., 2.

71. Thus, the two field armies remained divided by a gap, which was later exploited by the IDF forces for building a corridor to reach the waterline, cross the canal, and capture territory on the western bank.

72. *Captured Egyptian Document*, 851/0006, 3. The analysis takes into account the terrain and Egypt's view of the Israeli defense layout, including the IDF forces that would probably be counterattacking.

73. Ibid., 3–4.

74. Ibid., 4. On the use of landed forces in the planning stage and during the war, see the section on commandos in this chapter.

75. For instructions for building bridgeheads, and the plan for crossing the Suez Canal, see *Captured Egyptian Document*, 472/1, 3.

76. *Captured Egyptian Document*, 851/0006. 5.

77. The plan for crossing the Suez Canal, *Captured Egyptian Document*, 472/1, 3. All of the timetables are from this source.

78. Ibid.

79. According to Shazli, *Crossing the Canal*, 46, the chief of staff estimated that the bridgeheads would be consolidated at a depth of seven and a half kilometers and length of fifteen kilometers by H-Hour plus 18.

80. Ibid., 10

81. *Captured Egyptian Document*, 851/0006. 18.

82. On the theory and use of combat engineers in the war, see the section on combat engineers in this chapter.

83. *Captured Egyptian Document*, 851/0006, 22.

84. During my visits to the Suez Canal after the Yom Kippur War I saw a large number of diesel-based apparatuses for producing smoke — especially smoke generators.

85. *Captured Egyptian Document*, 851/0006, 22.

86. Ibid., 24–26. See also the section on artillery in this chapter.

87. As the war approached, orders were changed and the artillery preparatory barrage was extended to thirty-eight minutes, and then further increased to fifty-eight minutes. See *Captured Egyptian Document*, 149/11, the order from the Third Army's artillery commander for "Granite 2 Amended," September 1973.

88. On the missions of the first-echelon battalion and its crossing schedule, see *Captured Egyptian Document*, 129/11 (the decision of the battalion commander of the Seventy-fourth Brigade, Twenty-fourth Infantry for engaging in an attack while breaching the Suez Canal — reading the battalion commander's map), August 1973. 3

89. *Captured Egyptian Document*, 472/1, the plan for crossing the Suez Canal, 3.

90. This is how it appears in the 1972 instruction manual. Ibid., 26. In subsequent material the Egyptians postpone the capture of the strongholds until a later stage in the fighting.

91. On air defense plans and antiaircraft weapons, see *Captured Egyptian Document*, 268/12 (air defense for the reinforced infantry divisions during the crossing).

92. Ibid., 28. The Egyptians apparently preferred this method of defense and were ready to meet the IDF attack from a static position.

93. The IDF chose to counterattack on October 8 from the flanks and to the north of the Second Army's (Second Division) bridgeheads. Here, and especially at the bridgeheads, the IDF came up against stubborn Egyptian resistance reinforced with antitank units.

94. This subject was studied and drilled at the Nasser Higher Military Academy. See undated captured manual, "Defense of Captured Bridgehead by Infantry Division, C.S.C. 633."

95. This is how it appears in a 1972 instruction manual, see Ibid., 29. Chief of Staff Order No. 41 presents a more detailed structure. See Appendix A and the formula for deployment at the bridgehead at H plus 24.

96. See Appendix F.

97. "Defense of Captured Bridgehead by Infantry Division, C.S.C. 633," 10–11.

98. *Captured Egyptian Document* 805/7 (the IDF's defense system on the canal and seizing it by the attacking forces), 2. See Appendix F.

99. On the battery and incendiary facilities, see the section on the engineering problems that the Egyptians had to deal with.

100. *Captured Egyptian Document* 805/7, 12.

101. *Captured Egyptian Document* 851/0006, 12.

102. Ibid., 26–27.

103. Ibid., 14.

104. Only a small number of Israeli fortifications were attacked in the first stages of the fighting, mostly in the northern isolated sector.

105. See *Captured Egyptian Document* 805/7, 8.

106. On Soviet combat engineers, see Major L. N., "Soviet Combat Engineers — The Main Features of their Operations in the Past and Present," *Ma'arachot* 130 (August 1960), 66–71.

107. *Captured Egyptian Document* 851/8, July 1970 (engineering support of the brigade and division in an offensive).

108. A similar book dealing with combat engineers in a defensive battle fell into Israeli hands, "Combat Engineer Support of a Brigade and Division in a Defensive Battle," *Captured Egyptian Document* 851/10. The book was translated into Arabic and circulated in the Egyptian army in 1970. It became the basis of the fortification plan in the "Amalia 200" defense plan.

109. "Soviet Combat Engineers — The Main Features of their Operations in the Past and Present," 66. At the start of the Second World War, combat engineer field armies were established mostly for fortification work.

110. *Captured Egyptian Document* 195/11 (Battle Order No. 1/73 to Third Army, Nineteenth Division Engineer Headquarters, April 1973). According to the document, the division's Forty-ninth Combat Engineers Battalion was the primary engineering force in the offensive. The division was reinforced with the Fifty-first Engineering Battalion (109th Combat Engineers Brigade) which, according to the plan, became field army's reserve force (in addition to the bridging units) after the crossing.

111. Ibid., 3, provides details on the order of battle of the divisional engineering battalion. In addition to three companies of sappers, it included one company of road constructors, one company of mechanical engineering equipment, one engineer reconnaissance company, and one headquarters company.

112. See Major L. Merhav, "The Soviet Warfare Concept of the Offensive, the Different Branches and their Role in the Offensive," *Ma'arachot* 147 (October 1962), 26–27.

113. *Captured Egyptian Document* 851/8, 2. See also "Soviet Combat Engineers — The Main Features of their Operations in the Past and Present," 66–67. In battle conditions of the European theater, assistance to the crossing of a water obstacle was the primary mission in the advancing stage. The Egyptians adopted this move in the Suez Canal sector, integrating it into opening stage of the breakthrough of the enemy's defense lines.

114. According to *Captured Egyptian Document* 195/11, 2, the Forty-ninth Battalion's reconnaissance platoon was responsible in the preparatory stage for the following tasks: gathering information on the enemy's layout that require engineering solutions, such as strongholds, flanks and the dirt embankment in the division's sector; locating obstacles in the rear of the enemy's front lines; locating minefields on the eastern bank; locating areas suitable for a breakthrough; locating crossing areas suitable for rafts and bridges (on both banks); following enemy activity that indicates his plans to make a canal crossing.

115. Ibid. The reconnaissance platoon's missions in these stages: operating two mobile observation points at the bridgeheads; locating breaches and corridors through enemy obstacles and fortifications; checking and determining routes of advance; observing the enemy's engineering equipment and its use; locating obstacles and devising solutions to overcome them. As the battle develops, combat engineer recon units will carry out patrols ahead of and on the flanks of the main force, identifying minefields and obstacles, and testing the suitability of the roads for missions.

116. This includes minefields and obstacles in the attacker's territory, built as part of his defense system.

117. *Captured Egyptian Document* 851/8, 10–11, 29–30. The doctrinal chapter dealing clearing paths through the minefields discusses the number of paths needed for each unit, the size of the force, and its equipment and modus operandi (manually, pipe charges — Bangalore torpedoes — and rolling drums). Because of conditions at the Suez Canal, the Egyptians could dispense with this chapter. In the Yom Kippur War, the task of clearing obstacles included passageways in the dirt embankment on the eastern bank. For more information, see further in this section.

118. *Captured Egyptian Document* 195/11, 3. Two companies of the Forty-ninth Battalion acted as a mobile obstacle force. Company B with the antitank reserve No. 2, and Company C with the antitank reserve No. 1.

119. Roads will be blocked by the improvised planting of minefields. The company-sized mobile obstacle force will consist of six APCs with trailers for mine planting. The Egyptian companies had 1,800 mines, which were enough for 1,200 to 1,600 meters of minefields.

120. "Soviet Combat Engineers — The Main Features of their Operations in the Past and Present," 69–70.

121. *Captured Egyptian Document* 195/11, 3. Two companies from the division's engineer battalion had to fortify the division's headquarters in the preparatory stage of the campaign. The third company would fortify the battalion's assembly area.

122. Much of the document "Engineering Assistance for a Brigade and Division in an Offensive Battle" (*Captured Egyptian Document* 851/8) deals with fortification construction and preparation of positions for various weapons. The document discusses in detail the nature of the objective, personnel strength, and time required. According to *Captured Egyptian Document* 195/11, 9, at least 30 percent of the soldiers in each unit have to be allocated to fortification work, canal improvement, and layout maintenance in the preparatory stage.

123. According to *Captured Egyptian Document* 195/11, 9, fortification activity during the attack will require a quick entrenchment at each halt, with priority given to headquarters and firing positions for tanks and primary weapons. This engineering task will be carried out with dynamite.

124. Order No. 41.

125. Ibid., 22.

126. Ibid., 24.

127. Ibid., 23. Each team was given one infantry carriage.

128. Ibid., 23–24. The instructions describe in great detail the allocation of infantry carriages to all units. The goal is to have the largest possible number of mines transferred in as short a time as possible. Seventy-two carriages were allocated to the two first echelon brigades (and only twenty-seven to the second-echelon brigade).

129. On the mine-laying reserves' role, see *Captured Egyptian Document* 553/2, "Presentation of the Objective: The Engineering Company as a Mobile Mining Reserve Force in the Attacking Division," Sixth Division Headquarters, May 13, 1973.

130. Shazli, *Crossing the Canal*, 38.

131. *Captured Egyptian Document* 170/009, "Organizing Defense Forces against Chemical and Bacteriological Weapons in a Military Offensive while Engaging in a Planned Assault-Crossing of a Water Obstacle in the Direction of the Shore," Nasser Higher Military Academy, 1972.

132. Ibid., 8.

133. Shazli, *Crossing the Canal*, 40–41.

134. See, for example, "A Battalion Commander's Plan (24th Infantry Brigade) for Attack while Crossing the Canal," *Captured Egyptian Document* 120/11. The plan calls for the artillery to destroy the incendiary pipelines between H-Hour and H-Hour plus 22. See *Captured Egyptian Document* 614/2 that assigns the first wave the task of destroying (plugging up) the napalm canisters.

135. As intelligence officer in the Southern Command, I took part in the experiment. The dates are from an Egyptian military intelligence memo (July 11, 1973); the subject: "Flammable Facilities on the Canal's East Bank Dirt Embankment." *Captured Egyptian Document* 680/2.

136. Ibid., 1.

137. *Captured Egyptian Document* 116/013, "A Reconnaissance Patrol's Report — Fifth Brigade/Nineteenth Division, May 13, 1973."

138. Liwa (General) Ibrahim Fuad Mahmud Nasser, director of military combat intelligence.

139. *Captured Egyptian Document* 680/2, 2.

140. Gamasi, 309–310.

141. Lieutenant Colonel Avi-Shai, *Egypt on the Eve of the Yom Kippur War*, 35n25.

142. *Al-Akhbar* (Egypt), May 29, 1975.

143. The Egyptian armor commander also recalls in his memoirs the cutting and sealing of the pipeline with cement. See Kamal Hasan Ali, *Warriors and Peacemakers*, Ma'arachot, 1993, 45 [Hebrew translation].

144. Shazli, *Crossing the Canal*, 41.

145. Ibid., 161.

146. According to Shazli, *Crossing the Canal*, 38, the dirt embankment rose twenty meters above the canal.

147. Shazli considers this problem as one of the most serious challenges facing the planners. He refers to it as a "breakthrough" — a doctrinal term used in an offensive battle. *Crossing the Canal*, 39.

148. *Captured Egyptian Document* 851/0006, 21. The

1972 instruction manual on the water crossing still presented this option. The use of automatic water pumps is mentioned in another section.

149. Ibid., 40.

150. The job of opening the breaches fell on the combat engineers attached to the infantry brigades in the first waves. The engineers were reinforced, according to the battle order, with engineer units of the Nineteenth Division. *Captured Egyptian Document* 195/11, 3–4. The Fifty-first Engineers Battalion of the 109th Engineering Brigade reinforced the division: two companies to the Seventh Brigade and one company to the Fifth Brigade.

151. Ibid., 163–164.

152. See Gamasi, 312.

153. Shazli, *Crossing the Canal*, 166.

154. *Voroshilov Lectures*, 131.

155. The Soviet's main need in the Don and Stalingrad campaigns in 1942 was to buy time in order to organize the troops for the offensive. Ibid., 134.

156. Much can learned about the Egyptian army's defensive warfare doctrine — especially at the units' level — from the Egyptian Field Regulations (beginning in 1972), from instructional material and numerous captured documents on Egyptian defense layouts ("Amalia 200" plan), and other papers dealing with the construction of bridgeheads on the eastern side.

157. The main goal of the Egyptians' defensive deployment was to inflict heavy losses on the attacking enemy. This tactic was also used by the Soviets in the Battle of Kursk in 1943. See *Voroshilov Lectures, 133*.

158. Modern defense must be able to repel ABC attacks, tank offensives, air strikes, artillery barrages, and massive armor and infantry assaults. It must also prevent the enemy from landing forces from the sea and air, and have the capacity to destroy enemy forces that break through the defense layouts. See *Voroshilov Lectures, 140*.

159. At the higher levels of the field army and front, the battle layout will include additional elements, such as surface-to-surface rocket and missile groups, aircraft, and special reserves. For more information, see *Voroshilov Lectures, 158–159*.

160. On Egyptian plans to use artillery and antiaircraft forces, see the relevant sections.

161. The Egyptians attributed equal importance to each of the bridgeheads, on the assumption that local counterattacks, like the main ones, could be made against any one of them.

162. Additional divisional reserves — such as antitank forces, engineers, and chemical warfare units — were also deployed. See the relevant sections.

163. *Voroshilov Lectures, 159*.

164. For the first time in the history of warfare, the Egyptians reinforced the first-echelon battalion with a large quantity of antitank rockets. See the section on this subject in this chapter.

165. On the use of the Egyptian obstacle layout during the Yom Kippur War, see the section on combat engineering in this chapter.

166. *The Use of Ground Forces in the Soviet Warfare Doctrine*, 102–103.

167. Ibid., 117–118.

168. Phillip A. Karber, "The Soviet Anti-tank Debate," *Survival*, May–June 1975, 105–111.

169. Unlike the Egyptians, who put nearly all their faith in antitank rockets, the Syrians employed tanks as the main weapon against IDF armor.

170. The Egyptians termed the portable Sager rockets "Fahad," and the APCs carrying the BRDM-2 rockets "Leopard."

171. Zvi Lanir, *Fundamental Surprise — The National Intelligence Crisis*, 48–49.

172. On the "Sager's" unexpected appearance on the battlefield, see Dani Asher, "From 'Order 41' to 'Tahrir 41,'" 49.

173. Shazli claims that the Egyptians' innovation was not in new weapons, since they were common knowledge. The main innovations were in training, fighting techniques, and the army's determination and tenacity. *Crossing the Canal*, 56.

174. For more on this subject, see Lieutenant Colonel M. Hofman's comprehensive article, "Antitank Defense in the Soviet Doctrine," *Tzeklon* 7 (December 1980), 41–48.

175. Ibid., 42.

176. Ibid., 43.

177. The ideal Soviet solution for defense against enemy tanks was the proper integration and effective use of all task-oriented and other weapons. See Lieutenant Colonel Y. Volodin, "Antitank Weapons in Defense, *Soviet Military Review*, May 1975, 18–20.

178. The Soviets first developed rockets as the infantry's antitank weapons in 1955. See Col. B Antsiz, "Antitank Guided Missiles in Defense," *Soviet Military Review*, July 1975, 15–17.

179. Karber, "The Soviet Anti-Tank Debate," 107; and Major General G. Biryukov and Colonel G. Melnikov, *Antitank Warfare*, 79–86.

180. Ibid., 78–79.

181. Ibid., 82. The authors compare the effects of an antitank rocket on a tank to the effects of a machine gun, modern artillery shell, or aircraft on cavalry.

182. Ibid., 84.

183. On the doctrinal revolution in the world's armies since the absorption of antitank rockets, see B. Amidror, "Infantry and Warfare against Tanks on the Modern Battlefield," *Tzeklon*, 7, December 1980, 11. The author contends that the rocket succeeded the antitank cannon and recoilless gun as the main antitank weapon and has had a direct influence on tactical maneuvering in the fighting. The antitank weapon has become the mainstay in the infantry layout and is no longer merely a "support factor."

184. In Arabic the antitank guided missiles are *makthufat muwajaha nudad lil-dababat* (MMMD).

185. *Captured Egyptian Document* 693/M 64/27, "The Combat Principles of a Guided Missile Battalion against Tanks" (printed by the armed forces' Office of Publications, 1971).

186. The Soviet term for Sager missiles is "Malyutka."

187. The antitank battalions had an organic platoon of (apparently) three 82-millimeter mortars, mainly for providing illumination. The platoon was divided up — one mortar per antitank company.

188. On innovations and technical data for each antitank rocket and missile used during the Yom Kippur War, see Captain Richard F. Timmos, "A.T. Missiles in the Yom Kippur War," *Infantry*, January 1974, 18–22.

189. On the structure and quantity of weapons, see Dani Asher, "The Antitank Weapon as a Solution" (The Egyptians' plan for using antitank weapons in the Yom Kippur War), *Ma'arachot* 346 (February 1996), 6–8.

190. Shazli, *Crossing the Canal*, 24.

191. Third Army divisional plans that fell into Israel's hands reveal that the Nineteenth Division had fifty-four antitank weapons for each kilometer on the crossing front, and the Seventh Division had fifty-seven.

192. Ibid., 188. Shazli relates that each infantry division had 535 launchers.

193. Antitank rocket launcher.

194. The Egyptian infantry divisions performed the

canal crossing. The Nineteenth Division, for example, had an organic battalion of conveyable rockets, a BMP battalion in the mechanized brigade, and one company of conveyable rockets in the infantry brigade. The division was also reinforced with a mobile battalion from the Sixth Division and a company of conveyable rockets from the paratroop brigade. In sum, the sector had sixty ground teams, fourteen BRDMs, one BMP battalion, and twelve "Shmel" jeeps from the field army.

195. See Organization Order No. 2942, "Reorganization of the 'Fahad' antitank guided missile battalion in the Egyptian infantry division." *Captured Egyptian Document*, 468/007.

196. Shazli, *Crossing the Canal*, 24.

197. On the commando units, their organization and use in the war, see the section on commandos in this chapter.

198. BRDM-2 APCs were a new type of weapon that was absorbed in the Egyptian army under the name "Leopard" only a few months before the war. The warfare doctrine held that there were many similarities in the methods of employing APC-mounted launchers and man-portable rockets.

199. Shazli, *Crossing the Canal*, 144, notes that in the March 1973 arms deal Egypt acquired approximately 200 BMP-1 APCs capable of carrying Sager missiles. Some of the vehicles were immediately supplied, and the rest arrived in the third quarter of 1973. This was a new model APC that could convey an infantry squad on its side. It was armed with a smooth-bore, 73-millimeter antitank cannon, a deck-mounted Sager missile launcher, and four more missiles in its belly. Fifty portable missile launchers were also acquired in the same deal.

200. According to Shazli, 163, such a battalion was sent to reinforce each infantry division.

201. On the Soviet warfare doctrine's recommendations for the deployment of various antitank weapons, see Lieutenant Colonel Y. Volodin, "Antitank Weapons for Defense, *Soviet Military Review*, May 1975.

202. On the modus operandi of Egyptian tanks at the bridgeheads, Shazli writes: "The enemy employed his tanks as armor as usually employed. But we employed ours as mobile antitank artillery. This was not due to ignorance of military science but to the policy we chose and whose consequences we were fully aware of. This was done in order to cover up our weaknesses and deny the enemy his advantages." *Crossing the Canal*, 172.

203. The details come from Order No. 41 (Egyptian GHQ), "An Infantry Division Crossing a Water Obstacle."

204. On the use of commandos, see the section dealing with this in this chapter.

205. Obsolete "Shmel" antitank rockets were fired from jeeps.

206. On the Soviets' use of Sager antitank rockets, see Antsiz's article describing the modus operandi of a Sager battery in antitank missions. The article was published in July 1975 and may have applied the lessons of the Yom Kippur War.

207. *Captured Egyptian Document* 85/11, September 1973.

208. Egyptian planners allocated two rockets for the destruction of each enemy tank.

209. Infantry carriages were built according to the specifications of Chief of Staff Shazli when he was commander of the Red Sea sector in July 1971. He had found an Israeli carriage for mortar rounds that had been left in the field and ordered three thousand carriages built — each one capable of carrying 150 kilograms of weapons and equipment. Shazli, *Crossing the Canal*, 44–45.

210. Since the demand for antitank rockets during the war was greater than the supply, it received the highest priority in the Soviet airlift. Shazli, *Crossing the Canal*, 200.

211. *Captured Egyptian Document*, "Military Research Manual No. 78, published by the Egyptian War Ministry, February 14, 1973."

212. *Captured Egyptian Document* 463/1 relates to the training of tank hunters (Second Army), (Second Army Training Branch, July 6, 1973).

213. Gamasi, 309.

214. Colonel T. N. Dupuy, "'The '73 Arab-Israeli Conflict'— A Military Analysis," *Strategy & Tactics*, January–February 1982.

215. Israel Tal, *Israel's National Security, Few against Many*, 176.

216. Ibid., 190. Tal perceives that this was due to the air force's loss of firepower in the land battle.

217. Mukdam Hitham al-Ayubi, "Revolutionary Features in the Fourth Arab-Israeli War," *Ma'arachot* 234–235 (January–February 1974), 20.

218. Karber, 106. According to Marshal A. A. Grechko, *Armed Forces of the Soviet State*, second edition.

219. *Al-Ahram*, Egypt, "The Role that Egyptian Artillery Played, Including Antitank Weapons, in the First Stages of the Yom Kippur War." The Egyptian antitank layout was employed as part of and under the command of the artillery system.

220. Ibid., 30–31. See also the section (below) "The Operative Pause."

221. Ibid., 38. The October 14 attack did not begin with a serious softening-up barrage.

222. Ibid., 38–40. The air force was not used in the October 14 attack. Excluding the single landing of a commando platoon near the contact line south west of Tasa, no airborne troops were detected.

223. Ibid., 34. See the section below, "The Operative Pause."

224. The Syrians blamed the Egyptian pause at the bridgeheads and the nondevelopment of the attack eastward into Sinai's depth as one of the main reasons why they failed to retain their gains on the Golan Heights.

225. Sa'ad Aladin al Shazli, in an interview in the weekly *Al Arabi*, October 2000 [Arabic].

226. On the way the operative pause was perceived in Arab sources, see Shmuel Bar, *The Yom Kippur War in the Arabs' Eyes*, 36–38 [Hebrew].

227. Heykal, *The Road to Ramadan*, 215.

228. The executive summary of The Cairo Symposium (October 28–31, 1974), 153.

229. Hasan Badri, Taha Magdub, Hia al-Adin Zohari, *Harb Ramadan, al-Jula al-Arabiya-al-Israiliya al-Arba'a — Aktober 1973 (The Ramadan War — the Fourth Israeli-Arab Round — October 1973)* 92.

230. See Lieutenant Colonel M., "The Egyptian Army's 'Operative Pause' in the Yom Kippur War," *Ma'arachot* 327 (November–December 1992), 12–19.

231. Five infantry divisions reinforced with tank brigades, artillery, engineers, and antitank teams — all were under the protection an air defense umbrella.

232. Lieutenant Colonel Avi-Shai, *Egypt toward the Yom Kippur War*, 22.

233. Yona Bandman, "The Third Army Crosses the Suez Canal," *Ma'arachot* 296 (December 1984), 26–30 [Hebrew]. According to an article submitted to *Ma'arachot* in October 1979.

234. Ibid., 29.

235. According to Hanoch Bartov, *Dado — 48 Years and 20 Days*, Vol. II (Ma'ariv Publishers, 1978) 48–49 [Hebrew]; Aviezer Golan, *Albert* (The Albert (Avraham)

Mendler Memorial Foundation, Yediot Achronot, April 1977), 211–212 [Hebrew].

236. "The Third Army Crosses the Suez Canal," 29.

237. Zvi Lanir, *Fundamental Surprise—The National Intelligence Crisis*, 64 [Hebrew].

238. The armored and motorized divisions.

239. Lieutenant Colonel M., "The Egyptian Army's 'Operative Pause' in the Yom Kippur War," 13.

240. According to Dr. Shimon Naveh's August 1998 lectures on the advanced systems, the term appears in Clausewitz's seventh book describing the connection between defense and offense.

241. According to Clausewitz.

242. According to Dr. Shimon Naveh's August 1998 lectures on advanced systems.

243. Ibid.

244. See the section on the offensive combat doctrine.

245. Captured document, Nasser Academy Lectures — *Vol. V, Lecture No. 650*, 1970 (English) "A Field Army's Offensive Operation when Crossing a Water Obstacle on the Coastal Axis, in Conjunction with the Air Force, Navy, and Air Defense."

246. Captured document, *Anthology of Lectures on the Field Army in an Attack*, Egyptian Command and Staff College (English).

247. The Egyptians claimed that Soviet military thinking was based on its World War II experience where the fronts were 3,000 kilometers long, while the Egyptian army had to operate only on a 150-kilometer front. "Hassanein Heykal's Memoirs," *Ma'ariv*, April 28, 1975, 13 [Hebrew].

248. The battle order of Brig. Gen. Ahmad Shahin, Third Army artillery commander, for operation "Granit 2 Improved," dated September 1973, *Captured Egyptian War Document 149/11*, specifically mentions that the depth of the field army bridgeheads in the Al-Shat area (north of the Bay of Suez) and south of the lakes will be eight to ten kilometers.

249. The Soviets also refer to this issue, see Colonel R. Loskutov, "The Yom Kippur War — the Egyptian Army versus the IDF," *V.I.Z.H. USSR*, October 1988 (translated by Hatzav, June 8, 1989, 85). The Soviets claim that the Egyptians intended to reach the passes in the field army's following mission. However, mission depth was twenty-five to thirty kilometers, a distance that, to the best of my knowledge, would not even bring them to the western entrances of the passes.

250. In a later order on electronic warfare, issued by Third Army Headquarters on September 28, 1973, *Captured Egyptian War Document 116/11*, this was explicitly referred to as a "tactical pause" that would be made before the field army carried out its final mission. According to the document, the attack's opening stage would begin on D-Day plus 4 or 5. The direct mission stage — stabilizing and expanding the bridgeheads — had to be completed by D-Day plus 2. During the tactical pause, the field army's forces would have to fend for themselves and repulse the enemy's counterattack, which was expected to last two or three days.

251. Ibid. In the same exceptional document the Third Army's final line is mentioned: the Ras Sudar-Ras al Jundi-Sudar al Hitan line, east of the Al Gidi mountains. I would like to reemphasize that the above details are found only in this particular source, which is a marginal document as far as military hierarchy is concerned. The writer of the document, a low-ranking officer (lieutenant colonel), was probably uninformed about the cutback in mission dimensions.

252. I came into possession of an operations map issued by the Third Army Artillery Commander in January 1973. The map, approved by the commander of the army,

Major General Wasal, has a black arrow showing that the Fourth Armored Division's final objectives were in Bir Gafgafa area. Also appearing on the map in general terms are the Seventh and Nineteenth Infantry Divisions' axes of advance. The two divisions were planned to link up with the commando forces that landed in the mountain passes' western openings. It seems that this map, like similar ones from the Second Army that fell into Israeli hands, describes the plan's general objectives before orders were issued that were based on the plan's reduced dimensions in late January 1973. The electronic warfare document, *Captured Egyptian War Document 116/11*, also refers to the Fourth Armored and Sixth Motorized Divisions that were scheduled to attack from the bridgeheads toward al-Mlaz (Bir Gafgafa-Bir Tmada). It also notes that the Third Army would divert its main effort from south of the lakes to Jabel Sahaba and the al Mlaz airfield. However these directions do not correspond to the Wadi Mabuk axis which was taken on October 14 by the Fourth Division's Third Brigade. In other words, either the plan in this order was antiquated or the October 14 attack did not conform to the original plan.

253. For a comprehensive and detailed discussion on this issue, see Shmuel Bar, *The Yom Kippur War in the Arabs' Eyes*, 36–38.

254. Gamasi, 212, claims that the "Bader" plan assumed that the attack could be made eastward up to the line of the mountain passes either without or after "a tactical pause."

255. Heykal, *The Road to Ramadan*, 215.

256. *Tishrin*, "The Military and Strategic Results of the October War," Syria, October 4–5, 1979.

257. Shazli, *Crossing the Canal*, 36–37.

258. Gamasi, 377–400.

259. Bar, *The Yom Kippur War in the Arabs' Eyes*, 73–74.

260. Lieutenant Colonel M., in his article "The Operative Pause," 15, notes that "[t]he GHQ and southern command couldn't make heads or tails out of the enemy's moves in this attack. We found no reference to an Egyptian move of limited depth ... or any intention to transfer the armored divisions to the eastern bank at this stage. The impression was that [the safeguarding of] armor units was the main interest [not all of them crossed in the first stage of the war — D.A.], while the real meaning of Egypt's move in the first stage of the battle was still engulfed in fog." Zvi Lanir, in his book *Fundamental Surprise—The National Intelligence Crisis*, 64, states that for several days after the outbreak of the war, the Egyptians continued to demonstrate remarkable tenacity in sticking to their original plans, and the Israeli GHQ functioned as though the enemy's plans were unknown. This went on despite the detailed information in Israel's hands regarding Egyptian war plans. In my opinion, these descriptions prove that Israel did not have Egypt's final plans and failed to decipher their latest plan, at least not in the first week of the war.

261. Bar, *The Yom Kippur War in the Arabs' Eyes*, 36.

262. Shazli, *Crossing the Canal*, 182.

263. See *Captured Egyptian Document 224/11*, the war diary of the Twenty-fifth Armored Brigade's commander, October 7–16, 1973, 4. The October 13 order mentions "putting pressure on the forces opposite you." The October 14 order for the Twenty-fifth Tank Brigade was to assist Eleventh Brigade infantry forces that were advancing only as far as the junction (apparently the Gidi Axis-Artillery Road Junction).

264. Captured Egyptian Document, Third Army War Diary (dated October 13 and 14).

265. According to Shazli, *Crossing the Canal*, 180, only four tank and one motorized infantry brigade took part in the attack that required four independent breaches.

266. From the testimonies given by Egyptian war prisoners (including officers) and from statements by Israeli officers, a clearer picture comes into view of a sporadic attack of limited objectives, and under no circumstances a general attack, since their mission was to reach only as far as the mountain passes. For an expanded discussion on this point, see my article "From 'Order 41' to 'Tahrir' 41," *Ma'arachot* 332 (September–October 1993), 49–53; and Avraham Ayalon, "October 14, 1973, Why Was it Deleted from History in Sadat's Memoirs?" *Ma'arachcot* 266 (November 1978), 9–19 [both in Hebrew].

267. According to intelligence officer Col. (later Maj. Gen.) Yehoshua Sagi, in a conference commemorating the twentieth anniversary of the Yom Kippur War.

268. The path that the Fourth Division's Third Tank Brigade took in Wadi Mabuk led it to a dead end that may have enabled a local flanking maneuver toward the western opening of the Mitle. In any case, this was not the transportation axis planned for the divisions attacking the passes. In a captured map that came into my possession, the Fourth Division's lines of advance toward the Refidim Opening are clearly marked. For more information on the engagements that took place on this axis, see the article by Major Doron, (later Maj. Gen. Doron Almog) "The October 14 Battle in the Wadi Mabuk Sector," *Ma'arachot* 266, 20–27.

269. Several works attest to the number of Egyptian tanks destroyed on October 14. Some Egyptian writers have adopted the exaggerated number of 250, which appears in Israeli sources. Both Shazli and Gamasi, each for his own reasons, accepted this number, while the Egyptian spokesman announced (Sawt al Arabi on October 14, 1973) that the enemy suffered 150 damaged tanks and Egypt one hundred. Col. Avraham Ayalon, in his article "October 14, 1973, Why Was it Deleted from History in Sadat's Memoirs?" discusses in detail the reports about the wrecked tanks and gives the number as 200. Col. (res.) Emanuel Wald in his book *The Curse of the Broken Pieces*, 109, offers a more realistic number —150 Egyptian tanks destroyed out of the three hundred that tried to advance. The IDF, on the other hand, suffered twelve damaged tanks.

270. On the use of the antitank missile and tank-hunter teams, see the section on antitank warfare in this chapter.

271. On the amphibious brigade, see J. S. Bermudez, Jr., "The Egyptian 130th Amphibious Brigade," *Marine Corps Gazette*, June 1995, 59–68. For a detailed discussion on the brigade, see the rest of this section.

272. On the use of commandos for antitank missions, see the section on antitank warfare in this chapter.

273. Surprisingly, Shazli, in his book *Crossing the Canal*, omits a chapter on Egyptian commando operations, maybe because of their negligible achievements in the Yom Kippur War.

274. According to the captured document, "The Capture and Securing of the Mountain Passes during an Attack," that was published by the Third Army (*Egyptian Captured Document 470/1*, January 1972, translated into Hebrew and published in *Tziklon*, 8, Ma'arachot, May 1981, 21–26 (Chapter 3, Section 2) [Hebrew].

275. Ibid, Section 6. Chapter 3 of the document presents a detailed explanation of the method of capturing and securing the Mitle Pass by a paratrooper commando force. Section 8 deals with the method of capturing the Gidi and Khutumiya mountain passes.

276. According to the use of special airborne troops in the Soviet army, with an emphasis on the Spetznatz, see Ronald M. Bonesteel, "The Soviets 'Other' Forces," *Infantry*, November-December 1988, 26–28.

277. For a comprehensive work on Egyptian commando activity in the war and Israeli methods of countering it, see Colonel Eldad, Lieutenant Colonel (res.) Nachum, and Lieutenant Colonel (res.) Zvi, "Egyptian Commando Fighting in the Yom Kippur War" *Ma'arachot* 327, 20–25 [Hebrew].

278. For a description of the use of commando forces in the war, see Gamasi, 310–311.

279. *Captured Egyptian Document, 424/1.*

280. The electronic warfare orders in Operation "Granit 2 — Improved" were published by Third Army Headquarters on September 28, 1973, *Captured Egyptian Document 116/11*. The document revealed to Israeli analysts all aspects of Egypt's intended mission depth and led them to miscalculate the following events. In my opinion, the document was signed by a low-ranking officer (lieutenant colonel), an electronic warfare battalion commander, who was not updated on the changes in the Egyptian plan and the reduction in missions. The document discusses missions that had been planned earlier.

281. Gamasi considers (311) the commando action in Wadi Sudar as the most important commando operation in the war. This is understandable, given that no serious activity was made on the axis of the main effort.

282. Col. Eldad, Lt. Col. Nachum, and Lt. Col. Zvi. "Egyptian Commando Fighting in the Yom Kippur War." *Ma'arachot* 327, 21.

283. According to *Captured Egyptian Document 116/11*, the GHQ would send commando forces to the passes only between D-Day plus 1 and D-Day plus 2. I believe that the electronic warfare battalion commander, the author of the document, simply erred.

284. According to the Egyptian study, "The Capture and Securing of the Mountain Passes during an Attack," (Chapter 3, Section 7B), the force that was planned to capture the mountain pass would land in the area at least twenty-four hours before the beginning of the attack. The Egyptian planner lacked this amount of time to surprise the IDF. In my opinion, moving the hour of the crossing ahead should not be seen as the reason for failing to make in-depth landings.

285. Ibid.

286. According to Lieutenant Colonel Avi-Shai, *Egypt towards the Yom Kippur War*, 35, note 33, the First Motorized Brigade (Sixth Mechanized Division) was reinforced with an artillery battalion and antitank missile company. The brigade was planned to operate in the Red Sea Command and make the crossing on D-Day plus one (that is, October 7) at the southern bridgehead (the Nineteenth Division sector). The First Motorized Brigade would capture Ras Masala, gain control of Ras Sudar, continue south and deploy defensively ten kilometers south of A-Tur. In reality, the brigade made the crossing only on the evening of October 9 and halted in the vicinity of Ras Masala.

287. Gamasi, 311.

288. Order No. 1, Seventh Division, *Captured Egyptian Document 424/1*, defines the commando battalion's mission (the battalion that would be operating under the command of Group 127): "The battalion will embark on the first attack wave and operate in *majmu'ot* (combat teams) against the enemy's headquarters, artillery positions, and communications lines so as to confuse the enemy and cause him to lose control of his forces. The battalion will set up ambushes and plant mines on the dirt embankment in the close depth of the enemy reserve's routes of advance."

289. According to "The Capture and Securing of the Mountain Passes during an Attack," 20.

290. According to Order No. 1 (Seventh Division), *Captured Egyptian Document 424/1*, "the Thirty-third Commando Battalion's assignment (made up of one platoon and

two companies) will be to act as a reserve for the division commander and be prepared to carry out any assignment."

291. According to Lieutenant Colonel Avi-Shai, "Egypt on the Eve of the Yom Kippur War: War Aims and Attack Plans," *Ma'arachot* 250 (July 1976), 28, 36.

292. Order from the Third Army commander, 16, 20.

293. According to "The Capture and Securing of the Mountain Passes during an Attack," 23.

294. According to *Captured Egyptian Document 431/1 (8).*

295. On the brigade structure/formation, see *Egyptian 130th Amphibious Brigade*, 62.

296. Shazli, *Crossing the Canal*, 36–37.

297. According to *Egyptian 130th Amphibious Brigade*, 61, the brigade had seventy-four amphibious BTR-50 or OT-62 APCs and twenty PT-76 tanks.

298. Order No. 1 (Seventh Division), *Captured Egyptian Document 424/1*, states that a company from the Thirty-sixth Mechanized Infantry Battalion (Eleventh Motorized Brigade), a second-echelon brigade (from Seventh Division), and the 651st Antitank Battalion's Leopard Company would operate as a marine landing force. In addition to reinforcing the landing force, they would also strengthen the antitank layout on the bridgehead front before the other antitank forces arrived. The order also states that the task-force would operate as an antitank blocking line and prevent the enemy's local reserves from interfering with the Twenty-sixth Battalion's mission (to destroy the Israeli stronghold south of the lakes).

299. Ibid. The task was given to a company from the Thirty-third Commando Battalion that was short two platoons. A mortar battery was positioned on kilometer 57/12 on the Gidi Axis.

300. *Captured Egyptian Document 242/1.*

301. See Shazli, *Crossing the Canal*, 161 and Bermudez, *The Egyptian 130th: The Amphibious Brigade.*

302. *Captured Egyptian Document 116/11*, issued by Third Army headquarters, states that the attacking field army would make full use of the water areas [whose coasts were less protected — D.A.] for covering secondary units of the 130th Independent Mechanized Infantry Brigade, in order to strike at the enemy's flanks and rear which were concentrated in the Israeli front-line strongholds.

303. Shazli, *Crossing the Canal*, 161. The force numbered twenty tanks, eighty APCs, and one thousand troops.

304. Ibid., 37.

305. According to Bermudez, *The Egyptian 130th: The Amphibious Brigade*, 66.

306. Ibid.

307. According to Shazli, *Crossing the Canal*, 61, the Egyptians concentrated over 2,000 artillery pieces.

308. Shmuel Reshsef, chief artillery officer (1986–1989), in the forward to Chris Bellamy's book, *Red God of War: Soviet Artillery and Rocket Forces* (Tel Aviv: Ma'arachot, 1990).

309. Chris Bellamy, *Red God of War*, 15.

310. Major L. Merhav, "The Attack in the Soviet Warfare Concept, the Military Branches — and their Part in the Attack," *Ma'arachot*, 147 (October 1962), 2.

311. Bellamy, *Red God of War*, 15.

312. According to L. Merhav, *Ma'arachot* 147 (October 1962), 22, with the entry of nuclear weapons, senior Soviet officers believed that the artillery formation would be replaced by nuclear weapons. The concept was later revised: nuclear weapons could not be used for every mission, whereupon it was decided to develop the artillery and return it to its former status.

313. For more information on the Soviet doctrine's use of artillery in the modern age, see the section on "combat preparations in offensive operations of the front" in *Voroshilov Lectures*, 189–233.

314. *The Soviet Military Encyclopedia*, (1976) Vol. I, p. 22 [Russian].

315. The most significant of the translated publications that Israel captured was *Captured Document Mash-964/75*, "Rules of Field Artillery Fire Procedure" (Armed Forces Publications, 1971). The first part deals with the fire procedure at the battalion and group levels.

316. According to Bellamy, *Red God of War*, 197. See also L. Merhav, *Ma'arachot* 147 (October 1962), 23.

317. Full-density paralysis is intended to cause the enemy heavy losses (25–30 percent).

318. L. Merhav, *Ma'arachot* 147 (October 1962), 23, claims that the doctrine calls for sixty to ninety minutes of artillery softening-up.

319. Ibid., 25.

320. On the use of antitank in the war, see Dani Asher, "Antitank Fire as an Answer," and the section in this chapter on antitank weapons.

321. *Israeli Captured Egyptian Document 5000/10* (October 17, 1970) deals with "the lessons learnt from the artillery battles with the enemy on the Suez Canal between 1967 and 1970." The document was published by the military research branch, but was prepared by the artillery administration. It discusses the lessons learned by artillery units from the fighting on the Canal Zone, analyzes the battles, the application of artillery forces, and the distribution and administration of artillery fire (including direct laying fire, fire control, and corrections).

322. The battalion, equipped with SU-152 assault cannons, was strengthened to regimental size on the eve of the war.

323. A battalion grew to four companies on the eve of the war.

324. Dual-purpose 100-millimeter cannons were put on the hulls of T-34 tanks.

325. According to Shazli, *Crossing the Canal*, 144–145, the Scud three-battalion-strong missile brigade arrived in Egypt only in late July 1973, began training on August 1, and became combat ready in October.

326. See *Capture Egyptian Document 149/11*, battle order for Operation "Granite 2 Improved" (September 1973), Third Army artillery commander.

327. Target acquisition includes all the activity needed to pinpoint the objective and enable the fire echelon to hit it.

328. In an article on Egyptian artillery in *Al-Ahram* (December 22, 197), the author asserts that the War of Attrition gave Egypt the opportunity to pinpoint the enemy's artillery and positions, learn his modus operandi, and pick out additional objectives.

329. See *Captured Egyptian Document 964/75*, 11, Table No. 1 — how to find target coordinates.

330. The deployment of the various groups in the southern sector appears in the captured map of the Third Army's artillery deployment and targets, signed by the OC, Major General Wasal.

331. For more details on the barrages, see Third Army *Captured Document 149/11* for Operation "Granite 2 Improved" and *Captured Document 10/2*, which deals with the Sixth Division's artillery missions: "The Artillery Commander's Battle Order."

332. According to *Al-Ahram*, the security ranges were cut back from 300–400 meters to 200 and sometimes 100 meters in order to provide greater assistance.

333. See Third Army artillery commander's battle order and captured document — "The Third Army's Field Artillery Situation."

334. See details (in this book) of the artillery ORBAT and the map outlining its deployment in the Seventh Division sector.

335. According to *Egypt toward the Yom Kippur War*, 30, the Third Army had only two crossing sectors, but they were covered with 600–900 barrels of field artillery.

336. An *Al-Ahram* article (December 22, 1973) discusses the role that Egyptian artillery played in the first stages of the Yom Kippur War, and notes that the number of cannons on the western bank of the canal was double that used by both sides in the Battle for El Alamein in World War II. The article was entitled "A Cannon for Every 11 Meters and 175 Shells per Second."

337. On the crossing plan and transfer of forces across the bridgeheads, see *Captured Egyptian Document 766/4*.

338. *Captured Egyptian Document 149/11*.

339. On the various methods of fire for effect, see *Captured Egyptian Document 64/75*, chapter 2, 38–58.

340. On the various methods of counter-battery fire and the number of shells allotted to it, see *Captured Egyptian Document Mash-964/75* in the subsection: "Paralysis of the Enemy's Artillery and Mortar Batteries," 43–47.

341. *Captured Egyptian Document 502/1*. Statements to the same effect can be found in *Captured Egyptian Document 472/1*, 4–9.

342. Israel Tal, *Israel's National Security, Few against Many*, 206.

343. On Israel's artillery ORBAT in Sinai in the Yom Kippur War, see the article by Itai and Dani Asher, "The IDF Artillery on the Sinai Front in the Yom Kippur War," *Ma'arachot 354* (November 1997), 10–20.

344. On Third Army artillery commander's ORBAT, see *Captured Egyptian Document 149/11*.

345. According to the captured document "The Situation at the Seventh Infantry Division's Artillery Headquarters." *Captured Egyptian Document 131/11*.

346. *The Use of the Ground Forces in the Soviet Warfare Doctrine*, 190.

347. *Vorosholov Lectures*, 236.

348. Ibid., 237.

349. Ibid., 192.

350. Ibid., 194. The Egyptian army has a basic coefficient for calculating the amount of supplies allotted to the units, based on the amount of supplies that must be located at all the times in a particular branch or based on a single piece of equipment.

351. In the Egyptian case, the GHQ, serving as a front headquarters, is responsible for the maintenance and administration of the combat theaters above field army level.

352. *Voroshilov Lectures*, 237.

353. This is how it is in the Egyptian army. The only exceptions are the nonorganic units that "come under the command" of other units. They too carry the supplies of the superior command level and for this reason are provided with additional vehicles.

354. *The Use of the Ground Forces in the Soviet Warfare Doctrine*, 196.

355. *Captured Egyptian Document 851/0006*, 23.

356. *The Use of the Ground Forces in the Soviet Warfare Doctrine*, 200.

357. *Captured Egyptian Document 851/0006*, 23.

358. *The Use of the Ground Forces in the Soviet Warfare Doctrine*, 200–202.

359. *Voroshilov Lectures*, 254.

360. *Captured Egyptian Document 851/0006*, 24.

361. In Egypt the GHQ level is identical with the front level (following the Soviet doctrine).

362. There is almost no need for a water supply in the European theater. Pipelines are mainly laid to provide a regular flow of oil to the ground and air forces. See *Voroshilov Lectures*, 255.

363. The subject was taught in the Nasser Academy in 1971–1973 according to the manual entitled "Logistic Support to the Motorized Infantry Division in an Attack and Assault Crossing, C.S.C.," 134. (The manual was captured by the Israelis but not translated into Hebrew.)

364. Ibid., 3.

365. Ibid., 9.

366. The bridgeheads, of course, did not attain this range in any sector.

Appendices

1. Sources of the Soviet warfare doctrine on an attack at the field army level can be found in *Voroshilov Lectures* (265–271); in captured publications in English from the Nasser Higher Military Academy (1969–1970); and in Egyptian officer manuals, graduates of Soviet war colleges (including the Frunza Academy) 1966–1970. Israeli intelligence collected the material and published it in *The Field Army in an Attack* (December 1976).

2. According to *Voroshilov Lectures* (272), the Soviets differentiate between a fully staffed field army operable on various types of missions and an armored field army which is generally used only in the direction of the main strike in the attack. The Egyptians employed only two field armies in the Yom Kippur War.

3. *Voroshilov Lectures*, 271–272.

4. The Soviets differentiate between nuclear and conventional warfare. For the field army's missions in nuclear warfare conditions, see *Voroshilov Lectures*, 277.

5. For more information on the Egyptian missions and mission depth in the Yom Kippur War, see the section "The Operative Halt — Mission Depth."

6. *The Field Army in the Attack*, 7–8.

7. The field army's final mission may become the following mission when the field army makes a strategic attack in which the following mission is identical with the final mission in the same operation, as in the case of the Yom Kippur War.

8. According to the Soviet warfare doctrine from the late seventies, the rate of advance increases during the attack. The recommended rate is forty to fifty kilometers a day in conventional combat conditions. In nonconventional warfare the rate rises to fifty to eighty kilometers a day. See *The Use of Ground Forces in the Soviet Warfare Doctrine*, 15.

9. The Egyptian war plans that were prepared between 1969 and 1971 envisioned crossing all of the Sinai Peninsula, reaching the international border, penetrating it, and possibly linking up with the Gaza Strip. Such an operation demanded movement of up to 350 kilometers in a ten- to twelve-day period. For more information on the plan, see the relevant section in chapter 4.

10. On the missions and mission depth, see *The Field Army in an Attack*, 8–10.

11. The Soviet instructors in the Nasser Academy taught that Sinai's conditions required a field army's attack front to be sixty to eighty kilometers at the beginning of the operation, with the possibility of expanding it to 110–120 as the campaign progressed. The recommended dimensions were based on the Soviets' understanding of Egypt's needs. The Egyptians had two field armies in this period. The length of the canal front allowed for an attack to be made along a 140–160 kilometer line (the entire length of the canal was 170 kilometers, but the marshlands and Bit-

ter Lakes' littoral area were totally unfavorable to the development of combat efforts). The adaptation to Egyptian needs was doctrinally justified by claiming that Sinai's mountain area lacked a contiguous defense and only 50–60 percent of it was suited to developing an attack effort. During the war, the length of the Second Army's attack front, with three first echelon divisions, was approximately sixty kilometers; and the Third Army's front, with only two divisions, was twenty-eight kilometers. *The Field Army in an Attack*, 10.

12. Instructors at the Nasser Academy taught that the Egyptians had to penetrate Sinai to a depth of 240 kilometers in order to capture all of the area. For more on this subject, see the sections in chapter 5: "The Egyptians' Application of the Crossing Doctrine — The Plan" and "The Operative Pause."

13. *Voroshilov Lectures*, 280.

14. The lessons of World War II show that a high pace of an attack is attained when overwhelming superiority is created in narrow breeching sections. Factors such as accurate intelligence, paralysis of the entire length of the enemy's defense layout, increased density of tanks, correct application of second-echelon forces and reserves, and the effective use of armor and mobile forces during the breakthrough, resulted in an increase in the rate of advance. In 1941 the field army's rate of advance was four to six kilometers a day; in 1945 it reached forty to fifty kilometers a day, with armored forces attaining seventy to eighty kilometers a day.

15. According to *Voroshilov Lectures*, 279, the rate of the daily attack in modern battlefield conditions may be forty to sixty kilometers a day in regular terrain, and sometimes sixty to seventy kilometers when penetrating the enemy's deep layouts.

16. *Voroshilov Lectures*, 291.

17. For details on the field army's ORBAT, see *The Field Army in an Attack*, 13–16.

18. In exceptional cases the field army may employ two armored divisions. According to *Voroshilov Lectures*, 280, the Soviet field army was made up of five to six divisions (an armored field army had three to four divisions).

19. On the application of SF in the Egyptian army in general, and in the Yom Kippur War in particular, see chapter 5.

20. According to *Voroshilov Lectures*, 281, the air force will provide the field army with ten to fifteen fighters or bombers.

21. *Voroshilov Lectures*, 290.

22. *Voroshilov Lectures*, 287–288.

23. The Egyptians published much material on the IDF's view of defense on the Sinai front. One of the first works written in the Nasser Higher Military Academy was *Organization and Conduct of Defense* (Foreign View), High War College, A-17, 1969.

24. *The Use of Ground Forces in the Soviet Warfare Doctrine*, 14.

25. The Egyptians, like the Soviets, note the different types of enemy defense layouts — hasty, organized, and fortified — and the weapons and troops operating from them.

26. According to *Voroshilov Lectures*, 292, the first echelon may number four to five divisions, the size of Egypt's first echelons in the Yom Kippur War.

27. *The Use of Ground Forces in the Soviet Warfare Doctrine*, 14. See also *The Field Army in an Attack*, 17–18. The Egyptians reinforced each of their five divisions engaged in the first-echelon attack with an independent armored brigade or a brigade from the second-echelon divisions.

28. Ibid. See also *The Field Army in an Attack*, 17–18. According to *Voroshilov Lectures*, 292, armored divisions may be used as the field army's first echelon when the main battle with enemy armored forces is expected, but not when breeching the enemy's fortified layout.

29. See the section dealing with the artillery doctrine in chapter 5.

30. *Voroshilov Lectures*, 292, mentions that in conjunction with the surface-to-surface missile brigade operating in the field army, a larger number of artillery battalions (seven to nine) are also employed in the field army formation, according to the number of divisions that the field army has been able to muster.

31. On the organization of antiaircraft forces and their use in the battle, see *Captured Egyptian Document 851/0022*, "The Tactical Use of Antiaircraft Artillery for the Defense of Ground Forces." The document's first chapter deals with air defense for the attacking forces. The third chapter (61–81) discusses air defense for the field army during its attack moves. The document was circulated on October 20, 1975. In *Voroshilov Lectures*, 283, the air defense ORBAT in the modern period is three surface-to-air missile batteries, 450 personal antiaircraft launchers, 26–32 antiaircraft guns, and eighty mobile antiaircraft guns.

32. The subject of antitank helicopters was of relevance in the Yom Kippur War. On the other hand, older means, such as tank-busters and flamethrowers, are absent in contemporary doctrinal literature. On the use of antitank weapons and antitank reserves, see chapter 5.

33. These missions called for a commando battalion in each of the field armies. On the planning and use of SF in the Yom Kippur War, see the section on commandos in chapter 5.

34. *Voroshilov Lectures*, 347. The conditions for a successful attack are taken from modern battlefield experience, and may also be based on the lessons learned in the Yom Kippur War. A preemptive air strike does not appear in the Egyptian doctrinal-military literature prior to the Yom Kippur War. To the best of my knowledge the Egyptians realized that they were incapable of carrying out such an attack, given the IDF's air superiority.

35. *The Field Army in an Attack*, 20–24.

36. The Egyptian attack plan (see the relevant section in chapter 4) makes no mention of the axis or the field army's primary effort. First-echelon divisions are the only units that were employed in the divisional efforts. I claim that second-echelon divisions (armored or motorized) were not used in any stage of the attack. A close examination of the plan and its implementation fails to locate a real main effort in either of the two field army sectors.

37. See *Voroshilov Lectures*, 347–349.

38. On the Egyptians' plan, missions, and employment of landing forces during the Yom Kippur War, see the section on commandos in chapter 5.

39. On the use of airborne and seaborne forces, see the manual *The Army in the Attack*, 25–28.

40. During the Yom Kippur War the Egyptians landed an amphibious force east of the Little Bitter Lake. On the application of this force, see the relevant section in chapter 5.

41. Command-and-control activity includes the physical construction of headquarters and forward observation points for use during the attack.

42. On the recommended application of deceptive tactics according to the warfare doctrine, see the relevant section in chapter 4.

43. Much has been written on Egyptian deception activity in the preparatory stages of the war. Most of the activity was intended to conceal the true motive of the operation by presenting it as just another military exercise. In all

of my research, I found no deception activity during the actual course of the operation, no were any feints or false advances carried out by second echelon forces. On the application of deception, see the relevant sections in chapter 4.

44. The Egyptian planners would reduce the rate of advance between the different areas and the starting line by 25–50 percent. See *The Use of Ground Forces in the Soviet Warfare Doctrine*, 58.

45. This is where the Egyptians launched their attack.

46. According to the warfare doctrine, the Egyptian defense strip on the canal bank was made up of three layouts which provided the area with sufficient depth and were used for troop deployment.

47. Nearly all of the first-echelon divisions' organic units were positioned in their defense layouts on the west bank of the Suez Canal. The reinforced units, including the tank brigades that were attached to the infantry divisions, had to redeploy.

48. According to *The Use of Ground Forces in the Soviet Warfare Doctrine*, 11, the forces will be collected in rear assembly areas sixty to seventy kilometers from the front.

49. *Voroshilov Lectures*, 354–355.

50. In the initial stage of the war, the Egyptian assault forces generally circumvented the Israeli strongholds on the canal's banks, taking time to capture them a few days later.

51. *The Use of Ground Forces in the Soviet Warfare Doctrine*, 11.

52. The Egyptians carried out almost no commando operations in the Yom Kippur War because the war plan reduced the army's depth of movement.

53. *The Army in the Attack*, IDF Intelligence (1976), 43.

54. *The Use of Ground Forces in the Soviet Warfare Doctrine*, 11.

55. *Voroshilov Lectures*, 356–357.

56. *Voroshilov Lectures*, 304.

57. The field army's second echelon was not used in this way during the Yom Kippur War. The main reason seems to have been the reductions and cancellations of the breakthrough missions to the operative depth. The fact that the second-echelon divisions remained on the western bank — only some of them were sent to reinforce the first echelon — is another indication that the Egyptian planners were satisfied with the reduced objectives in the tactical depth.

58. The Egyptian October 14 armored attack included several tank brigades — some from the second-echelon divisions, most from the center of the first-echelon divisional bridgeheads rather than from the flanks or gaps. In no case was a serious effort detected. See the sections dealing with the plan, the war's reduced dimensions, and the October 14 attack.

59. According to a number of scholars, one of the reasons the Egyptians did not order the second echelon into battle was the fear of what might happen if they left the air defense umbrella.

60. On the engagements and pursuit battles, see *The Army in the Attack*, 47–51.

61. For more information, see the section "The Operative Pause."

62. In the introduction to book *The Divisions (Brigade) in the Attack*, 3, the author, Major General Pelekh (apparently a Russian general) discusses the Egyptian armed forces' experience from combat exercises, especially regarding their structure, weapons, equipment, and the geographical conditions in the Sinai theater of operations. According to Pelekh, the book was written by a group of instructors at the Nasser Academy and was designed for brigade and divisional level officers and cadets at Egypt's military colleges.

63. *The Use of Ground Forces in the Soviet Warfare Doctrine*, 43.

64. *The Division (Brigade) in the Attack*, 3.

65. *The Use of Ground Forces in the Soviet Warfare Doctrine*, 44. This preference is of special importance in a war that had the potential of developing into a nuclear engagement.

66. According to "The Organization and Use in the Infantry or Mechanized Infantry or Armored Division in Various Stages of the Battle," *Captured Egyptian Documents 511/I*, 2, the attack (the breakthrough of the enemy's defenses) is the division's main role, and one requiring field army support.

67. Ibid., 9–10.

68. *Voroshilov Lectures*, 304. The division will move out from assembly areas forty to sixty kilometers to the rear of the first echelon division.

69. On the division's activity in the advanced stages of the attack battle, see *Captured Egyptian Document 851/0005*, "The Armored Division in the Advance and in Engagement Battle" (Armed Forces GHQ, Military Research Branch).

70. *The Use of Ground Forces in the Soviet Warfare Doctrine*, 45.

71. The daily mission will not be established at levels lower than the divisional level because the mission will probably change due to unexpected developments in the enemy's layout.

72. *The Division (Brigade) in the Attack*, 12–13.

73. On the doctrinal view of mission depth in the Yom Kippur War relative to the missions assigned to the first echelon divisions, see the section in chapter 4 on the war's reduced dimensions.

74. The Soviet doctrine holds that the enemy's layout should be studied as though it was proceeding according to the doctrine's recommendations.

75. Soviet experts in Egypt attempted to fit the warfare doctrine to the needs of the Sinai theater. They did this by presenting the Israeli defense layout on the eastern bank as though it were built a considerable distance from the canal. The line of strongholds was considered a protective envelope and the force operating in it was regarded as covering troops.

76. *The Division (Brigade) in the Attack*, 15.

77. Ibid., 16.

78. The doctrine states that the rate of advance of an armored division in battle is twenty kilometers an hour in daylight and fifteen kilometers at night. Its range is forty to sixty kilometers, and it is capable of fighting three to five consecutive days to a distance of 250 kilometers. See "The Organization and Use in the Infantry or Mechanized Infantry or Armored Division in Various Stages of the Battle," 8. These figures do not seem to correspond to Egypt's needs and abilities in the Yom Kippur War. The Egyptian armored divisions were not used in this way during the war.

79. *The Division (Brigade) in the Attack*, 16–17.

80. According to *Voroshilov Lectures*, 302, a division's attack front will be fifteen to twenty kilometers in length.

81. *The Division (Brigade) in the Attack*, 18, 28–29. According to the doctrine's calculations, the attacking divisions will need a fortified layout to concentrate 300 barrels on the breakthrough sector with seventy to eighty guns on each kilometer of the front. The artillery density during the attack and the softening-up fire in the breakthrough battle are carried out with the same numbers of weapons. Page 28 mentions eighty-five barrels for each kilometer of front. For details on artillery fire, see the relevant section in this book.

82. *Voroshilov Lectures*, 303.

83. *The Division (Brigade) in the Attack*, 19.

84. The Egyptians perceived the Israeli layout on the canal's banks as an organized or hastily set up defense by the doctrine's standards. This enabled an easier breakthrough. The water obstacle, that naturally called for a greater effort, was regarded a problem. See "The Organization and Use in the Infantry or Mechanized Infantry or Armored Division in Various Stages of the Battle," 3.

85. With the growth in armored and mechanized layouts since World War II, this force is capable of almost any type of attack.

86. *The Use of Ground Forces in the Soviet Warfare Doctrine*, 52.

87. *The Division (Brigade) in the Attack*, 20.

88. "The Organization and Use in the Infantry or Mechanized Infantry or Armored Division in Various Stages of the Battle," 2–3.

89. On the artillery, its grouping, deployment, and modus operandi, see the section on artillery in chapter 5.

90. On the structure, deployment, and use of mobile obstacle-laying forces and antitank reserves, see the relevant section in chapter 5.

91. The tank brigade operating as an advanced force of the division may reach and gain control of objectives fifty kilometers from the main force. See "The Organization and Use in the Infantry or Mechanized Infantry or Armored Division in Various Stages of the Battle," 9. This distance did not suit Egypt's needs. The tank brigades in the Yom Kippur War were appended to the infantry divisions at the bridgeheads and not outside them.

92. *The Division (Brigade) in the Attack*, 21–22.

93. In principle this is the mission of the airborne forces in the depth of field army's layout. The mission appears in "The Organization and Use in the Infantry, Mechanized Infantry, or Armored Division in Various Stages of the Battle," 3.

94. On the commando missions at various levels, see the section on SF in chapter 5.

95. The preparatory fire stage includes artillery softening-up and air softening-up. Other weapons — tanks and antitank guns — are also used in direct trajectory fire in this stage. *The Division (Brigade) in the Attack*, 24.

96. On the artillery's formation, organization, warfare doctrine, and modus operandi, see the section on artillery in chapter 5.

97. *The Use of Ground Forces in the Soviet Warfare Doctrine*, 71.

98. According to *The Division (Brigade) in the Attack*, 26, a division requires 342 guns and mortars for indirect fire, and an additional forty-five to sixty guns for direct fire.

99. On the "preparatory fire," support fire, fire concentrations, and fire screens, see the section on artillery in chapter 5.

100. *The Use of Ground Forces in the Soviet Warfare Doctrine*, 68.

101. *The Division (Brigade) in the Attack*, 33–34. See also the section on tactical air support, in *The Use of Ground Forces in the Soviet Warfare Doctrine*, 144–151.

102. Ibid., 35–36. See also the section on air defense in *The Use of Ground Forces in the Soviet Warfare Doctrine*, 138–143.

103. *The Use of Ground Forces in the Soviet Warfare Doctrine*, 169–174.

104. See *Capture Egyptian Document 170/009*, "The Organization of Defending the Attacking Forces against Chemical and Bacteriological Weapons while Making a Planned Assault Crossing of a Water Obstacle in the Direction of the Shore" (Nasser Higher Military Academy, 1972) [Arabic].

105. *The Division (Brigade) in the Attack*, 38.

106. *Captured Egyptian Document 116/11*, "The Instruction of Electronic Warfare 73/1," Third Army Headquarters, September 28, 1973, provides details on the use of electronic warfare at the field army level as operation "Granite 2-Improved" approached.

107. Ibid., 39–40. See also the section on engineering assistance in *The Use of Ground Forces in the Soviet Warfare Doctrine*, 160–169. On the engineers' mission and methods of operation, see the section on engineers in chapter 4.

108. Ibid., 41–42.

109. Ibid., 42–44.

110. An alternative headquarters will be set up next to the headquarters. "The Organization and Use of an Infantry, Mechanized Infantry, or Armored Division in Various Stages of the Battle," 9.

111. On command-and-control and organizing headquarters according to the Soviet doctrine, see *The Use of Ground Forces in the Soviet Warfare Doctrine*, 186–189. On the adaptation of the Soviet doctrine to Egyptian military needs, see *Captured Egyptian Documents 963/12*, military research publication No. 55, "The Organization of Control Centers and the Protection of Continuous Wireless Contact during Attack Operations while Breeching a Water Obstacle" (Egyptian War Ministry Publications, The Department for "High" Military Studies, May 20, 1970). The document is signed by Sa'ad al Shazli, Armed Forces Chief of Staff.

112. Colonel-General Malinkov, "The Soviet Perspective — Deception at the Operational Level," *Voyenno Istoricheskiy Zhurnal*, April 1982, in "Battlefield Deception," 16, (*GHQ Warfare Doctrine*, November 1992) [Hebrew].

113. On activity in the deception layout as part of the intelligence warfare in the Battle of Kursk in July 1943, see David M. Glantz, "Soviet Operation Intelligence (Razvedika) in the Kursk Operation, July 1943, *Intelligence & National Security* 5, no. 1 (1990).

114. During the crossing of the Dnieper in October 1943, for example, a smoke screen was laid down simultaneously over thirteen sectors on a thirty-kilometer front.

115. While preparing for the Battle of Kursk "bulge" in 1943, the 340th Division and an engineering battalion, engineering company, and platoon of sappers for mine laying were allocated to the Thirty-eighth Field Army in order to camouflage the actual missions.

116. For a detailed study describing the Soviet deception (*maskirovka*) and its application on various levels, emphasizing the general tactical level for deception and concealment, see Jennie A. Stevens, Henry S. Smith, "Surprise and Deception in Soviet Military Thought," *Military Review*, July 1982, 24–35.

117. The Egyptians made massive use of smoke screens, mainly for concealing bridging activity and the forces crossing the canal. During my inspections and tours of the western canal bank I encountered scores of smoke devices fed by diesel fuel that had been used with great intensity and effectiveness in the first days of the crossing.

118. Colonel Y. V. Iganov, "Surprise and Deception: The Foundation of a Successful Operation," *Military Thought* (*Voennaya Mysl*) 8/93, 30.

119. *Captured Egyptian Document 766/4*. The document has been edited for the reader's convenience.

120. It is not clear if this refers to the field army's second echelon. These divisions, it will be remembered, did not cross the canal in the first stages of the war.

121. As previously mentioned, all five infantry divisions were reinforced with independent tank brigades or brigades from second-echelon mechanized and armored divisions.

122. *Captured Egyptian Document 91/11*. The document

was found on the battlefield. It has been edited directly and accurately from the source.

123. The "strongholds" may have been in the area's depth since another force had already been assigned the task of dealing with them.

124. *Captured Egyptian Document 434/1.* The document has been edited and omits less important portions, such as details on the enemy's moves, the ORBAT, and brigade-level secondary-unit missions. The order is missing a complete date but is apparently from early 1973 and was probably issued before all of the details were determined in the "limited plan."

125. This stage was not developed in the plan, nor was it implemented in the war.

126. The landing was not carried out in the war, therefore there was no need to link up with it.

127. The entire 130th Amphibious Brigade (two battalions) crossed the lakes during the war.

128. *Captured Egyptian Document 805/7.* The document was found in the Second Army's battle zone. Its address is not clear and appears to have been hastily written. Some sentences are disjointed and others are simply incoherent. Parts of the translated document have been omitted and others reedited for the reader's convenience. They are accurate renditions of the original.

129. On western bank of the canal?

130. This apparently refers to "Or Yikarot's" burn system.

131. The intention seems to be to neutralize the artillery in or after the preparatory stage.

132. The intention may have been limited range of weapons operating from the stronghold that cover only part area of the canal front.

133. My emphasis.

134. This seems to refer to electronic jamming and disruption of communications systems and electronic warfare.

135. This apparently refers to the "snapirs" [fins] that were built on the flanks of the positions.

136. Only in the capture of the strongholds.

137. My emphasis.

138. I believe that this refers to the artillery of the general defense layout and not only that of the strongholds. In a few strongholds, for example, "Budapest," artillery pieces were positioned (excluding the mortars in every stronghold).

139. My emphasis.

140. This may refer to the tank-hunter force.

141. The intention may have been long-burning ones.

142. The reference may be to man-portable antitank missile companies.

Bibliography

All Hebrew titles are presented here in English translation.

Books — In Hebrew

Adan, Avraham (Bren). *On Both Banks of the Canal.* Jerusalem: Idanim, 1979.

The Agranat Commission. The Investigating Committee of the Yom Kippur War, *The Agranat Report*, Vols. I & II. Jerusalem, 1974.

Ajami, Fuad. *Arab Identity and the Arabs Since 1967.* Tel Aviv: Yidiot Achronot, 2001.

The Army in the Attack. IDF Intelligence, 1976.

Bellamy, Chris. *Red God of War — Soviet Artillery and Rocket Forces.* Tel Aviv: Ma'arachot, 1990.

Bar, Shmuel. *The Yom Kippur War in the Arab's Eyes.* Tel Aviv: Ma'arachot, 1986.

Bar-Yosef, Uri. *The Guard That Slept on His Watch: The Origins of the Surprise in the Yom Kippur War.* Lod: Zmora-Bitan, 2001.

Baron, Aryeh. *Moshe Dayan in the Yom Kippur War.* Jerusalem: Idanim/Yidiot Achronot, 1993.

Bartov, Hanoch. *Dado — 48 Years and 20 Days*, Vols. I & II. Tel Aviv: Sifriat Ma'ariv, 1978.

Ben Israel, Yitzhak. *Dialogues on Science and Intelligence.* Tel Aviv: Ma'arachot, 1989.

Ben-Porat, Yoel. *Enclosure.* Tel Aviv: Idanim, 1991.

The Division (Brigade) in the Attack. IDF Intelligence, 1976.

Gelber, Yoav. *The History of Intelligence,* Vol. III. Tel Aviv: Ministry of Defense, 1998.

Gluska, Emanuel. *The Road to the Six-Day War.* Jerusalem: Hebrew University, 2000.

Golan, Aviezer. *Albert.* The Major General Albert (Avraham) Mendler Memorial Foundation, Yidiot Achronot, April 1977.

Guy, Carmit. *Bar-Lev.* Tel Aviv: Am Oved, Sifriat Hapoalim, 1998.

Dayan, Moshe. *Story of My Life.* Jerusalem, Tel Aviv: Idanim, 1976.

Harkabi, Yehoshafat, ed. *The Arabs and Israel: An Anthology Translated from Arabic.* IDF Intelligence Branch, 1975.

_____. *The Arabs' Lessons from Their Defeat.* Am Oved, 1972.

_____. *The Arabs' Position in the Arab-Israeli Conflict.* Tel Aviv: Dvir, 1968.

_____. *Changes in the Arab-Israeli Conflict,* Tel Aviv: Dvir, 1978.

_____. *War and Strategy.* Tel Aviv: Ma'arachot, 1990.

Kabahah, Mustafa. *The War of Attrition as Reflected in Egyptian Sources.* Tel Aviv University, 1995.

Kam, Ephraim. *Surprise.* Tel Aviv: Ma'arachot, 1990.

Kamal, Hasan Ali. *Warriors and Peacemakers.* Tel Aviv: Ma'arachot, 1993.

Lanir, Zvi. *Fundamental Surprise — The National Intelligence Crisis.* Center of Strategic Studies, Tel Aviv University, 1983.

Leonard, Roger Ashley, ed. *On War: A Short Guide to Clausewitz.* Tel Aviv: Ma'arachot, 1967.

Levite, Ariel. *Israel Military Doctrine — Defense and Offense.* Jaffee Center of Strategic Studies, Tel Aviv University, 1988.

The Lexicon of the Warfare Doctrine, IDF Publications, General Staff, 1996.

Meir, Golda. *My Life.* Tel Aviv: Ma'ariv, 1975.

Meital, Yoram. *Egypt's Political Development in the Conflict with Israel: 1967–1977.* PhD thesis, Haifa University, July 1991.

Merchav, L., ed. *Soviet Military Thinking in the Nuclear Age.* Tel Aviv: Ma'arachot, April 1969.

Napoleon. *War Maxims.* Tel Aviv: Ma'arachot, 1991.

Naveh, Shimon. *The Art of Battle: The Evolution of Military Excellence.* Tel Aviv: Ma'arachot, 2001.

Sadat, Anwar. *The Story of My Life.* Jerusalem: Idanim/Yidiot Achronot, 1978.

Segev, Shmuel. *Sadat, The Road to Peace.* Masada: Givatayim, 1978.

Shamir, Shimon, ed. *The Decline of Nasserism, 1965–1970: The Waning of a Messianic Movement.* Tel Aviv: University Press, 1979.

Shazli, Sa'ad al-Din. *Crossing the Canal.* Tel Aviv: Ma'arachot, 1987.

Shiftan, Dan. *Attrition: Nasser's Political Strategy in the Wake of the Six-Day War.* Tel Aviv: Ma'arachot, 1989.

Solomon, Michel. *Red Star over the Middle East.* Tel Aviv: Ma'arachot, 1972.

Tal, Israel. *Israel's National Security, Few against Many.* Tel Aviv: Dvir, 1996.

The Use of Ground Forces in the Soviet Warfare Doctrine, Hatzav, 830/001 October 1981, translated and published by the United States Army Training Branch.

Vald, Emanuel. *The Curse of the Broken Pieces.* Tel Aviv: Schocken, 1984.

Vitan, Ariel (Alex). *Soviet Involvement and Intervention in Egypt, 1967–1972, The Military Aspect*, IDF History Branch, March 1990.

Wallach, Yehuda. *The Development of Warfare Theory in the 19th and 20th Centuries*, (translated into Hebrew from German). Tel Aviv: Ma'arachot, 1977.

_____. *Not on a Silver Platter*. Carta, 2000.

Whaley, Barton. *Codeword Barbarossa*. Tel Aviv: Ma'arachot, 1980.

Zeira, Eli. *The October '73 War: Myth against Reality*. Tel Aviv: Yidiot Achronot, 1993.

Articles — In Hebrew

Al-Ayubi, Hitham Mukdam. "The Revolutionary Features of the Fourth Arab-Israeli War," *Ma'arachot* 234–235 (January–February 1974), 20.

Amidror, B. "Infantry and Antitank Warfare on the Modern Battlefield." *Ziklon 7* (December 1980), 11.

Arad, Aryeh. "Yom Kippur — The War that Launched the Missile Era," *Davar*, October 6, 1992.

Asher, Dani. "Allenby's Operational Use of Deception to Conquer Eretz-Israel." *Ma'arachot* 329 (March–April 1993), 20.

_____. "Egyptian Artillery in the Yom Kippur War." *Ma'arachot* 361 (November 1998), 2–13.

_____. "From 'Order No. 41' to 'Tahrir 41' — from the Egyptian Warfare Doctrine to War." *Ma'arachot* 332 (September–October 1993), 46–55.

Asher, Itai, and Asher, Dani. "IDF Artillery on the Sinai Front in the Yom Kippur War." *Ma'arachot* 354 (November 1997), 10–20.

Avi-Shai, Lt. Col. "Egypt on the Eve of the Yom Kippur War: War Aims and Attack Plans." *Ma'arachot* 250 (July 1976).

_____. "The Yom Kippur War in the Eyes of the Egyptians." *Ma'arachot* 245 (July 1975), 29–39.

Avraham, Col. "Sadat's View on the Reasons for the Yom Kippur War." In *Sadat, War, and Peace*, Education Branch, September 1979.

Ayalon, Avraham, "October 14, 1973 — Why this Date was Omitted from Sadat's Memoirs," *Ma'arachot* 266 (November 1978), 9–19.

Bandman, Yona. "The Third Army Crosses the Suez Canal, October 6–8, 1973." *Ma'arachot* 296 (December 1984), 26–30 (according to the article submitted to *Ma'arachot* in October 1979).

Ben Dor, Gavriel. "Evaluating Arab Strategy in the Yom Kippur War." In *In the Shadow of Yom Kippur*. Haifa University, 1976.

Ben Israel, Yitzhak. "If Only I Could Reveal the Truth as Easily as I Refute the Lie." *Davar*, September 24, 1993.

Ben-Porat, Yoel. "The Yom Kippur War — Blunder in May, New Facts on the Yom Kippur Surprise." *Ma'arachot* 299 (July–August 1985), 1–9.

Binor, Yoram. "We Avenged Uur Revenge." *Hadashot*, special edition, September 24, 1993, 52–55.

Doron, Major. "The Battle of October 14 in the Wadi Mabuk Sector." *Ma'arachot* 266, 20–27.

Eitan, Zeev. "'Dovecote' — Planning and Implementation under the Test of Fire." *Ma'arachot* 276–277 (October-November 1980), 38–46.

Eldad, Col., Lt. Col. Nachum, and Lt. Col. Zvi. "Egyptian Commando Fighting in the Yom Kippur War." *Ma'arachot* 327, 20–25.

Froika, Lt. Col. "Equipment for Crossing Water Obstacles." *Ma'arachot* 234–235 (January–February 1974). The article was also published before the war in *Ma'arachot* 230.

G., A. "Military Strategy in Soviet Eyes." *Ma'arachot* 156 (December 1963), 9–10.

Gamasi, Muhammed. "How We Tricked Israeli Intelligence." *Ma'ariv*, October 8, 1989.

Golan, Shimon. "The Army as a Tool in Egypt's Foreign Policy in the Yom Kippur War." *Ma'arachot* 338 (October–November 1994), 22.

Harkabi, Yehoshafat. "The Weak Point in Nasser's Army, Social Weaknesses." In *The Decline of Nasserism, 1965–1970: The Waning of a Messianic Movement*, Shamir, Shimon, editor. Tel Aviv: University Press, 1979.

Hasdai, Yaakov. "The Yom Kippur War — Surprise or Victory?" *Ma'arachot* 275 (August 1980), 7–13.

Hendel, Michael. "Dissimulation, Deception, and Camouflage on the Eve of the Yom Kippur War." *Ma'ariv*, September 1, 1977.

_____. "Intelligence and Deception." In *Intelligence and National Security*, Ofer, Z. & A. Kover, editors. Ma'arachot, 1987.

Heykal, Hassanein. "Memoirs." *Ma'ariv*, April 28, 1975.

_____. "Memoirs." *Ma'ariv*, April 30, 1975, 15.

Hofman, M. "Antitank Defense in the Soviet Doctrine." *Ziklon 7* (December 1980), 41–48.

Jacobs, Walter Darnel. "Strategy 'Sokolovsky Style.'" *Ziklon 11*, *Ma'arachot* 155 (November 1963), 6–11.

Lemov, N. "On War and Weapons." In *Soviet Military Thinking in the Nuclear Age*, Merchav, L., editor. Tel Aviv: Ma'arachot, April 1969, 30.

Levran, Aharon. "Surprise and Warning — A Look at Basic Questions." *Ma'arachot* 276–277 (October–November 1980), 17–20.

Lewis, Bernard. "Israel and the Arabs and the Blocs in the Middle East." *Ma'arachot* 217–218 (September 1971), 10–15.

M., Lt. Col. "The Egyptian Army's 'Operative Halt' in the Yom Kippur War." *Ma'arachot* 327 (November–December 1992), 12–19.

Mayzel, Matti. "The Soviet Union's Objectives in the War of Attrition." *Ma'arachot* 335 (May 1994).

Merchav, L. "Firepower in Attack Operations." *Ma'arachot* 156 (December 1963), 12–17.

_____. "On the Eve of the Attack." *Ma'arachot* 148 (December 1962), 9–15.

_____. "The Soviet Attack and War Perspective — The Military Branches and their Part in the Attack." *Ma'arachot* 147 (October 1962), 21–27.

Milman, Yosi. "The Story that Remains Unlocked," from Lt. Col. Shabtai Bril, Director of MI's Information Collection Division. *Ha'aretz*, August 18, 1996.

N., Major L. "The Soviet Corps of Engineers, its Application in the Past and Present." *Ma'arachot* 130 (August 1960), 66–71.

Naveh, Shimon. "The Operative Art and Theory of General Operations." *Ma'arachot* 354–355 (December 1995–January 1996), 2–15.

Pa'il, Meir. "The Yom Kippur War — An Historical

Look at the Strategic Level." *Ma'arachot* 276–277 (October–November 1982), 2–10.

Raviv, Haim. "The Pressure of the War of Attrition, Expression of Public Misery." In *The Decline of Nasserism, 1965–1970: The Waning of a Messianic Movement*, Shamir, Shimon editor. Tel Aviv: University Press, 1979.

Reshef, Shmuel. Preface in *Red God of War — Soviet Artillery and Rocket Forces*, by Chris Bellamy. Tel Aviv: Ma'arachot, , 1990.

Rozansky, A. "The Revolution in the Art of War and Units' Tactics." *Soviet Military Thinking in the Nuclear Age* Tel Aviv: Ma'arachot, April 1969, 63–74.

Samanov, V. A. "A Short Article on the Development of the Soviet Art of Operations." Moscow, 1980 [translated to Hebrew by IDF Intelligence Branch].

Sh., Col. "The Cognitive Failures in Deterrence in the Yom Kippur War and What Can be Learned from Them." *Ma'arachot* 230 (October–November 1994), 10–15.

Shaked, Yochai. "The Contribution of Compartmentalization to Egypt's Surprise in the Yom Kippur War." *Ma'arachot* 373 (November 2000), 42–51.

Shamir, Shimon. "Formulating the Perspective of the October Attack." In *Egypt under Sadat's Leadership*. Tel Aviv: Dvir, 1978, 88.

Shiftan, Dan. "From the Six-Day War to the War of Attrition." *Ma'arachot* 257 (August 1977), 8–13.

_____. "Strategy toward Israel at a Dead End — From the Six-Day War to the War of Attrition." In *The Decline of Nasserism, 1965–1970: The Waning of a Messianic Movement*, Shamir, Shimon, editor. Tel Aviv: University Press, 1979.

Sokolovsky, V. & M. Cherdechenko. "The Art of War in New Stages of Development." In *Soviet Military Thinking in the Nuclear Age*, L. Merchav, editor. Tel Aviv: Ma'arachot, April 1969.

Sushko, N. "On War." *Soviet Military Thinking in the Nuclear Age*. Tel Aviv: Ma'arachot, April 1969, 11.

Tamari, Dov. "The Yom Kippur War: Concepts, Assessments, Lessons." *Ma'arachot* 276–277 (October–November 1980), 2–10.

Timofiev, A. "The Russians Planned the Yom Kippur War." Originally in *Novaya Vremya*, translated into Hebrew and published in *Bamahane*, May 3, 1989, 53.

Vitan, Ariel (Alex). "Soviet Involvement and Intervention in Egypt 1967–1972, the Military Aspect." *Ma'arachot* 289–290 (October 1983), 65–70.

Wallach, Yehuda. "The Omnipotent Tank..." *Ma'arachot* 276–277 (October–November 1980), 22–26.

Yiftach, Shimon. "Missiles in Egypt." *Ma'arachot* 217–218 (September 1971), 19.

Ysraeli, Rafi. "President Sadat: The Image of the Leader." In *Sadat, War, and Peace*, Education Branch, September 1979.

Zeevi, Aharon. "The Egyptian Deception Plan." In *Intelligence and National Security*, Ofer, Z. & A. Kover, editors. Ma'arachot, 1987. 430–438.

_____. "The Egyptian Deception Plan." *Ma'arachot* 289–290 (October 1983), 39–42.

_____. "Political Aspects of the Egyptian Deception Plan in the Yom Kippur War." *Ma'arachot* 338 (October–November 1994), 6.

Zeoyalov, Lt. Gen. "The Soviet Warfare Doctrine." In *Soviet Military Thinking in the Nuclear Age*, Merchav, L., editor. Tel Aviv: Ma'arachot, April 1969.

Zohar, Avraham. "The War of Attrition." *Ma'arachot* 257 (August 1977), 15–18.

Translated Reviews and Reports

Cairo Symposium. An executive report of the Cairo symposium, a symposium on war issues, October 28–31, 1974 (translated into Hebrew and circulated by Hatzav).

"A Detailed Report of Russian Training, Equipment, and Techniques for Crossing a Water Obstacle," a British intelligence document dated August 28, 1970, was published in the Lebanese newspaper *Al-Anwar* on September 7, 1970. (The article was translated into Hebrew.)

Egyptian and Warsaw Pact Means for Crossing a Water Barrier. Israeli Intelligence Branch Survey, January 1970.

Lobachev, G. "Speed of Attack as a Condition for Victory." In *Attack Speed as an Important Factor in the Soviet Warfare Doctrine*, published and translated by Hatzav 832/03, July 20, 1978.

Melnikov, Col. Gen. "The Soviet Perspective — Deception and the Operational Level." Originally published in *Voyenno Istoricheskiy Zhurnal*, April 1962; translated into Hebrew and edited in *Battlefield Deception*, IDF General Staff Branch, November 1992, 16.

The Principles of Crossing a Water Barrier according to the Soviet Army's Warfare Doctrine. Israeli Intelligence Branch Survey, July 1970.

Books — In Arabic

Badri, Hasan; Tah Magdub; Theya Aldin Zahari. *Harb Ramadan — Aljoula Alarabiya — Alisrailiya Alarba'a* [The Ramadan War, the Fourth Arab-Israeli Round — The October 1973 War]. Cairo 1974.

Fawzi, Mahmud. *Harb Althalat Sanuat 1967–1970 — Mithrakat al Farik Awal Mahmud Fawzi Wazir al Harabiya al Asbak* [The Three Year War, Memoirs of Former War Minister Mahmud Fawzi]. Cairo, 1984.

_____. *The 1973 October War*. Chapters of the book appeared in *Al-Shara* (Lebanon), August–October 1988.

Gamasi, Muhamad. *Mazkarat Al-Gamasi, Harb Oktober 1973* [Gamasi Memoirs, The October 1973 War]. Paris 1990.

Hamad, Gamal. *Alma'arach Alharabiya ala Algabha'a Almisriya* [The Campaign on the Egyptian Front]. Cairo 1989.

_____. *Min Sinai Ela Algolan* [From Sinai to the Golan]. Cairo 1988.

Heykal, Mahmud Hassanein. *Anid Mitparak Altarak Harb Oktober* [On the Crossroads, The October War]. Cairo 1983.

Teh, Magdub al-. "Aljish Almisri ba'ad Yunio 67" [The Egyptian Army after June '67]. *Harb Yunio 1967 ba'ad 30 Sana* [The June 1967 War 30 Years Later]. Cairo, 1998, 115–147.

Articles in the Arab Press

"A Cannon on Every 11 Meters and 175 Shells Every Minute: The Role that Egyptian Artillery, Including Antitank Missiles, Played in the First Stages of the Yom Kippur War." *Al-Ahram* (Egypt), December 22, 1973.

Lahwi, Fuad, Jibril Batar, and Adiv Almor. "Military and Strategic Results of the October War." *Tishrin* (Syrian army journal), October 4–5, 1979.

Riad, Mahmud. *Mithkarat* [Memoirs] (Jordan), November 1, 1981.

Shazli, Sa'ad al-Din. An interview with the Yom Kippur War's chief of staff. *Al Arabi*, October 15, 2000.

Books in Other Languages

Ananyev, I. M. *Tank Army in the Offensive.* JPRS UMA-88–020-L, Moscow, 1988.

Badri, el Hassan, et al. *The Ramadan War, 1973.* Virginia: T. N. Dupuy Associates, 1978.

Bar-Siman-Tov, Yaacov. *The Israeli—Egyptian War of Attrition 1969–1970.* New York: Columbia University Press, 1980.

Beaufre, André. *An Introduction to Strategy.* New York: Praeger, 1965.

Biryukov, G. & Melnikov G. *Antitank Warfare.* Moscow: Progress, 1972.

Borets, I. G. "*Taktika.*" *SVE*, 1979.

Draper, T. *Israel and World Politics of the Third Arab-Israeli War.* New York: Viking Press, 1968.

Erlich, Haggai. *Students and University in 20th Century Egyptian Politics.* London: Frank Cass, London, 1989, 65.

Glantz, David M. *The Soviet Conduct of Tactical Maneuver: Spearhead of the Offensive.* London: Frank Cass, 1991.

_____. *Soviet Military Intelligence in War.* London: Frank Cass, 1990.

Glasman, Jan D. *Arms for the Arabs.* Baltimore: Johns Hopkins University Press, 1975.

Grechko, A. A. *Armed Forces of the Soviet State.* 2nd ed. Moscow, 1975.

_____. "*Voyennya Nauka*" [Military Science]. *SVE*, 1979.

Hendel, Michael I. *Perception, Deception and Surprise: The Case of Yom Kippur War.* Jerusalem: Hebrew University, 1976.

Heykal, Mohamed. *The Road to Ramadan.* New York: Ballantine Books, 1975; London: Collins, 1977.

_____. *The Sphinx and the Commissar.* London: Collins, 1978.

Hussini, Mohrez Mahmoud el-. *Soviet-Egyptian Relations, 1945–85.* London: Macmillan, 1987.

Israelyan, Victor. *Inside the Kremlin during the Yom Kippur War.* Pennsylvania State University Press, 1995.

Kulikov, V. G. "*Operativnoye Iskusstvo*" [Operational Art]. *SVE*, 1978.

Lester, Robert. *The Lyndon Johnson National Security Files: The Middle East, 1963–1969.* Frederick, MD: University Publications of America.

Liddell Hart, B. H. *Strategy.* New York: Praeger, 1954.

Meital, Yoram. *Egypt's Struggle for Peace Continuity and Change, 1967—1977.* University Press of Florida, 1997.

_____. *The Road to Peace: Egypt's Policy towards the Conflict with Israel, 1967–1977.* University of Haifa, The Jewish–Arab Center, 1996.

Naveh, Shimon. *In Pursuit of Military Excellence, the Evolution of Operational Theory.* London: Frank Cass, 1997.

Ogracov, N. V. "*Voyennaya Strategiya*" [Military Strategy]. *SVE*, 1979.

Ro'i, Yaacov. *From Encroachment to Involvement.* New York: John Wiley, 1974.

Rubinstein, Alvin Z. *Red Star on the Nile.* Princeton, NJ: Princeton University Press, 1977.

Selected Soviet Military Writings, a Soviet View. Translated and published by the U.S. Air Force. U.S. Government Printing Office, 1977.

The Soviet Army: Operation and Tactics, FM 100–2-1. Washington D.C.: Department of the Army, July 16, 1984.

The Soviet Military Encyclopedia, Vol. I. 1976 [Russian].

Thibault, George, editor. *The Art and Practice of Military Strategy.* Washington, DC: National Defense University, 1984.

The Voroshilov Lectures. Graham Hall Turbiville, Jr., general editor. Material from the Soviet General Staff Academy, Volume III, "The Art of Operations." Washington, DC: National Defense University Press, 1992.

Whaley, Barton. *Stratagem: Deception and Surprise in War.* Cambridge, MA: MIT, 1969.

Wohlstetter, Roberta. *Pearl Harbor, Warning and Decision.* Stanford, CA: Stanford University Press, 1962.

Zisk, Kimberly Marten. *Engaging the Enemy: Organization Theory and Soviet Military Innovation, 1955–1991.* Princeton, NJ: Princeton University Press, 1993.

Non-Hebrew, Non-Arab Articles and Documents

Antsiz, B. "Antitank Guided Missiles in Defense." *Soviet Military Review,* July 1975, 15–17.

Bermudez, J. S. Jr. "The Egyptian 130th: The Amphibious Brigade." *Marine Corps Gazette,* June 1995, 59–68.

Bonesteel, Ronald M. "Soviets 'Other' Forces." *Infantry,* November–December 1988, 26–28.

Dupuy, T. N. "'73 Arab Israeli Conflict'—A Military Analysis." *Strategy & Tactics,* January–February 1982.

Glantz, David M. "Soviet Intelligence Operations in the Kursk Operation, July 1943," *Intelligence & National Security* 5, no.1 (1990).

Gross-Stein, Janice. "Military Deception, Strategic Surprise and Conventional Deterrence: A Political Analysis of Egypt and Israel, 1971–73." *Journal of Strategic Studies,* 16/5/1, March 1982, 95–120.

Karber, Phillip A. "The Soviet Anti-Tank Debate." *Survival,* May–June 1975, 105–111.

Kozlov, L. "Antitank Defense (Based on the Experience of the Great Patriotic War of 1941–45)." *Soviet Military Review,* July 1975.

Kulish, V. "Nachalo Voiny: Schet k Staliny" [The Beginning of the War: Stalin's Regime]. *Sputnik* 10, no date.

Meital, Yoram. "The Khartoum Conference and Egyptian Policy after the 1967 War: A Reexamination." *Middle East Journal* 54 (Winter 2000), 64–82.

_____. *The Road to Peace: Egypt's Policy towards the Conflict with Israel, 1967–1977, Working Paper No. 2* (no date).

Sevorov, V. "GUSM — The Soviet Service of Strategic Deception." *I.D.R. Swiss*, August 1985.

Stevens, Jennie A., & Henry S. Marsh. "Surprise and Deception in Soviet Military Thought." *Military Review*, July 1982, 24–35.

Timmos, Richard F. "Antitank Missiles in the Yom Kippur War." *Infantry*, January 1974, 18–22.

United States: The Nixon Project, *White House Central Files*, 1974.

Volodin, Y. "Antitank Means in Defense." *Soviet Military Review*, 1975, 18–20.

Other Translated Articles

Luskotov, R. & O, Letushko. "The Yom Kippur War — the Egyptian Army versus the IDF," *V.I.Z.H.*, Soviet Union, October 1988 (translated by *Hatzav*, June 8, 1989).

Makravsky, V. & B. Pavlov, B. "The Crossing of the Water Obstacle — Lessons of the Yom Kippur War," *V.I.Z.H.*, Soviet Union, July 1987 (translated by *Hatzav*, March 18, 1988).

Interviews and Speeches

Field Marshal Ismail Ali Ahmad in an interview with Hassanein Heykal, *Al-Anwar*, November 18, 1973.

General Jamal Hamad, lecture delivered before the al-Wafad Party's Information Committee, Egypt, November 11, 1987.

Nasser speech, April 10, 1968, *Al-Ahram*, April 11, 1968.

Sadat interview on Lebanese television, October 9, 1974.

Sadat, interview with Drs. Takla and Darwish, the authors of *The Six Hour War*; chapters from the book were published by Faruk Altawil in the weekly *A'akhar Sa'ah*, May 8, 1974.

Sadat, *Radio Cairo*, September 28, 1974, speech on the fourth anniversary of Nasser's demise.

Egyptian Military Documents

(captured by Israel in the Yom Kippur War — most without date or provenance)

Army Offensive Operations in the Great Patriotic War, training aid A-171, Nasser Higher Military Academy. 1969 (Israeli war booty, not translated).

C.S.C. 134, Logistic Support to Motorized Infantry Division in Offensive with Assault Crossing, Nasser Higher Military Academy. (The document fell into Israeli hands but was not translated.)

C.S.C. 633, Defense of Captured Bridgehead by Infantry Division, Nasser Higher Military Academy, textbook, no date. (The document fell into Israeli hands but was not translated.)

Captured Egyptian Document (8) 431/1, lessons learned from the IDF's landing in the Abu al-Daraj and al-Zafrana area on September 23, 1969.

Captured Egyptian Document (8) 471/12, capturing and securing the mountain passes during the Third Army's attack operation, prepared in January 1972 for the Nineteenth Division brigade commanders' meeting.

Captured Egyptian Document 10/2, the Sixth Division's artillery assignments.

Captured Egyptian Document 27/10, Egyptian Chief of Staff Shazli's Order No. 4 — the defense strongholds, including a diagram of a reinforced infantry company defending a stronghold, September 25, 1971.

Captured Egyptian Document 64/27 693/M, the principles of combat operations for an antitank guided missile battalion. Armed Forces' Publishing Unit.

Captured Egyptian Document 81/11, the plan for crossing the canal and the participating forces. (See Appendix C in this book.)

Captured Egyptian Document 85/11, comparative research on the way Egyptian and Israeli mechanized infantry brigades are organized, September 9, 1973.

Captured Egyptian Document 116/11, electronic warfare instructions for Operation "Granite 2 Improved," issued by Third Army Headquarters, September 28, 1973.

Captured Egyptian Document 116/013, reconnaissance patrol report — Fifth Brigade, Nineteenth Division, May 13, 1973.

Captured Egyptian Document 120/11, the plan of the commander of the Seventy-fourth Battalion (Twenty-fourth Infantry Brigade) for attacking while crossing the Suez Canal. Reading the battalion commander's map, August 1973.

Captured Egyptian Document 131/11, Seventh Infantry Division, Artillery Command.

Captured Egyptian Document 149/11, battle order for Operation "Granite 2 Improved" from the Third Army's artillery commander, Brigadier General Ahmad Shahin, September 1973.

Captured Egyptian Document 170/009, organizing the defense of the troops against chemical and bacteriological warfare in an attack operation while crossing a water obstacle in an assault on the shore. Nasser Higher Military Academy, 1972.

Captured Egyptian Document 195/11, battle orders to engineering units No. 1/73 from the Engineering Headquarters of the Nineteenth Division, Third Army, April 1973.

Captured Egyptian Document 268/12, air defense for a reinforced infantry division when crossing a water obstacle.

Captured Egyptian Document 290/12, the order for the "Tahrir" 41 exercise, Third Army, Operation Branch, September 30, 1973.

Captured Egyptian Document 424/1, battle order from Seventh Division Headquarters for Operation "Granite 2 Improved." Battle Order No. 1 was apparently issued in early 1973. (See Appendix D in this book).

Captured Egyptian Document 463/1, notes on training soldiers in tank-hunting teams. Training Branch Second Army, September 9, 1973.

Captured Egyptian Document 468/007, organizational order No. 2942, reorganization of the "Fahad" antitank guided missile battalion, Egyptian infantry division.

Captured Egyptian Document 470/1, doctrinal research on capturing and securing the mountain passes during an attack operation by the Third Army, January 1972. Translated and published in *Ziklon* 8, Ma'arachot Publishers, May 1981, 21–26.

Captured Egyptian Document 472/1, the plan for crossing the Suez Canal. The document, untitled and without date or name of publisher, was apparently written by the Third Army's artillery commander close to the outbreak of the war.

Captured Egyptian Document 474/005, orders for organizing the armed forces' modus operandi, January 29, 1969.

Captured Egyptian Document 511/1, organizing and employing infantry, mechanized infantry, armored divisions in various stages of the battle.

Captured Egyptian Document 533/2, the engineering company as a mobile mine-laying reserve for the attacking division: Sixth Division Headquarters, Sixth Engineering Battalion, May 13, 1973.

Captured Egyptian Document 614/2, notebook.

Captured Egyptian Document 680/2, memo from the Egyptian military intelligence branch on the inflammable systems on the dirt embankment east of the canal, July 11, 1973.

Captured Egyptian Document 766/4 Order No. 41, the Egyptian chief of staff's order for an infantry division crossing a water obstacle (Suez Canal) — details on the forces, equipment, and priorities in the crossing, March 20, 1973 (see Appendix A in this book).

Captured Egyptian Document 784/6, Soviet advisors' 1973 work program.

Captured Egyptian Document 805/7, the IDF's defense system on the canal and overpowering it with assault forces. (See Appendix B in this work)

Captured Egyptian Document 851/0005, the armored division in an engagement battle and advance, Armed Forces General Staff, Military Research Branch.

Captured Egyptian Document 851/0006, training manual that sums up Plan-50, Nasser Higher Military Academy. The requirements for carrying out special operations for securing the bridgeheads at the Suez Canal and proceeding to an attack from the bridgeheads, 1972.

Captured Egyptian Document 851/0022, the tactical use of antiaircraft artillery for defending the ground forces.

Captured Egyptian Document 851/8, engineering assistance to the brigade and division in the attack. July 1970.

Captured Egyptian Document 851/10, engineering assistance to the brigade and division in the defensive battle. The book was issued to the Egyptian army in 1970.

Captured Egyptian Document 963/12, Military Research Publications No. 55, organizing a control center and securing radio communications in an attack operation while breaking through a water obstacle. Egyptian War Ministry, "Hiya" Military Research Branch, May 20, 1970.

Captured Egyptian Document 964/75-MSH, the rules

for field artillery fire direction. Armed Forces' Publishing Unit, 1971.

Captured Egyptian Document 5000/10, lessons learned from studying the enemy's artillery engagements on the canal front 1967–1970. The document was published by the Military Research Branch, Artillery Command, October 10, 1970.

Captured Egyptian Document, Egyptian Chief of Staff Shazli's Order No. 37, fighting in a battle zone under enemy air control, March 3, 1973.

Captured Egyptian Document, instructions for safeguarding Operation "Granite 2 Improved," September 30, 1973.

Captured Egyptian Document, Nasser College Lectures — Vol. V, Lecture No. 650 (in English): "The field army's attack while crossing the water obstacle on the coastal axis, in coordination with the air force, navy, and air defense," 1970.

Captured Egyptian Document, Training Brief No. 68/2, organizing tactical training of a reinforced infantry company for an attack while crossing a water obstacle. Armed Forces Training Branch, 1968.

The Division (Brigade) in Offensive Combat, textbook, Nasser Higher Military Academy, a Soviet doctrinal book that was translated into English for the Academy's training program in 1971. The book was translated into Hebrew under the title *The Division (Brigade) in the Attack*, General Staff Training Branch, 1974.

Lectures on the subject: the field army on the attack, from the Egyptian Command and Staff College (in English). (The document fell into Israeli hands but was not translated.)

Organization and Conduct of Defense (Foreign View), Nasser Higher Military Academy. (The document fell into Israeli hands but was not translated.)

Peculiarities of an Offensive Involving a Water Barrier Crossing, C.S.C. 122, Nasser Higher Military Academy. 1969 (Israeli war booty, not translated).

Pelekh, Major General, Candidate of Military Science, Docent, in the introduction to his book *The Division (Brigade) in Offensive Combat*, Nasser Higher Military Academy (Israeli war booty, not translated).

Strategic Offensive Operations, (lecture), A-163, Nasser Higher Military Academy. 1969, (Israeli war booty, not translated).

Maps and Figures

Figures and maps from Egyptian doctrinal material that fell into Israeli hands.

Operational map printed by the Third Army's artillery headquarters in January 1973. The map was approved by the army's commander, Major General Wasal.

Various operational maps of Egyptian brigade and battalion commanders dealing with the canal-crossing technique in an attack to secure the bridgeheads and capture the strongholds, and the plans for establishing the defense layout at the bridgeheads' front.

Index